PIETY IN PIECES

Piety in Pieces

How Medieval Readers
Customized their Manuscripts

Kathryn M. Rudy

OpenBook Publishers

https://www.openbookpublishers.com

The University of St. Andrews Library Open Access Fund supported this Open Access publication. The Leverhulme Trust has generously contributed towards the research for this volume.

The Leverhulme Trust

ISBN Paperback: 978–1-78374–233–2
ISBN Hardback: 978–1-78374–234–9
ISBN Digital (PDF): 978–1-78374–235–6
ISBN Digital ebook (epub): 978–1-78374–236–3
ISBN Digital ebook (mobi): 978–1-78374–237–0
DOI: 10.11647/OBP.0094

Cover image: Opening from a book of hours at the incipit of the *Hours of the Holy Spirit* with original and added parchment and decoration. The Master of Gijsbrecht van Brederode painted the historiated initial around 1465. Around 1510 the Masters of the Dark Eyes supplied the full-page miniature depicting the Coronation of the Virgin on separate parchment. The Hague, Koninklijke Bibliotheek, BPH 151, fol. 71v-72r. Published with permission from the Koninklijke Bibliotheek—the National Library of The Netherlands.

All paper used by Open Book Publishers is SFI (Sustainable Forestry Initiative), PEFC (Programme for the Endorsement of Forest Certification Schemes) and Forest Stewardship Council(r)(FSC(r) certified.

Printed in the United Kingdom, United States, and Australia
by Lightning Source for Open Book Publishers (Cambridge, UK)

Invisible threads are the strongest ties.
— Friedrich Nietzsche

I dedicate this book to my father, Dr Donald J. Rudy,
who taught me how to paddle, fly, and achieve more topspin.

Contents

Notes to the reader

This book grew out of an Arbeitsgespräch titled *Manuscripts Changing Hands: Handschriften wechseln von Hand zu Hand*, held at the Herzog August Bibliothek, Wolfenbüttel, from 20–22 June 2012. It was organized by Dr Volker Schier (Arizona Center for Medieval and Renaissance Studies) and Professor Dr Corine Schleif (Arizona State University), to whom I am grateful. The study, which at that time was titled "Pimp my Manuscript," also benefitted from helpful comments by others present at this event.

This study also developed thanks to Martin Kauffmann at the Bodleian Library, who invited me to Oxford to give a masterclass on this topic. This event invigorated me intellectually and socially at a time when my batteries were running low.

The work was funded by a Leverhulme Trust Research Fellowship; I thank the Trust heartily, as the fellowship allowed me to spend time in Cambridge and Oxford to conduct research and also to buy the relevant images. This work would not have been possible without their support. I also thank the School of Art History, University of St. Andrews, for supplementing the image budget for this study. The University of St. Andrews Library Open Access Fund supported Open Access publication. I thank Alessandra Tosi, Marc Mierowsky, and Bianca Gualandi at Open Book for the hundreds of small ways in which they enabled the production of this book.

Years ago I held a grant from the Dutch Research Council (NWO) that allowed me to study medieval manuscripts in libraries across the Low Countries nearly every day for three years. During these stimulating years, I gathered ideas and materials that have fed into every project

I have subsequently done, including this one. Thank you, NWO, for making it possible for me to collect material for a decade's worth of ideas. My gratitude goes out to Erik Geleijns, Kate Greenspan, Peter Gumbert, Marlene Hennessy, Klaas van der Hoek, Erik Inglis, Erik Kwakkel, James Marrow, Johan Oosterman, Katharina Smeyers, and Mark Trowbridge who provided images or helped shape my thinking. I thank Lisa Regan and Jeffrey Hamburger for comments on drafts and Emily Savage for her perspicacious reading. I am also indebted to individuals from manuscript repositories around Europe, the UK and North America, who have granted me access to manuscript and provided me with invaluable information, especially Karin Zimmermann (Heidelberg), Ann Kelders (Brussels), Suzanne Paul (Cambridge), and Martin Kauffmann (Oxford).

Finally, I thank the two anonymous peer reviewers who made valuable suggestions, all of which I have taken up.

A note about the images: I have told the story in this book with words and pictures. Words are cheap. Pictures cost. Their price varies considerably from one institution to the next. As of this writing, high-resolution digital images from the Koninklijke Bibliotheek in The Hague cost about €5, about as much as an artisanal latte. Those from the Fitzwilliam Museum in Cambridge cost £40 for the tiff, plus £35 for new photography, plus VAT. Thus, ten images from the Fitzwilliam cost more than my car. Financial considerations and not just intellectual ones have, by necessity, dictated my choice of examples.

Institutions that do not allow hand-held photography make it difficult to me to develop ideas, because it often takes me weeks or months to make sense of a manuscript's structure, and doing so usually involves building diagrams and models based on notes and photographs. Institutions that currently prohibit photography include Trinity College Dublin, the Fitzwilliam Museum, and Lambeth Palace Library. As a result of these policies, I find myself avoiding those libraries and throwing my intellectual efforts at materials held in libraries that do allow photography in the reading room. Institutions with policies that encourage and facilitate research are those that are well-represented in my study.

In order to contain publication costs (so that this book can be free for you) while presenting all the necessary images, I have decided to concentrate on reproducing those images that are not otherwise available on the Web, and to provide links to those that are. Furthermore, Cambridge University Library and I are also conducting an experiment in this book: I used part of my Leverhulme fellowship funds to pay for the digitization of folios from manuscripts in their collection. They have agreed to mount these images on their own website so that readers of this book (and in fact, anybody) can view them. That way, you can see them in higher resolution, and you can use the images in your own study (if, for example, you should disagree with me vociferously and feel the need to write an illustrated counterargument). And I can use the publication budget to reproduce more obscure items, or items in collections that have no digitization plans (such as the Koninklijke Bibliotheek van België in Brussels).

All translations from Latin and Middle Dutch are mine, as are the Middle Dutch transcriptions and interpunctuations.

Abbreviations used in this book

AUB	Universiteitsbibliotheek van Amsterdam
Baltimore, WAM	Baltimore, Walters Art Museum
Berlin, SPK	Staatsbibliothek zu Berlin — Preußischer Kulturbesitz
BKB	Brussels, Koninklijke Bibliotheek van België
BPH	Biblioteca Philosophica Hermetica collection within the HKB
Edinburgh, NLS	Edinburgh, National Library of Scotland
Enschede, RMT	Enschede, Rijksmuseum Twenthe
HKB	The Hague, Koninklijke Bibliotheek — The National Library of The Netherlands
HMMW	The Hague, Museum Meermanno-Westreenianum
KA	Koninklijke Nederlandse Akademie van Wetenschappen (Royal Dutch Academy of Sciences) collection within the HKB
LBL	London, British Library
Nijmegen, RU	Nijmegen, Radboud Universiteit
Paris, BA	Paris, Bibliothèque de l'Arsenal
Paris, BnF	Paris, Bibliothèque national de France
Cambridge, UL	Cambridge, University Library
's-Heerenberg, HB	Collection Dr. J.H. van Heek, Huis Bergh Foundation, 's-Heerenberg, The Netherlands
UB	Universiteitsbibliotheek (Dutch) or Universitätsbibliothek (German)

Introduction:
A new approach to codicology

In response to an event in the Soviet Union in 1953 George Orwell wrote, "He who controls the present controls the past, and he who controls the past controls the future." He was referring to an incident that involved a strategic adjustment to a book. Stalin had just died, and Lavrentiy Pavlovich Beria, the chief of Stalin's secret police, had fallen out of favor. The *Great Soviet Encyclopedia*, issued since 1926, had a positive article on Beria that was now an embarrassment. This meant that the article had to be amended. Rather than reprint the entire encyclopedia, which would have cost time and resources, the Soviets instead found a cheaper solution: to write an addendum page—an extended article about the Bering Strait—and then send it to all registered owners of the volumes, with instructions that they should paste the new page over the Beria article, thereby obfuscating it.[1] The motivations for issuing this new article were clearly political (expunge Beria!) and economic (do it cheaply!). Speed was also a motivation: the paste-over allowed the book to keep pace with events in a manner faster than making a whole new book.

While the content of this action was dedicated to maintaining a sense of Soviet historical purity, the actual procedure used continued a practice that had been widespread in the Middle Ages. In this study I explore the ways in which medieval book owners adjusted the contents of their books to reflect changed circumstances. Such circumstances were not

---

1   Julian Assange, the founder of WikiLeaks, describes the situation in an interview, "History Deletes Itself," *Harper's Magazine*, December 2011, pp. 27–28.

                    http://dx.doi.org/10.11647/OBP.0094.06

usually so overtly political, but they nonetheless reveal other fears and motivations. Religious, social or economic reasons could also motivate such emendations. Augmentations to a book reveal strong emotional and social forces. These are often difficult to identify in manuscripts, because the new parts often blend in with the old. Furthermore, modern audiences often see manuscripts as products of a single "genius" mind, when in fact all manuscripts were made in a group effort over months, years or even decades.

When a manuscript enters a public collection, it is stabilized, preserved, frozen. In the Middle Ages, however, the manuscript was not a static entity, but rather an object whose content and structure were dynamic. Although all medieval manuscripts could, in theory, have texts and images added to them, in the current study I concentrate on Netherlandish prayerbooks, because certain aspects of their production lent them to upgrades. Assembled in layers from the beginning, Netherlandish prayerbooks were uniquely able to accommodate revisions. Generations of owners added physical material, texts, and objects, and with them, layers of meaning. These changes often reveal their owners' fears and desires. By manipulating the past (in the form of the received book) and making adjustments to it, book owners felt as if they could control the future, which for Christian believers often meant controlling their own eschatological outcome: the fate that would befall them at the end of time. Many prayers added to Netherlandish prayerbooks were designed to secure an eternal place in heaven for their users. As the technology of salvation became ever more complicated, people needed "devotional upgrades" in their manuscripts. They added prayers that promised ever-greater indulgences to reduce their purgatorial sentences after death.

A manuscript under normal circumstances would outlive its original owner and probably outlive its next ten owners. After stone slabs with lapidary inscriptions carved into them, parchment is one of the most enduring substrates for preserving a text. When owners died, the manuscripts changed hands, except in the rare cases where people were buried with their books.[2] Normally, the book passed to another member

---

2   On church burials where people were buried with books or book clasps, see Janne Harjula, "Underground Literature: Archaeological Finds of Books and Book Elements from Finnish Churches," *Mirator* 16 (2015), pp. 160–90.

of the living. These important moments in a manuscript's history often led to changes in the manuscript's form: adjustments to keep the old manuscript relevant to a new owner. In this study I lay out a scheme for organizing the kinds of changes that medieval people made to their manuscripts.

I concentrate on Netherlandish manuscripts and the changes made to them in the fifteenth century, because this was a particularly dynamic time and place for books. (I do occasionally draw on examples from neighboring regions, especially for earlier examples, because Netherlandish book production started quite late but then sped rapidly in its technological development.[3]) With manuscripts produced in both convents and in secular ateliers, the Northern and Southern Netherlands had some of the most robust markets for manuscripts in Europe. Because so many Netherlandish prayerbooks made for local consumption were in the vernacular, they had a far greater social reach than in France and England, where most of the books of hours and prayerbooks were copied in Latin and were therefore limited to the most highly educated. These forces exerted pressure on Netherlandish book production to create more manuscripts, cheaper, faster and more efficiently, and to reach ever-broader audiences. Production was so successful in the Southern Netherlands (mainly Bruges), for example, that stationers exported books of hours (in Latin) to England, where the demand was greater than the supply. It is this dynamic market setting that I intend to investigate, because these conditions inspired new techniques and operations for producing new books and upgrading old ones.

To adjust a manuscript, one could either add or subtract contents or change the organization. One could make marks upon existing material or insert new material that provides space for further marks, or even add new material with marks already in place. Obversely one could scrape out existing marks, thereby creating a palimpsest, or cut out material altogether. Subtractions could mean cutting out folios, removing quires, scraping out texts, and defacing images, either through iconophilia

---

3   On the development of book culture in this region, consult J. P. Gumbert, *The Dutch and Their Books in the Manuscript Age* (London: British Library, 1990); Kathryn M. Rudy and Ed van der Vlist, "Het geschreven boek in Nederland tot omstreeks 1400: continuïteit en emancipatie," *Jaarboek voor Nederlandse boekgeschiedenis* 17 (2010), pp. 15–51.

or iconophobia. I concentrate here on additions to manuscripts: how manuscripts, which could be considered complete and discrete objects, might be made to accommodate new materials. One manuscript's gain was sometimes another's loss, and to the extent that that's the case this study deals in images that were cut from one manuscript to arrive in another. But throughout the following pages, my interest is in the act of acquisition and insertion of images and text, by which the book might gain, rather than lose, contents.

Some cutting inevitably took place in the Middle Ages, but the systematic harvesting of images from books began in the modern era, and as such, is beyond the scope of this study. Furthermore, recent studies have already dealt with cutting things out. Most notably, the topic of collecting cuttings has been addressed in an exhibition mounted by Sandra Hindman and Nina Rowe that showcased the practice of gleaning images from medieval manuscripts (especially in the nineteenth century) to suit the tastes of collectors.[4] Whereas the modern collector desired a variety of the best examples to put on display, which led to the fragmentation of books, the medieval owner collected prayers and images, which led to the expansion of the manuscript. I am primarily interested in the manuscript itself as the site of collection.

Studying how medieval users in the Netherlands augmented their books can give insight into a different spectrum of information about how people used them. Whereas receiving a book is a passive act, and buying a used book is an act of selection and consumption, taking an already-complete book and making the effort to add something to it is fundamentally active (rather than passive) and includes elements of

---

4   Sandra Hindman et al., "Reconstructions: Recuperation of Manuscript Illumination in Nineteenth- and Twentieth-Century America," in *Manuscript Illumination in the Modern Age: Recovery and Reconstruction*, ed. Sandra Hindman and Nina Rowe (Evanston: Northwestern University Press, 2001), pp. 215–74. Before this, Rowan Watson, *Vandals and Enthusiasts: Views of Illumination in the Nineteenth Century: An Exhibition Held in the Henry Cole Wing of the Victoria and Albert Museum, 31 January-30 April 1995* (London: Victoria and Albert Museum, 1995), and Roger S. Wieck, "Folia Fugitiva: The Pursuit of the Illuminated Manuscript Leaf," *The Journal of the Walters Art Gallery* 54, Essays in Honor of Lilian M. C. Randall (1996), pp. 233–54; and Christopher De Hamel, *Cutting up Manuscripts for Pleasure and Profit*, The Sol M. Malkin Lecture in Bibliography 11 (Charlottesville: Book Arts, 1996), also addressed the topic.

production (rather than just consumption).[5] If someone adds images or texts to a book, he or she has probably read the book thoroughly enough to know that certain desired components are missing. This new owner has addressed that lack by initiating a series of steps, which may result in commissioning artists, scribes and binders to break the book apart, change it, and put it back together. Until now the strong desires that have been considered have chiefly been the destructive ones—the forces of iconoclasm, on the one hand, and the collector's desire for ownership, on the other.[6] But in fact, strong desires could provide an opposite force and lead to a book's burgeoning.[7] A believer's powerful needs could make his book swell with the desire for more outlets for his love. More words, more images, more pages could make the book burst out of its binding. Studying the physical book and its additions can help to track these desires. I consider the augmented book as the result of a particular need.

Throughout this study, therefore, my essential questions are these: when an owner possessed a complete, finished manuscript, how could he or she add things (texts, images, physical material) to it to reflect its (new) ownership? And what would he gain by doing that? In the period of flourishing literacy, what basic changes to the structure of manuscripts made it possible for him to do this? This study is ostensibly about the material life of objects—medieval books—as they accumulated layers of stuff from one or more owners. But of course, the study is really about people, and what of their desires can be found among those layers. The study rests at the intersection of human desire and codicology.

Codicology—the archeology of the book—has been a concern in manuscript studies ever since scholars such as L. M. J. Delaissé and Peter Gumbert underscored its importance for understanding the medieval book. In this study, I approach codicology in a new way, offering up

---

5   J. P. Gumbert, *The Dutch and Their Books in the Manuscript Age* (London: British Library, 1990), pp. 72–73 discusses the market for second-hand books in Deventer.

6   On iconoclasm see David Freedberg, *The Power of Images: Studies in the History and Theory of Response* (Chicago: University of Chicago Press, 1989).

7   Virginia Reinburg, *French Books of Hours: Making an Archive of Prayer, c. 1400–1600* (Cambridge and New York: Cambridge University Press, 2012), pp. 2, 44 and passim notes that older books of hours were updated to keep them in circulation, although this is not the thrust of her larger project.

an original account of the processes that produced augmentations.[8] Considering the book as a physical object allows me to think about the adjustments to it as something both historically bound and cumulative. By that I mean that various techniques for manipulating the contents of the finished book developed over the history of the codex's existence, accumulated, so that by the fifteenth century, when literacy and book production rose sharply, book makers and users had a panoply of methods from which to draw. I hope to reveal these exploitations in a systematic way, which to some extent also maps onto a history of the book. By taking the structure of the book as my starting point, I will extend Delaissé's initial research. Of course, I won't describe the exact physical structure of every manuscript in the book, or discuss every text and image in every book, as that would be tedious.

I have chosen to focus on Netherlandish manuscripts because of their unique circumstance, poised at a moment when broad demand for books driven by popular piety necessitated rapid production, but before the printing press allowed for a process of mass production. In the Netherlandish manuscript, economic, social, and individual interests come together to create a variety of methods for creating and adapting books—methods one can pick apart via stratigraphy to reveal the interests of the owners. While such a reconstructive effort might be possible for any of the many genres of medieval manuscripts (Ovids, Bibles, bestiaries, sermons, etc.), I have focused on prayerbooks because of the fierce demand for them, their large-scale production, and the rapidity with which indulgences and local variations required that they be updated to suit their owners' needs. And I have focused on Netherlandish prayerbooks because of the ways their innovative manufacture encouraged users to think—not only about their relationship to newly procured books, but also to old ones.

I begin by explaining what I am calling the "modular method," with which some—but by no means all—books of hours were made in the fifteenth century in the Netherlands. I dwell on this because this method represents not only a way in which new books could be made, but also a change in mindset about how older books could be updated

---

8   Eamon Duffy, *Marking the Hours: English People and Their Prayers 1240–1570* (New Haven and London: Yale University Press, 2006), pp. 38–39, uses the term "devotional accretion" to describe images and texts added to prayerbooks.

and adjusted. I then turn to the two large categories I have defined: adjustments *not* requiring binding, and those requiring binding. In fact, both kinds of adjustments become much more widespread in the fifteenth century because of the modular method. Assembling a book from modules left many areas of parchment blank (for example, the backs of single-leaf miniatures and the ends of text quires) and thus provided naked surfaces for new owners to fill in. This could be done without rebinding. Secondly, the modular method promoted the idea that a book could be built in segments, thereby opening the possibility for all kinds of new added parts. Making such additions predates the fifteenth century, and my examples demonstrate this, but the practice rises to a crescendo just as printing makes its debut. I have chosen to concentrate on manuscripts made in the Netherlands (both Northern and Southern) in the fifteenth century because these represent bookmaking at a moment of extraordinary expansion in literacy, when the demands of buyers impelled producers to seek more efficient production techniques. The modular method was developed there to make more affordable books that would cater to the newly literate. It was a place and time when readers were eager to get their hands on books, and when new books were being made in new ways with proto-assembly-line methods.

Types of augmentations

Manuscripts were part of the luxury goods that were passed down from one generation to the next. Instead of existing in a linear economy (take resources, make an object, use it, dispose of it after use), a manuscript reentered the system after one person finished using it and therefore participated in a circular economy (take resources, make an object, use it, refurbish it wholly or in components, recirculate it). In this way, manuscripts were like expensive plate or clothing that formed part of a trousseau. Plate was melted and reshaped into new, fashionable wares; old clothing was reused, turned into linings, or had the buttons or other costly pieces removed for repurposing.[9] So was it also with books. Old

---

9   Susan Mosher Stuard, *Gilding the Market: Luxury and Fashion in Fourteenth-Century Italy* (Philadelphia: University of Pennsylvania Press, 2006); Brigitte Buettner, "Past Presents: New Year's Gifts at the Valois Courts, ca. 1400," *Art Bulletin* 83, no. 4 (2001), pp. 598–625.

books did not leave the system quickly. New ones were made faster than the old ones were thrown out, and the old ones were updated so that they could stay in circulation even longer.

In fact, books were made ever-more efficiently and in ever-greater numbers in the later Middle Ages. Therefore, the structural division I propose between manuscript augmentations that required rebinding and those that didn't is accompanied by a temporal division. I begin by examining the structure of the prayerbook before and after ca. 1390, because doing so reveals a growing culture around making augmentations, which the post-1390 book structure facilitated. Most pre-1390 prayerbooks were planned and made in a unified campaign of work. But after this time book culture changed rapidly and moved to more mechanical means of production, just as rising literacy was creating a demand for more books, and private devotion was changing such that votaries demanded prayers with ever-higher spiritual rewards. Escalating book production triggered cheaper ways to make them. It also meant that more people had access to the raw materials of book making, such as parchment. Access to time and materials plus creativity and zeal but without much training led to the production of new kinds of books and images as well as autonomous images. After 1390 the modular method gradually became the dominant method of producing books of hours (except for those at the very top and very bottom of the market[10]), and was one of the great innovations of the late Middle Ages (discussed at length in Part I). It was also wasteful of materials, because it resulted in many blank folios. However, books' recipients would fill those blanks up with all kinds of stuff.

Some books were not completed during the lifetime of the copyist, miniaturist, or patron, and it is easy to see why recipients would consider these in need of further work. For example, the Limbourg Brothers died of the plague before they could finish *Les Très Riches Heures du Duc de Berry* (1412–16, Chantilly, Musée Condé, Ms. 65). Jean Colombe completed it in 1485 at the court of Savoy, partly copying the Limbourgs' style, and partly finishing illuminations in his own visual

---

10   Buyers at the top of the market continued to order individualized, bespoke books
     made according to traditional design principles, and those at the bottom of the
     market might make themselves a book with home-spun decoration.

idiom.[11] Likewise, the *Sforza Hours* (LBL, Add. Ms. 34294) was made in two distinct campaigns of work. Giovan Pietro Birago executed the first round of illuminations around 1490 for Bona of Savoy, widow of Galeazzo Sforza, Duke of Milan. He delivered only part of the work to the patron, and the final tranche of this work was stolen before he could deliver it. The book thus remained incomplete until Margaret of Austria, who inherited the book 30 years later, commissioned Gerard Horenbout to finish the miniatures in 1517–20. Thus, three decades and the Alps separate the two campaigns of illuminations for this book.[12] One can understand the impulse to finish a nearly-finished book, to have a complete entity rather than one in which blanks call attention to themselves.[13]

Other forces, however, drove book owners to add texts and images to books that anyone would have considered complete. These forces included: a desire to personalize the book; a desire to respond to newly available texts and visual subjects; a desire to show devotion to new feasts and cults; a desire to make the book reflect the financial strength of the book owner; a desire to raise the level of decoration to make the book more colorful; a desire to systematize the decoration; a desire to incorporate loose images, sometimes given as gifts, into the book, thereby turning it into a memory album. This final desire is one I have discussed at length in a previous book.[14] In the current study, I concentrate on the others.

Then as now, the *nouveaux riches* often swathed themselves in visually loud accouterments. To this end, merchants and other wealthy urbanites added extra decoration to their prayerbooks, an arena in which they could lay on gold, decoration, abundant color while at

---

11 Patricia Stirnemann, "The King of Illuminated Manuscripts: The Très Riches Heures," in *The Limbourg Brothers: Nijmegen Masters at the French Court, 1400–1416*, ed. Rob Dückers and Pieter Roelofs, *exh. cat., Museum het Valkhof, Nijmegen* (Ghent: Ludion, 2005), pp. 113–19, at p. 113. In the same volume, see p. 219, fig. 13, for an example of the two campaigns of work on a single folio.

12 Mark L. Evans, *The Sforza Hours* (London: British Library, 1992).

13 Lucy Freeman Sandler, "Notes for the Illuminator: The Case of the *Omne Bonum*," *The Art Bulletin* 71, no. 4 (1989), pp. 551–64, analyzing an example of later illuminators finishing an English encyclopedia of the fourteenth century, performs a close codicological reading.

14 Kathryn Rudy, *Postcards on Parchment: The Social Lives of Medieval Books* (New Haven and London: Yale University Press, 2015).

the same time remaining humble and godly. Votaries also wished to remain devotionally current, which is why people from all walks of life expressed their personal desires by adding newly available texts, including new prayers, especially those that presented indulgences that would secure them a place in heaven. Or they wanted to record a fact or oath in a book that was as close to the word of God as possible, for this lent it gravitas.

I first catalogue the means by which new images and other kinds of objects might find their way into books—the various gluings, sewings, scribblings, scribings, and stitchings. These cultural activities turned the book into an interactive object—a porous object—that would absorb the desires of an owner, or of a series of owners over time. While the techniques for making additions and emendations had existed since the advent of the codex, they became almost *de rigueur* in the years after 1390 for three reasons: first, the number of lay readers increased significantly, meaning that more people had books and traded ideas about how to use them. Second, techniques for making books of hours were adapted to the structure of this book type, which brought together discrete texts. When these were made in modular form, the fissures between sections generated blank parchment, which invited and even demanded additions. Third, prayer culture changed significantly in the fifteenth century, so that new prayers, especially those promising apotropaic benefits or indulgences, quickly became popular, and book owners wanted to incorporate these into their volumes to keep them up to date. Once owners conceptualized their books of hours as absorbent objects, they made ample use of them as repositories for prayers, notes, familial and historical information, small devotional objects. In other words, their books became platforms upon which to express themselves, and at the same time, places to store memory items. Upon the death of the owner, the manuscript would be given or sold to a new owner and not be thrown out. That new owner might adjust the book to keep it relevant. In short, manuscripts belonged to a circular economy: they circulated through multiple owners, rather than being discarded.

Updating manuscripts could involve small or large interventions. Jotting down a new prayer or drawing a figure onto the existing blank (sometimes ruled) parchment of an older prayerbook formed the smallest interventions. The second level: adding single leaves, pasting or sewing small objects, including bits of parchment, leather, paper, metallic badges to the blank areas of the parchment. Third: inserting single leaves into the book so that they become part of the book's structure. Fourth: adding entire quires to the beginning or end of an existing manuscript. Fifth: adding material, such as quires, to the interior of the manuscript in such a way that the contents are restructured. Only some of these forms of updating could be accomplished within the original binding of the book.

The second part of my argument is this: while the parchment book block lasts a long time, a book's binding does not. Bindings fall apart after a few years of hard use. Consequently, users often had their books rebound if they used them heavily. Doing so also afforded them the opportunity to add more material before the book was resealed into its new binding. Ateliers even sprung up that specialized in dismantling, refurbishing and rebinding books, as I argue toward the end of this study. In what follows I have organized these strategies for augmenting the book, from the simplest to the most complex, and as such have divided the augmentations into two conceptual categories: those that are relatively superficial and do not require rebinding the book; and those that do require structural changes, and therefore rebinding. These I take up in Parts III and IV, respectively.

To rebind a manuscript was an operation that required the assistance of a professional, and with it the provision of time, money, and planning. Rebinding signals a high degree of desire, even desperation, to keep a book useful and in circulation. Book owners who have their books rebound have either worn them so heavily that they have no real alternative, or have such a strong desire for certain texts and images that they are willing to part with considerable resources to create the books they want. Both scenarios reveal a strong attachment to the book and also signal that more was at stake than merely the object itself. Augmenting the prayerbook was augmenting the spiritual self, and making that altered spirituality manifest materially. Such physical interventions are therefore an order of magnitude more complicated than changes that can be wrought without rebinding. Those that don't require rebinding, conversely, are considerably more casual and could be cheap or even free. They could be as simple as adding some scrawls to a blank page. The structure of those changes provides the structure of this study. They are as follows:

Additions made to manuscripts

Category I: Changes that did not require rebinding
Correcting the text
Adding text to blank folios and interstices
Augmenting the existing decoration
Drawing or painting images directly onto the blank parchment
Adding physical material superficially

Category II: Changes that required rebinding
Incorporating end leaves into the book during rebinding
Adding single leaves into the structure (textual or with an image)
Adding a bifolium
Adding a quire
Changing the structural order of the quires
Multiple and more complicated changes

Nearly every surviving medieval book has had something done to it during the intervening centuries, and therefore, nearly every manuscript would be eligible as fodder for the present study. You will be relieved to know that this study is not meant to be an exhaustive catalogue of medieval manipulations to the book, but its goal is to organize such manipulations, and by doing so, to foster awareness of them, to think about them structurally, and to seek patterns. That said, a manuscript that has one sort of augmentation often has several, for an owner who considered his book incomplete might initially write some additional text on the blank end leaves, but then find that he had even more text to add, and therefore wanted to bind in some more pages. Moreover, the people who wrote in their books and affixed objects to them were also the people who used their books most heavily, thereby wearing out the bindings and necessitating an additional round of work. In my classification, these measures would qualify as two kinds of manipulation, one from Category I (changes without rebinding) and

Category II (changes that require rebinding). Therefore, some of the manuscripts I introduce early in this study reappear later on.

Documentary photography can capture some of these augmentations.[15] Most commercial photography produced by museums and libraries does not present the manuscript as an entity, but flattens out single folios (usually by pressing them under glass) and shows them as if they were not connected to a book. I have therefore included some of my own amateur photos of manuscripts, which often provide a better sense of the object as a layered, three-dimensional object. Regardless of the type of photography, the more complicated the intervention, the more photos that are required to show it. For some of the more multifold interventions near the end of the study, I have also employed diagrams to illustrate my points.

In summary, therefore, my premise is this: understanding the fears, hopes, and desires of people who lived half a millennium ago through the murky lens of time is often fruitless, but by studying the images and texts that owners *added* to their books, one can see what drove and inspired them. It took effort to change a book once it was already made. These changes, in demonstrating what owners were willing to add even at the expense of some inconvenience, precisely index those texts they most desired. Devotion, as a series of habits, was never finished. The committed votary collected ever more ways to venerate his or her object of devotion, while the parchment manuscript was an ever-expanding unit of layered memory that could grow in step with the shifts in one or more owners' lives. Reactions to marriage, children, sin, and fear of the fiery afterlife, all entered books and structured sets of gestures. These gestural habits, mediated by the manuscript, molded the mind and body.

---

15   On a related set of concerns, see Rowan Watson, "The Illuminated Manuscript in the Age of Photographic Reproduction," in *Making the Medieval Book: Techniques of Production: Proceedings of the Fourth Conference of the Seminar in the History of the Book to 1500, Oxford, July 1992*, ed. Linda L. Brownrigg (Los Altos Hills and London: Anderson-Lovelace & Red Gull Press, 1995), pp. 133–43, who details the early history of documentary photography for manuscripts, which was crucial to their being entered in the canon.

Part I: The modular method

Toward the end of the fourteenth century, the manner in which manuscripts were made changed dramatically. In the late fourteenth and throughout the fifteenth centuries, book makers created their wares increasingly with what I call the *modular method*, an approach to construction that takes into account a division of labor and a need for efficiency, and that presupposes an owner who would expand the book later. This had serious implications for the ways in which book owners could make augmentations to their books.

Along with a shift in production methods came a shift in book type. Before ca. 1260, the psalter was the main text for private devotion. Psalters contain the 150 psalms, which a supplicant would read in fixed groups over the course of days or weeks, and thereby work through the entire text from cover to cover. A psalter's text was therefore static. Although psalters continued to be made and used for the duration of the Middle Ages, beginning around 1260, the book of hours gradually replaced the psalter as the predominant book for private devotion.[1]

---

1   For late medieval psalters, see A. Bennett, "The Transformation of the Gothic Psalter in Thirteenth-Century France," in *The Illuminated Psalter: Studies in the Content, Purpose and Placement of Its Images*, ed. F. O. Büttner (Turnhout: Brepols, 2004), pp. 211–21, as well as the other essays in this volume. See also studies about individual manuscripts: Jane Geddes, *The St. Albans Psalter: A Book for Christina of Markyate* (London: British Library, 2005); Kathryn Gerry, "Cult and Codex: Alexis, Christina and the St. Albans Psalter," in *Der Albani-Psalter. Stand und Perspektiven der Forschung / the St. Albans Psalter. Current Research and Perspectives*, ed. Jochen Bepler and Christian Heitzmann, *Hildesheimer Forschungen, Band 4* (Hildesheim, Zürich and New York: Georg Olms, 2013), pp. 69–95; Stella Panayotova and Andrew Morris, *The Macclesfield Psalter: "A Window into the World of Late Medieval England"* (Cambridge: Fitzwilliam Museum, 2005); Lucy Freeman Sandler, *The*

     http://dx.doi.org/10.11647/OBP.0094.01

Because of the canonical status of the psalms, and the longevity of
the physical book, the process of change was slow. Psalters, of course,
continued to be made, and combination books, such as the Liège
Psalter-Hours, featured below, provided a transitional form.[2] Books
of hours contained some standard texts: calendar, Little Office of the
Virgin, Penitential Psalms and Litany, and Office of the Dead. They
often appeared in this order, but their sequence was by no means
fixed. Furthermore the book of hours usually contained other texts as
well, such as the popular prayers *O Intemerata* and *Obsecro te*. Books
of hours became increasingly widespread in France, England and the
Netherlands in the mid- to late fourteenth century. In the early years
of production, say, until ca. 1390, the book of hours was often made
as a bespoke product, with a planner mapping out the entire book as
one unit. Texts developed coevally with cycles of imagery—including
infancy and passion cycles—which differed regionally and in which
there was plenty of latitude.[3]

Psalter of Robert De Lisle in the British Library (London and New York: Harvey Miller
& Oxford University Press, 1983); Lucy Freeman Sandler, *Illuminators & Patrons
in Fourteenth-Century England: The Psalter & Hours of Humphrey De Bohun and the
Manuscripts of the Bohun Family* (London: The British Library, 2014); Anne Rudloff
Stanton, "The Psalter of Isabelle, Queen of England 1308–1330: Isabelle as the
Audience," *Word & Image: A Journal of Verbal/Visual Enquiry* 18, no. 4 (2002), pp. 1–27;
James H. Marrow, "Text and Image in Two Fifteenth-Century Dutch Psalters from
Delft," in *Spiritualia Neerlandica: Opstellen voor Dr. Albert Ampe hem door vakgenoten
en vrienden aangeboden uit waardering voor zijn wetenschappelijk werk* (Antwerp:
UFSIA-Ruusbroecgenootschap, 1990), pp. 341–52. For early books of hours, see
Claire Donovan, *The De Brailes Hours: Shaping the Book of Hours in Thirteenth-Century
Oxford*, Toronto Medieval Texts and Translations (Toronto and Buffalo: University
of Toronto Press, 1991).

2   Studies of individual examples include Judith Oliver, "Reconstruction of a Liège
     Psalter-Hours," *The British Library Journal* 5, no. 2 (1979), pp. 107–28; Alexa Sand,
     "Vision, Devotion, and Difficulty in the Psalter Hours 'of Yolande of Soissons,'"
     The Art Bulletin 87, no. 1 (2005), pp. 6–23; Alexa Sand, "A Small Door: Recognizing
     Ruth in the Psalter-Hours 'of Yolande of Soissons,'" *Gesta* 46, no. 1 (2007), pp.
     19–40; Alexa Sand, "*Cele Houre Memes*: An Eccentric English Psalter-Hours in the
     Huntington Library," *Huntington Library Quarterly* 75, no. 2 (2012), pp. 171–211;
     Richard A. Leson, "Heraldry and Identity in the Psalter-Hours of Jeanne of Flanders
     (Manchester, John Rylands Library, Ms Lat. 117)," *Studies in Iconography* 32 (2011),
     pp. 155–98.

3   Dominique Vanwijnsberghe, "The Cyclical Illustrations of the Little Hours of the
     Virgin in Pre-Eyckian Manuscripts," in *Flanders in a European Perspective: Manuscript
     Illumination around 1400 in Flanders and Abroad: Proceedings of the International
     Colloquium, Leuven, 7–10 September 1993*, ed. Maurits Smeyers and Bert Cardon
     (Leuven: Peeters, 1995), pp. 285–96; Dominique Vanwijnsberghe, "Le Cycle de
     l'Enfance des Petites Heures de la Vierge dans les Livres d'Heures des Pays-

Just as the psalter might be read completely from beginning to end, it was also written in the same way, from beginning to end. In contradistinction to that, the book of hours contained many different texts, intended to be read on an as-needed basis. Users would dip into the texts that were appropriate for the moment, reading, for example, just the litany in one sitting, or just the vespers of the Hours of the Virgin. They might read the Hours of the Cross in the week before Good Friday, the Hours of the Holy Spirit to prepare for Pentecost, and the Penitential Psalms during Lent. Seasonal appropriateness and personal interest could determine which texts to read at any given hour and day. Whereas a psalter was canonical, there was never an entirely standard set of texts that made up the book of hours. Their composition always varied, both at the time of production and by force of an owner's interests and desires.[4]

Furthermore, literacy increased considerably from the thirteenth to the fifteenth century, and new literate urban classes demanded more affordable books. These two forces—reading style and economics—meant that books of hours were written and designed differently from psalters. Books of hours (at least in the Netherlands) were made increasingly in smaller segments that could be brought together during binding. In other words, they were both read *and produced* in units—that is, modularly.[5]

Bas Méridionaux," in *Manuscripten en miniaturen: studies aangeboden aan Anne S. Korteweg bij haar afscheid van de Koninklijke Bibliotheek,* ed. J. A. A. M. Biemans, et al., *Bijdragen tot de Geschiedenis van de Nederlandse Boekhandel* (Zutphen: Walburg Pers, 2007), pp. 355–65.

4 See Paul Henry Saenger, "Books of Hours and the Reading Habits of the Later Middle Ages," in *The Culture of Print: Power and the Uses of Print in Early Modern Europe,* ed. Alain Boureau and Roger Chartier (Cambridge: Polity, 1989), pp. 141–73; Paul Henry Saenger, *Space between Words: The Origins of Silent Reading* (Stanford: Stanford University Press, 1997); Kathryn M. Rudy, "Dirty Books: Quantifying Patterns of Use in Medieval Manuscripts Using a Densitometer," *Journal of Historians of Netherlandish Art* 2, no. 1 (2010).

5 Farquhar, "The Manuscript as a Book," pp. 40–41, describes the modular method in brief (although he does not use this term). Farquhar's essay also draws on Delaissé, "The Importance of Books of Hours for the History of the Medieval Book." Reinburg, *French Books of Hours: Making an Archive of Prayer, c. 1400–1600,* pp. 22–26, discussing a similar situation in France, calls books of hours assembled from parts "shop copy manuscripts." However, in examples she gives such as Baltimore, Walters Art Museum, Ms. W. 269, fol. 76r, the miniatures are integral with the text pages and therefore do not reveal a physical separation of copyists from illuminators and therefore do not exemplify the production methods I am outlining here.

A. Modular and non-modular, compared

To explain the modular method of manuscript construction with a concrete example, I compare two manuscripts, an earlier psalter-hours, and a later book of hours. The psalter-hours was made in the second half of the thirteenth century in Liège (HKB, Ms. 76 G 17). It is written in Latin and French and was made for a Beguine at the beguinage of St. Agnes in Maaseyck. This book's structure is typical of many thirteenth-century productions. Historiated initials mark major text divisions with corresponding gold and painted decoration in the margin. Major psalm divisions, with their extra decoration, can occur on a recto or verso, at the top of the folio or in the middle. For example, the initial for Psalm 26, which depicts Christ healing a blind man, appears near the bottom of a verso folio (HKB, Ms. 76 G 17, fol. 20v; fig. 1).[6] When the scribe set out to write this text, he simply began at the beginning and continued to the end, filling the requisite number of quires. He left space for the rubrics and the decorated initials as he went along. The placement of historiated initials was by default dictated by the scribe.[7] The painter who made the bar borders was either the same person as, or else worked closely with, the person who painted the figures. These painters then sent their work back to the scribe, who at that point filled in the labels identifying St. John the Baptist and Moses, figures occupying the bas-de-page. The scribe also filled in Moses's scroll. This manuscript reveals the degree to which the production required careful coordination between scribes and illuminators, who may have been working under the same roof. By contrast, in the late fourteenth and fifteenth centuries, scribes and planners had a different concept of book production, one marked by a sharper division of labor.

---

6   Folio from a psalter, with a historiated initial showing Christ healing a blind man, Psalm 26. The Hague, Koninklijke Bibliotheek, Ms. 76 G 17, fol. 20v. http://manuscripts.kb.nl/zoom/BYVANCKB%3Amimi_76g17%3A020v

7   J. P. Gumbert, "Times and Places for Initials," *Quaerendo* 39 (2009), pp. 1–24.

Fig. 2 Modular book of hours, opened at the beginning of the Vigil for the Dead. Special
Collections of the Universiteitsbibliotheek van Amsterdam, Ms. I G 54, fol. 32v-
33r. Image © Universiteitsbibliotheek van Amsterdam, CC BY 4.0.

A book of hours now in Amsterdam reveals that it was constructed
according to a different set of principles (AUB, Ms. I G 54; fig. 2). I
could have used any one of hundreds of books of hours to complete
this comparison, but I chose this one because its binding is loose, which
allows one to see the structure more easily. Each new text begins on the
top recto of a fresh quire. Though the texts vary in length, the scribe
simply used as many quires as were necessary for that text. He then
began the next text on a blank recto at the beginning of a new quire.
Some blank, ruled parchment invariably fell at the end. This book's
scribe has composed each section as a separate packet, and then sewn
them together. A close look at the photograph reveals the division
between two modules.

Changing fashion for types of devotional literature both necessitated
and encouraged a new mode of production; that new mode of
production in turn spurred further changes in devotional literature.

Several forces—including literacy rates, new forms of private devotion, and economic forces—coalesced to fundamentally change how manuscripts were made in the decades just before the printing press. A closer look at the structure of the book of hours clarifies how this procedure developed. Let me explain.

Books of hours proved so popular that a high demand encouraged new, cheaper methods of production, which would also allow a wider audience to buy them. In Bruges around 1390, a new development occurred: a group of illuminators known as the Masters of the Pink Canopies began making full-page miniatures in ateliers separate from where the texts were written. These miniatures could then be inserted into the book-block before binding. Primarily they made full-page miniatures for books of hours for export to England. These were made in considerable quantities. Nicholas Rogers has identified 170 surviving books of hours made for this export market between 1390 and 1520.[8] The Masters of the Pink Canopies were some of the first artists to systematically exploit the new production and design concepts I have been outlining, which allowed production to swell. Pink Canopy manuscripts have for the most part been discussed in the art historical literature, because scholars have been interested principally in the miniatures and not in the bookish substrates those miniatures lived in.[9] Consequently there is no comparable name for the group of copyists who inscribed the books that contains their work. The fact that they form a group of "masters" with no identifiable individuals among them suggests that their labor was as interchangeable as the miniatures they made. The rather large number of surviving manuscripts containing their wares points to an efficient atelier (or group of ateliers) making miniatures for an export market of non-bespoke manuscripts.

---

8   Nicholas Rogers, *Books of Hours Produced in the Low Countries for the English Market in the Fifteenth Century* (M. Litt. thesis, Cambridge University, 1982), p. 1.

9   For example, see LBL, Sloane Ms. 2683, made in Bruges, ca. 1390–1400, and a description in Scot McKendrick, *Flemish Illuminated Manuscripts, 1400–1550* (London: British Library, 2003), fig. 2. Surprisingly little has been written about the "Pink Canopies" group of manuscripts. Consult: Maurits Smeyers, *Naer Natueren Ghelike: Vlaamse Miniaturen voor Van Eyck (ca. 1350-ca. 1420)* (Leuven: Davidsfonds, 1993), pp. 90–91; Susie Vertongen, "Herman Scheerre, the Beaufort Master and the Flemish Miniature Painting: A Reopened Debate," in *Flanders in a European Perspective: Manuscript Illumination around 1400 in Flanders and Abroad: Proceedings of the International Colloquium, Leuven, 7–10 September 1993*, ed. Maurits Smeyers and Bert Cardon, *Corpus van Verluchte Handschriften = Corpus of Illuminated Manuscripts* (Leuven: Peeters, 1995), pp. 251–65.

For example, they produced a packet of images that was then bound into a book of hours for Sarum use in the last decade of the fourteenth century (Cambridge, UL, Ms. Ii.6.2).[10] This packet included images added to the Hours of the Virgin: an Annunciation, a Visitation, a Nativity, an Annunciation to the Shepherds, the Adoration of the Three Magi, the Massacre of the Innocents, the Flight into Egypt, and the Presentation in the Temple (fig. 3).[11] Included in this manuscripts are also single-leaf miniatures depicting single standing saints to preface short suffrages at the beginning of the manuscript, as well as a miniature depicting the Virgin in a radiant sunburst to preface the *Salve Regina*; a Crucifixion to preface a prayer to Christ's limbs; an image of Christ as Man of Sorrows with the *arma Christi* which preface the Seven Penitential Psalms (fig. 4);[12] and a funeral service to preface the Office of the Dead (fig. 5).[13] These images were designed to enhance a book of hours, to make it more colorful and appealing, and to roughly gauge the interests of a recipient (piety to Mary and to Christ's suffering, and to an assortment of popular saints).

Two features are striking about these images: first, their large number for such a relatively modest book of hours; and second, their sheer clumsiness. Although the full-page miniatures marking each canonical hour of the Virgin represent a lavish outlay of color, the individual paintings rely heavily on formulas and lack convincing spatial illusion. Patterned backgrounds—such as the swirling gold filigree on the black backdrop behind the Presentation in the Temple—add opulence, but in fact required little skill to apply. Likewise, voluminous drapery fills the

---

10 Paul Binski, P. N. R. Zutshi, and Stella Panayotova, *Western Illuminated Manuscripts: A Catalogue of the Collection in Cambridge University Library* (Cambridge and New York: Cambridge University Press, 2011), pp. 343–44.

11 Opening in a book of hours, with a full-page miniature by the Masters of the Pink Canopies depicting the Presentation in the Temple, facing complines of the Hours of the Virgin. Cambridge, University Library, Ms. Ii.6.2, fol. 55v–56r. http://cudl.lib.cam.ac.uk/view/MS-II-00006–00002/106 and http://cudl.lib.cam.ac.uk/view/MS-II-00006–00002/107

12 Opening in a book of hours, with a full-page miniature by the Masters of the Pink Canopies depicting Christ as Man of Sorrows among the *arma Christi*, facing the Seven Penitential Psalms. Cambridge, University Library, Ms. Ii.6.2, fol. 75v–76r. http://cudl.lib.cam.ac.uk/view/MS-II-00006–00002/144 and http://cudl.lib.cam.ac.uk/view/MS-II-00006–00002/145

13 Opening in a book of hours, with a full-page miniature by the Masters of the Pink Canopies depicting the Mass for the Dead, facing the Vigil for the Dead. Cambridge, University Library, Ms. Ii.6.2, fol. 94v–95r. http://cudl.lib.cam.ac.uk/view/MS-II-00006–00002/182 and http://cudl.lib.cam.ac.uk/view/MS-II-00006–00002/183

pictorial space with color and patterns, but it obfuscates anatomy and structure. In the Presentation, an altar mostly covers Simeon's lower body—his upper body appears as an indistinct swirl of drapery—while Mary's body appears as a blue area of fabric. For the funeral service, the artist has reduced the number of figures to two and has avoided showing the figures' hands, no doubt because they are difficult to draw. Instead the artist has filled most of the available space with a coffin, which—like the body of the Virgin earlier—is entirely covered with drapery. For the artist of limited skill, pattern (such as the red dots on the fabric) trumps volume, because showing three-dimensional forms in space is difficult. Flattened, patterned colorful shapes apparently fulfilled the buyers' desires well enough, for the Masters of the Pink Canopies did a swift trade in miniatures. The opportunity to own colorful images, even incompetent ones, must have played a significant role in the rising popularity of the book of hours.

By allowing ateliers to specialize—to just make full-page miniatures, without having to copy all the texts—the division of labor streamlined production and also changed the imagery by simplifying and standardizing it. The Masters of the Pink Canopies began each sheet by drawing a standard-sized frame, topped with an eponymous pink canopy. These choices were givens. They then filled in popular subjects, often using patterns to further reduce the labor of having to come up with new compositions. For example, the composition with Christ as Man of Sorrows among the *arma Christi* (fig. 4) is one that appears in other manuscripts. A close free-hand copy appears in another book of hours made in Bruges for export to England (LBL, Sloane Ms. 2683; fig. 6).[14] This subject must have been a calculated choice for replication, because the image could be used in front of a variety of texts. In Cambridge, UL, Ms. Ii.6.2, it prefaces the Seven Penitential Psalms, whereas in Sloane 2683 it prefaces a prayer to the wood of the cross, to the crown of thorns, to the Five Wounds (taken one at a time), to the Virgin, and to St. John. A rubric prefacing the prayer indicates that it should be read before an image of the crucifix. The Pink Canopy miniature provides the required

---

14   Folio in a book of hours, with a full-page miniature by the Masters of the Pink Canopies depicting Christ as Man of Sorrows among the *arma Christi*, facing a prayer to be read before an image of the crucifix. London, British Library, Sloane Ms. 2683, fol. 65v. http://www.bl.uk/manuscripts/Viewer.aspx?ref=sloane_ms_2683_fs001r

image of the crucifix alongside several other items mentioned in the prayer. Thus, this image was flexible and therefore interchangeable: it could find a home in nearly any book of hours. Second, its simplicity must have appealed to the half-trained Masters of the Pink Canopies. Depicting the naked figure of Jesus provided challenges for the artists, but they followed a formula, which made it easier. Otherwise, most of the surface is given to the *arma Christi*, which comprise simple geometric shapes and posed little challenge even to a maladroit painter. Part of the appeal and popularity of the *arma Christi* as a devotional aid must have been the ease with which it could be reproduced with little skill. By churning out ubiquitous infancy imagery, popular saints, and flexible motifs such as the *arma Christi*, these "masters" could contribute image-modules to accompany text-modules produced elsewhere.

Other examples confirm that the new high-volume miniaturists sought out simple imagery. Among the miniatures included in Cambridge, UL, Ms. Ii.6.2 is the Face of Christ (fig. 7).[15] Various elements of the standard iconography have been reduced, abstracted, or obfuscated. Veronica herself is missing altogether, and the face has swollen to nearly the full width of the page. Either the face was traced from a template or copied freehand based on transcribing simple geometric shapes. While visually "elevating" the subject, the cloth of honor obviates the need for drafting recessional space, which is difficult to depict convincingly. On the cloth and throughout the image, the artist used pattern (which is simple and repetitive) instead of modeling (which requires more skill to achieve nuanced gradations). These artists were not capable of achieving logical coherence: a blue blob below the central boss of the highly formulaic canopy makes no structural sense. A checkerboard floor indicates an attempt at depicting recession, although the artist has not quite understood the principle, and the floor just looks wonky. The features visible in this opening speak to a strong division of labor (painter, copyist, manager who assembles components), and to the deskilling of painters, whose work was reduced to copying boilerplate models. This yielded symmetrical designs, expressionless figures and

---

15   Opening in a book of hours, with a full-page miniature by the Masters of the Pink Canopies depicting the Face of Christ, facing the prayer "Salve sancta facies." Cambridge, University Library, Ms. Ii.6.2, fol. 12v-13r. http://cudl.lib. cam.ac.uk/view/MS-II-00006–00002/30   and   http://cudl.lib.cam.ac.uk/view/ MS-II-00006–00002/31

unmodulated areas of color, but ultimately, richly colored books of hours. Using under-skilled labor must have driven prices down far enough to create a demand. The English ate it up.[16]

That the book of hours—and no other kind of book—initiated this production method makes intuitive sense, because its makeup is inherently predisposed to being assembled in modules. In fact, the conceptualization of the book as modular might have arisen from the ways in which the calendar was produced. Because calendars were typically made on two quires of three bifolia, to make twelve pages for the twelve months, and because they were ruled differently from the rest of the manuscript, they were made in a separate campaign of work. In the Southern Netherlands, special ateliers may have developed just to produce calendars (more research will have to be done to understand that situation for certain). Book makers must have realized that other texts could similarly be made of components that could be slotted into place. Thus, instead of producing entire books of hours, makers could produce components, and let customers choose which texts to bind together into a book of hours. This reduction to components became especially useful in the suffrages, where ateliers in Bruges produced single leaves with images of saints, and single leaves with prayers to those saints. Customers must have been able to select the saints they wanted according to desire and budget. For customers living further afield (such as the English clientele for Bruges books of hours), either the customer could send an agent, or the producer could roughly anticipate the consumer's desires by including some of the most popular saints,

---

16   Libraries all over the British Isles hold books of hours made in the Southern Netherlands for export. Consult Nicholas Rogers, *Books of Hours Produced in the Low Countries for the English Market in the Fifteenth Century*; Nicholas Rogers, "Patrons and Purchasers: Evidence for the Original Owners of Books of Hours Produced in the Low Countries for the English Market," in *Als Ich Can: Liber Amicorum in Memory of Professor Dr. Maurits Smeyers*, ed. Bert Cardon, et al., *Corpus of Illuminated Manuscripts = Corpus van Verluchte Handschriften* (Leuven: Peeters, 2002), pp. 1165–81; Saskia van Bergen, "The Production of Flemish Books of Hours for the English Market: Standardization and Workshop Practices." In *Manuscripts in Transition: Recycling Manuscripts, Texts and Images: Proceedings of the International Congres* [Sic] *Held in Brussels (5–9 November 2002)*, edited by Brigitte Dekeyzer and Jan van der Stock. Corpus of Illuminated Manuscripts, pp. 271–83 (Leuven: Peeters, 2005); Saskia van Bergen, *De Meesters van Otto van Moerdrecht. Een onderzoek naar de stijl en iconografie van een groep miniaturisten, in relatie tot de productie van getijdenboeken in Brugge rond 1430* (PhD thesis, University of Amsterdam, 2007).

including Sts George and Thomas, whom the English adored. Each customer could then further specify these by using local labor.

Book makers used modules as the basis of bare-bones books of hours, which owners could expand not only with further images, but also with further texts. An owner might want, for example, a "basic" book of hours, but with a copy of the Short Hours of the Cross. A scribe could produce this desired text in a single quire, and it, along with the relevant imagery, could then be incorporated in the final book. This modular manuscript construction had wide implications for bringing down the costs of books of hours and also for allowing owners to "personalize" them. It led to increased standardization and more variety at the same time. It also allowed owners to buy as many images as they cared to, or could afford. Medieval books were expandable, but this feature led to further design limitations, because book design still had to conform to long-established ideals around decoration.

B. The hierarchy of decoration

This new modular method had to take into account the hierarchy of decoration that already governed text-image decisions scribes and illuminators made when they produced manuscripts. Although this concept is widely understood by those who study manuscripts, the "hierarchy of decoration" often forms an unspoken set of assumptions in works of modern scholarship.[17] In a nutshell, the hierarchy of decoration means that the decoration of a book reiterates and reinforces the structure of the text. Each manuscript has its own internally consistent design logic. A manuscript can be highly decorated or barely

---

17   Articles that have addressed this topic directly rather than implicitly include Claire Donovan, "The Mise-en-Page of Early Books of Hours in England," in *Medieval Book Production: Assessing the Evidence; Oxford, July 1988*, ed. Linda L. Brownrigg, *Proceedings of the Conference of the Seminar in the History of the Book to 1500* (Los Altos Hills: Anderson-Lovelace, 1990), pp. 147–61; Michael T. Orr, "Hierarchies of Decoration in Early Fifteenth-Century English Books of Hours," in *Tributes to Kathleen L. Scott: English Medieval Manuscripts: Readers, Makers and Illuminators*, ed. Marlene Villalobos Hennessy (London: Harvey Miller, 2009), pp. 171–95. Although it discusses the development of penwork initials primarily and only the hierarchy of decoration secondarily, a fundamental work remains Patricia Stirnemann, "Fils de la Vierge. L'initiale à Filigranes Parisiennes: 1140–1314," *Revue de l'Art* 90 (1990), pp. 58–73.

decorated at all. Regardless of the degree of embellishment, the design of a medieval book's page layout is always organized around an initial.[18] One finds the largest and most lavishly painted initials marking the beginnings of the most important texts. With the largest initials always placed at the top left corner of a page, their decoration can spread vertically upward and laterally into the margin. Smaller initials might mark either subdivisions within that text, or less important texts; these could come partway down a page. Historiated initials (those containing narrative scenes in their letter frames) are higher in the hierarchy than decorated initials (with no figures). Decorated initials of cascading sizes mark further divisions. The number of rulings it fills up indicates an initial's size. For example, a manuscript might have 12-line historiated initials to mark the major texts, and three-line decorated initials to mark the internal divisions within the text, and one-line initials in alternating red and blue ink to mark new sentences or phrases.

Using initials of varying sizes to signpost the structure of the text could be likened to our modern system of making outlines, beginning with Roman numerals, then capital letters, then Arabic numerals, then lowercase letters, and so forth. Note also that in an outline each subsection begins on a fresh line and is indented appropriately. Increasing indentation fills the same role in a modern outline as the descending size of the initial in a medieval manuscript. In both systems the goal is to make the structure of the text manifest in the layout of the page.

Two rules governing the hierarchy of decoration are that each kind of initial should accompany a specific level of border decoration, and border decoration always emanates from an initial. A border decoration's grandeur can be quantified by how many sides of the page it fills up, and by its material, which may be (in descending order of grandeur): gold and painted figures, gold and painted abstract designs, just paint, or penwork. In this system, gold trumps paint. Paint trumps penwork. Figurative imagery trumps abstraction. Within a single manuscript, initials of various sizes correspond to flourishing of respective intensities. When a book's decorative program breaks these rules, it usually signals a later intervention, an unplanned component,

---

18   Gumbert, "Times and Places for Initials," pp. 1–24.

an impromptu addition. An owner's desire was often stronger than a decorative program's consistency.

According to the hierarchy of decoration, miniatures of cascading sizes also correspond to the grandeur of the initials, with the full-page miniature at the top of the chain, followed by column-wide miniatures, and then small miniatures that don't fill a column, and so on down. Each of these levels corresponds to a level of border decoration. For example, 12-line historiated initials painted in tempera and framed in gold might accompany painted and gilded border decoration on four sides, while in the same manuscript four-line decorated (painted) initials accompany painted border decoration on one side.

All this decoration helps orient the book's user. More colorful pages signal the beginnings of more important texts. Smaller initials, with their accompanying decoration that spilled out into the margins and was therefore visible when one was flipping through the book, helped users find other text passages. Within a single manuscript the internal logic should be consistent; if it is not, then that is a sign that the manuscript was pieced together from disparate parts.

From the time when parchment codices were first made in the fourth and fifth centuries, the hierarchy of decoration was planned from the outset, because producing a manuscript followed these steps: the parchment was first ruled; then the scribe would write the text; the illuminator would then apply the paintings and decoration; and finally the book block would go to a binder. The system of the hierarchy of decoration required that scribes know from the beginning what size all of the initials should be and where the miniatures should go, because they would have to leave appropriate space for them. In other words, for the first 800-or-so years of codex production, the scribe knew what all the texts and decoration would be in finished work. It was all planned from the beginning.

With the new modular system, the scribe and the illuminator would work in separate ateliers. An illuminator would not make images for a particular book, but rather make "interchangeable parts" that could be added to any book. A book's scribe would not know where, or even if, images would be added to his work. There was little contact between painters and scribes, because a manager (sometimes called a stationer) would direct their labor. With this system, the hierarchy of decoration could not be anticipated from the beginning. Separating the painters from the copyists suddenly made certain page layouts extremely inconvenient, namely, those that had both figurative paintings and inscribed words. Consequently, the new system suppressed certain design elements, including column-wide miniatures and other kinds of painting that the scribe would have to anticipate.[19] This is not to say that book makers abandoned illuminations. On the contrary, they used images even more fanatically. The old hierarchy of decoration and the new separation of the text copying from the image making meant that images would primarily be conceived as full-page miniatures, painted on single leaves, because such images could be slotted into the book at the beginning of the quire, and scribes would not have to plan for them. In order to face the text they accompanied, miniatures would almost always be inserted from now on as versos, that is, on the left side of the opening. This situation created a new standard.

Among the structural changes that followed from this shift was that now all new texts had to begin on a fresh quire so that the initial began on a fresh recto. Since the miniature had to precede the initial, the only place for it to go was on the preceding folio as a full-page miniature. Thus, with the new modular method, nearly all books that bore miniatures would have those miniatures on the left side of the opening, to face a text that began on the right side. In the pre-modular system, on the other hand, design elements would fall where they may. Page layout therefore ossified under the new modular method. Whereas in the past, each book was hand-designed and planned (at great mental cost and labor), now manuscripts could be made according to a general set of principles, so that the interchangeable units could be made remotely.[20]

All of the examples of the Pink Canopy Masters' work, given earlier, follow this standard: full-page miniature on the left of the opening, incipit on the right. In the opening with the Face of Christ, for example, someone (the stationer?) has inserted the image across from the prayer *Salve Sancte Facies* (fig. 7). The image has clearly been made in a separate

---

19   Ibid.

20   This trajectory maps onto the history of the car industry in the early twentieth century. Henry Ford's great breakthrough was to make interchangeable parts and put them together on an assembly line. This made the cars much cheaper than previous models that were made one at a time. Efficiency demanded more standardized components and created more regular results.

campaign of work from the text, as the two sides of the opening have different border decoration. Moreover, the decoration around the text block has been reduced to a minimum. Scribes and initial painters were undoubtedly under as much pressure as illuminators to apply their respective *technes*, repeatedly and efficiently, and to the minimum standard that the consuming public would permit. Initial painters would do only a cursory job. Most of the decoration in the manuscript would be borne by illuminators such as the Masters of the Pink Canopies. If customers wanted more decoration, they could pay for it by adding more miniatures.

Conventions for a hierarchy of decoration mandated that major texts be flagged with illumination and that major text breaks be flagged with large initials. It follows also that minor text breaks begin on a new line, and that items in a list each occupy a separate line. When major texts had to begin on a fresh quire, the remainder of the previous quire would remain blank. The backs of the miniatures were also blank, when they were added to an already-complete text. In the opening before the Face of Christ, for example, this modularization process generated one-and-a-half folios of blank parchment (Cambridge, UL, Ms. Ii.6.2; fig. 8).[21] The more modularized book making became, the more blank space it left in its wake. In short, the new production method multiplied the negative space of the book.

C. Modules and blank space

Another principle of medieval design was *horror vacui*, the fear of empty spaces. With its addition of newly blank spaces, the modular method came into direct conflict with this design principle. As components were added, blank space was created, and it demanded decoration. Scribes, illuminators, and book users often had the urge to fill those blank spaces up. A pervasive urge to fill empty space was already in play in the early Middle Ages, as on the text pages of the Book of Kells, where an illuminator has filled the line endings with colorful geometric

---

21   Opening in a book of hours with two blank folios in a row, immediately before the Face of Christ. Cambridge, University Library, Ms. Ii.6.2, fol. 11v-12r. http://cudl.lib.cam.ac.uk/view/MS-II-00006–00002/28 and http://cudl.lib.cam.ac.uk/view/MS-II-00006–00002/29

shapes, and in one case a horse and rider, and has even gone so far as to fill the empty space of the round letters with pools of color (Dublin, Trinity College, Ms. 58; fig. 9).[22] Avoiding trapped and blank white space remains a design principle today.

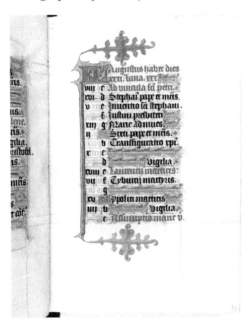

Fig. 10 Calendar folio from the Hours of Catherine of Cleves, with painted line endings and beginnings. New York, Morgan Library and Museum, Ms. M. 917, p. 17. Image © The Morgan Library and Museum, all rights reserved.

Using line endings and following the basic principle of filling empty space continued throughout the manuscript era, and resulted in some flamboyant displays of color and gold, all in the interest of preventing blank parchment within the text block, for example, in the calendar copied into the Hours of Catherine of Cleves (New York, Morgan Library and Museum, Ms. M. 917; fig. 10). A scribe has begun each saint's name on a fresh line because the alternating blue and gold initials in this manuscript demand a fresh line according to the hierarchy of decoration. Starting each on a fresh line creates unsightly blanks at the ends of the

---

22 Text folio from the Book of Kells, gospels, written and illuminated ca. 800, possibly on Iona. Dublin, Trinity College, Ms. 58, fol. 89r. http://digitalcollections.tcd.ie/home/index.php?DRIS_ID=MS58_089r

lines. The decorator has solved this problem by painting "line endings," long and narrow geometric forms painted in bold colors and gold. Book makers had varying degrees of tolerance for blank space in other parts of the book, but the new modular method generated space at the ends of quires that sometimes proved too much to fill.

Modular manuscripts made in the Southern Netherlands for English export created excessive empty space. In England in the two centuries before the Henrician Reformation, book makers could not keep up with demand, which is why England imported so many books of hours from the Low Countries. Bruges book makers were put under pressure by the sheer scale of the demand to find new means of production, and began using more workers whose tasks became more divided. Now, each worker (or atelier) was delivering components, and the people making them never had oversight over the whole, finished product. In and around Bruges, this method of production created demand for stationers who assembled the components and must also have been able to guide production, so that suppliers made enough Jesuses and not too many Barbaras and just the right number of Vigils of the Dead. At the other end, post-consumption, a small industry must have grown up in England for scriveners to fill some of that blank space with English prayers, that is, to refine the roughly tailored products.

Cambridge, UL, Ms. Ii.6.2 had pages and pages of blank parchment when it was shipped from Bruges to England, and its English owners responded by filling it in. Much of this blank space appears on the backs of the 20 miniatures supplied by the Masters of the Pink Canopies. The first miniature in the book depicts the Trinity (fig. 11).[23] The English recipient responded to its blank back by writing on it, or more likely, by hiring several scriveners to write on it (fig. 12).[24] An English hand added one short prayer to the top of the page, and then someone else added a second. Emendations of this sort lent themselves to brief texts which would not exceed the available space. Scribes often chose a fresh blank

---

23 Opening in a book of hours, with a full-page miniature by the Masters of the Pink Canopies depicting the Throne of Mercy, facing a prayer to the Trinity. Cambridge, University Library, Ms. Ii.6.2, fol. 10v. http://cudl.lib.cam.ac.uk/view/MS-II-00006–00002/26

24 Folio in a book of hours, the reverse of the Throne of Mercy miniature, with prayer texts added in an English hand of the fifteenth century. Cambridge, University Library, Ms. Ii.6.2, fol. 10r. http://cudl.lib.cam.ac.uk/view/MS-II-00006–00002/25

page to begin a new prayer; therefore, additional prayers fill the top sections of many of the blank backs of other miniatures.

Sometimes the locations of the additions are significant. One the back of the miniature of the personal angel (Cambridge, UL, Ms. Ii.6.2; fig. 13)[25] the owner has added a prayer in which words are interspersed with crosses, probably signaling that the reader should cross him- or herself at those points (fig. 14).[26] Such prayers were understood to form a shield around their performer, who covered him- or herself with signs. The owner may have chosen this spot—in close proximity to the angel— who was also understood to protect the bearer, in order to concentrate the protective prayers in one area of the book. Deeper in the manuscript, sixteenth-century owners have added birth dates of family members to the back of the image of the Annunciation (fig. 15).[27] These notices have been added in English over a period of decades, the scribes layering them so that they form a chronology for the family. Of course by writing the names on the same piece of parchment as the Annunciation (fig. 16),[28] the family associated itself with the Ur-Christian birth.

Not only were the full-page miniatures made on singletons, but some of the prayer texts were, too, specifically the suffrages. Short texts that rarely fill a single folio recto and verso, suffrages provided a main vehicle for honoring the saints of whom worshippers had grown visually fond, in sculpted or painted form. They demanded images of them alongside the prayers. This posed a problem for manuscripts made in the modular method, for if the suffrage texts were copied continuously into a quire, it would not be possible to slot full-page miniatures into the packet. A solution was to treat both the images and the prayer texts as singletons,

---

25 Opening in a book of hours, with a full-page miniature by the Masters of the Pink Canopies depicting the personal angel battling a dragon, facing a suffrage to the personal angel, inscribed in Bruges on a singleton. Cambridge, University Library, Ms. Ii.6.2, fol. 14v-15r. http://cudl.lib.cam.ac.uk/view/MS-II-00006–00002/34 and http://cudl.lib.cam.ac.uk/view/MS-II-00006–00002/35

26 Folio in a book of hours, with two prayer texts, written in an English hand of the fifteenth century, added to the blank back of a miniature. Cambridge, University Library, Ms. Ii.6.2, fol. 14r. http://cudl.lib.cam.ac.uk/view/MS-II-00006–00002/33

27 Folio in a book of hours, with birthdays added to the blank back of a miniature in an English sixteenth-century hand. Cambridge, University Library, Ms. Ii.6.2, fol. 33r. http://cudl.lib.cam.ac.uk/view/MS-II-00006–00002/61

28 Folio in a book of hours, with a full-page miniature by the Masters of the Pink Canopies depicting the Annunciation, painted on a singleton. Cambridge, University Library, Ms. Ii.6.2, fol. 33v. http://cudl.lib.cam.ac.uk/view/MS-II-00006–00002/62

then fold and glue them into modules. In Cambridge, UL, Ms. Ii.6.2, an entire quire of suffrages, filling fols 10–17, comprises singletons: single-leaf images glued to single-leaf text pages for form four bifolia, which can then be nested and sewn to a thong. In other words, each bifolium is a confection, glued together from two halves, rather than a continuous sheet.

The result of this production method was empty space. For example, suffrage to the personal angel, like most suffrages, is quite short. It fills only the recto of fol. 15, which is a singleton, as is the full-page miniature facing it, depicting the personal angel doing battle (fig. 13). Both folios are therefore blank on the back. That blank faces another blank, the empty back of the next full-page miniature, forming two blanks in a row. An English scribe has been commissioned, however, to write out a Latin prayer in a bookhand to fill this otherwise blank parchment (fig. 17).[29]

Similar situations occur throughout the suffrages in Cambridge, UL, Ms. Ii.6.2. To take another example, the full-page miniature depicting St. George faces a short suffrage to that saint, both units produced as singletons (fig. 18).[30] Turning the page reveals two blanks facing each other, which have served as extra parchment for the English owners' whims (fig. 19).[31] Three scribes have been hired to add prayers in Latin and in English to this otherwise blank opening. The final prayer added in this group is dedicated to St. Erasmus, who became popular in the late fifteenth century but was not originally included in this early fifteenth-century manuscript. These prayers in this opening have been written by different hands, and different again from the hands on the previous folios. It would appear, then, that adding prayers to the blank areas in the book was a cumulative process, that the owner looked for space as his or her needs changed.

---

29 Opening in a book of hours, with blank space filled with prayers in an English hand. Cambridge, University Library, Ms. Ii.6.2, fol. 15v-16r. http://cudl.lib.cam.ac.uk/view/MS-II-00006–00002/36   and   http://cudl.lib.cam.ac.uk/view/MS-II-00006–00002/37

30 Masters of the Pink Canopies, St. George, full-page miniature painted on a singleton. Cambridge, University Library, Ms. Ii.6.2, fol. 22v. http://cudl.lib.cam.ac.uk/view/MS-II-00006–00002/46 and http://cudl.lib.cam.ac.uk/view/MS-II-00006–00002/47

31 Blank space in the book of hours, filled with prayers in an English hand. Cambridge, University Library, Ms. Ii.6.2, fol. 23v-24r. http://cudl.lib.cam.ac.uk/view/MS-II-00006–00002/48 and http://cudl.lib.cam.ac.uk/view/MS-II-00006–00002/49

Not only did the English scribes write on the blank backs of painted and inscribed singletons, but they also found space at the ends of quires, which usually offered ruled parchment. To the extra ruled lines at the end of the Hours of the Virgin, an English scribe has carefully added a prayer to St. Botolph (Botwulf) of Thorney, an English abbot (fig. 20).[32] St. Botolph was understood to protect travellers, which is why medieval churches dedicated to him were situated at the major gates of London: at Aldersgate, Aldgate, Billingsgate and Bishopsgate. This prayer was but one of many that the English owners added to the book to make the foreign product locally relevant.

Cambridge, UL, Ms. Ii.6.2 is but one of many manuscripts made with the modular method in Bruges for export to England, which produced not only an attractive product for English buyers, but one that buyers could adapt. These cumulative inscriptions suggest that a cottage industry developed in England for scribes to add texts to the blank areas of books of hours. The example I have discussed above, and many others, all have additions made by multiple hands, as if updating the manuscript were a continuous process. English patrons could add prayers as they came into fashion and thereby keep their books fresh and up to date. An impressive amount of empty space was opened up in these books by the modular method, and therefore they were capable of hosting significant additions, without having to add new parchment.

Modular manuscripts often contain blank folios, because scribes typically started new texts on a fresh recto. In doing so they were anticipating that a (future) owner could insert a full-page miniature to the book on the left side of the opening, so that it would face the initial on the right. The southern Netherlands produced the most extreme cases of wasted parchment. These manuscripts were extremely modularized.

D. Precursors of book modules

Some of the elements of the modular method were already present in earlier systems of making manuscripts: account books made out of single leaves; thirteenth-century Parisian Bibles copied with the pecia

---

32 End of the Hours of the Virgin (inscribed in Bruges), and prayer to St. Botolph (added in England). Cambridge, University Library, Ms. Ii.6.2, fol. 58v. http://cudl. lib.cam.ac.uk/view/MS-II-00006–00002/112

system; image cycles prefacing psalters; and compilation volumes made in monasteries. I take these in turn and discuss how producers of books of hours drew on their innovations and streamlined them in the fifteenth century.

Accountants and merchants used a bundling technique to make booklets from single leaves. They would organize receipts generated by impaling them on a nail on the wall so that these sheets, once collected and bound, would become books. Jan Gossaert's portrait of a merchant of around 1530 depicts such a record-keeping system (fig. 21).[33] A merchant has gathered single sheets one after the next on his nail. When the bundle is sufficiently thick, or a particular period had passed, say, a month, he would take the leaves off the wall and bind them. In this way, the resulting booklets would then serve as a chronological record of transactions. This departed from the regular way in which books were made on pre-ruled bifolia that were nested into stacks to form quires, which were then sewn into a binding.

When Southern Netherlandish stationers applied this idea to the illuminated manuscript, they were using an idea from work-a-day books and applying it to manuscripts that occupied a higher social stratum. With this new method of manuscript production, careful planning was unnecessary. In books of hours with suffrages to saints, the manuscript-makers compiled single sheets: a full-page image of a saint, followed by a single text sheet with a prayer to that saint, followed by the image and prayer to the next saint. Patrons could have as many saints as they wanted. As I will show later, book makers in the Southern Netherlands (which had a vigorous mercantile culture) took full advantage of this construction principle and made some packets out of single leaves arranged in a particular order. This also turned the manuscript-making procedure upside-down. In the past, the book would be planned, and the text inscribed with spaces left for the miniatures. But here, in this section of suffrages, the book maker begins with full-page singletons

---

33 I owe this observation to Peter Stallybrass. He discussed it in a lecture at the 6th Annual Lawrence J. Schoenberg Symposium on Manuscript Studies in the Digital Age in Philadelphia, November 21, 2013. Jan Gossaert, Portrait of a Merchant, ca. 1530. Washington, National Gallery of Art. https://www.nga.gov/collection/gallery/gg41/gg41–50722.html

with images; it was the text quires that had to be cut up to accommodate them. They're all singletons, just like the merchant's receipts.

Another earlier book-making technique that the proponents of the modular method developed came from the way in which Bibles were copied. The university of Paris was founded around 1200 and flourished in the thirteenth century, attracting students from all over Europe. They created a high demand for the Bible, which was the main textbook used. Students needed a single-volume Bible that was handier and more economical than the enormous multi-volume Bibles that until then had been the norm. The new "Paris Bible" was small and made on thin parchment and written in highly abbreviated words so that it was physically manageable and as inexpensive as possible. Furthermore, it was copied according to a standard canonical exemplar so that all students would have the same texts in the same order.[34] Efficiency and standardization often go hand-in-hand. Although many used copies were in circulation by the end of the thirteenth century, the demand for small bibles far exceeded the supply in the first half of the century. This put pressure on the system to invent new ways to bring the costs down and to increase the speed of production, while maintaining a standard of quality. Taking manuscript production out of the hands of monks and putting it into the hands of secular urban scribes was the first step to increasing efficiency. In addition to urbanizing production and making the bible much smaller so that it would require less physical material, book makers began copying it in a new way, namely with the pecia system, which means "piece." The university authorized copies of the bible and of other key works. These served as exemplars. Students could hire professional scribes who would each have access to one piece of the bible and could copy a volume as a team, each member with his own piece. In this way, the book was broken into modules and copied through a group effort.

---

34 Richard H. Rouse and Mary A. Rouse, "The Book Trade at the University of Paris, c. 1250-c. 1350," in *La Production du livre universitaire au moyen age: Exemplar et Pecia: Actes du Symposium tenu au Collegio San Bonaventura de Grottaferrata en mai 1983*, ed. Louis J. Bataillon, Bertrand G. Guyot, and Richard H. Rouse (Paris: Editions du Centre national de la recherche scientifique, 1983), pp. 41–123; Christopher De Hamel, *Glossed Books of the Bible and the Origins of the Paris Booktrade* (Woodbridge: D. S. Brewer, 1984); J. J. G. Alexander, *Medieval Illuminators and Their Methods of Work* (New Haven: Yale University Press, 1992), pp. 22–23.

This system, however, is different from the modular method of making books of hours, in that the quires of a bible did not correspond to discrete texts and were not therefore "stand-alone" units. For a bible to be a bible, it had to be complete and canonical. A book of hours, on the other hand, could comprise multiple units combined according to a buyer's wishes. To be complete, it required very few units: owners often demanded more. Whereas the goal of the bible-copying pecia system was efficiency, regularity, and cost-cutting, the goals of the modular method in the fifteenth century were interchangeability, expandability, and of course cost-cutting as well.

Widespread in the fifteenth century, the practice of adding a quire made elsewhere may stem from an earlier practice of adding prefatory images to psalters. Certain luxury psalters were provided with a packet of images that formed a quire or two at the beginning of the text. They appeared in some quantity in the thirteenth century, resulting in semi-autonomous groups of folios containing pictures and no texts.[35] The exact composition of these images fluctuated but often included full-page images depicting saints, and perhaps a Passion cycle that served as elaborate frontispieces for the book. The images, which depicted post-biblical saints and a passion cycle based on the New Testament, did not "illustrate" the psalter, which is a text that comes from the Old Testament. Rather, they framed the psalter by imposing a Christian context onto it and provided a visual means by which to pray. Structurally these prefatory images were made separately from the text pages and the textual and visual components were only brought together later.

Modules that were made separately tended to come apart at the seams. Some image cycles have survived into the modern era loose, which has led some to believe that such image-only modules simply circulated as separate entities. For example, it is not clear whether a particular cycle of images made in Northern France, which now forms a separate book, was ever the prefatory cycle from a psalter (HKB, Ms. 76 F 5; fig. 22).[36] If it did, then the psalter has not survived or cannot be

---

35　Caroline S. Hull, "Rylands Ms French 5: The Form and Function of a Medieval Bible Picture Book," *Bulletin of the John Rylands University Library of Manchester* 77, no. 2 (1995), pp. 3–24.

36　J. P. J. Brandhorst, "The Hague, Koninklijke Bibliotheek Ms 76 F 5: A Psalter Fragment?," *Visual Resources* 19 (2003), pp. 15–25. Opening from a "picture bible" or a prefatory cycle from a psalter. The Hague, Koninklijke Bibliotheek, Ms. 76 F

identified as such. What is clear is that illuminators designed image-oriented modules, and copyists did not need to plan for them from the outset. In the Northern French cycle, the illuminator has divided the page not according to the needs of a copyist, but for the needs of the pictorial unfolding of the story, where geometric separators hold the vignettes apart. Each page has been bisected horizontally and vertically to create four frames. However, for the story of Moses parting the Red Sea on fol. 7r, the illuminator has used the full width of the page rather than dividing it vertically by a bar, because he needed a wider landscape to tell the story. In short, no scribe planned the space for these images, and they have been made without respect to a particular text or word-oriented page layout. In that sense, they anticipate image-making procedures of the late fourteenth and fifteenth centuries.

Building a book of hours out of modules is closely related to making composite volumes out of separate parts or booklets. However, building manuscripts out of bookles was distinct from compiling texts. Whereas *compilatio* was a literary activity, assembling composite volumes was a physical activity. The former involved copying texts together, and the latter involved binding codicological units together.[37] Making a composite volume was a way to bring together small loose booklets, sewing them together into a set, and placing them in a single binding, which would protect them. A composite volume from the convent of Canonesses Regular of St. Agnes in Maaseik has several modules, each

---

5, fol. 6v-7r. http://manuscripts.kb.nl/zoom/BYVANCKB%3Amimi_76f5%3A006v and http://manuscripts.kb.nl/zoom/BYVANCKB%3Amimi_76f5%3A007r

37   Compiling, the act of selecting ideas from existing texts and arranging them into a new text, is a literary activity which compounds the auctoritates of the authors cited. Compilatio, which emerged in the thirteenth century, resulted in a new genre of literature, including the encyclopedia, whose goal was usefulness for the reader. On compilatio, see M. B. Parkes, "The Influence of the Concepts of Ordinatio and Compilatio on the Development of the Book," in *Medieval Learning and Literature: Essays Presented to Richard William Hunt*, ed. J. J. G. Alexander and M. T. Gibson (Oxford: Clarendon Press, 1976), pp. 115–41; Alastair J. Minnis, "Late-Medieval Discussions of Compilatio and the Role of the Compilator," *Beiträge zur Geschichte der deutschen Sprache und Literatur* 101 (1979), pp. 385–421; Diane Mockridge, "The Order of the Texts in the Bodley 34 Manuscript: The Function of Repetition and Recall in a Manuscript Addressed to Nuns," *Essays in Medieval Studies* 3 (1986), pp. 207–16; Neil Hathaway, "Compilatio: From Plagarism to Compiling," *Viator* 20 (1989), pp. 19–44.

apparently copied by a different sister. These were brought together into a rigid binding and given as a gift to the sisters' mother superior. In this way, the fact that the composite volume includes the labor of several sisters is integral to its function as a collective gift.[38]

In 1980 Pamela Robinson first called attention to volumes containing separate codicological units that have different scribes, and she applied the term "booklets" to them.[39] A booklet forms an autonomous unit and may comprise any number of quires. As such, the content, author, copyist, and date of one booklet may have nothing to do with that of its binding mates. According to Denis Muzerelle in his *Vocabulaire codicologique* of 1985, a manuscript made of booklets is a *volume composite*. He defined the *volume composite* as "a volume created by combining independent codicological units." But as Peter Gumbert points out, this definition "leaves no room for the numerous cases where units are combined which are not quite independent and yet distinct."[40] For example, the books of hours I discuss in this study comprise parts that were made as distinct units, but would not function independently. Gumbert suggests that the production of such books could be described as "articulated in blocks," which could often mean that they were copied by different scribes. I agree and emphasize that the blocks of a book of hours might not be pre-determined at the outset of production; that the blocks could be interchangeable; and that they could be bound in many different configurations, most often with the calendar first, the Vigil last, and the texts in the middle varying widely. In criticizing the codicological terms defined by Muzerelle and by Maniaci,[41] Gumbert urges scholars to make "provisions for the many shades between 'made in one piece'

---

38 Rudy, *Postcards on Parchment*, pp. 77–79, with further references.
39 For the definition of a booklet, see Pamela R. Robinson, "The 'Booklet:' A Self-Contained Unit in Composite Manuscripts," *Codicologica: Towards a Science of Handwritten Books* 3 (1980), pp. 46–67; and Ralph Hanna III, "Booklets in Medieval Manuscripts: Further Considerations," *Studies in Bibliography*, 39 (1986), pp. 101–12.
40 Gumbert, "Codicological Units: Towards a Terminology for the Stratigraphy of the Non-Homogenous Codex," *Segno e testo* 2 (2004), pp. 17–42, at p. 19. Erik Kwakkel uses the term "production units," in his article: "Towards a Terminology for the Analysis of Composite Manuscripts," *Gazette du livre médiéval* 41 (2002), pp. 12–19.
41 Marilena Maniaci, *Terminologia del Libro Manoscritto* (Rome and Milan: Istituto centrale per la patologia del libro; Editrice Bibliografica, 1996).

and 'built up out of independent items,' and between 'sensible' and 'random' combinations."

Rather than using the term "booklet," "codicological unit," or "production units" (a term Erik Kwakkel uses), I am using the term "modules," because it's more concise, has an adjectival form and can refer to single leaves and to parts of books of hours, which were made (semi-) independently. Building manuscripts out of modules has a long history. One of the earliest illustrated copies of the Gospels—the Rossano Gospels of the sixth century—has an "author portrait" of St. Mark that is probably not original, but added later.[42] St. Mark appears on a bifolium, which according to Kresten and Prato, has been added to the book. Retrofitting manuscripts to make them conform to new standards (i.e., having author portraits) by adding physical material to them is a practice nearly as old at the codex itself. As the Rossano Gospels demonstrates, book makers had been adding images made on separate leaves to existing books for a thousand years, but it was only in the final century of the codex on parchment that the production and insertion of such images became routine.

The modular method of producing and adding to manuscripts as practiced in the fifteenth century would take this idea—of separating labor and assembling books from components—to a higher degree of systemization. Responding to pressure to make more books (especially books of hours) cheaper, but to supply them with dazzling color and personality, book makers in the fifteenth century looked to the past for some ideas, and then updated those ideas and deployed them on a large scale.

---

42 See O. Kresten and G. Prato, "Die Miniatur des Evangelisten Markus im Codex Purpureus Rossanensis: eine spätere Einfügung," *Römische historische Mitteilungen* 27 (1985), pp. 381–403. William Loerke, "Incipits and Author Portraits in Greek Gospel Books: Some Observations," in *Byzantine East and Latin West: Two Worlds of Christendom in Middle Ages and Renaissance. Studies in Ecclesiastical and Cultural History*, ed. Deno John Geanakoplos (New York: Harper & Row, 1966), pp. 377–81. Loerke tries to refute Kresten and Prato, but according to John Lowden he has not succeeded. See John Lowden, "The Beginnings of Biblical Illustration," in *Imaging the Early Medieval Bible*, ed. John Williams, *Penn State Series in the History of the Book* (University Park: Pennsylvania State University Press, 1999), pp. 9–60, here: pp. 20–21.

E. Implications of the modular method

This new strategy for building books out of components has several implications. First, when manuscripts are made in modules, every major division falls on the recto of a new quire. This makes it very easy to slip a full-page miniature into the book so that it faces the incipit. Artists and groups of artists working in a similar style exploited this fact by constructing packets of single-leaf miniatures that owners could buy later and easily bind into their books.[43]

Fig. 23 Book of hours made in the modular method, unbound. Special Collections of the Universiteitsbibliotheek van Amsterdam, Ms. I G 50. Image © Universiteitsbibliotheek van Amsterdam, CC BY 4.0.

This appears, for example, in book of hours in the University Library at Amsterdam that is now unbound, which allows one easily to see the

---

43 For an interpretation of what happens when votaries add images to manuscripts that were not made in the "modular method," see my study of Liège, UL, Ms. Wittert 35 in Rudy, *Postcards on Parchment*.

quires fanned out. Some of the quires contain a complete text, and other longer texts require multiple quires (AUB, Ms. I G 50; fig. 23). The first text, the Hours of the Virgin, fills five quires. The next text, flagged by a large decorated initial, fills two quires, and so on. It is clear the scribe did not produce this book of hours from beginning to end, but rather, as a series of booklets that could be arranged in any order and assembled just before binding. In fact, this is one of the reasons that Netherlandish books of hours come in so many varieties, with no standard organization. Often the Hours of the Virgin appears first, right after the calendar, but the Hours of Eternal Wisdom can also be first. Sometimes books of hours contain the Long Hours of the Cross, sometimes the Short Hours of the Cross, and sometimes both. Sometimes they contain one or two quires of prayers to the sacrament, or other non-essential prayers, such as indulgenced prayers. Clearly an array of possibilities was fostered by the new method of construction.

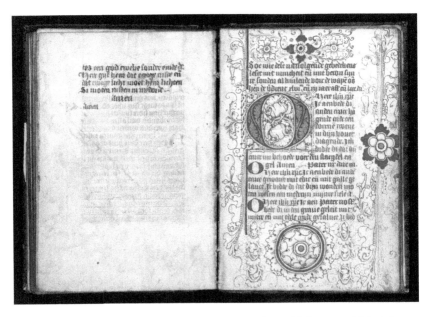

Fig. 24 Original production (left of the gutter) and an added quire, with incipit of an indulgenced prayer (right of the gutter). Special Collections of the Universiteitsbibliotheek van Amsterdam, Ms. I G 54, fol. 64v-65r. Image © Universiteitsbibliotheek van Amsterdam, CC BY 4.0.

Second, conceptualizing the book as a series of packets means that there is suddenly plenty of empty space—blank parchment—that could be filled later with more texts. Using packets was essentially wasteful, because the end of the text rarely fell at the very end of a packet. If it ended before the final folio, the rest of the quire would be left blank. In AUB, Ms. I G 54 (fig. 2), the end of the quire has six lines of ruled, empty parchment, while the new text begins on the fresh quire with an enormous gilt *M*. Many manuscripts built with the same procedure (using modules) have an entire folio of blank space at the ends of gatherings. Rarely did the scribe fill the quire perfectly, right up to the last inscribed line. Instead, the procedure usually left at least a few blank lines. That same scribe—or a different one—could fill these ruled lines with short texts; I have designated a category of brief texts used for this purpose as "quire fillers." One convent (the St. Ursula convent in Delft, discussed later) made a virtue of these leftover spaces and kept short texts on hand to fill up these otherwise blank areas.

Third, it meant that books could be easily expanded. One could buy a book now with an eye to expanding it later. In fact, AUB, Ms. I G 54, introduced earlier, received an extra quire at the end (fig. 24). This packet was made in a different campaign of work, as the jarringly new borders reveal: the added modules have cheaper pen borders and lack gold, and they were clearly not made by the same decorator as the rest of the quires in the book. One can easily see that the style of decoration strongly contrasts with those of the original production. This quire also has a text that begins at the top of the first recto. The texts that this quire contains are heavily indulgenced and could be considered optional: they are not necessary components to a complete book of hours. They begin with the *Adoro te*, for which the reader of this booklet will receive 46,003 years' and 59 days' indulgence. The owner of the book, it would seem, received a basic book of hours, and later had it expanded with a quire full of indulgenced texts. This was easy to do, since such a packet was available as a module that could be slotted into the existing book. Doing so in no way disrupted the structure of the book's contents, which were modular anyway.

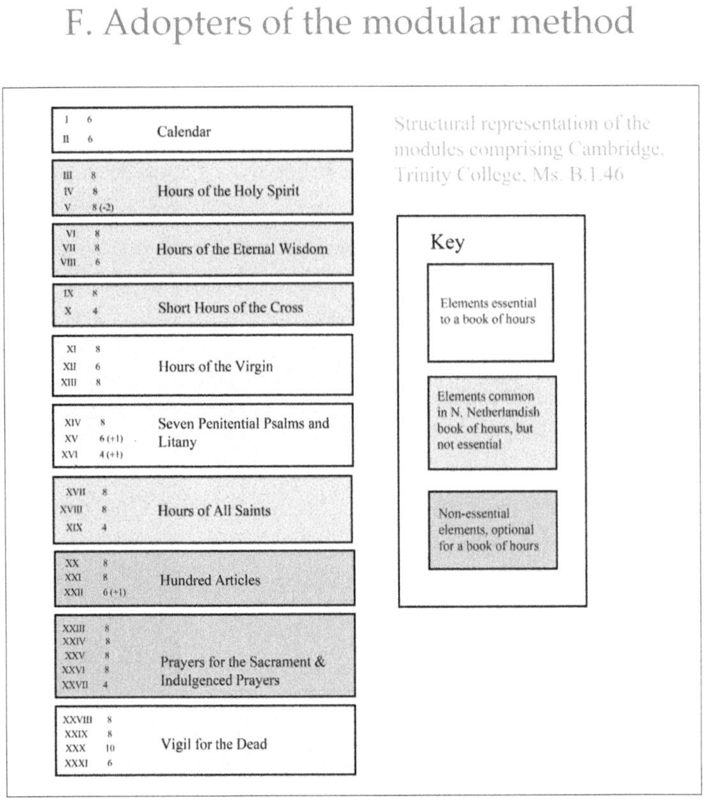

F. Adopters of the modular method

I	6	Calendar
II	6	
III	8	Hours of the Holy Spirit
IV	8	
V	8 (-2)	
VI	8	Hours of the Eternal Wisdom
VII	8	
VIII	6	
IX	8	Short Hours of the Cross
X	4	
XI	8	Hours of the Virgin
XII	6	
XIII	8	
XIV	8	Seven Penitential Psalms and Litany
XV	6 (+1)	
XVI	4 (+1)	
XVII	8	Hours of All Saints
XVIII	8	
XIX	4	
XX	8	Hundred Articles
XXI	8	
XXII	6 (+1)	
XXIII	8	Prayers for the Sacrament & Indulgenced Prayers
XXIV	8	
XXV	8	
XXVI	8	
XXVII	4	
XXVIII	8	Vigil for the Dead
XXIX	8	
XXX	10	
XXXI	6	

Structural representation of the modules comprising Cambridge, Trinity College, Ms. B.1.46

Key

Elements essential to a book of hours

Elements common in N. Netherlandish book of hours, but not essential

Non-essential elements, optional for a book of hours

Fig. 25 Modular method at the convent of St. Ursula. Diagram showing the modules comprising Cambridge, Trinity College, Ms. B.1.46. Diagram © Author, CC BY 4.0.

Although this is not a monograph about any particular atelier, a few production studios—secular workshops in Bruges and convents in Delft—will make multiple appearances. One of these is the St. Ursula convent in Delft, founded in 1454 or 1457, which probably produced manuscripts for its own use and for sale outside the conventual walls (or for donation to patrons, with the expectation of a gift in return). These sisters built many books of hours from modules. Manuscripts connected to this convent share a certain set of "brand" features. They all have St. Ursula and the 11,000 Virgins listed in the litany as the first virgin; they all have painted or penwork borders typical of Delft; and they all have a particular kind of even, blocky script. A book of hours with the typical red and blue penwork of Delft and simple painted imagery was probably made by and for one of the inmates of this Franciscan convent in the 1470s (Cambridge, Trinity College, Ms. B.1.46).[44] At least two and possibly more closely related hands copied the manuscript in modules, so that the text for each office stands as a production unit.[45] A diagram of Cambridge, TC, Ms. B.1.46 demonstrates how the parts fit together (fig. 25). Modules in yellow are required in a book of hours. Those in green are common but not required. Those magenta and orange, the eighth and ninth modules, respectively, are idiosyncratic, and the book's owner would have had to specify them or have them made separately. A single text fills the entire eighth module: the Hundred Articles, which apparently circulated only in female monastic houses. The ninth module contains prayers for the sacrament and indulgenced prayers.

In the cities of the western Netherlands (including Delft, Amsterdam, Haarlem, and Leiden), conventual scribes wrote in a corporate hand, which minimized the differences between the individual scripts.[46] As a result, this book of hours (Cambridge, TC, Ms. B.1.46) looks quite uniform, just as a Bible made in the pecia system looks quite uniform. Packets of quires comprise the normal texts (Hours of the Cross, Hours of the Virgin, etc.), as well as the texts that individuate this book. Based on these clues, I suspect that the sisters of St. Ursula probably assembled B.1.46 for their own use. It contains, for example, a prayer "to those who give us alms," which, with its first-person plural form and the social relationship it implies, would make the prayer appropriate for a sister in a convent. Furthermore, a generalized convent sister is depicted in the margins of several folios. In manuscripts decorated for their own use, the sisters did not create lavish painted borders or gold, but rather limited themselves to penwork borders, albeit ones with some painted figures and historiated initials.

---

44 The manuscript is not in M. R. James, *The Western Manuscripts in the Library of Trinity College, Cambridge: A Descriptive Catalogue*, 4 vols. (Cambridge: Cambridge University Press, 1900).

45 Kwakkel, "Towards a Terminology for the Analysis of Composite Manuscripts," pp. 12–19.

46 There are far more recognizable conventual scribes from German convents, and Cynthia Cyrus has identified an impressive number of them. See Cynthia J. Cyrus, *The Scribes for Women's Convents in Late Medieval Germany* (Toronto: University of Toronto Press, 2009).

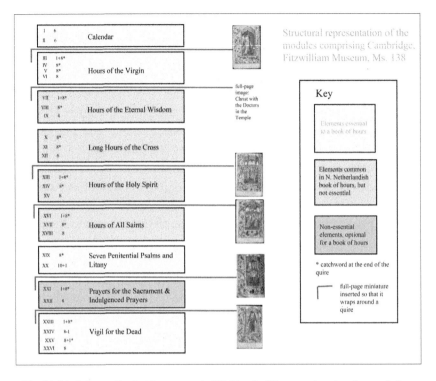

In those cases where an individual owner was purchasing the manuscript,
the owner could apparently order a manuscript from the convent with
just the text inscribed. He or she could then take the textual skeleton to a
professional artist to have full-page miniatures added, as well as having
the textual folios decorated in a matching style. This is what happened
with a manuscript book of hours now in the Fitzwilliam Museum (Ms.
138; fig. 26). Bare modular quires, comprehending only text and no
decoration, were all that the sisters of St. Ursula initially supplied. A
professional artist easily slipped full-page miniatures in front of each
module, because a new text always begins on a new quire. I suspect that
the professional atelier then painted the incipit text folios so that they
matched the borders around the illuminations. The resulting openings
look uniform, as it they had been carefully planned from the beginning,
when in fact, they are built out of components.

My discussion above has largely involved the *sisters* of St. Ursula and St. Margaret—for religious women produced many if not most of these modular quires. This is itself something new. Standard manuscript history, by contrast, goes like this: *In the early Middle Ages, monks copied manuscripts in monasteries, largely for their own use. Around 1200, the University of Paris attracted students, who needed copies of the bible, which was the main textbook. Monasteries could not meet this demand, and a new, secular urban production of book making ensued. At the end of the fifteenth century, the market in manuscripts gave way to printed books.* This is largely true, but there's another, unexpected chapter: monasteries continued making manuscripts and existed alongside professional ateliers.

Around 1400, in the Northern Netherlands and in Germany, monasteries again became major players in manuscript production, this time making not bibles necessarily, but all kinds of manuscripts for use within the convent and especially outside it.[47] In fact, they overshadowed professional ateliers in the quantity of their production. For example, the Franciscan convent of St. Barbara in Delft produced manuscripts and acquired other manuscripts from outside the convent; their librarian produced a catalogue of their book holdings, which is nine folios in length and lists 109 items (HKB, Ms. 130 E 24).[48] (Later in the century they also operated some of the earliest printing presses, but that is the subject of a different book.[49]) Monastic inmates made books of hours and prayerbooks for themselves, but also for sale (or donation) outside the conventual walls. These manuscripts contain clues about their production in their script, decoration, calendars and litanies (in

---

47 Whereas Cynthia Cyrus has systematically studied the German material, conventual scribes in Netherlandish convents have not been the subject of an analogous study. Karl Stooker and Theo Verbeij, *Collecties op Orde: Middelnederlandse handschriften uit kloosters en semi-religieuze gemeenschappen in de Nederlanden*, 2 vols, Miscellanea Neerlandica (Leuven: Peeters, 1997), have catalogued all known manuscripts from Netherlandish convents, both male and female, and have identified scribes where possible.

48 The great nineteenth-century bibliophile Willem Moll made an edition of the catalogue in 1857, which was enlarged and corrected in Willem Moll, "De Boekerij van het St. Barbara-Klooster te Delft, in de tweede helft der vijftiende eeuw: eene bijdrage tot de geschiedenis der middeleeuwsche letterkunde in Nederland," *Kerkhistorisch archief* IV (1866), pp. 209–86 (24–28).

49 Ina Kok, *Woodcuts in Incunabula Printed in the Low Countries*, transl. by Cis van Heertum, 4 vols. (Leiden: Brill, 2013).

which the patron saints of the scribe's monastic house are listed first among the confessors and virgins). Some of the convents had artists and illuminators, who could make miniatures. However, many convents did not, and they teamed up with professional artists, or pasted in prints purchased on the open market, to make a product complete with figurative images.[50]

In other cases book buyers purchased the written components from a convent, and then bought the miniatures separately from a professional, and then had all of the components bound together. Manuscript makers took advantage of this division of labor, and also took advantage of the collective labor in a convent in order to further streamline production. In order to make an internally consistent book of hours, which was actually written by five, six, or more hands, the sisters in a given convent had to learn to write in a similar, corporate style so that their efforts would be interchangeable and indistinguishable. Most convent sisters did not sign their work, but one group of sisters did: the sisters of St. Margaret in Gouda.[51] They collectively produced books that look as if a single scribe could have written them, but yet multiple people signed them. They were, in effect, anticipating by 500 years Henry Ford's assembly line production, which relies on identical (or at least highly similar) fungible parts.

In the Northern Netherlands in the fifteenth century, urban convents made the bulk of surviving books of hours. Most of these convents housed women (although a few male monastics also produced manuscripts). Some professional ateliers also made books of hours, especially at the end of the century. Chief among them were the Masters of the Dark Eyes,

---

50 On convent sisters making manuscripts illustrated with pasted-in prints, see Ursula Weekes, *Early Engravers and Their Public: The Master of the Berlin Passion and Manuscripts from Convents in the Rhine-Maas Region, ca. 1450–1500* (London: Harvey Miller, 2004).

51 According to the book's colophon, five sisters together (sister Aef Dircsdochter, sister Jacob Gherijtsdochter, sister Aechte Claesdochter, sister Maria Martijnsdochter, and sister Maria Gherijtsdochter) copied Jan van Ruusbroec, *Vanden gheesteliken tabernakel* (HKB, Ms. 129 G 4) in 1460. Fol. 207r: "Ende is ghescreven uut minnen des heilighen daghes ende buten die tijt des ghemenen arbeyts totter eeren gods ende salicheit der sielen alle der gheenre diet lesen ende horen lesen. Int jaer ons heren m cccc ende lx. van suster Aef Dircs dochter. suster Jacob Gherijts dochter. suster Aechte Claes dochter. suster Maria Martijns dochter ende suster Maria Gherijts dochter. nonnen. haren gheminden susteren tot een testament ende een ewighe ghedenckenisse na haerre doot. welker namen ghescreven moeten wesen inder herten gods. Amen."

who will reappear several times later. The large number of surviving books of hours indicates that they were affordable. In the north using the labor of women, which is nearly always more poorly remunerated than men's, contained costs. In the Southern Netherlands, there were many more professional ateliers, and fewer monastic ones. In Bruges and its environs professionals made books of hours more affordable by dividing labor, reducing decoration of text pages as far as possible, and using simple templates to repeat motives. Manuscript makers in Bruges in the fifteenth century streamlined their production techniques so that most of the figurative imagery was executed on single-leaf miniatures, which were then brought together with text pages inscribed elsewhere. Both northern convents and southern ateliers used the modular method.

With the modular method book makers gained some efficiency by dividing labor, but at the same time they lost some material efficiency, as the new procedures wasted significant parchment. Manufacturing a book with single-leaf miniatures created empty parchment in the book, not only the blank backs of the miniatures, but the ends of the quires just before the inserted miniature. One suspects that demand for books was rising, labor costs were high, and the costs of raw materials, parchment in particular, were coming down, or else such wastefulness would not have justified the savings on labor. Above I showed how manuscripts made in Bruges and its environs often had enormous amounts of blank parchment in them. As a result, the exported books had plenty of room for the English owners to assert their personalities. Sisters at the convent of St. Ursula must have had lists of short religious texts on hand, because they left almost no ruled parchment blank. Instead, they filled it up with short sayings from church fathers, or brief prayers, or other texts I call "quire fillers." In so doing, they trapped no white space on the page. They smoothed over the seams between modules. And they offered their customers even more value.

Blank parchment has not been discussed before because nearly all art historians concentrate on the fronts of miniatures. Photographs of blank pages make for boring plates. But I contend that the blank pages are key to understanding how the books were produced so efficiently, and how their new owners used them. Space was opened up by the modular process that might be used for two new kinds of products, both independently created to fill these spaces: quire-fillers and single-leaf miniatures.

G. Complicated stratigraphy

In the fifteenth century English book producers could not supply enough books for lay votaries' demands. As a result, the English imported books from the Southern Netherlands, where certain ateliers and artists specialized in making books of hours for Sarum use. Such manuscripts were made in modules, which resulted in many folios of blank or wasted parchment (the backs of full-page miniatures, and the blank ends of modules) bound into the book. English owners received their new, generalized books and almost always augmented them. Notating these layers of production is challenging; ideally a description should communicate the original and added physical material, as well as the original and added texts. When a manuscript is originally built out of components, designating "original" from "added" can be a slippery exercise.

Cambridge, UL, Ms. Ff.6.8 was made in the Southern Netherlands for export to England. It has prayer texts written in Latin, in brown ink by competent Netherlandish scribes, and numerous full-page miniatures, which have been bound in as singletons so that they face their relevant texts. The blank folios are concentrated at the beginning and end of the book and in areas with a high density of images. There are nearly as many hands among these additions as there are additions, suggesting that texts were added continually by several book owners.

The original modules are: the calendar; the suffrages; the Hours of the Virgin; Seven Penitential Psalms, Litany, and Vigil for the Dead; *Commendatio animarum*; and the Psalter of St. Jerome. Notable here is that the Penitential Psalms, Litany of Saints, and Vigil for the Dead form a single module. Whereas the litany invariably follows the Penitential Psalms and forms a unit with it, here the scribe has also tacked on the Vigil, which is a necessary and defining text of a book of hours. The scribe copied these texts together in order to make a somewhat larger module. Perhaps he did this for the sake of efficiency, as he knew that anyone ordering a book of hours would require these texts in this sequence.

On the other hand, the *Commendatio animarum* and the Psalter of St. Jerome were optional texts. These the scribe has copied in such a way that they each fill one quire. They could be slotted in easily, or omitted, as necessary. Further research may reveal that scribes manipulated these texts so that they would fill exactly one quire. In the two modules of suffrages, which each comprise a series of singletons, the solution was to alternate between image-text-image-text, so that the image of the saint always faces his or her prayer.

The scribe treated the Hours of the Virgin and various Marian prayers as one module. A full-page miniature appears on the left of the prayer's incipit, and a text with a decorated initial stands on the facing folio (Cambridge, UL, Ms. Ff.6.8; fig. 27).[52] This is the standard design solution within the modular method. Clearly the manuscript met with approval. How much did the early readers have to use this book in order to rub off the bottom third of the miniature through handling? On the facing folio the text has also been heavily used, but has held up better, suggesting that the parchment and the paints were prepared in a different way. This further underscores the fact that the miniatures were made in one atelier, and the texts in another (and the decoration around the text folios in yet another), and that the various ateliers sourced their materials from different places and did not necessarily swap recipes. The paint of the miniature has not stuck well and has practically thrown itself from the page. Within the Hours of the Virgin, the scribe began some of the subtexts on a verso side (such as lauds, on 28v; fig. 28),[53] indicating that he or she did not anticipate a miniature to accompany the individual hours. On the other hand, the scribe left space at the end of the Hours of the Virgin in order to start the next prayer, the *Salve Regina*, on a fresh recto. This has allowed the book maker to insert a full-page miniature before the *Salve Regina*, specifically, an image depicting the Virgin of the Sun (fig. 29).[54] One can see at the opening with the Marian prayer beginning on fol. 51r that the text pages were painted at some distance from where the marginal decoration around the facing miniature was executed. Simply stated, the borders don't

---

52 Matins of the Hours of the Virgin. Cambridge, University Library, Ms. Ff.6.8, fol. 23v-24r. http://cudl.lib.cam.ac.uk/view/MS-FF-00006–00008/47 and http://cudl.lib. cam.ac.uk/view/MS-FF-00006–00008/48

53 Lauds of the Hours of the Virgin. Cambridge, University Library, Ms. Ff.6.8, fol. 28v. http://cudl.lib.cam.ac.uk/view/MS-FF-00006–00008/58

54 Virgin of the Sun, full-page miniature inserted into a book of hours before the *Salve Regina*. Cambridge, University Library, Ms. Ff.6.8, fol. 51v-52r. http://cudl. lib.cam.ac.uk/view/MS-FF-00006–00008/104 and http://cudl.lib.cam.ac.uk/view/ MS-FF-00006–00008/105

match. Painters making single-leaf illuminations such as this one must have gotten significant mileage from this image type. Not only was it easy to paint—with the Virgin's red and gold radiance represented as simple geometric shapes and patterning and most of the figure covered in drapery—but the image activated an indulgenced prayer, the *Ave, sanctissima virgo Maria*, which was much in demand. It could also be inserted before most other Marian prayers, such as the *Salve Regina* or the *Magnificat*.

The previous text in Ms. Ff.6.8—the Hours of the Virgin—finished on fol. 50r (fig. 30).[55] This means that the bottom of 50r and the entirety of 50v, consisted of blank ruled parchment, and that fol. 51r, which is the back of the full-page miniature, was also blank (fig. 31).[56] To transition from the end of one text to the jubilant, decorated beginning of the next cost 2 ½ pages of blank parchment. However, the English recipient has considered this white space an invitation to add further texts. On fol. 50r, he or she has inscribed the incipit of the Book of John, "In principio erat verbum…." This particular text was considered thaumaturgic, so that anyone carrying it would be protected from sudden death, without reading it. By no means a necessary text, it was nevertheless considered highly desirable to have in one's book, and is therefore among those that owners most often squeeze in or find room for.

Wider and less confident, the English script of the "In principio" contrasts with the fine, even, decorous script of the Netherlandish scribe at the top of the folio. Notice, though, that the English scribe's ink has flaked off severely, but the first campaign of work has stayed in place for more than half a millennium. It is easy to see from this page alone that the Netherlanders had a more developed book-making culture and could do a better job cheaper and faster than could the English at the time. That is why the English imported their books from their neighbors across the channel in the first place.

An English owner added (or commissioned from a scrivener) another prayer to the bottom of fol. 50v (fig. 31). This hand, also English,

---

55 End of the Hours of the Virgin (original scribe) and beginning of a text added in England. Cambridge, University Library, Ms. Ff.6.8, fol. 50r. http://cudl.lib.cam.ac.uk/view/MS-FF-00006–00008/101

56 Prayer added to a formerly blank area. Cambridge, University Library, Ms. Ff.6.8, fol. 50v. http://cudl.lib.cam.ac.uk/view/MS-FF-00006–00008/102

contrasts with that at the top of the folio and makes it clear that many additions were made to the empty space in this book, possibly over a period of several decades. Whereas the inscription of the incipit of the Book of John was made seemingly in that spot because there was sufficient space, the placement of this added text was not careless: the bottom of this folio had seven ruled blank lines, more than enough to inscribe a rhyming prayer to the Virgin, which then precedes her image.

Blank, ruled parchment also provided an opportunity to inscribe a prayer to St. Ethelburga, an English saint with a small cult (Cambridge, UL, Ms. Ff.6.8; fig. 32).[57] Stationers in Bruges must have been able to successfully make products for their English market, and this meant that the customers had ways of making their requests known through agents or middlemen. Netherlandish book makers apparently did not receive the message that Ethelburga was in demand, and her suffrage remained to be added locally.

An English owner found an entire blank opening before the image depicting Christ in Judgment, which prefaces the Seven Penitential Psalms (fig. 33[58] and 34).[59] That owner has, in fact, added a prayer to the Virgin in this blank area, one that has little to do with the Christological texts that preceded it or the Psalms that followed it (97v-98r). These additions, while sometimes placed carefully to give the new item a particular context are at other times added opportunistically, because the extra space was available.

This added Marian text appears in yet another rather poor-quality English hand. These additions suggests that either a single owner paid several scribes over a period of time to continually update the book, or else that a later owner took a stab at further personalizing the book. One of my observations, made after studying hundreds of such

---

57   Added prayer to St. Ethelburga (below a prayer to St. Thomas of Canterbury, later crossed out). Cambridge, University Library, Ms. Ff.6.8, fol. 16v. http://cudl.lib.cam. ac.uk/view/MS-FF-00006–00008/34

58   Prayer text added to the formerly blank parchment. Cambridge, University Library, Ms. Ff.6.8, fol. 97v-98r. http://cudl.lib.cam.ac.uk/view/MS-FF-00006–00008/196 and http://cudl.lib.cam.ac.uk/view/MS-FF-00006–00008/197

59   Christ in Judgment, full-page miniature, formerly blank on the back, inserted before the Seven Penitential Psalms. Cambridge, University Library, Ms. Ff.6.8, fol. 98v-99r. http://cudl.lib.cam.ac.uk/view/MS-FF-00006–00008/198 and http://cudl.lib. cam.ac.uk/view/MS-FF-00006–00008/199

augmentations, is that a book that contains one is likely to contain many. Seeing one augmentation seems to encourage an owner to add more.

Overall, English scribes were worse than the Netherlandish scribes, even though the Bruges copyists were making hash out of some of the pages. I suspect that multiple people in Bruges wrote the various modules, which is one of the reasons to adopt a modular system in the first place, as several individuals could collaborate on a single product if they could work in a similar style. Such a system relies on standardization, although one can nevertheless see the seams between hands in the original part of the book, for example on fol. 11r, where there is a change of hand half-way down the page (Cambridge, UL, Ms. Ff.6.8; fig. 35).[60] (Compare the two instances of the word "Deus" above and below the seam in the middle of the page.) Saskia van Bergen has investigated the nature of ateliers in Bruges and found the workers picked up casual contracts, so that scribe *A* did not always work with artist *B*, but rather, they operated in an ever-changing and fluid network.[61] This is relevant to both the ways in which the books were produced and consumed.

Just as multiple hands can be seen at work in the script, the same is true of the images, which might be built up out of many pieces of different origin, and shoved together to reflect local interests. Text and image might be adapted to each other as part of this process, in a feedback loop of production (where new images need accompanying added text and vice versa). Cambridge, UL, Ms. Ff.6.8 speaks to a form of production in which it was possible to construct highly decorated manuscripts out of component parts. Studying the codicological structure of this manuscript reveals another aspect of this process: the suffrages (quires III and IV) have been assembled entirely out of singletons: an image singleton, followed by a relevant prayer text copied onto a singleton, followed by another image page, another text page and so on. Each of these folios has a stub that has been folded down so that all of the loose pages can be joined up and sewn together. In effect, the Southern Netherlandish book makers were assembling many codicological units, some comprising just a single folio, to build the suffrage modules. Single

---

60   Seam between hands. Cambridge, University Library, Ms. Ff.6.8, fol. 11r. http:// cudl.lib.cam.ac.uk/view/MS-FF-00006–00008/23

61   van Bergen, *De Meesters van Otto van Moerdrecht.*

leaves depicting saints in full-page miniatures were quickly becoming the norm. In order to ensure that these images accompanied their relevant suffrages, the scribes had to adopt the same method: copying a single suffrage on a single leaf. This must have resulted in a situation by which customers could simply choose from stacks of saints those they wanted to include. They "expressed themselves" in this act of shopping. English customers had agents in Bruges who aided in these transactions. Alternatively stationers must have also assembled books of hours speculatively for the English market. In this case, they could stick to safe choices: the most popular female saints, plus the English saints George and Thomas of Canterbury, and St. Christopher, the most popular protective saint. Regardless of who was making the final selection, this form of book construction results in blank parchment that early owners could then fill.

Its English owner(s) added several prayers to Ms. Ff.6.8, including the apotropaic incipit of the Book of John; a suffrage to St. Sebastian (142v), who was thought to ward off the plague; an incantation to the names of Yahweh (143r); and a prayer headed "Tetragramaton" that lists the 72 names of Yahweh interspersed with red Maltese crosses (143v). It is clear, therefore, that the English owner(s) used the blank space to turn the book of hours into an apotropaic object, which would provide personal protection. It is also clear from the dirt ground into the pages and the wear incurred on the miniatures that they used the manuscript as prescribed, as a daily guide to prayer, reading it habitually and keeping it close at hand. They employed the blank parchment as a vehicle to carry new texts, especially apotropaic ones, thereby multiplying the functions of their beloved imported book.

* * *

Analyzing the book structurally, noting which material is original and which is added, and considering the blank areas and the additions made post-production help to illuminate the stratigraphy of the book. Noticing these features reveals workshop practices and shows how book makers in cities such as Bruges and Delft adopted a modular system. Not every atelier in the Netherlands built manuscripts out of modular units. Those that did seemed to be tapping into a manuscript production method that would allow multiple scribes to work on a single manuscript; to produce manuscripts at varying levels of decoration; to include several standard texts, but allow for the expansion with other, less popular texts; and possibly to streamline production, thereby reducing its attendant costs. It also allowed the manuscript to be expanded later, when more components could be added at the beginning, at the end, and at the fissures.

Whereas book makers in Bruges worked primarily in secular workshops, those in Delft, Amsterdam, Haarlem, and other cities in the Northern Netherlands were largely organized in convents. In the discussion above I have used Bruges manuscripts as examples, because their extreme form of modular construction is easily graspable. Later, I will treat manuscripts from other centers, which were made according to similar principles.

One might be inclined to think that the maker of the manuscript, locked in his atelier, and the owner who later glues a scrap of parchment into that manuscript or adds a quire to the end, stand at opposite ends of the manuscript's life. But in fact, the processes of production and alteration of manuscripts could be stutter-stepped, incremental, and intertwined. A manuscript might go through several stages of "making," involving many hands—including those of its owner, who might intervene in this creation on multiple occasions—from initially having the book constructed via a modular method that suited, as much as was possible at that initial moment, his prayer needs. He or she might intervene repeatedly to keep that book as it had been at its initial creation—up to date. Circumstances, devotion, and motivations would change as a book aged with its various owners. Book production methods were, from the 1390s onward, fully prepared to accommodate this fact.

People who owned books—especially books of hours—in the fifteenth century, made all kinds of modifications to them. Some of these modifications resulted from a new production method—what I'm calling the modular method. Building the book from additive and modular parts paved the way for owners to add even more modules (some of them quite chunky), to fill in the otherwise wasted space with text, and to slip in images at quire divisions. While the idea of modifying books had been around for centuries, here for the first time the methods of book making anticipated post-production alterations.

In the following two parts, I analyze these types of modifications structurally, from the simplest to the most complex, using examples drawn from a millennium of book making. People have modified books as long as books have been made. Owners of books of hours in the fifteenth century — the century of the greatest rise in literacy, the largest manuscript production and expanded markets for books — was also the era of the most book modification. They borrowed simple techniques of augmentation that did not require rebinding, as well as more complicated techniques that did. All of these interventions, from the full rebinding to the work of the quire-filler, will be considered within the larger frame of the contemporary use of books. In short, I want to reveal not just what was done to these books, but also what motivated owners to intervene.

Part II: Changes that did not require rebinding

My discussion thus far has shown that the modular way of making manuscripts multiplied the amount of blank space in them, which owners often desired to fill. Nearly all manuscripts, whether they were made modularly or not, also have blank space at the very beginning and very end of the book, in the form of flyleaves and paste-downs. But many votaries wanted a full book, and they took opportunities to fill up any blank space. Book owners, or the scribes they hired, could simply write in these blank spaces without having to take the book apart. In this part, I systematically work through the types of additions they could make to the book without rebinding.

A. Correcting the text

How does someone amend the text once it's already neatly formed in the text block? Early medieval author portraits show that the scribe wrote with a pen in one hand and a knife in the other. The knife was for sharpening the quill, but also for scraping out errors. If the scribe caught an error immediately, he could scrape it out and write over the now-velvety and slightly weakened parchment. If he caught the error after one or more lines of text were already inscribed, he could "expunctuate" it, that is, make little dots under a wrong word, signaling the reader to ignore it. An example is a child's ABC, written in the Southern Netherlands in the fifteenth century in silver and gold

 http://dx.doi.org/10.11647/OBP.0094.02

letters on stained parchment, in which the repeated words "adveniat regnum" have been expunctuated with gold dots (New York, Columbia University, Plimpton Ms. 287; fig. 36).[1] In the Bruges book of hours, made for English export explored above (Cambridge, UL, Ms. Ii.6.2), the English owner found an error in the manuscript and must have taken the book to a professional copyist to have the problem rectified (fig. 37).[2] The English scribe has scraped out the offending passage but then has reinscribed the ruling in the erased section using bright red, and then used a dark brown ink to write the correct words. The scribe probably did this without taking the book apart.

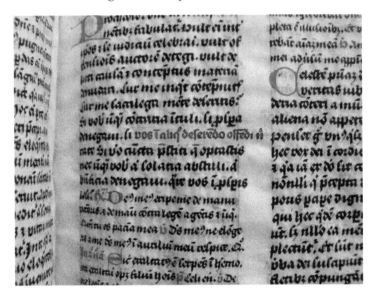

Fig. 38 Folio in a breviary made by the convent of St. Agnes in Delft revealing text painted out and corrected. Delft, Prinsenhof, no number. Image © Author, CC BY 4.0.

A little-known way of correcting the text was to use the medieval version of typewriter correction fluid. A manuscript probably made at the convent of St. Agnes in Delft on very fine parchment has employed this

---

1   Folio of a child's ABC, with expunctuation, made in the Southern Netherlands, ca. 1450–1500. New York, Columbia University, Rare Book and Manuscript Library, Plimpton Ms. 287, fol. 1r. http://vm133.lib.berkeley.edu:8080/xtf22/search?rmode=d igscript;smode=basic;text=plimpton 287;docsPerPage=1;startDoc=1;fullview=yes
2   Writing over an erasure. Cambridge, University Library, Ms. Ii.6.2, fol. 93r. http:// cudl.lib.cam.ac.uk/view/MS-II-00006–00002/179

technique (fig. 38). The parchment here is so thin that it would not have withstood scraping with a knife, which may explain why the copyist chose instead to cover over her errors with a layer of white. Using this method indicates that the scribe had access to thick, lead-based white paint of the sort used by illuminators. In the period after 1400, this method was employed seldom because scribes were writing in ateliers in which there was no paint. Paint was kept in painters' ateliers instead. (The Augustinian convent of St. Agnes in Delft, whose sisters both wrote and illuminated manuscripts, was an exception and therefore had white paint on hand.)

Occasionally, to cover large errors, a scribe would paste over a sheet of paper or parchment with the new, corrected text, in the way that the Soviet government did to get rid of Beria and add the Bering Strait. This involved introducing small amounts of new material. This solution to correction appears in a prayerbook now at Columbia University (Columbia RBML, Ms. X096.C286; fig. 39).[3] This book has been pieced together from dozens of dismembered "parent" manuscripts and some printed fragments. The owner has built the first folio out of two columns of text pasted to a parchment page (so that the verso is not visible). Not only is the text glued to the page, but the decorated initials, which were cut out of different manuscripts, have been pasted down on top, to create a page that is several layers thick.[4] In addition to these layers, the book's user has pasted a correction to the text in the second column. This approach to correcting an error is consistent with the user's approach toward illuminating the book: this person in fact glued in decoration as well, using an extra strip of parchment for a small correction was an extension of the same thinking.

---

3 For a full manuscript description, search the Digital Scriptorium (http://bancroft. berkeley.edu/digitalscriptorium/basicsearch.html) with the term "X096.C286." Consulted 25 May 2016. Folio with decoration and a correction glued on. New York, Columbia University, Rare Book and Manuscript Library, X 096.C286, fol. 1r. http://vm133.lib.berkeley.edu:8080/xtf22/search?rmode=digscript;smode=basic;text=X096.C286;docsPerPage=1;startDoc=1;fullview=yes

4 Likewise, Cambridge, Trinity College, Ms. O.4.16, an English Psalter made ca. 1250–1275, includes pasted-in decorations cut out of other manuscripts. See Paul Binski, "The Illumination and Patronage of the Douce Apocalypse," *The Antiquaries Journal* 94 (2014), pp. 1–8, n. 13.

A similar solution also appears in a booklet made with prints, now disassembled and housed in the British Museum. Each folio of the booklet consists of a printed engraved image on the recto, which has then been highly decorated with multiple colors (fig. 40).[5] Each sheet's verso contains densely written prayer text, written in a West Flemish dialect of Middle Dutch (fig. 41).[6] Fitting the long text into the small area of the back of the print gave the scribe tremendous difficulty. When she made an error, she was in trouble. Because this was paper not parchment she could not scrape out the error. Often a scribe would add a missing piece of text to the margin and signal its correct position by placing a carat in the text, but she had no room at the bottom to do so. The solution was to clip a small piece of paper onto the error and inscribe the correct text on top. This has been done in a different hand, similar to the first (which suggests a corporate similarity, an adherence to an impersonal style typical of female convents), but slightly less slanted. Thus, the corrector was using a solution that anticipates the fiasco around the Soviet encyclopedia by 500 years.

B. Adding text to the blank folios and interstices

One way to augment an existing, finished manuscript was simply to write in its blank areas. Both the modular and the uniform methods leave several possible blank spaces in a manuscript, including its pastedowns, front and back flyleaves, and margins. The former also leaves blank spaces at the ends of quires and the backs of full-page miniatures. Nearly every existing medieval manuscript has had at least some text added to its interstices. Because the reasons for doing so were extensive,

---

5   Weekes, *Early Engravers and Their Public*, pp. 121–43. Lamentation, printed engraving, hand-colored with an inscription in Middle Dutch. London, British Museum Department of Prints and Drawings, inv. no. 1846,0709.49. http://www.britishmuseum.org/research/collection_online/collection_object_details/collection_image_gallery.aspx?partid=1&assetid=48947001&objectid=1361029

6   Reverse of the Lamentation, with hand-written prayer text. London, British Museum Department of Prints and Drawings, inv. no. 1846,0709.49v. http://www.britishmuseum.org/research/collection_online/collection_object_details/collection_image_gallery.aspx?partid=1&assetid=378290001&objectid=1361029

I do not pretend that this list is comprehensive. Nevertheless, there are a few major patterns that emerge:

1. Noting who owned, commissioned, and paid for items

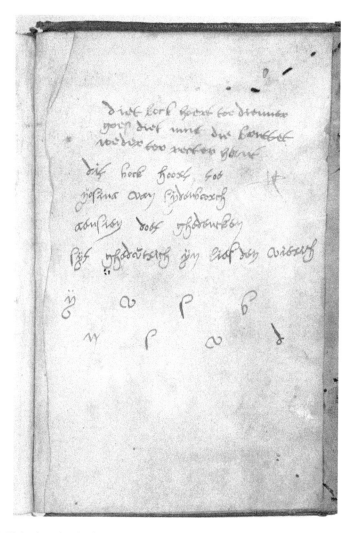

Fig. 42 Flyleaf in a book of hours, inscribed with notes of ownership and practice letters. The Hague, Koninklijke Bibliotheek, Ms. 132 G 38, fol. 140r. Image © Koninklijke Bibliotheek—the National Library of The Netherlands, CC BY 4.0.

Fig. 43
Folio in the Missal of the Guild
of St. Mary Magdalene at
Bruges, showing an iconic Mary
Magdalene surrounded by scenes
from her *Life*, made in 1475–76.
's-Heerenberg, The Netherlands,
Collection Dr. J. H. van Heek, Huis
Bergh Foundation, Ms. 16; inv. no.
285, fol. 201v. Image © The Huis
Bergh Foundation, CC BY 4.0.

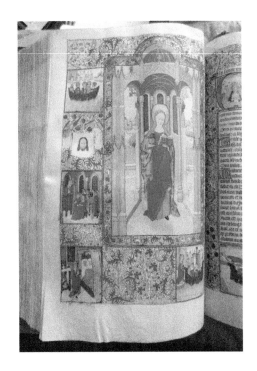

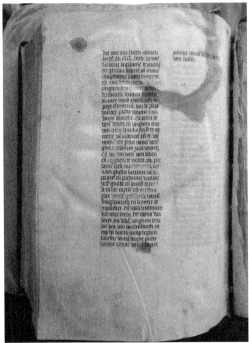

Fig. 44
Final folio in the Missal of the
Guild of St. Mary Magdalene at
Bruges, listing the the patrons
who paid for the manuscript.
's-Heerenberg, The Netherlands,
Collection Dr. J. H. van Heek,
Huis Bergh Foundation, Ms. 16;
inv. no. 285, fol. 250v. Image
© The Huis Bergh Foundation,
CC BY 4.0.

Owners inscribed pleas to return the book if found.[7] In a similar vein, owners added their names to the front or the back of the book to lay claim to their property. The front and back usually had space in the form of flyleaves and a paste-down. In writing there owners followed a tradition of scribal colophons that appear at the end of the writing and record part of the book's history. In writing notes in the back of the book, owners were perhaps extending this tradition by placing themselves in the book's history. For example, two female book owners record their ownerships of a book of hours from South Holland (to be discussed at length below; HKB, Ms. 132 G 38; fig. 42). Diewer Goes and later Josina van Sijdenburch record their names in shaky hands on the final folio.[8] Josina was particularly insecure as a scribe and seems to have practiced a few of the letters first in the middle of the page.

A more fulsome addition to the back of a richly decorated missal tells the story of its patronage ('s-Heerenberg, HB, Ms. 16; inv. no. 285).[9] Made for the Guild of St. Mary Magdalene in Bruges in 1475–1476, the missal contains voluminous decoration, with the life of Mary Magdalene in vignettes around her iconic image (fig. 43). Willem Vrelant may have illuminated the book, but if he did, he apparently was not important enough to mention in the record on the last page (fig. 44). Instead, important were the patrons who paid for it. While the rest of the manuscript was written in Latin, the note of patronage was added in the vernacular (Dutch). The patrons, whose names include Lenaert Brouke, Oliver vander Abeele, Jan de Pape Temmerman, Jan de Pape Vulder, Pieter Lowijc, Joos vanden Broucke, amongst others. The inscription also lists the guild masters: Jooris Weilaert, Jan van Haerdenburch, Iacob van Craylo, Iacob Beghin Silvester van den Berghe, Pieter Lowijc, Adrian vanden Moere, Arnout vanden Abeele and Jacob van Hulst, who were the decision makers in the Guild of Mary Magdalene, which

---

7   Marc Drogin, *Anathema! Medieval Scribes and the History of Book Curses* (Totowa: Allanheld & Schram, 1983), collects many examples.

8   The inscriptions read: "Diet bock hoert toe Diewer Goes. Diet vint die brnttet weder ter recten hant;" and "Dit bock hoort toe IJosina van Sijdenburch aensien doet ghedencken sijt gheduerich ijn liefden vierich." For a fuller description of the manuscript and further literature, see Hanneke van Asperen, *Pelgrimstekens op Perkament: Originele en nageschilderde bedevaartssouvenirs in religieuze boeken (ca 1450-ca 1530)* (PhD thesis, Radboud Universiteit Nijmegen, 2009), no. 46, pp. 327–28.

9   A. S. Korteweg, *Catalogue of Medieval Manuscripts and Incunabula at Huis Bergh Castle in 's-Heerenberg* ('s-Heerenberg: Stichting Huis Bergh, 2013), cat. 70, pp. 122–26.

commissioned the book. According to the inscription, they used alms
to pay for it. One can see why they would have needed to take up a
collection, as the decorative cycle is full and would have been expensive.
Whereas most missals include only one full-page miniature, this one
contains two, both with elaborate border decoration, plus 18 historiated
initials, numerous images in the margin, painted initials on all pages
and penwork initials on some. The canon was quite heavily used, as
one can see from the pages discolored from handling at the center of the
book. These pages would have also been partially visible when the book
was used, and anyone who had access to the altar during mass would
have seen flashes of color from its rich illumination.

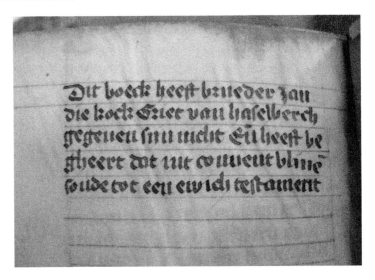

Fig. 45 Folio near the end of a book of hours, with a note of ownership. The Hague,
Koninklijke Bibliotheek, Ms. 135 G 10, fol. 163v.Image © Koninklijke
Bibliotheek—the National Library of The Netherlands, CC BY 4.0.

Sometimes notes record more complicated information about the
transfer of a book. A book of hours made in the Southern Netherlands
has this note on the final folio: "Dit boeck heeft brueder Jan die Kock
Griet van Haselberch gegeven sijn nicht. Ende heeft begheert dat int
convent bliven soude tot een ewich testament" (Brother Jan die Kock
gave this book to his niece, Griet van Haselberch. He has requested that it
shall remain in the convent as an everlasting testimony (HKB, Ms. 135 G
10, fol. 163v; fig. 45). Although Brother Jan die Kock is giving the book to
his niece, he is ostensibly giving it to the convent so that the other sisters

can continue to remember him after she is dead. His real motivation was to secure prayers for his soul in perpetuity. Internal evidence suggests that he was not the book's original owner; namely, three figures who may represent the original patrons, appear in a miniature depicting the Elevation of the Host (fig. 46).[10] A moneybag hangs from the belt of the man in the image, who sports a full head of hair, both indications that he is not a "brother." Somehow, the book passed to Brother Jan die Kock, who then gave it to his niece, Griet van Haselberch. In other words, he was giving his niece (and her convent) a used book, not one made expressly for them with their interests reflected.

2. Adding family information

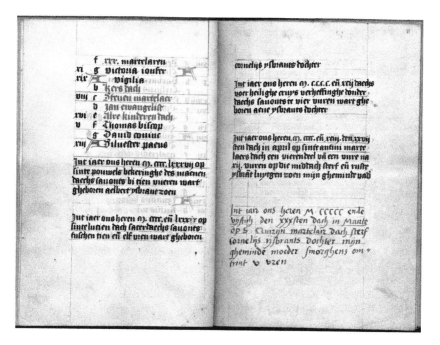

Fig. 47 Family information added to the end of the calendar of a book of hours made in Enkhuizen. The Hague, Koninklijke Bibliotheek, Ms. 79 K 6, fol. 10v-11r. Image © Koninklijke Bibliotheek—the National Library of The Netherlands, CC BY 4.0.

---

10 Layman with a money bag (the original donor?) and two women in contemporary garb witnessing the elevation of the Eucharist. The Hague, Koninklijke Bibliotheek, Ms. 135 G 10, fol. 123v. http://manuscripts.kb.nl/zoom/BYVANCKB%3Amimi_135g10%3A123v

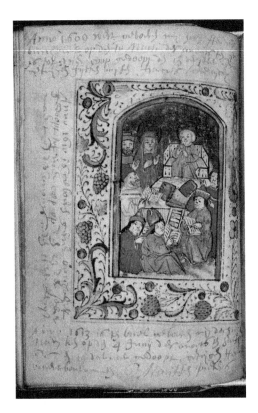

Fig. 48
Christ teaching in the temple,
Book of hours from Delft,
hand-colored prints instead of
miniatures. Brussels, Koninklijke
Bibliotheek van België, Ms. IV
142, fol. 47v.Image © Koninklijke
Bibliotheek van België, all rights
reserved.

While some augmentations might record smaller transitions, such
as the gift of a book, other augmentations, taken collectively, also
record large-scale transitions in the way people used the book itself.
Most significantly, private prayerbooks went from being exclusively
repositories of devotional material to being family heirlooms that might
fill devotional purposes. One kind of annotation that signals this shift
is notes recording birth and death information and family history. Such
notations appear, for example, in a book of hours probably made in
Enkhuizen, where several generations of owners added this information
at the end of the calendar (which is also the end of a quire) (fig. 47).
Here an expanse of blank parchment formed a powerful invitation to
the owner, who obligingly filled the void. The dates incorporated in
such additions, and the style of handwriting in which they are inscribed,
indicate that birth and death notices were often made in the post-
medieval period, and well-after the Reformation, when the structures

and content of prayer had changed significantly. In other words, books of hours often changed function, from prayerbook to family heirloom. People understood their books of hours to be time machines that would continue to have relevance to their progeny's progeny. A book of hours made in Delft, with printed full-page "miniatures," for example, has some of its margins filled with just this kind of family information, added in the seventeenth century (BKB, Ms. IV 142; fig. 48). While the margins around the Last Judgment print are left blank, those around the image of Christ preaching in the temple as a child are filled with a family's birth records, as if they wanted to associate their progeny with the clever young Jesus.

For several reasons families chose a book of hours as the repository of such information.[11] First, books of hours were made on parchment, a far more durable surface than paper, which has a finite lifespan. Families wanted to record their important information on a material they considered suitable for the job. Second, families in the sixteenth century chose a book from the previous century in which to record data in order to extend the existing record, demonstrate the antiquity of their family, and provide a sense of continuity. Third, recording this information is an extension of recording obits in calendars. Having such information in a book of hours reminded one to read the Vigil for the Dead, on the anniversaries of loved ones' deaths. One of the functions of a book of hours was to pray for the long dead and recently departed. If the book stays in the family for several generations, then one is ideally praying for the person who had bequeathed that very book of hours.[12] Fourth, owners considered the book of hours a vessel in which to store

---

11　Kathleen M. Ashley, "Creating Family Identity in Books of Hours" *Journal of Medieval and Early Modern Studies Volume* 32, no. 1 (2002), pp. 145–66, discusses books of hours as loci for family memory. She posits reasons different from mine for the book of hours taking up this role. Anne-Marie Legaré, "Livres d'Heures, Livres de Femmes: Quelques Examples en Hainaut," *Eulalie* 1 (1998), pp. 53–68, with a series of case studies, shows how women passed books of hours down the maternal line. Several of her examples postdate the medieval period and probably represent manuscripts that were being used not as vehicles for prayer but for storing family history.

12　On this point, see Geneviève Hasenohr, "L'Essor des bibliothèques privées aux xive et xve siècles," in *Histoire des Bibliothèques Françaises, Vol. 1: Les Bibliothèques Médiévales du vie Siècle à 1530*, ed. André Vernet (Paris: Éditions du Cercle de la Librairie, 1989), pp. 215–63, esp. 229–30.

all manner of objects and concepts, including pilgrims' badges, other religious tokens, loose images, and talismans.

Eamon Duffy and Kathleen M. Ashley have discussed this kind of change of use, from prayerbook to family heirloom.[13] In the present study I am primarily interested in changes made to the book in the medieval period, roughly before 1550, and will therefore set aside annotations that signal an early modern change of function.

3. Adding legal documents

People also used religious manuscripts to inscribe legal transactions. An eighth-century Anglo-Saxon gospel book had some empty space at the end of a column just before the incipit of the Gospel of Matthew. Into this space someone in the tenth-century has inscribed a manumission document in Old English under King Athelstan (LBL, Royal Ms. 1 B VII, fol. 15v; fig. 49).[14] Beyond simply improvising in the face of parchment shortages, medieval users may have added such a manumission document to a gospel book with the intent of giving the documents greater gravitas and a more binding character, by virtue of the fact that the Gospel of Matthew witnessed them. The added text is formulaic, but it has been inscribed, and possibly pronounced aloud, in the presence of sacred scripture. This manumission document is not an isolated event: several manumission documents have been inscribed into the folios of a compilation manuscript begun in the eighth century, the Leofric Missal (Oxford, Bodl. 579, fol. 11v). Nicholas Orchard has sorted out the manuscript's complicated stratigraphy, with its phased genesis that lasted several hundred years.[15] The manumission documents appear in the earliest parts of the manuscript. Such documents attest to the

---

13   Duffy, *Marking the Hours*; Ashley, "Creating Family Identity in Books of Hours," pp. 145–66.

14   Michelle Brown, *The Lindisfarne Gospels: Society, Spirituality and the Scribe*, British Library Studies in Medieval Culture (London: British Library, 2003), pp. 55–56. See also David Anthony Edgell Pelteret, *Slavery in Early Mediaeval England: From the Reign of Alfred until the Twelfth Century*, Studies in Anglo-Saxon History (Woodbridge: Boydell, 1995), esp. pp. 131–33. Manumission document added to Gospel of Matthew. London, British Library, Royal Ms. 1 B VII, fol. 15v. http://www.bl.uk/catalogues/illuminatedmanuscripts/ILLUMIN.ASP?Size=mid&IllID=50424

15   Nicholas Orchard, *The Leofric Missal*, vol. v, pp. 113–14 (Woodbridge; London: Boydell Press for the Henry Bradshaw Society, 2002).

ways in which gospel and liturgical books took on functions other than their religious ones.[16] They could also symbolize terrestrial power and therefore serve as witness to civic oaths and legal agreements. Added text could therefore expand the functions of the manuscript. Legal records such as this do not appear frequently in private prayerbooks in the later Middle Ages, because separate systems for recording legal documents were more fully developed by the thirteenth century and had greater legal authority than recording something in a prayerbook would have had.

Fig. 50
Christ crucified between Mary and John, full-page miniature in a missal. Zutphen, Regionaal Archief, Ms. 7, fol. 144v. Image © Regionaal Archief Zutphen, CC BY 4.0.

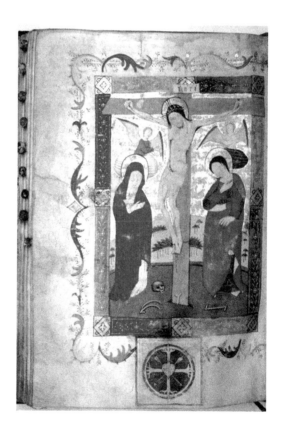

16　For gospel books used as objects for swearing testimony, see: Eyal Poleg, "The Bible as Talisman: Textus and Oath-Books," in *Approaching the Bible in Medieval England, Manchester Medieval Studies* (Manchester: Manchester University Press, 2013), pp. 59–107.

Fig. 51
Formerly blank back of a full-page miniature of Christ crucified, with inscriptions added in the fifteenth and sixteenth centuries. Zutphen, Regionaal Archief, Ms. 7, fol. 144r.Image © Regionaal Archief Zutphen, CC BY 4.0.

Manumission documents were irrelevant after the twelfth century, when serfdom replaced slavery. The legal system had also evolved, and with it came the rise of charters, land deeds, legal documents, and secular institutions to deal with civic cases, which obviated the need to inscribe that kind of legal information in other (religious) books. One kind of legal document that continued to be inscribed into books, however, was transactions about the book itself. A fascinating example appears in a missal made in the mid-fifteenth century (Zutphen, Ms. 7; fig. 50).[17] It

---

17   J. P. Gumbert, *Manuscrits datés conservés dans les Pays-Bas; Catalogue paléographique des Manuscrits en Écriture Latine portant des Indications de Date; T. 2. Manuscrits d'Origine Néerlandaise (xive-xvie siècles), et Supplément au Tome Premier (Cmd-Nl 2)*, 2 vols. (Leiden: Brill, 1988), no. 774; Korteweg, *Kriezels, Aubergines en Takkenbossen: Randversiering in Noordnederlandse Handschriften uit de Vijftiende Eeuw*, p. 119; H. L. M. Defoer et al., *The Golden Age of Dutch Manuscript Painting*, 1st ed., Exh. Cat. Rijksmuseum Het Catharijneconvent, Utrecht and the Pierpont Morgan Library, New York (Stuttgart: Belser Verlag, 1989), p. 78.

has a canon page—an image of Christ crucified—made by the Masters of Otto van Moerdrecht in the second quarter of the fifteenth century.[18] Someone has made an inscription in the vernacular on the back of the canon page (fig. 51).[19] It indicates that "this missal" was sold in 1473 to the "altar of St. Anthony." Guild brothers of St. Anthony paid for it, with the provision that it must never be sold or removed but would serve on the altar for daily service.

Two items need to be mentioned here: First, the inscription serves as a testament to a transaction—the sale of this very missal to the brotherhood of St. Anthony in Zutphen in 1473. Second, the position of the inscription serves a symbolic and ritual function. The scribe was instructed to write these words not at the beginning of the book, on, say, a flyleaf, but rather in the middle of the book, right on the back of the canon page. That same canon page initiates the most important part of the mass, the part of the ceremony involving ritualized actions that culminate in the transubstantiation. Here a crucifixion miniature initiates and signals the canon page in the book, all the more so because it is the only large miniature in this (and most other) missals. Though the parchment is thick, it is slightly lipidinous, rendering it translucent and allowing the bold colors and heavy gold delineating the figures and background to be visible through the parchment membrane. By inscribing the back of this miniature, the scribe was placing his words as closely as possible to the body of Christ, and therefore as closely as possible to the moment of transubstantiation. In fact, he has written the words at the faint feet of Jesus, and used the body of St. John to demarcate the left side of the text block, and the frame of the miniature to define the right side. In this way, the inscription is made as a response to, and in relation to, the image. The testament becomes more powerful because it is laid at the feet of the lord and only a thin membrane away.

---

18   For an overview of the canon images by these masters, see Hanns Peter Neuheuser, "Die Kanonblätter aus der Schule des Moerdrecht-Meisters," *Wallraf-Richartz-Jahrbuch* 64 (2003), pp. 187–214.

19   The inscription reads: Inden iaer ons heren m.cccc.lxxiii hebben samentliker hand ghekoft to sunte Anthonijs altaer dyt missael. Testamentoers seligher gedachten hen allen bulkens vicarious des altaers. Ende die ghemein ghilde broeders van sunte Anthonijs. In vorwarden dat men dit missale to genre tijt noch om ghenen noeden verkopen ofte versetten sal, mer den behoerliken dienst des altaers daer uut daghelikes te betalen.

One situation I observed in the course of writing *Postcards in Parchment* is this: once a book has some objects pasted into it, this addition gives the owner, and later owners, license to add more images and objects. By their presence, previously added images inherently convey the idea of adding more images, and tacitly give permission to do so. This idea has broad applications, and is in effect the idea behind Malcolm Gladwell's book, *The Tipping Point*.[20] Among numerous examples that explain phenomena in our modern world, he shows that once a wall bears some graffiti, it becomes a magnet for further graffiti. In a similar way, the Zutphen missal became a target for further inscriptions that bear testaments, in particular a note describing the book's conservation:

> This book has been renewed and repaired at Deventer in the house of Florence in the year 1539. The payment and expenses as regards this missal were paid by the venerable master Reyner Bruckinck, who died in the year of our lord 1550. Please pray to God for him.

> Hic liber innovatus et reparatus est Daventrie in domo Florencii. Anno domini 1539 Stipendiis et expensis venerabilis domini Reyneri Bruckinck. istius altaris vicarii. ad quod spectat hoc missale. Qui obiit anno domini m v^c l. Oretis propter deum pro eo [Zutphen, Ms. 7, flyleaf]

In 1539 the manuscript was therefore repaired, and the person who paid for the restoration was to be memorialized within the very object in whose longevity he had invested. Stating that the work was done in Deventer, the inscription refers to a monastic house there, that of the Brothers of the Common Life, who were dedicated to St. Mary and St. Gregory and St. Jerome, and whose house was also known as the House of Master Floris. At this point this missal still belonged to the brothers of St. Anthony. The inscriptions trace the various owners and their investments in the book.

I make three observations about this situation. First, the fact that the missal needed to be rebound in 1539 suggests that it was heavily used in the preceding decades. Thus the brothers of St. Anthony used the book quite vigorously. Secondly, and more tenuously, I hypothesize that if the testament of purchase had not been inscribed in the book in 1473,

---

20   Malcolm Gladwell, *The Tipping Point: How Little Things Can Make a Big Difference*, 1st ed. (Boston: Little, Brown & Co., 2000).

that master Reyner Bruckinck would not have had the idea to add his own testament in 1539 when he had it repaired. Writing in the book once makes it more likely that someone will write in it again. Such a statement as his, detailing the terms of the book's conservation, are rare. The previous testament gave him the idea of adding his own.

Thirdly, the way in which the book was constructed, with the crucifixion miniature on a separate leaf that was slotted in to preface the text commencing *Te Igitur*, meant that the page had a blank back, which the new owners could exploit. A new function was suggested by the structure of the book itself, that of making testaments witnessed by Jesus, Mary, and John on the very flesh that made them manifest. Most of what I am discussing in this book concerns prayerbooks, but some aspect of the method of production could was also applied to other types of books in the Netherlands, including Missals. Namely, the single image could be made in a separate atelier, which meant that the back would normally be blank, and therefore available for fill.

4. Adding a gloss

One of the simplest ways to add text to a finished manuscript is by writing in the margins, so that the added notes relate spatially to the main text. One can add words, signs, or manicules ("little hands"). All of these additions could be called glosses. They function by bringing a reader's notes into a relationship with what's already on the page. The meaning of a gloss comes from its content and its position on the page.

A gloss can reveal how someone used a book. A thirteenth-century psalter made in Amiens for an abbey was written in two columns with a small amount of blank space at the end of the column, just before the initial for Psalm 109.[21] Because the scribe needed six lines for a historiated initial, but only had five available at the end of column 1, he has begun the Psalm at the top of column 2. This has left five empty lines

---

21 Psalter from Amiens, possibly the Abbey of St. Fuscien, late thirteenth century, with comments added shortly thereafter in the otherwise empty space of col. 1. New York, Pierpont Morgan Library and Museum, Ms. M.796. For an image, see John Plummer, *Liturgical Manuscripts for the Mass and the Divine Office* (New York: Pierpont Morgan Library, 1964), no. 47, pp. 38–39, plate 17.

of ruled, uninscribed parchment. In this blank space at the end of the column, a user has squeezed eight lines of text, in very small and highly abbreviated script. These added words provide an indication of how he used the manuscript. A fragment from the Psalms, "Confitebor domino nimis in ore meo," forms the first line, which repeats the psalter text at the top of this very page.[22] It is also an antiphon used in the liturgy. Specifically, it is sung on Saturdays, at matins, as the third antiphon in the second nocturne. Other texts to be sung during the Saturday liturgy were noted by the book's user in the squeezed-in list. His notations are therefore oriented to the space of this page.

These notes are:

Marginal note	In which part of the Saturday liturgy the text is used	Inventory number in Dom René-Jean Hesbert, *Corpus Antiphonalium Officii.* 6 vols. Rome: Herder, 1963–79
Confitebor domino nimis in ore meo	Ad Matutinam, In secundo nocturno, Antiphon 3	CAO 1874
Responsus Domine exaudi oratio nem me am et clamor	Ad Matutinam, In primo nocturno, Responsory 2	CAO 6494
Benigne fac in bona volun tate tua domine	Ad Laudes, Antiphon 1	CAO 1736
Bonum est confiteri domino	Ad Laudes, Antiphon 2	CAO 1744
Metuant dominum omnes fines terre	Ad Laudes, Antiphon 3	CAO 3749
Et in servis suis domine miserebitur	Ad Laudes, Antiphon 5	CAO 2705
In cymbalis benesonan tibus laudate dominum	Ad Matutinam, In secundo nocturno, Antiphon 2	CAO 5471
In viam pacis dirige nos domine	Ad Laudes, Antiphon	CAO 3310

22   For the contents of the medieval liturgy, based on autopsy of specific manuscripts, see the Medieval Music Database, housed at Latrobe University (Australia), http://arrow.latrobe.edu.au/store/3/4/5/4/2/public/MMDB/Feasts/l04067000.htm

The texts he has listed in the extra space relate to the Psalm at the top of the page, because that Psalm is part of the Saturday liturgy and he provides the first few lines of the other texts used in the same service. But his list deviates somewhat from the standard order of the Saturday liturgy, as given in the second column of my chart. This suggests that he is either using his psalter to follow along with some non-standard antiphonal, or to sketch out a few adjustments, but it is difficult to know whether the list is descriptive or prescriptive. What is clear is that the person who made these notes knew Latin, knew how to write, knew quite a bit about the liturgy, and was using the psalter not just as an aid to private meditation, but as a tool for organizing the liturgy. His reason for using this particular space in the book to record this list was not simply opportunistic, but also closely related to the contents of the page.

As I show below, the ways in which Netherlandish prayerbooks were made meant that there was a great amount of blank parchment, which owners could fill. Sometimes these additions relate to, or comment upon, what is already present on the page. But the many empty spaces simply created opportunities for additional comments and texts, images and items. What kinds of things were added, and how they were added, shifted considerably in the fifteenth century. It appears that a cottage industry opened up to add marginal glosses to empty space, because the opportunities were so numerous.

5. Adding calendrical data

There is typically blank space in the vicinity of the calendar, because saints' names are too short to fill an entire line, and because usually not every day is filled in. There were often blank lines with no saints, especially in calendars from before, say, 1430: calendars before this date are often sparsely populated. Such open areas seem to have called out to owners, including one who felt the need to fill some of the empty space with a grinning, waving figure (Paris, Bibl. Sainte-Geneviève, Ms. 95; fig. 52).[23] As the century wore on, a new fashion for very full calendars grew,

---

23 Grinning waving figure added to a calendar, in a missal for the use of Beauvais, made in the early twelfth century, with the drawing added later. Paris, Bibl. Sainte-Geneviève, Ms. 95, fol. 5v-6r. http://initiale.irht.cnrs.fr/ouvrages/ouvrages. php?imageInd=5&id=3148

as if scribes themselves were responding to the need to fill these spaces by finding saints, so that most calendars made around 1500 have a saint for every day, and therefore less space for frivolities.

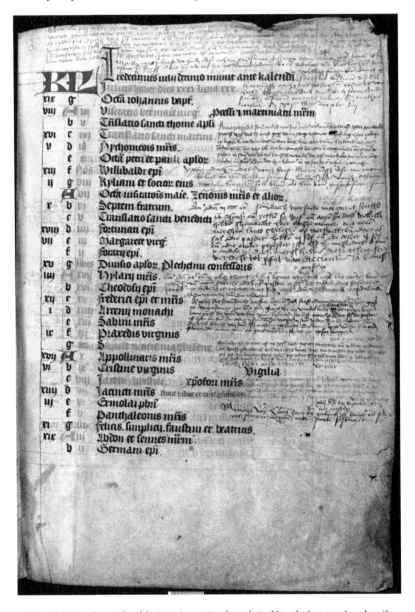

Fig. 53 Calendar with additions, in a missal made in Utrecht but used on Lopik. Utrecht, Universiteitsbibliotheek, Ms. 405, fol. 3r. Image © Utrecht, Universiteitsbibliotheek, CC BY 4.0.

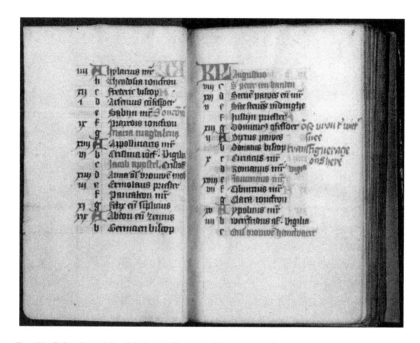

Fig. 54 Calendar with additions. Glasgow, University Library, Ms. Hunter, H186, fol. 7v-8r. Published by permission of University of Glasgow Library, Special Collections. Image © University of Glasgow Library, all rights reserved.

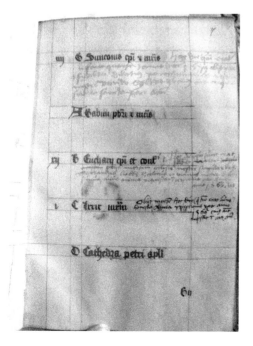

Fig. 55
Necrology, filled in by various scribes. Utrecht, Museum Catharijneconvent, BMH h 127, fol. 7r. Image © Museum Catharijneconvent, Utrecht, CC BY 4.0.

Users often added notes to the calendar in order to turn this part of the manuscript into an annual memory aid. For example, a missal made in the middle of the fifteenth century has extensive annotations written in the calendar (Utrecht, UB, Ms. 405; fig. 53). Although the manuscript contains pen-flourished initials in an Utrecht style, it was brought to the parish church in Lopik, where it was used for years, as names of the benefactors of that church have been added to the book.[24] The addition of the names also marks a change in function for the book. By adding cumulative death information to the calendar, the corporate owner of this missal has turned it into a necrology. An added benefit was putting the names of the benefactors on the altar, where the missal was used. In effect, the priest performed the mass and said a blessing over the very inscriptions that stood for the benefactors.

Book owners frequently amended the calendar by adding names and events. For example, the owner of a book of hours made c. 1440–1460 in North Holland (Haarlem?) has a calendar to which a late-fifteenth- or early-sixteenth-century owner has added two entries to the calendar (Glasgow, UL, Ms. Hunter 186; fig. 54). That owner may have been Trijntijn Pietersdochter, who inscribed her name and statement of ownership three times on an unnumbered folio before the calendar: "Dit boek hoert to Trijntpieters," and again "dit boeck hoort to Trijntijn Pieterdr. van Delft;" and again, "dit boek hoort tot Trijntijn Pieters dochter van sint Catherine (?) convent." It is as if she were practicing her new skill of writing as much as asserting her existence and ownership of the book. She may have been the person who, under the rubrics of August in calendar (fol. 8r), added a feast in red to Aug 5: "Onse vrou ter witter snee" (Our Lady of the White Snow), which refers to a miracle of the Virgin in the snow in the middle of summer.

Some calendars structurally demanded later additions, such as memorial books, which consist of a calendar ruled with enormous spaces after each saint. One such book, which has a note of ownership indicating that it belonged to the Church of St. Dionysius in Reissum, contains death notices of people from the parish, written in a variety of hands. In this case the calendar serves as a perpetual reminder to

---

24 Gisela Gerritsen-Geywitz, "Kaarsvet en Kerkwijding," in *Rapiarijs: Een Afscheidsbundel voor Hans van Dijk*, ed. S. Buitink, A. M. J. van Buuren, and I. Spijker (Utrecht: Instituut De Vooys voor Nederlandse taal- en letterkunde, 1987), pp. 45–47.

say masses for the souls of those individuals on the anniversaries of their deaths (Utrecht, Museum Catharijneconvent, BMH h 127; fig. 55). It therefore represents a neatened-up version of the kind of calendar in Utrecht, UB 405, and this time the necrological function designed in the planning stage.

Because calendars were the sites of memory, they were frequently amended. A book of hours made in London ca. 1405 contains a calendar manipulated by an early owner named Nicholas (Cambridge, UL, Ms. Ee.1.14).[25] He had several additions made to the calendar in red: St. Wynwaloy (3 March, fol. 4r); the translation of the relics of his name saint, Nicholas (on 9 May, fol. 5r); and the dedication of the church of St. Mary in Bury St. Edmunds (4 October, 7v). Such particular calendrical additions, as well as the style of some of the other emendations, confirm that they were executed at Bury St. Edmunds around 1440. While these feasts have been added in a neat *textualis* of a professional scribe, he may have himself added a note at 27 November (8r): "my moder departyd to god." When Nicholas brought the manuscript to Bury St. Edmunds, presumably fifteen years after the book was originally made, he therefore added texts to make the book appropriate for its new environment, with local saints, a nod to the new owner's name saint, and a reminder to pray for his mother's soul on the anniversary of her death. Later, I will detail more of the extensive changes he made to this book.

6. Changing a text to reflect updated circumstances

Owners could silently declare that the book, as received, was insufficient. Since their prayerbook was an object they spent considerable time with, and read over and over again, they knew the contents intimately. As my work on "Dirty Books" has shown, book owners picked and chose certain texts and ignored others.[26] Certain texts, such as the litany of the saints, were often locally determined, so that the contents would reflect regionally venerated saints. When prayerbooks changed hands, or moved physical location, their litanies could be out of kilter.

---

25 Binski, Zutshi, and Panayotova, *Western Illuminated Manuscripts: A Catalogue of the Collection in Cambridge University Library*, no. 191, pp. 180–81.

26 Rudy, "Dirty Books: Quantifying Patterns of Use in Medieval Manuscripts Using a Densitometer."

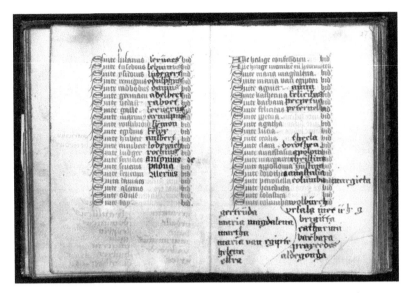

Fig. 56 Opening in a book of hours, showing a litany with added saints. Special Collections of the Universiteitsbibliotheek van Amsterdam, Ms. I G 54, fol. 26v-27r. Image © Universiteitsbibliotheek van Amsterdam, CC BY 4.0.

Fig. 57 Folio in a book of hours, with morning prayers added as quire filler. Bruges, Stadsbibliotheek, Ms. 334, fol. 33v-34r. Image © Bruges, Stadsbibliotheek, all rights reserved.

Many cared deeply about the litany and read it to the point of heavilywearing the folios on which it was written. They must have therefore paid close attention to the saints' names. Some were clearly not satisfied. That is the message that the owner of a book of hours has communicated by nearly doubling the number of saints in the litany by squeezing them onto the half-empty lines and the margins (AUB, Ms. I G 54; fig. 56). This scribe appears unsteady, possibly old or infirm. He or she has attempted to keep the saints in their established groups, by adding more confessors to fol. 26r, beginning with Franciscus and Dominicus and adding more female saints to the list of virgins on fol. 27r, beginning with St. Anne. Adding St. Anne dates the additions to the end of the fifteenth century or the beginning of the sixteenth, when this saint's cult flourished.[27] This manuscript returns again below, as the owner also added quires to it.

While Southern Netherlandish manuscripts for English export present extreme cases of "wasted parchment" that the English recipients then filled up with personalizing prayers, these are not the only books that received such modifications. Manuscripts made in the Northern Netherlands also had blank leaves and spaces as a result of production with the modular method. The owner of a book of hours made in South Holland (now in Bruges, SB 334) saw the blank space at the end of the quire and used it to add a prayer to say when waking up in the morning (fig. 57). This marks a shift, at the end of the fifteenth century, from prayer texts organized around the canonical hours, to those organized around clock time. Urban votaries in particular lived by clock towers heard throughout the city; this shift served their needs.

---

27 Many fifteenth-century missals have a feast of St. Anne added to them at the end of the fifteenth or beginning of the sixteenth century. Another such example is BKB, Ms. 15073, a missal probably copied in Utrecht in the second quarter of the fifteenth century, with illumination by the Masters of Otto van Moerdrecht. The added Mass of St. Anne has been attached to a bit of blank parchment at the end of the Temporal and before the beginning of the Sanctoral (fol. 151v). For St. Anne, see *Sint Anna in De Koninklijke Bibliotheek: ter Gelegenheid van de vijfenzestigste verjaardag van Anne S. Korteweg* (Amsterdam & The Hague: Buitenkant & Koninklijke Bibliotheek, 2007), with further references.

7. Adding text to make a book appropriate as a didactic tool

Added words can reveal a manuscript's former didactic context. As Michelle Brown has argued, the Holkham Bible Picture Book began as a series of quires bearing images only. Events to be portrayed seem to have been chosen by the artist based on degree of drama, action, and bloodshed. Only when the artist had constructed an entire non-verbal "cartoon"-like version of the Old and New Testaments did a scribe add text to the pages. This meant ruling the small areas—the bits of parchment in the interstices—in order to wedge in a text that would match the lively images. This manuscript is therefore unique in several regards, including its stratigraphy, beginning as it did with images. Nearly all other manuscripts begin with text, to which images are added. Adding the text to the interstices of the image-centered book changed the nature of the object and turned it into a didactic tool.

I believe that certain "picture Bibles," including Rylands, French 5, were made for, or rather adapted for children.[28] This manuscript presents the biblical stories as full-page miniatures so that they are extra large, sharp, clear, schematic, and for all these reasons, well suited to instruction. But even if the images are clear, they are unintelligible to those who do not know the stories. An instructor, or confessor, has used the blank areas at the upper and lower margins to write short descriptions. The *tituli* provide the young learner with the names of the characters and the place names. Most subjects, such as Noah's ark, seem to be those that might appeal to children (fig. 58).[29] "This is Noah's ark," the writer has added, though this is something that anyone who had already mastered the rudiments of the religion would know. Possibly to further entertain or engage a child, the teacher has also used pen and ink to add a bird.

---

28   Neither Robert Fawtier, *La Bible Historiée Toute Figurée de la John Rylands Library* (Paris: Pour les Trustees et gouverneurs de la John Rylands library, 1924), in his monograph on the manuscript, nor Hull, "Rylands Ms French 5: The Form and Function of a Medieval Bible Picture Book," pp. 3–24, in her analysis of the function of this manuscript, propose that it was tailored to the needs of teaching children.

29   Dove returning to Noah's ark with an olive branch, folio with large miniature and added inscription, in a picture bible made ca. 1250. Manchester, Rylands Library, Ms. French 5, fol. 14r. http://luna.manchester.ac.uk/luna/servlet/detail/Man4MedievalVC~4~4~989875~142711

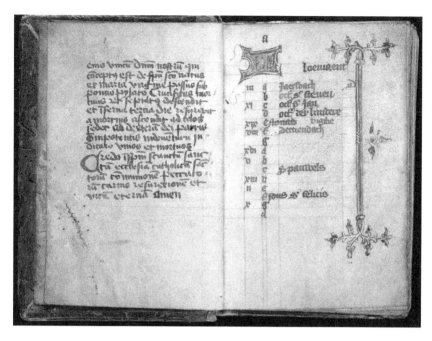

Fig. 59 Prayer added before calendar. The Hague, Koninklijke Bibliotheek, Ms. 135 K 17, fol. 1v-2r. Image © Koninklijke Bibliotheek—the National Library of The Netherlands, CC BY 4.0.

Fig. 60
Folio from the Hours of the Virgin, with a writing lesson in the margin. The Hague, Koninklijke Bibliotheek, Ms. 135 K 17, fol. 112r. Image © Koninklijke Bibliotheek—the National Library of The Netherlands, CC BY 4.0.

Fig. 61 Christ before Pilate, full-page miniature with a scribble added before prime. The Hague, Koninklijke Bibliotheek, Ms. 135 K 17, fol. 77v-78r. Image © Koninklijke Bibliotheek—the National Library of The Netherlands, CC BY 4.0.

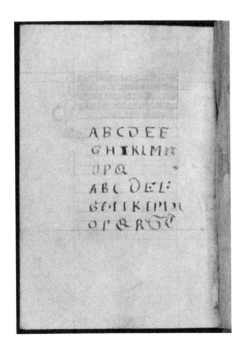

Fig. 62
Folio in a book of hours, with an alphabet added to the otherwise blank area at the end of a quire. Cambridge, University Library, Ms. Dd.15.25, fol. 66v. Image © Cambridge University Library, all rights reserved.

Like picture bibles, books of hours were sometimes adapted for children.[30] One fifteenth-century book of hours, copied in the diocese of Liège, had a modest program of decoration including single-leaf miniatures added at the major text openings (HKB, Ms. 135 K 17). The owner converted some of the blank space for didactic purposes. For example, the manuscript had a blank flyleaf. It was ruled as part of the calendar but originally left blank, possibly because it contains a large flaw in the parchment, which had been sewn. Its owner later used that folio to inscribe the *Pater Noster*, *Ave Maria* and *Credo*, the basic prayers of Christendom. These prayers, which were taught to children, turn the book of hours into a teaching tool (fig. 59). Someone has also assigned the letters *a-m* to the months, so that the letter *a* appears over *January*. Was the teacher trying to impart knowledge of the 12 months of the year along with the alphabet? Deeper in the same manuscript, the teacher has turned the book 90° and used the margin as a place to teach someone how to write. Specifically, the teacher has written a sentence in the margin, which the student has tried to copy (fig. 60). The writing lessons have gotten out of hand on fol. 77v, where the learner has scribbled in the lower margin (fig. 61). Like many fifteenth-century manuscripts, this has been preserved in a sixteenth-century binding, suggesting that it was heavily worn during its first 50 years of use, which warranted rebinding, but then was put on a shelf as an heirloom after the Reformation.

A South Netherlandish book of hours for Sarum use likewise had an owner who used it as a space for teaching (Cambridge, UL, Ms. Dd.15.25, fol. 66v-67r; fig. 62). He has copied out the alphabet in firm capitals on a bit of blank parchment in order to guide his students in practicing their forms. His student gets rather flustered mid-alphabet and abandons the project. No doubt the task was made even more difficult with the judging

---

30 On teaching medieval children, see: Nicholas Orme, *Medieval Children* (New Haven and London: Yale University Press, 2001); Roger S. Wieck, "Special Children's Books of Hours in the Walters Art Museum," in *Als Ich Can: Liber Amicorum in Memory of Professor Dr. Maurits Smeyers*, ed. Bert Cardon, et al., *Corpus of Illuminated Manuscripts = Corpus van Verluchte Handschriften* (Leuven: Peeters, 2002), pp. 1629–39; Kathryn M. Rudy and René Stuip, "'Martin Fights in July, and He Strikes St. Vaast with the Font.' A Cisiojanus and a Child's Alphabet in Oxford, Bodleian, Ms Rawlinson Liturgical E 40," *Cahiers de Recherches Médiévales et Humanistes / A Journal of Medieval and Humanist Studies* 19 (2010), pp. 493–521; Roger S. Wieck, "The Primer of Claude de France and the Education of the Renaissance Child," in *The Cambridge Illuminations: The Conference Papers*, ed. Stella Panayotova (London: Harvey Miller, 2007), pp. 167–72; Kathryn M. Rudy, "An Illustrated Mid-Fifteenth-Century Primer for a Flemish Girl: British Library, Harley Ms 3828," *Journal of the Warburg and Courtauld Institutes* 69 (2006), pp. 51–94.

Christ leaking through the opposite page. This same impatient child may be the person responsible for adding pen drawings throughout the book, including several funny heads and a camel.

8. Adding prayers

More than anything else, what owners most frequently added to prayerbooks was more prayers. Because it usually did not have a fixed text, a prayerbook could be ever-expanded to include any fashionable, or indulgenced texts, new prayers to reflect recently ratified feasts, or prayers belonging to growing cults. Like all additions, these reveal how the owner used the book, and often expose his desires and fears. They reveal steps owners have taken to keep their books relevant across time.

In a fifteenth-century copy of the "Contemplations of Walter Hilton," preceded by "A comfortable tretyes to strengthyn and confortyn creaturys in the feyth specially hem that arn symple and disposyd to fallyn in desperacyon," a fifteenth-century scribe has added a note to a blank folio at the beginning of the book. He writes: "Unto every man or woman that seyth this prayere folwyng: Benedictum sit dulce nomen Domini nostri Iesu Christi et gloriosissimae virginis Mariae matris ejus in eternum et ultra: Amen. Nos cum prole benedicat virgo Mariae: Amen. ar grauntyd iii yer of pardon tociens quociens of pope Clement the fourth atte the requeste of seynt Lowys kyng of Fraunce" (Cambridge, Parker Library, Ms. 268, fol. iiiv).[31] In other words, the scribe used the empty space at the beginning of the book to add a very short prayer for which the reader would earn an indulgence. Possessing prayers that would yield indulgences or promised to multiply existing indulgences motivated many book owners to amend their books, in margins, in blank areas, or on added sheets (as I will demonstrate below).

Not all added prayers promised indulgences; others promised bodily protection. An English book of hours introduced above (Cambridge, UL, Ms. Ee.1.14) had two blank leaves at the beginning of the quire containing the calendar. An owner or several owners have inscribed (or commissioned from a scrivener) various prayers for these precious pages. A professional scribe has been charged with the task of squeezing two longish prayers onto fol. 2r into the space (Cambridge, UL, Ms. Ee.1.14, fol. 1v-2r; fig. 63).

---

31   M. R. James, *A Descriptive Catalogue of the Manuscripts in the Library of Corpus Christi College, Cambridge*, 2 vols. (Cambridge: Cambridge University Press, 1912), cat. 268, pp. 24–25.

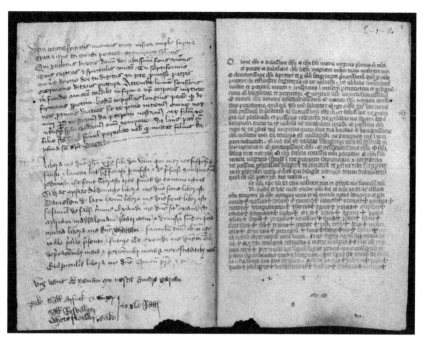

Fig. 63 Opening in a book of hours, with prayers added by several English scribes.
Cambridge, University Library, Ms. Ee.1.14, fol. 1v-2r. Image © Cambridge
University Library, all rights reserved.

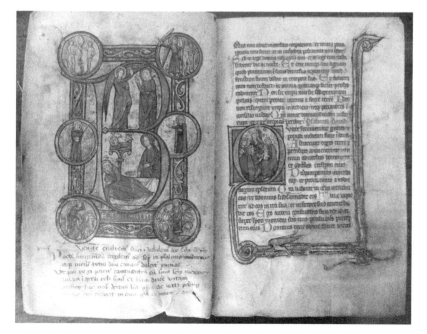

Fig. 64 First opening from a psalter-hours first made in 1275–1280 in Liège.
's-Heerenberg, The Netherlands, Collection Dr. J. H. van Heek, Huis Bergh
Foundation, Ms. 35. Image © The Huis Bergh Foundation, CC BY 4.0.

One is "O bone Ihesu..." and the other is the "72 names of Jesus," in which each name is interspersed with a red cross. Of these, the former was understood to be amuletic, to protect the bearer from sudden death; the latter harks back to incantations to the "72 circumlocutions of Yahweh," which were originally spoken because the name of God was too powerful to be uttered. The circumlocutions, and eventually the "72 names of Jesus," were thought to be so powerful that they would ward off evil.[32] To fit these in, the scribe has ruled this page (and only this page) with very narrow lines. Marks of wear on the page, including a dark thumbprint at the bottom margin, indicate that these were among the owner's favorite prayers.[33] Once he paid someone to add them, he justified his choice by reading it intensely.

In other cases it is not clear exactly why an owner desired a particular prayer, but he or she has added it in response to a particular image. Such is the case with a psalter-hours produced in 1275–1280 in Liège (fig. 64; 's-Heerenberg, HB, Ms. 35, inv. no. 225).[34] It opens with the psalter. A full-page initial *B*, for "Beatus vir," serves as a frontispiece. The Annunciation and Nativity are depicted in the two large loops of the *B*, and vignettes from the Old Testament in the corner roundels. In other words, it is organized around prefigurations at the edges, and redemption at the center. An early owner, as if responding to the Annunciation and Nativity,

---

32 For amuletic prayers and manuscripts, see Willy Louis Braekman, "Enkele zegeningen en krachtige gebeden in een Vlaams devotieboek uit de vijftiende eeuw," *Volkskunde* LXXIX (1978), pp. 285–307; Braekman, *Middeleeuwse Witte en Zwarte Magie in het Nederlands Taalgebied: Gecommentarieerd Compendium van Incantamenta tot Einde 16de Eeuw* (Gent: Koniklijke Academie voor Nederlandse Taal- en Letterkunde, 1997); Kathryn Rudy, "Kissing Images, Unfurling Rolls, Measuring Wounds, Sewing Badges and Carrying Talismans: Considering Some Harley Manuscripts through the Physical Rituals They Reveal," *eBLJ (The Electronic British Library Journal)* special volume: Proceedings from the Harley Conference, British Library, 29–30 June 2009 (2011); Don C. Skemer, *Binding Words: Textual Amulets in the Middle Ages*, Magic in History (University Park: Pennsylvania State University Press, 2006); Jean Vezin, "Les Livres Utilisés comme Amulettes et comme Reliques," in *Das Buch als Magisches und als Repräsentationsobjekt*, ed. Peter Ganz, *Wolfenbütteler Mittelalter-Studien* (Wiesbaden: Harrassowitz, 1992), pp. 101–15.

33 Rudy, "Dirty Books: Quantifying Patterns of Use in Medieval Manuscripts Using a Densitometer."

34 Korteweg, *Catalogue of Medieval Manuscripts and Incunabula at Huis Bergh Castle in 's-Heerenberg*, cat. 62, pp. 112–13; Judith Oliver, *Gothic Manuscript Illumination in the Diocese of Liège (c. 1250-C. 1330)*, vol. 2–3, Corpus van Verluchte Handschriften uit de Nederlanden = Corpus of Illuminated Manuscripts from the Low Countries (Leuven: Peeters, 1988), I, pp. 27, 54–55, 159–160; II, pp. 293–94, no. 41.

has inscribed a prayer in the lower margin, writing "Venite exultemus domino…," Psalm 95, a song of triumph that Christians were supposed to read in the mornings. Perhaps the book's user inscribed this at the front of the manuscript so that it would be handy first thing.

A book that is most altered is likely to be most heavily used. While people who have only one book are inclined to both use it and alter it, it is surely also the case that the act of altering the book kept it up to date, and therefore more likely to be relevant for longer. By the same token, the obverse is also true: the Hours of Catherine of Cleves, for example, was not altered (until an unscrupulous dealer broke it up much later), and likewise has no signs of use at all.[35] Perhaps she considered commissioning a lavish book of hours a devotional act in itself, one that did not necessitate actually reading it. In some ways I am really asking: How physical was the owner's relationship with the book? To what degree was it part of the person's daily habit? Did the book's owner think of it as an interactive object that would respond to his needs? In the case of this example, the answers are largely negative. But that is far from the norm.

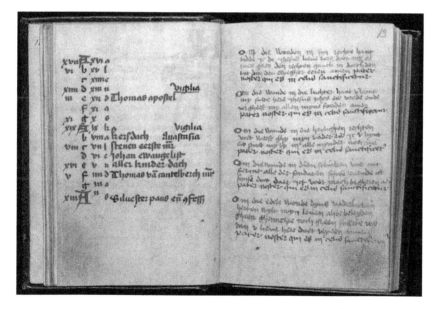

Fig. 65 The Colnish Pater Noster added after the calendar. The Hague, Koninklijke Bibliotheek, Ms. 133 D 10, fol. 12v-13r. Image © Koninklijke Bibliotheek—the National Library of The Netherlands, CC BY 4.0.

35 For images, see http://www.themorgan.org/collection/Hours-of-Catherine-of-Cleves

Fig. 66 Trinity, full-page miniature in a book of hours, with an added inscription.
The Hague, Koninklijke Bibliotheek, Ms. 133 D 10, fol. 147v-148r. Image
© Koninklijke Bibliotheek—the National Library of The Netherlands, CC BY 4.0.

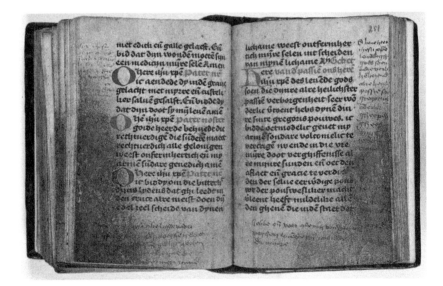

Fig. 67 *Adoro te* (5-verse version) with more verses added in the margin. The Hague,
Koninklijke Bibliotheek, Ms. 75 G 2, fol. 250v-251r. Image © Koninklijke
Bibliotheek—the National Library of The Netherlands, CC BY 4.0.

An added text is the one the reader desired the most, and often shows the most signs of wear. For example, HKB, Ms. 133 D 10, a book of hours, has a text added to the blank leaf after the calendar (fol. 15v-16r, fig. 65). The added prayer is the Colnish Pater Noster, a highly physical prayer directed toward (an image of) Christ Crucified. Some copies of the prayer instruct the votary to read particular segments into the wounds of Christ. Votaries may have performed this prayer while holding an image, such as a small sculpture of the body of Christ, and uttering the spoken text into the represented hands and feet. This text was rarely provided with a miniature, so one should imagine the supplicant performing this prayer with an image that is external to the book. Dirty fingerprints at the bottom of the page indicate that the owner spent considerable time with this text.[36] In the same manuscript, the fingerprints again reveal that she or he has paid particular attention to the image of and prayer to the Trinity (fig. 66). He or she has also written what appears to be a motto under the image, as if asserting a presence there. Again, he or she pays the greatest attention to these self-augmented parts of the book. The augmentation both constructs and reflects the reader's relationship to the text and to the book.

Likewise, the owner of a heavily worn prayerbook showed particular interest in the folios that were augmented (HKB, Ms. 75 G 2, fig. 67). This manuscript has a calendar for the bishopric of Liège that includes an entry for the dedication of the Church of Tongeren (7 May) in red, suggesting that the manuscript came from a convent in or near that city. Female pronoun endings indicate that the owner was probably a woman. She may have come from an Augustinian convent, as Augustine appears first among the confessors in the litany, while Mary Magdalene is first among the Virgins. One possibility is that she belonged to the Canonesses Regular of St. Catharine (Sinte-Katharijnenberg/Magdalenezusters) in Tienen, which is very close to Tongeren. She has augmented her book of hours with some unusual prayers, including a prayer to the Virgin's body parts, the Hours of St. Catherine, and the Hundred Articles of the Passion, which circulated almost exclusively in

---

36   Densitometer data reveal that this was one of the most handled texts in the book (HKB, Ms. 133 D 10), with a sharp spike at fol. 16. For the empirical results, see Rudy, "Dirty Books: Quantifying Patterns of Use in Medieval Manuscripts Using a Densitometer."

monastic houses. The manuscript also has a number of added images, which I have discussed elsewhere.[37] It also has a number of annotations in the margin, particularly around the *Adoro te*.

This prayer, the *Adoro te*, was one of the most heavily indulgenced texts of the late Middle Ages. It came in several versions, including a shorter version with just five verses, each one beginning with the letter *O*. Toward the end of the fifteenth century, versions with 7, 9, 10, or even 11 verses circulated. These longer versions were copied with rubrics promising ever-greater indulgences. Her original book had the five-verse version of the Verses of St. Gregory, carrying an indulgence for 20,000 years, but she augmented this with what appear to be four additional verses in the margins. In most instances, the longer versions carried a much greater spiritual reward than the 5-verse version. The additions, however, are impossible to read, as she handled this text so voraciously that she rubbed the words away through use. Indeed, she employed her manuscript so heavily that she left her dark, shiny black fingerprints on nearly every folio. But by the time the owner had rubbed the words away, she had probably memorized them. In the process of using the text, she obliterated it from the page and impressed it onto her mind.

Many prayers were added to the interstices of prayerbooks during the last decades of the fifteenth century and the first decades of the sixteenth. A large number of these supply indulgences. For example, a book of hours with spectacular and unusual illuminations associated with Spierinck has been made modularly, with the full-page miniatures on separate singletons (HKB, Ms. 133 H 30; fig. 68).[38] Filling more than one quire, the Hours of the Virgin finishes on fol. 55r in the middle of the page (fig. 69). There were several blank pages left in the quire, however, and the scribe has filled two of them by inscribing the indulgenced prayer, *Adoro te*, in its Dutch translation (fig. 70).

---

37 Ibid.

38 For this artist see Klaas van der Hoek, "The North Holland Illuminator Spierinck: Some Attributions Reconsidered," in *Masters and Miniatures: Proceedings of the Congress on Medieval Manuscript Illumination in the Northern Netherlands (Utrecht, 10–13 December 1989)*, edited by K. van der Horst and Johann-Christian Klamt, pp. 275–80 (Doornspijk: Davaco, 1991). Opening of the Hours of the Virgin, with a full-page miniature depicting the Annunciation. The Hague, Koninklijke Bibliotheek, Ms. 133 H 30, fol. 16v-17r. http://manuscripts.kb.nl/zoom/BYVANCKB%3Amimi_1 33h30%3A016v_017r

Fig. 69 End of the Hours of the Virgin, with blank parchment at the end of the
quire. The Hague, Koninklijke Bibliotheek, Ms. 133 H 30, fol. 54v-55r. Image
© Koninklijke Bibliotheek—the National Library of The Netherlands, CC BY 4.0.

This prayer carries an enormous indulgence of "xx" or "xc" *dusent iaer*, that is, 20,000 or possibly 90,000 years (the Roman numeral is unclear). The scribe has left the next page—that before the following module—blank (fig. 71). Thus, even though the Hours of the Virgin does not relate directly to the *Adoro te*, the scribe used the invitation of the blank parchment to add it. While the text was added as an afterthought, and is discontinuous with the text that precedes it, it appears to have been written by the same scribe. Thus, additions can occur at any time: immediately after the core text is written, or years later. It appears, also, that two layers of border decoration were executed in this book. They compete on the page, as on fol. 55v (above). One painter ornamented the page with bands of decoration above and below the text. But it seems that the owner was not satisfied with this degree of decoration, and ordered more highly-gilded and painted decoration on the side margin. Added decoration of this sort is the next category of change to the book.

Fig. 70 *Adoro te*, in its Dutch translation, used as quire filler. The Hague, Koninklijke Bibliotheek, Ms. 133 H 30, fol. 55v-56r. Image © Koninklijke Bibliotheek—the National Library of The Netherlands, CC BY 4.0.

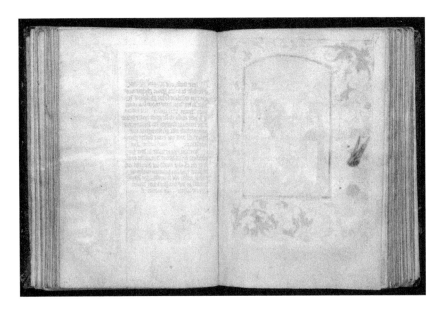

Fig. 71 A blank opening at the transition between text and image. The Hague, Koninklijke Bibliotheek, Ms. 133 H 30, fol. 56v-57r. Image © Koninklijke Bibliotheek—the National Library of The Netherlands, CC BY 4.0.

Fig. 72
Prayer to St. Francis and his
stigmata added to the back of
the Crucifixion miniature in
the Gouda Missal. The Hague,
Koninklijke Bibliotheek, Ms. 135 H
45, fol. 101r. Image © Koninklijke
Bibliotheek—the National Library
of The Netherlands, CC BY 4.0.

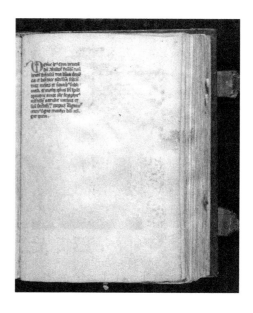

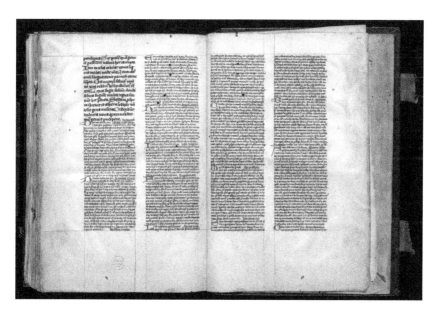

Fig. 73 Feasts added to the end of the Gouda Missal, including one (the first one)
dedicated to the Immaculate Conception of the Virgin. The Hague, Koninklijke
Bibliotheek, Ms. 135 H 45, fol. 215v-216r. Image © Koninklijke Bibliotheek—the
National Library of The Netherlands, CC BY 4.0.

Liturgical books could also receive additional prayers. For example, the Gouda Missal (HKB, Ms. 135 H 45) was made in several campaigns of work beginning in 1450–55.[39] Franciscan men in Gouda used and possibly commissioned the manuscript, which contains, for example, a Franciscan calendar, with feasts in red that include St. Bernardinus (May 20); the Translation of St. Francis (May 25); St. Anthony abbot (June 13); St. Clare (Aug. 12); and St. Francis (Oct. 4). A note of ownership appears on the inside front cover: "Pro conventu fratrum minorum in gouda diocesis traiectensis," which indicates that the book belonged to the house of Franciscan minderbrothers in Gouda. They owned the book, used it hard, and adjusted it in several ways. Among their additions is a prayer on fol. 101r, which is the otherwise blank back of the full-page Crucifixion miniature (fig. 72). This prayer praises St. Francis for receiving the stigmata, the "sign of the crucified body of our lord," imprinted into his own body in recognition of his merits and virtues. Although the fifteenth-century minderbrother could have inscribed this prayer anywhere in the codex, he chose to do so on the membrane that shares and image of Christ crucified. Praise for his patron is as close their model as possible, just a few microns of parchment away. St. Francis is literally the flip side of Jesus: they are of the same flesh.

At the very end of the manuscript some blank, ruled parchment remained that proved inviting to the Franciscan scribes (fig. 73). Into this space a later (but still fifteenth-century) scribe has used the opportunity to squeeze in texts for several feasts. To do this, he has had to write in script less than half the height of the original text, and to abbreviate it extensively. The first added feast is dedicated to the Immaculate Conception of the Virgin, a controversial feast that was championed by the Franciscans. As published in bulls of 1476 and 1477, Pope Sixtus IV extended an indulgence to those who celebrated this Office. This feast

---

39   Ina Kok, "Een Houtsnede in een Handschrift," in *Manuscripten en Miniaturen: Studies aangeboden aan Anne S. Korteweg bij haar afscheid van de Koninklijke Bibliotheek*, ed. J. A. A. M. Biemans, et al., *Bijdragen tot de Geschiedenis van de Nederlandse Boekhandel* (Zutphen: Walburg Pers, 2007), pp. 231–42, analyzes the woodcut prints made directly on the ruled parchment; Kathryn Rudy, "The Birgittines of the Netherlands: Experimental Colourists," in *Printing Colour 1400–1700: Histories, Techniques, Functions and Reception*, ed. Elizabeth Upper and Ad Stijnman (Leiden: Brill, 2014), pp. 82–90, discusses the technological shift from manuscript to print with respect to HKB, Ms. 135 H 45.

was probably inscribed at the end of the Gouda missal after 1476, and is a further indication that the male Franciscans in Gouda used the book and were responsible for the augmentations as they updated an older missal and retained its relevancy. They also added some extra texts for the feasts for the Nativity of Christ and the Epiphany to augment the existing text; to the feasts of St. Agnes and to St. Ursula with her Eleven Thousand Virgins, and to the dedication of a church. As the church and its feasts expanded, so did this book. (It is a manuscript to which I will return below, as it also has some other, more complex augmentations.)

C. Augmenting the existing decoration

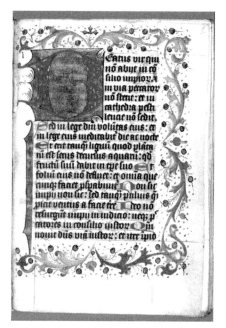

Fig. 74
Incipit of the psalter with a border painted in an eastern Netherlandish style. Special Collections of the Universiteitsbibliotheek van Amsterdam, Ms. V H 26, fol. 1r. Image © Universiteitsbibliotheek van Amsterdam, CC BY 4.0.

Fig. 75
Folio with a major psalm division, with an initial *S* decorated in two campaigns of work. Special Collections of the Universiteitsbibliotheek van Amsterdam, Ms. V H 26, fol. 64r. Image © Universiteitsbibliotheek van Amsterdam, CC BY 4.0.

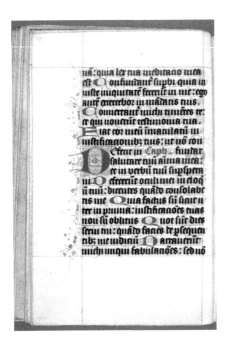

Fig. 76
Division within psalm 119, with
penwork decoration added in
North Holland. Special Collections
of the Universiteitsbibliotheek van
Amsterdam, Ms. V H 26, fol. 124v.
Image © Universiteitsbibliotheek van
Amsterdam, CC BY 4.0.

AUB, Ms. V H 26 is a psalter made in the eastern part of the Northern Netherlands in the middle of the fifteenth century. When the manuscript was written, it was embellished with both pen flourishes and some painted decoration, so that the first folio has a gilt and painted border in an eastern Netherlandish style (fig. 74), and some Psalms received a six-line decorated initial with pen-flourishes in an eastern style, such as the one on fol. 64r (fig. 75). At the end of the century, someone apparently brought the manuscript to North Holland and had decoration added to it, so that several folios, including 64r, also have painted decoration in a North Holland style applied to the other margins. This folio looks highly unusual because the added painted decoration does not emanate from the initial, but fills the other three borders.

By adding painted flourishes the new decorator has shifted the hierarchy of decoration across the entire manuscript. According to the original plan, only the first folio received painted decoration, and the psalms at the major divisions received large initials with pen flourishes. In order to rationalize the new regime, the manuscript has apparently undergone a second round of decorative augmentations. Namely, the major Psalm divisions were heightened to receive colorful painted decoration, and the divisions within the psalms also received decoration, so that, for example, the modest initial marking a chapter division within psalm 119 was given pen flourishing in one margin in a North Holland style (fig. 76) (*caph defecit in salutare tuum*). In other words, these initials were also elevated as the hierarchy shifted when the manuscript was redecorated ca. 1500 in North Holland.

A similar story describes what happened with a psalter and lay breviary now in Oxford's Bodleian Library (Ms. Broxb. 89.10; fig. 77).[40] Oddly, the manuscript was copied on paper and only the first two folios are on parchment. It was made in North Holland and has penwork decoration typical of that region, extending from the initials. For example, fol. 193r, which is the incipit for the Hours of Easter, has an eight-line *L* with North Holland penwork emanating from it. This same kind of penwork appears around fol. 169r, with the Hours of Christmas (fig. 78).[41] Multiple bright colors including purple and green, applied with broken symmetry, characterize penwork from this region. This type of original penwork fills only the left margins of these pages.

These two folios also reveal another, competing kind of decoration, which an artist has applied to those borders not already filled by penwork decoration. On fol. 193r, the painted borders are arranged around a gold and painted baguette, with "bunches of twigs" painted designs, another decorative form typical of North Holland. On fol. 169r, the painted decoration is not anchored to a baguette. On neither folio is the painted decoration anchored to the initial. This is a clue that the decoration was not original, for in Netherlandish manuscripts border decoration always emanates from the initial. But this added decoration cannot approach the initial, because that space was already filled by penwork (although I will show examples below in which the artist applying the supplementary decoration simply paints over the top of the existing penwork).

I suspect that what happened to this manuscript is that the entire manuscript was copied on paper for a person in a monastery (for monastics alone form the audience for breviaries). It was written and decorated with penwork in Haarlem. It contains a calendar for the

---

40 Hours of Easter, with decoration made in two campaigns of work: penwork from North Holland, and decoration supplemented with painted leaves. Oxford, Bodleian Library, Ms. Broxb. 89.10, fol. 193r. http://bodley30.bodley.ox.ac.uk:8180/luna/servlet/view/search/what/MS. Broxb. 89.10?q=broxb. 89.10

41 Hours of Christmas, with two campaigns of decoration: penwork from North Holland and decoration supplemented with painted leaves. Oxford, Bodleian Library, Ms. Broxb. 89.10, fol. 169r. http://bodley30.bodley.ox.ac.uk:8180/luna/servlet/view/search/what/MS. Broxb. 89.10?q=broxb. 89.10

bishopric of Utrecht but with St. Adalbert (June 25), the patron saint of Haarlem. (Haarlem was situated within the bishopric of Utrecht.) Furthermore, the manuscript was made in a Franciscan milieu, for St. Francis is not only mentioned first among the confessors in the litany, but he is called "o gloriose vader Franciscus." Likewise, St. Margaret (called "o gloriose moeder sancta Margrieta") is mentioned first among the Virgins. The book may therefore have been made for (and by) the Tertiaries of the convent of St. Margaret in Haarlem.

Once the manuscript was completely copied on paper and decorated with Haarlem penwork, however, why then were the two lonely parchment folios added to the beginning? I suspect that this decision indicates yet another process of augmentation, in which the scribe, shortly after the manuscript was finished, was instructed to add a full-page miniature of David with his harp (fig. 79).[42] It is not clear whether the owner already had this at hand, or whether she commissioned the image just for this book. The former seems more likely, since the folio is not quite the right size for the book, and the binder needed to wrestle this piece of parchment into the binding. Consequently, the justification is off, and the image slips partly into the gutter. In order to add this leaf on parchment, the scribe may have removed the first paper folio of the psalter and then recopied it on parchment. The paper incipit folio may have been replaced with a parchment one because parchment takes paint better than paper does. A colorful parchment incipit would give the opening visual coherence, with the full-page miniature on the facing page. Perhaps it was when the full-page miniature was added to the beginning of the book (and this is all speculative) that the painter also raised the level of the hierarchy of decoration across the manuscript, so that folios with a decorated initial would take four sides of decoration instead of just one. In short, the addition of the David miniature may have provided the impetus for the scribe and painter to make adjustments throughout the book, raising its overall level of sumptuousness, before bringing it to the binder. The manuscript is still in its late fifteenth-century binding, panel-stamped with an image of the blessing Christ. This suggests that the tampering occurred in the fifteenth century, not later.

---

42   David with his harp, facing the incipit of the psalter, with painted decoration typical of Haarlem. Oxford, Bodleian Library, Ms. Broxb. 89.10, fol. 17v-18r. http:// bodley30.bodley.ox.ac.uk:8180/luna/servlet/view/search/what/MS. Broxb. 89.10?q= broxb. 89.10

Late medieval book owners continuously exploited the possibilities for expanding and decorating their books. In a book of hours with elaborate, column-wide initials, a book owner added more decoration to the text pages when full-page miniatures were introduced (HKB, Ms. 131 G 3; fig. 80).[43] The manuscript could have been considered complete with just the initials, but the owner has added full-page miniatures to preface them. This book of hours with illuminations attributed to the Bible Masters of the First Generation, who are called the Gethsemane Master and Master Azor. These masters were apparently active in Utrecht around 1430. The manuscript contains 208 folios and is written in *littera textualis* in Middle Dutch, with an Utrecht calendar, and several full-page miniatures. As the online catalogue description points out, "all border decoration in Utrecht style (elongated green leaves, tri-petals)."[44] However, an inspection of the major text openings reveals that the story is more complex than the catalogue description would make it seem.

For one thing, there is considerable variation of style across these openings, suggesting that the various texts were actually made by different teams, and brought together for assembly. Furthermore, different hands, which are rather rough and sloppy, have inscribed the various texts. This evidence suggests that different scribes in fact wrote the modules. These scribes, however, had not been trained to write in a disciplined, corporate style, as the sisters in the convents of St. Ursula and St. Agnes had been. I suspect therefore that this manuscript was either copied in a convent with less regimented training, or was copied by professionals working together in a loose relationship.

Secondly, the catalogue description does not mention the book's complicated stratigraphy. When the book's owner added full-page miniatures to the openings, this necessitated additional changes to the book, as owners sought to preserve the visual continuity across the entire opening. Borders of green leaves and gold balls came with the miniatures. When the owner added the paintings, he or she had the facing text pages augmented with that same kind of decoration, which frames the frame, so that there is a sense of visual continuity across the full opening. This situation I will discuss below, in a chapter dedicated to changes that required rebinding. Here, however, I want to point out

---

43 Annunciation, and incipit of the Hours of the Virgin. The Hague, Koninklijke Bibliotheek, Ms. 131 G 3, fol. 13v-14r. http://manuscripts.kb.nl/zoom/BYVANCKB %3Amimi_131g3%3A013v_014r

44 http://manuscripts.kb.nl/show/manuscript/131+G+3, consulted 25 April 2016.

that the decorator has added a layer of ornamentation around both the miniatures and the facing text pages in order to unify them visually. When the Annunciation was added, the decorator added analogous embellishments ("elongated green leaves, tri-petals") to the outer border of the facing text page, even though this page already had full and complete border decoration executed in gold and body color. The same scenario occurred at the opening for the Hours of the Eternal Wisdom (HKB, Ms. 131 G 3; fig. 81).[45] When the owner added the full-page miniature, he or she also had the text folio paged with the typical Utrecht decoration so that it would match. At the opening for the Hours of the Holy Cross, the person who added the full-page miniature did not have enough space around the facing text folio to add the extra layer of decoration, so this fol. 118r was left un-augmented (fig. 82).[46] However, there was plenty of room around the incipit page of the final opening with full-page miniature, so this page did receive the green leaves. A noticeably different hand copied the final major text in the manuscript, prayers for the sacrament, suggesting that the production was a group effort with the modular method by scribes who had mastered the corporate style with varying degrees of success (fig. 83).[47] This text did not originally receive a historiated initial, suggesting that the planner (or scribes) were not anticipating a full-page illumination to face this text, which would demand (according to the hierarchy of decoration established earlier in the book) that full-page illuminations accompany historiated initials. When the full-page miniature was added, the facing folio had to be fully embellished. In this way, decoration not only ornaments the word of God, but it helps to smooth over the seams of a production assembled from disparate components.

An owner who had a physical relationship with his book was likely to update it by making physical emendations to it, and was also likely to handle it often, as part of a daily habit. HKB, Ms. 131 G 3 was handled repeatedly. That this book was heavily used is evidenced by the grime

---

45 Christ as Salvator Mundi, and the incipit of the Hours of Eternal Wisdom. The Hague, Koninklijke Bibliotheek, Ms. 131 G 3, fol. 79v-80r. http://manuscripts.kb.nl/zoom/BYVANCKB%3Amimi_131g3%3A079v_080r

46 Christ carrying the cross, and the incipit of the Hours of the Holy Cross. The Hague, Koninklijke Bibliotheek, Ms. 131 G 3, fol. 117v-118r. http://manuscripts.kb.nl/zoom/BYVANCKB%3Amimi_131g3%3A117v_118r

47 Christ sitting on the cold stone, and the incipit of prayers to be said for the sacrament. The Hague, Koninklijke Bibliotheek, Ms. 131 G 3, fol. 157v-158r. http://manuscripts.kb.nl/zoom/BYVANCKB%3Amimi_131g3%3A157v_158r

ground on the margins and the poor state of some of the miniatures. Its owner(s) used the book so heavily that the binding wore out, and it had to be replaced with its current blind stamped brown leather in the sixteenth century. It is possible that this represents not the book's second binding, but its third.

D. Drawing or painting images directly onto bound parchment

Book owners occasionally commissioned professional painters to add imagery to books that were already complete. Such a set of added paintings appears in the margins of a typological Life of Christ in Middle Dutch (Leiden, UB, Ms. Ltk 258). It was copied by a single hand on paper in North Holland, probably in Haarlem, around 1470.[48] This book may have been made by or for the tertiaries of St. Margaret in Haarlem. A few small illuminations—which depict the incarnation of Christ and the Three Magi—have been added to the margins of its 207 folios.

Fig. 84
Folio from a typological Life of Christ in Middle Dutch, with an added marginal painting representing the Annunciation. Leiden, Universiteitsbibliotheek, Ms. Ltk 258, fol. 8v. Image © Leiden, Universiteitsbibliotheek, CC BY 4.0.

---

48   J. A. A. M. Biemans, *Middelnederlandse Bijbelhandschriften: Verzameling van Middelnederlandse Bijbeltekstencatalogus*, Verzameling van Middelnederlandse Bijbelteksten (Leiden: Brill, 1984), no. 168; and Gumbert, *Manuscrits Datés Conservés dans les Pays-Bas, T. 2 (Cmd-Nl 2)*, no. 477 (where he suggests that the copyist of Ltk 258 may be identical with that of HKB, Ms, 78 J 63).

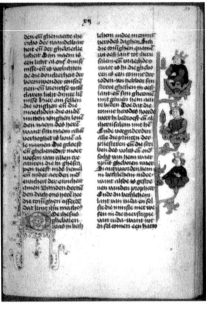

Fig. 85
Folio from a typological Life of Christ in
Middle Dutch, with an added marginal
painting representing the Nativity.
Leiden, Universiteitsbibliotheek, Ms.
Ltk 258, fol. 14r. Image © Leiden,
Universiteitsbibliotheek, CC BY 4.0.

Fig. 86
Folio from a typological Life of Christ
in Middle Dutch, with an added
marginal painting representing the
Magi. Leiden, Universiteitsbibliotheek,
Ms. Ltk 258, fol. 20r. Image © Leiden,
Universiteitsbibliotheek, CC BY 4.0.

Although the scribe did not plan these illuminations, a painter
(possibly an amateur) has added them to the margins, after the fact.
The painting representing the Annunciation, for example, does not
quite fit into the space of the margin. Likely tracing from a model of
a fixed size, the artist slid the model to this position, and placed it so
that the Virgin's head sticks up through the columns of text (fig. 84).

Further along in the book, the artist has painted another vignette in
the margins, this time turning the bottom margin into Bethlehem and
the side margin into the hills where the shepherds pasture their sheep

(fig. 85).[49] Again, the artist may have been tracing a model, and even adjusted the position of the infant Jesus upward. If the infant were on the same horizontal as the Virgin's knees, his mandorla-shaped form would have created trapped white space, which is anathema to designers then and now. By moving the baby up to the level of her hands, he fills what would have been white space (but he disconcertingly appears to be levitating).

Likewise, the artist has added an image of the Three Magi, each bearing his gift, to the relevant text in Ltk 258 (fig. 86).[50] He or she has tried to orient them to the text column, but they defy a major principle in manuscript design: that all decoration should emanate from an initial. Floating in space, the Magi are untethered to the letter. These features underscore the *ad hoc* nature of the images, which were not planned from the start. It is extremely odd visually to have loose images floating in marginal space and not anchored within frames. Their presence suggests that the owner was desperate to visualize them on the page, to make the incarnation and the recognition of Christ's divinity visual features of the book, rather than just mental illusions built by text in the mind.

Owners sometimes made amateur drawings on the blank parchment. As I have described above, manuscripts made in the Southern Netherlands for export to the British Isles were constructed with a form of the modular method that resulted in large blank areas of parchment. One such manuscript, now in Cambridge, had an owner who could not resist the opportunity to add his own tronies to the page (Cambridge, UL, Ms. Dd.15.25; fig. 87). They seem to interact with the professional painting on the other side of the membrane, which is leaking through. By adding his gruesome faces to the back of the image, he can comment on the scene without defacing it.

---

49 Folio from a typological Life of Christ in Middle Dutch, with an added marginal painting representing the Nativity. Leiden, Universiteitsbibliotheek, Ms. Ltk 258, fol. 14r. https://socrates.leidenuniv.nl/ (and search for "Ltk 258").

50 Folio from a typological Life of Christ in Middle Dutch, with an added marginal painting representing the Magi. Leiden, Universiteitsbibliotheek, Ms. Ltk 258, fol. 20r. https://socrates.leidenuniv.nl/ (and search for "Ltk 258").

In another book of hours, a nun floats in the space of a sparsely populated calendar; evidently this much blank parchment was too much to bear (HKB, Ms. 76 G 22; fig. 88).[51] Nun and crucifix are made in different styles, as if to suggest that the crucifix is a picture of a picture. With the exception of pointing fingers that draw attention to passages of text, added drawings rarely appear in finished manuscripts. I suspect that this is because a bound manuscript curves in its binding rather than lying flat, and thus creates a quite difficult object to draw on. Whoever

---

51 Nun praying before a crucifix, pen drawing with prayer, added to a calendar. The Hague, Koninklijke Bibliotheek, Ms. 76 G 22, fol. 3r. http://manuscripts.kb.nl/zoom/BYVANCKB%3Amimi_76g22%3A003r

added this drawing, possibly an Augustinian nun herself, did so on a blank area of parchment near the beginning of the book. She drew on the right side, and I suspect that she was right-handed and was able to hold the book down flat with her left hand while she drew.

In fact there are relatively few examples in which a painter in the fourteenth or fifteenth century added imagery to the blank areas of an already-bound book. In this period, a new cultural habit circulated, namely, painting images on loose leaves and inserting them into the book after they had dried. This was an even more efficient way to fill empty space.

E. Adding physical material superficially

So far the additions I have discussed have not added mass to the book but have taken advantage of empty spaces within the book as received. Owners could also add certain kinds of physical material to the bound book without needing to rebind it. Such additions are superficial, on the surface. Below I revisit physical additions but consider those that did require rebinding and are not on the surface, being instead worked into the structure of the book and integrated into its binding. The motivation for adding superficial physical material was largely to incorporate badges, sheets of paper, parchment or cloth that were ready-made and could thereby extend the book's function as a maker of meaning and a holder of memory.

1. Attaching parchment sheets to blank areas of the book

It is difficult to paint or draw on bound sheets, because one has to negotiate the gutter, the curvature of the book block, the tendency of the folios to buckle, and the soft cushion that a stack of parchment leaves makes. Book owners could more easily add drawings and paintings to their books by pasting or sewing in images made separately and executed on a flat, hard surface. Votaries often attached images to blank areas of their books. This was a way of preserving small sheets that were otherwise loose and vulnerable. Loose images must have been in circulation throughout the fifteenth century, and a fraction of them landed in manuscripts that became storage chests for small flat things. Small images were given as gifts, or formed objects of reciprocal gifting with or between convents. Images exchanged in such a way must have triggered specific memories for their owner, who cared enough about their preservation to secure them into a treasured manuscript that would certainly outlive the owner.

That may have been the motive behind the inclusion of a small drawing depicting the Virgin *in sole* pasted into a book of hours made in Ghent, probably in the second quarter of the fifteenth century (Ghent, UB, Ms. 2750; fig. 89). This simple pen drawing may have been traced from a model and given away as a spiritually valuable gift. It is difficult to date with precision, but may have been made around 1470, 20 to 50 years after the manuscript was made. Its recipient was apparently the owner—possibly the second or third owner—of the book, which was probably made in Ghent. Like other scrapbookers, this book owner may have been making a mark in the book and changing its function. Not having the appropriate prayer in the manuscript, the owner of the book of hours from Ghent therefore stuck it in where it would fit.

Fig. 89 Opening in the Van der Vlaest Hours from Ghent, at the end of terce and the beginning of sext, with a drawing on parchment sewn onto a blank area. Ghent, Universiteitsbibliotheek, Ms. 2750, fol. 55v-56r. Image © Universiteitsbibliotheek Ghent, CC BY-NC-SA 2.0.

Fig. 90 Opening in a book of hours, with a blank folio before vespers that formerly had a rectangular object sewn onto it. Nijmegen, Radboud Universiteit, Ms. 283 fol. 91v-92r. © Radboud Universiteitsbibliotheek, CC BY 4.0.

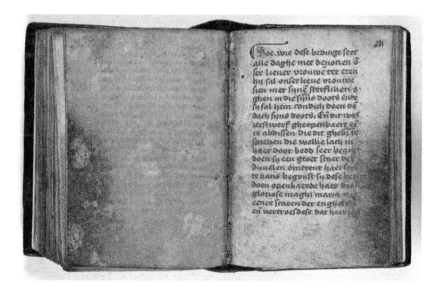

Fig. 91 Opening in a prayer book, with a blank folio before a rubric that formerly had an object glued to it. The Hague, Koninklijke Bibliotheek, Ms. 75 G 2, fol. 220v-221r. Image © Koninklijke Bibliotheek—the National Library of The Netherlands, CC BY 4.0.

Close inspection reveals that at one time manuscripts were even more full of added images than they presently appear, since just as things made their way into the book they made their way out as well, whether through hard use or opportunistic excision. Such is the case with a book of hours written possibly in Utrecht or the eastern part of the Northern Netherlands in the first quarter of the fifteenth century (Nijmegen, RU, Ms. 283; fig. 90). Nearly every canonical hour begins on a fresh recto; this left many surfaces of blank parchment. This was filled up with sewn-in and pasted objects, including large rectangular things, possibly prints or parchment paintings, to preface every new hour. These, however, have all been removed. For example, before vespers of the Hours of the Cross, one finds a blank, ruled page bearing holes at the top, bottom, and left side revealing that a rectangular object was formerly stitched there. That the person wielding the needle could not add stitches to the right side indicates that the book was already bound when the object was added. Furthermore, a frame of dirt around this rectangular ghost object indicates that the image was added early in the book's life, after which it received considerable wear. Other holes throughout this manuscript (for example, on folios 8, 61, 76, 91v) reveal that an early owner enthusiastically filled up as many of the blank spaces as possible. This manuscript was manipulated in other ways, as well, as I discuss later.

An even more dramatic case appears in HKB, Ms. 75 G 2, fol. 221v-222r, a prayerbook encountered above (fig. 91). The recto side of the opening presents a rubric indicating that the votary who reads the accompanying prayer with devotion in her heart would see a vision of the Virgin on her deathbed. Dark fingerprints on this opening reveal that this was among the owner's most beloved and intensely read prayers. Glue stains indicate that an object—most likely an image of the Virgin that would help prime the reader for her deathbed—had formerly been stuck to the page, but was worn off through use.

A Netherlandish prayerbook now in Heidelberg (UB, Cod. Sal. VII,4d) confirms an algorithm of use: the more marks of wear it has, the more likely that it has undergone changes in form and content. It has text pages heavily darkened from use, to the point that some of the script is worn off. Fol. 67v, which is now blank, has a rectangle of negative dirt, indicating that it once had an object stuck to it, mostly like an image (fig.

92).[52] This also points to a problem with glue on parchment: it rarely sticks forever as does glue on paper.

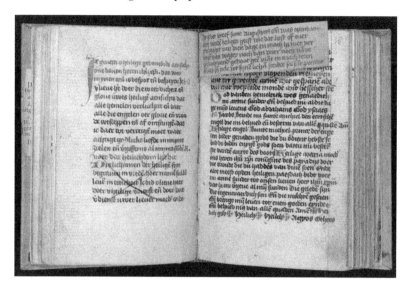

Fig. 93 Opening in a prayer book with an added rubrics inscribed on a separate sheet of parchment that has been slipped in behind the quire. Special Collections of the Universiteitsbibliotheek van Amsterdam, Ms. I G 35, fol. 37v-38r. Image © Universiteitsbibliotheek van Amsterdam, CC BY 4.0.

Fig. 94
Parchment sheets with extra prayers pasted into the back inside cover of the Gouda missal. The Hague, Koninklijke Bibliotheek, Ms. 135 H 45, back inside cover. Image © Koninklijke Bibliotheek — the National Library of The Netherlands, CC BY 4.0.

52 Opening in a prayerbook that formerly had an object pasted to the verso folio. Heidelberg, Universitätsbibliothek, Cod. Sal. VII, 4d, fol. 67v-68r. See http://digi. ub.uni-heidelberg.de/diglit/salVII4d

Owners could also slip in small sheets, securing them around a quire, without having to rebind. This was the technique used by the owner of a prayerbook—which was assembled out of a group of booklets—who used such sheets to smooth over the transition between assembled parts (AUB, Ms. I G 35; fig. 93). Assembling them into a coherent whole required some adjustments. For example, she has crossed out a partial text on fol. 37v: because the end of the text was missing, the beginning was not worth reading. Fol. 38r starts with a new prayer, but the owner wanted to add a rubric to it, so has written it on a separate scrap of parchment and looped it behind the quire. This sheet is small so that it fits behind the quire, just above level of the first sewing. It is held into the binding by friction alone. (In fact, this book therefore proposes an elegant solution to the problem faced by the fifteenth-century scribe in the Perth manuscript, analyzed above.)

Book owners could also paste in sheets with texts, if there were blank spaces that would accommodate them. A number of different kinds of augmentations appear in the Gouda Missal, made 1450–55 (HKB, Ms. 135 H 45) introduced above. As I have shown, a later scribe wrote extensive texts for celebrating feast days added directly to the blank quire ends. Furthermore, owners have pasted onto the back cover several sheets of parchment bearing prayers (fig. 94). In this position, against the hard boards of the cover, they would not bend, strain the glue and fall off. Short prayer texts, all written in Latin, fill these added sheets. The larger of the two pasted sheets was previously folded, indicating that it had a career as an autonomous entity before entering the manuscript. Several prayers dedicated to St. Anne appear on the scrap, but they are inscribed in two different hands. Because devotion to St. Anne became extremely popular in the 1490s, she is one of the most common subjects for added prayers.

2. Adding other objects to blank parchment

Medieval owners of books—especially of books of hours—used them to store small devotional objects, such as pilgrims' badges, metal souvenirs from having taken the Eucharist, gifted loose images, and any other flattish objects that they wanted to remember, store and associate with a devotional context. Another item they sewed in was curtains. Sewing curtains into books added opulence and value to manuscripts made, for example, at the Ottonian courts.[53] Small pieces of precious imported silk, made with subtle patterns woven according to unfathomably time-consuming procedures, could be stitched into a book both to protect the image below it and also to add the ritual of its unveiling to the procedures of reading the book.

Very few actual curtains survive in fifteenth-century books, but what does survive are the thousands of needle holes in parchment, in the marginal area above miniatures, which signal that someone once sewed a curtain there. To take one of dozens or hundreds of possible examples: Cambridge UL, Ms. Ii.6.2, fol. 12v has a row of telltale holes above the pink canopy (fig. 7). With a cloth of honor hanging behind his head, and a physical curtain hanging in front of his face, Christ was encased in curtains, which could be parted each time the viewer wanted a glimpse of the man. In fact every full-page image in this modest manuscript has such sewing holes, indicating that it was once aflutter with curtains. There seems to be an inverse correlation between the quality of the miniatures and the likelihood that an English owner would sew a curtain over the top, as if the owners were lending additional dignity to their images to capture for them some of the glory associated with imperial splendor, when in fact they were made by workshop hacks. Sewing in curtains is yet another procedure from the earlier Middle Ages that fifteenth-century book owners adopted and developed. But they changed the meaning of the gesture when they began making such curtains commonplace, rather than reserving them for only the most ornate display volumes.

* * *

My discussion above has systematically treated the techniques that book owners had at hand when they wanted to adjust the contents of their books. They added texts and images both formally and informally,

---

53 Christine Sciacca, "Raising the Curtain on the Use of Textiles in Manuscripts," in *Weaving, Veiling, and Dressing: Textiles and Their Metaphors in the Late Middle Ages*, ed. Kathryn M. Rudy and Barbara Baert, *Medieval Church Studies* (Turnhout: Brepols, 2007), pp. 161–90.

which is to say, they made scrawls and doodles in their bound books, but they also commissioned professionals to add inscriptions or to make images or to inscribe texts on separate leaves, which could then be attached to the book with glue, thread, or mere friction. Other items, such as loose paintings, found a home in books in a symbiotic relationship: the leaves embellished the books, while the books protected the leaves. Many of these additions reveal the changed circumstances of the book, such as a change in ownership, or a new devotion. With such alterations the book becomes a witness before God for manumission and other legal documents, and it becomes a treasure trove in which a series of owners can store and remember small things. Everyone wanted to get in on the new devotion, even if it meant altering the book physically. Physical changes to the book became changes in the owner's relationship—including physical relationship—to that book, as the new additions created new spaces of worship or intensified the owner's ability to manifest devotion.

In many cases, the placement of these additions contributed to their meaning. Glosses make most sense next to the texts they explicate. Owners added prayers in response to particular images. People made inscriptions on the backs of particular images, in order to bring the words as close as possible to the figures represented on the other side of the parchment membrane. Owners wanted to assert their ownership either at the very beginning or the very end of the book, thereby commanding the entirety. Thus, many inscriptions are positionally charged.

Other additions were made as space permitted. Owners had an interest in adding desired texts and images to the front of the book, not only because there was often space available for doing so, but also because the front was a privileged position. As most books of hours were put together with the Hours of the Virgin at the front, and the Vigil for the dead at the back, with the Penitential Psalms in the middle, they frame a world-view bookended by conception (the Annunciation) and death, with sinning and guilt in the middle. People were drawn to the front end of this array.

This part has considered images and texts written into available space, as well as pre-existing pieces of inscribed parchment that have been affixed to the book later, occasionally with needle and thread, but usually with glue. Gluing objects in added to the page's stiffness, and there was a limit to the amount of stuff that could be glued in before the book would not properly open. The way to add multiple parchment sheets was not to glue them in, but to take the book out of its binding and sew them along its spine.

Part III: Changes that required rebinding

The augmentations outlined above did not require the book owner to take the book apart. Owners and users simply made use of the blank and available space, and filled it with desired words and images. Every doodle, and most notes of ownership inscribed into the fronts (or backs) of books comprise additions of this sort. Yet the rest of the additions discussed in this study require adding physical material in such a way that it became structurally integrated with the original book. Most of this ancillary physical material came in the form of parchment. It provided more substrate for texts and images.

Single leaves were the simplest additions. Of course, there was an entire industry for the production of single-leaf miniatures. I have discussed this above in conjunction with a new way of conceptualizing book production that divided labor physically, resulting in manuscripts that were pieced together in such a way that the seams often showed quite clearly. After the 1390s many miniatures, which were made primarily for books of hours, were produced separately from the textual components of the manuscript. A stationer or book owner could slip such full-page miniatures into the book so that they prefaced major incipits, so long as each new text began on a fresh recto with an enlarged initial. Placed as a verso the image could thereby mark the beginning of key text passages. As long as books were constructed according to the modular method, then new texts automatically started at the beginning

   http://dx.doi.org/10.11647/OBP.0094.03

of a fresh quire on the recto side. And a stationer could simply add an image to the front of the quire.

Leaves added to manuscripts reveal owners' strong desires, even if that desire was simply to leave a mark. Physical alterations made the manuscript more attractive, more useful, more modern, and more personal. Owners could add single leaves or multiple quires. At their most extreme, the manipulations could transform the type of manuscript altogether. Earlier I discussed how the shift from psalter to book of hours accompanied a shift in production methods. In at least one case, the shift from psalter to book of hours appears within a single book over time: an owner of a thirteenth-century psalter added multiple quires to the manuscript in the second quarter of the fifteenth century. Specifically, he or she added quires containing the Hours of the Virgin and other prayers so that the new texts fell between the calendar and the psalter. This person in effect upgraded the manuscript, transforming a psalter into a psalter-hours. Later in the fifteenth century, another owner added even more quires to the end of the end of the book. These contain the Hours of the Holy Spirit, the Hours of the Cross, and other prayers.[1] This owner, in effect, continued the book's slow metamorphosis from psalter to book of hours. One wonders whether this later fifteenth-century owner took a cue from the earlier additions and saw that the book could be taken apart, emended, and sutured together again to form an improved, more modern book. Every emendation yielded not only additional content, but also communicated the very idea that structural additions were possible if one were willing to rebind the volume.

Rebinding

Until the early twentieth century, bookbinders were common in Western European cities. During the printing age, indeed until recently, many

---

1   The manuscript is in a private collection. It was formerly owned by Les Enluminures (Paris), for which see http://www.lesenluminures.com/inventory/expo-22443/ medieval-psalter-hours-use-of-st--omer-diocese-of-therouanne--20645, where it is listed as "Psalter-Hours by the Illuminator of Cambrai 87." For the illuminator of the eponymous manuscript, consult A. Bennett, "Devotional Literacy of a Noblewoman in a Book of Hours of Ca. 1300 in Cambrai," in *Manuscripts in Transition: Recycling Manuscripts, Texts and Images: Proceedings of the International Congres [sic] Held in Brussels (5–9 November 2002)*, ed. Brigitte Dekeyzer and Jan van der Stock (Leuven: Peeters, 2005), pp. 149–205.

books were sold in soft paper covers that merely held them together until they could be properly bound. That way, an owner could bind them in his house style and they would match the other volumes on the shelves. Likewise, medieval book binders did a swift trade binding and rebinding manuscripts.

Having handled over a thousand medieval manuscripts over the last twenty years and having seen bindings in all states of repair, I have come to some conclusions about them. Repeatedly opening and closing a book with a leather binding eventually weakens the leather. When leather is bent and unbent hundreds of times, the fibers in the outer, most stretched layers begin to fray. When they break, then the hinge, as it were, grows thin, and the remaining leather grows weaker even more quickly especially at the point of greatest wear. When the leather breaks all the way through, the binding can no longer protect the book block, because the unsecured covers slide and pivot, causing friction. One of the functions of a clasped binding is to serve as a book press, to keep the parchment folios from snapping back into the shape of a calf.

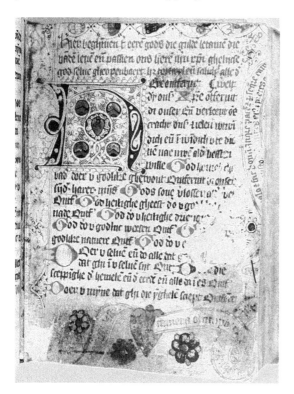

Fig. 95
Folio from a prayerbook that has been heavily worn and trimmed. Tilburg, Universiteitsbibliotheek, Ms. 11 (formerly TFK 10), fol. 48r. Image © Tilburg Universiteitsbibliotheek, CC BY 4.0.

Fig. 96 Binding with metal loops for suspending the book, early sixteenth
century. Tilburg, Universiteitsbibliotheek, Ms. 11 (formerly TFK 10).
Image © Tilburg Universiteitsbibliotheek, CC BY 4.0.

I contend that, even in the Middle Ages, a binding under intense use
might only last for the duration of a single owner, and that subsequent
owners would often rebind manuscripts and incorporate new parts
into them. I have therefore seen many heavily used fifteenth-century
manuscripts in early sixteenth-century bindings. Many surviving
medieval bindings are likely therefore not their true original
bindings. In medieval manuscript descriptions, what are often called
"contemporary" bindings (i.e., contemporary with the book block) may
in fact be their second or third bindings. If the book looks worn or has
been trimmed, but the binding is medieval, then the binding probably
dates from the period immediately after the manuscript was heavily
used. For example, a late fifteenth-century prayerbook (Tilburg, UB, Ms.
11) was so vigorously used by its early owners that the folios are now
soiled and damaged (fig. 95). Someone rebound it in the late fifteenth
or early sixteenth century, probably because the binding was damaged
from heavy use and the book was falling apart. Trimming the pages—
which usually occurred with books that were rebound—advertently
or inadvertently excised much of the dirt, but plenty of dirt and other

signs of wear remain. These signs reveal the motivation for the early rebinding.

Even though one would be tempted to date it from the same general period as the book to which it belongs, the medieval binding that the manuscript is now in is therefore not its original one (fig. 96). Rings attached to the bottom of the upper and lower covers indicate that the owner carried the book on a rope or chain in order to keep it close at hand when traveling. All of these signs are indicators that the early owner(s) spent a great amount of time reading and handling this book. Those who handled their books vigorously were also likely to make structural changes to them.

Updates and additions made by votaries to their prayerbooks at the end of the fifteenth century can reveal how they responded to new devotions and indulgences. When owners added texts or images to their manuscripts, they did so because they strongly desired those texts and images and actively selected them. Whereas an owner might purchase a book of hours off the shelf or inherit it from a deceased family member, thereby acquiring a manuscript with a particular set of texts over which he had little control, the added texts represent volitional acts. Sometimes the measures that owners took to update their manuscripts reveal that they were so eager to include certain texts that they were willing to adjust the structure of their books in order to accommodate them. These choices often embraced texts that had come into circulation only after the manuscript had been completed. In what follows, I consider manuscripts whose added images and/or texts reveal the voracious appetites of late medieval believers for the newest, latest, and most fashionable prayers.

Sometimes these changes came at the cost of entirely restructuring their prayerbooks by having them augmented and rebound; and other times the new essential prayers were squeezed into available space, such as on extra ruled lines at the end of quires, on the backs of the blank inserted miniatures, or on the flyleaves at the beginning or end of the book. Sometimes the one necessitated the other. Around 1500 someone in South Holland acquired a book of hours, made thirty years earlier with exquisite non-figurative painted decoration by the Master of Gijsbrecht van Brederode, and summarily tore the manuscript apart (HKB, Ms. BPH 151, hereafter: BPH 151). The owner then interpolated dozens of new images (including the Veronica, the Mass of St. Gregory, and the Last Judgment with the saved escorted to heaven) and several quires with prayers promising indulgences, and then bound the old parts together with the new to make a manuscript containing the most fashionable, colorful, and indulgence-rich prayers, but one that was still an heirloom. (This manuscript will be discussed further in Part IV below.)

Such augmentations were not unusual: medieval manuscripts had a long shelf life and often changed hands many times. Made of durable parchment—supple as paper but tough as leather—they could easily serve multiple owners and users over a period of decades or even centuries. Laypeople often handed their books down the generations or sold them. Updates people made to a family heirloom often reveal the new fashions in prayer culture, and along with that, their culturally constructed hopes and fears. This study treats prayerbooks made in the century before the Reformation; although it uses the methodology of codicology and stratigraphy to study books closely, it is really about people and what they revealed about themselves through their manipulations. A wealth of evidence shows that at the end of the fifteenth century, purgatory began to weigh heavily on people's minds—and therefore on their prayerbooks. Indulgences will feature in the discussion in the context of adding images, texts and entire quires to prayerbooks.

In the late Middle Ages, a layperson who owned a single book was likely to own a prayerbook; these far outnumbered Bibles or secular manuscripts. Rather than read from cover-to-cover, votaries would dip into the multiple texts these books contained. An individual owner's needs might change over the lifetime, and the book was flexible enough to allow for the insertion of new images and texts, especially when its owners married, bore children, or died, necessitating a change in ownership. Sometimes the measures that owners took to update their manuscripts revealed that they were even willing to adjust the structure of their books. These choices often embraced texts that had come into circulation only after the manuscript had been completed. These changes and additions precisely index those elements they desired most.

Certain Netherlandish studios specialized in updating older manuscripts. A group of artists known in modern scholarship as the

Masters of the Dark Eyes, for example, worked closely with scribes to take older books of hours, fill in blank folios with new prayers, and to add single folios as well as entire quires to bring manuscripts up to the standards of an image- and indulgence-hungry public in the decades flanking 1500. While the Masters of the Dark Eyes probably worked in secular, urban ateliers, other ateliers within convents similarly added new, desired components to existing prayerbooks. These convents included that of St. Ursula of Delft (Franciscan tertiary women), and that of St. Agnes, also in Delft (Augustinian canonesses). The current study will consider both isolated cases of manuscript meddling, as well as the systematic approach that these studios applied to update and personalize books.

With these forces at play, the only books that escaped the Middle Ages without some additions were those that were unused, for example, the Hours of Catherine of Cleves, which looks as if it were barely touched.[2] One wonders whether the book was even designed to be used, or whether ordering and paying for such a richly decorated book of prayers counted itself as a good deed, for which actually reading the book was not required.

What is clear is that, while expensive bespoke manuscripts continued to be made well into the sixteenth century, newer, cheaper ways of making the book were being explored, and these methods involved making components and then building a book from them. Assembling books with an additive method had a major impact on the mind-set of book makers and users, who exploited the possibilities of modules by treating them as opportunities to add new bits to old books. But the "modular method" also has other rather unexpected consequences, which will be important for both simple augmentations (not requiring rebinding) as well as more complex augmentations (requiring rebinding). Considering this modular method therefore provides the backdrop for new attitudes toward the book-in-flux.

---

2 For images, analysis and further bibliography, see Rob Dückers and Ruud Priem, *The Hours of Catherine of Cleves: Devotion, Demons and Daily Life in the Fifteenth Century* ([Antwerp]: Ludion, 2009).

A. Adding leaves bearing texts

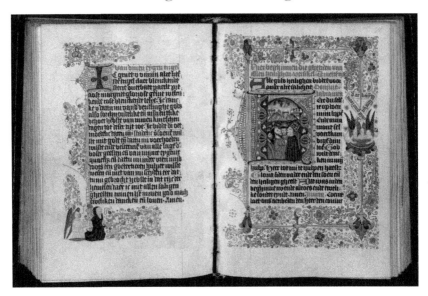

Fig. 97 Opening with the beginning of the Hours of All Saints (on the right), and a prayer to one's personal angel copied on a single, added leaf (on the left). Cambridge, Trinity College, Ms. B.1.46, fol. 110v-111r. Image © Trinity College Cambridge, CC BY 4.0.

Fig. 98 Opening revealing the stub from an added text leaf. Cambridge, Trinity College, Ms. B.1.46, fol. 105v-106r. Image © Trinity College Cambridge, CC BY 4.0.

A book of hours made for and by the sisters at the St. Ursula convent in Delft, introduced above, bears a single added leaf (fol. 110), which is inscribed with a prayer to the sister's personal angel and a small image depicting an angel watching a Franciscan sister's back (Cambridge, TC, Ms. B.1.46; fig. 97). This leaf was inserted at the end of one quire and the beginning of the next so that it faces the Hours of All Saints. One can see that it is an added leaf, because the stub sticks out from the opening eight folios earlier (fig. 98). At first glance, the script of the added leaf (fol. 110) closely resembles that in the rest of the book. I suspect that all of the women in this convent learned a "corporate script." Their ideal was to make their script indistinguishable from that of their sisters. In that way, the scribe-nuns could all work collectively on the same book projects, and their individual identities would be minimized.

A prayer to one's personal angel was not a common prayer. It did not fit neatly into any of the existing categories of standard texts for the book of hours. The owner may have added the additional folio at this location in the book in order to forge a connection between her personal angel and "All Saints," both entities which may be considered forms of protection. I speculate that the prayer to one's personal angel may have circulated in the form of single sheets, although I know of no examples that survive; however, I can imagine that someone who could not afford an entire prayerbook might be able to buy the protection that a prayer to a personal angel afforded.

Armed with the skills of both scribes and illuminators, the convent of St. Agnes in Delft also produced manuscripts. A full analysis of the work of this convent awaits. It is highly likely that the "Master of the Fagel Missal" was a woman, an inmate at the convent. She was active in 1459–60, the dates given within the Fagel Missal, and she also worked on some other books that the convent created.

This missal, which shows images of St. Augustine and St. Agnes, the convent's patrons, must have been made for their own chapel. They apparently used it for several decades. At some point in the early sixteenth century, the sisters needed another image for the book, for they wanted to celebrate the feast of St. Anne with more panache.

Fig. 99
Single leaf with prayers for the feast of St. Anne, with a historiated initial painted by the Masters of the Dark Eyes (South Holland, ca. 1500), inserted into the Fagel missal (Delft, 1459–1460). Dublin, Trinity College, Ms. 81, fol. 186r. Reproduced with kind permission of the Board of Trinity College Dublin. © Trinity College Library Dublin, all rights reserved.

Fig. 100
Incipit of the Sanctoral, with prayers for the feast of St. Andrew, with a historiated initial painted by the Master of the Fagel Missal (Delft, 1459–1460). Dublin, Trinity College, Ms. 81, fol. 187r. Reproduced with kind permission of the Board of Trinity College Dublin. © Trinity College Library Dublin, all rights reserved.

This saint had sharply risen in popularity at the end of the fifteenth and early sixteenth centuries, and furthermore, Anne was the patroness of the other Augustinian female convent within Delft, with which the Agnes convent had a necessary relationship. However, the "Master of the Fagel Missal" must have died by that point, for the sisters commissioned the Masters of the Dark Eyes to produce a folio with the Mass to St. Anne and an accompanying column-wide miniature (Dublin, TC, Ms. 81; fig. 99). They were then able to fit this new leaf into their book as fol. 186, just before the Sanctoral, which begins, as usual, with St. Andrew (fig. 100). Because the Sanctoral begins on a new quire, the binder was able to easily slip the new leaf before the beginning of the quire.

A comparison between the St. Anne page and the St. Andrew page reveals that the Masters of the Dark Eyes attempted to maintain the same page layout as the original part of the book, but they did not attempt to copy the style of the Fagel "master" or to copy the borders. (Whereas the Fagel Master/Mistress always frames the heads of figures from sacred history in a burnished gold halo, and fills space with labor-intensive patterning, the Masters of the Dark Eyes lack these features and create less stiff figures.) The work of the Masters of the Dark Eyes appears in many manuscripts, especially those made in South Holland. These masters worked with scribes to produce entire books of hours and prayerbooks, and they also supplied single leaves to fit into existing manuscripts, such as the leaf they created for the Fagel Missal.

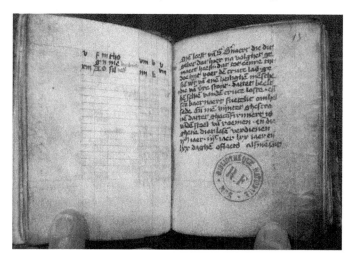

Fig. 101 Added folio (inserted at the break between two quires), bearing a rubric relevant to the following prayer. Paris, Bibliothèque nationale de France, Ms. Néerl. 111, fol. 12v-13r. Image © Author, CC BY-NC 4.0.

Fig. 102
Calendar with a highly
abbreviated Cisiojanus. Paris,
Bibliothèque nationale de France,
Ms. Néerl. 111, fol. 3r. Image
© Author, CC BY-NC 4.0.

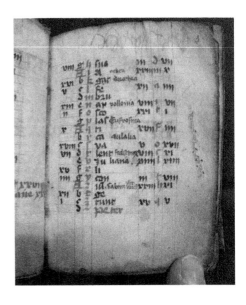

New prayers, such as the Mass of St. Anne, may have circulated on small single sheets. These could be copied into prayerbooks, or pasted in (in the case of the Gouda Missal, examined above), or incorporated into the binding. A Netherlandish prayerbook now in Paris has a prayer added on a separate folio, which has been later incorporated into the manuscript immediately after the calendar (Paris, BnF, Ms. Néerl. 111; fig. 101). This prayerbook was made in the mid-fifteenth century in the eastern part of the Northern Netherlands, to judge by the script and penwork decoration, the dialect and the page layout.[3] Measuring only 90x70 mm, with a text block measuring only 54x41 mm, the manuscript is quite small, and is the epitome of an object made for private devotion—a private devotion that could be further personalized. Some of the folios have been cut out—presumably the ones with the most elaborate decoration. Those that remain reveal that a group of people, probably sisters in a convent near the Dutch-German border, collectively made

---

3   1r: computational table (highly rubbed), with dates beginning 1415. However, the
     manuscript looks younger to me, and I suspect that the date was just slavishly copied
     from the exemplar. Ruling only defines a text box, and the individual lines are not
     ruled. The scribes therefore write a variable number of lines per folio. This is typical
     of German manuscripts, but less common in Netherlandish ones, suggesting that
     this manuscript came from the Dutch German border area, a hypothesis confirmed
     by the dialect, with words such as *mit* instead of *met*. Unusually, the script begins
     above the top line.

a manuscript out of production units, which they adjusted on the fly. Some of the adjustments yielded blank "inviting" parchment, to which indulgences and images were added; these were also added on single leaves.

The manuscript has been made in production units that correspond with the quires. A computational circle and a calendar with a cisiojanus comprise the first quire (Paris, BnF, Ms. Néerl. 111, fol. 1–12).[4] But the manuscript is tiny, and there was not enough room to fill in the entire calendar, so only the cisiojanus letters are present. Dutch saints do not match the Latin cisiojanus very well. February's folio reveals how frustrated the owner was (fol. 3r; fig. 102). In an attempt to make the abbreviations more intelligible, someone has tried with a tiny pen to go back and fill them in, but he or she has only done this sporadically. That same folio also reveals the extent to which the owner treated the book as a surface on which to make emendations and to record new thoughts.

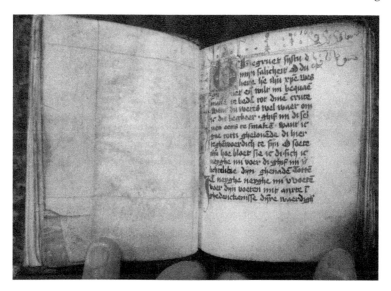

Fig. 103 Opening revealing the blank verso of an added folio (inserted at the break between two quires), and a prayer that's part of the original campaign of work. Paris, Bibliothèque nationale de France, Ms. Néerl. 111, fol. 13v-14r. Image © Author, CC BY-NC 4.0.

---

4   For a discussion of a cisiojanus in another manuscript, with further bibliography, consult Kathryn M. Rudy and René Stuip, "'Martin Fights in July, and He Strikes St. Vaast with the Font.'" A Cisiojanus and a Child's Alphabet in Oxford, Bodleian, Ms Rawlinson Liturgical E 40," *Cahiers de Recherches Médiévales et Humanistes / A Journal of Medieval and Humanistic Studies* 19 (2010), pp. 493–521.

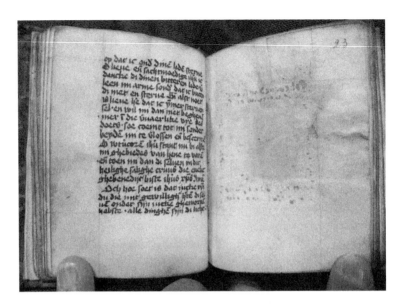

Fig. 104 Opening revealing the blank recto of an added folio (inserted at the break between two quires), and the end of a prayer that is part of the original campaign of work. Paris, Bibliothèque nationale de France, Ms. Néerl. 111, fol. 22v-23r. Image © Author, CC BY-NC 4.0.

Fig. 105 Opening revealing an added folio (inserted at the break between two quires), with a textual frame circumscribing a round object (now missing); and the beginning of a prayer that's part of the original campaign of work. Paris, Bibliothèque nationale de France, Ms. Néerl. 111, fol. 23v-24r. Image © Author, CC BY-NC 4.0.

Further aspects of the working methods are revealed by the second quire (Paris, BnF, Ms. Néerl. 111, 13r-22v). This quire contains a prayer to body parts of Christ, attributed to Bernard. It begins on fol. 14r with a decorated, three-line initial (fig. 103) and finishes on fol. 22v, with cramped letters as the scribe tried to squeeze the prayer into the available space (fig. 104). A quire comprises ten bifolia, which is two more than the usual eight. I suspect that what happened is that the scribe realized as she was nearing the end of the eight-folio quire that she could not fit the whole prayer in. She therefore added another bifolium, wrapping it around the outside of the packet. This, however, made a blank sheet at the beginning (fol. 13). Later someone added a text to that inviting parchment, in the form of a rubric on fol. 13r. A different scribe, working slightly later, inscribed that rubric (in black ink). The scribe therefore took the opportunity to add an indulgence to the beginning of the prayer, because the added parchment had inadvertently made space for it.

On fol. 13r the indulgence that the scribe opportunistically added reads:

> *rub:* One reads about St. Bernard, who wrote this following prayer, that one time he was reading it before a cross [and he was] observed by a holy person who stood there for hours. That image loosened itself from the cross and sweetly embraced St. Bernard. It is written that this has been confirmed by the See of Rome, and that anyone who reads [it] will earn 2370 years and 70 days of indulgence, as one can see.

> *rub:* Men leest van S Bernaert die dit gebet dat hier na volghet gemaect heeft dat tot eenre tijt doe hijt voer dat crucs las gesien uut van enen heilighen mensche die van ure stont dattet beelt hem selven vanden cruce loste. Ende sce baernaert suetelic omhelsede. Ende men vijntet ghescreven dattet gheconfirmeert is vanden stoel van Roemen ende die ghene diet lasen verdienen ij^m iaer iij^c iaer lxx iaer ende lxx daghen oflaets alsmen seit. [Paris, BnF, Ms. Néerl. 111, fol. 13r]

The prayer to the body parts, attributed to Bernard, therefore begins on fol. 14r, with fol. 13v blank. A later scribe took the opportunity presented by the resulting blank sheet at the beginning of the quire to add an introduction to the prayer that made it much more lucrative in the spiritual economy. Thus, what the owner has done is to add a frame to the prayer, which gives the prayer added relevance and benefit. It also presents a model for prayer, in the form of St. Bernard, who was able to make the image come alive by the power of his belief.

A similar situation may have ensued with the quire beginning with fol. 23r. On fol. 24r the first prayer begins (Néerl. 111; fig. 105), but the scribe realized that she needed more writing space, and therefore added an extra bifolium to the end of the quire. This created a blank leaf (fol. 23), which another scribe then filled with a most unusual design on the verso side, so that it faces the beginning of the new prayer. Comparing the script and decoration with the rest of the prayer texts, one can see that the sheet was made in a separate campaign and only added later. A roundel (approximately 31mm diameter, possibly accommodating a pasted-on engraving) was once affixed to the verso side but it has now been lifted. It may have depicted the face of Christ, as this is the prayer on the facing folio. A frame of words spirals around the image. The page has buckled, probably because someone steamed off the print, making the text difficult to make out: "rou ghelijc is minen rou. In hem en was gheen gedaen..." What is clear is that the added material has given the scribe license to experiment. What had been a tiny manuscript, one so cramped that the calendar had to be abbreviated beyond usability, became, with the addition of these two bits of material, a sufficient space for the scribes to take some chances.

Fig. 106 Folio added in the middle of the Hours of the Cross. The Hague, Koninklijke Bibliotheek, Ms. 133 D 1, fol. 99v-100r. Image © Koninklijke Bibliotheek—the National Library of The Netherlands, CC BY 4.0.

When book owners added material, they did not always consider where it went; they were simply desperate to get it in somewhere. A book of hours written in Dutch has such an added folio (HKB, Ms. 133 D 1, fol. 100; fig. 106) in the middle of the Hours of the Cross (fol. 89–109). It has a calendar with St. Jeroen in red, which suggests that it was made in the diocese of Utrecht; and the decoration around the miniatures is "blue acanthus," typical of Leiden. Whereas the rest of the book is in the vernacular, the added fol. 100 contains a prayer in Latin. The prayer is dedicated to St. Margaret. Was the owner's name Margaret? A peculiar floral border decoration adorns the sheet, which did not originate in South Holland, but rather in the Southern Netherlands, perhaps in Ghent or Burges. Were single-folio prayers sold or made for the purpose of personalizing manuscripts with people's name saints? What is clear is that the owner had to take the book apart in order to bind this sheet into it, or have this done at cost and effort. It was clearly important to the owner. More often, though, owners added sheets to incorporate more images.

B. Adding leaves bearing images

Roger Wieck writes that one of the reasons that books of hours exist was to provide a vehicle for images, such that very few books of hours are unillustrated.[5] I would like to qualify this: few books of hours exist *in American collections* that are unillustrated. Collectors in the nineteenth century bought manuscripts because they had images. Morgan, Walters, and the other great collectors passed over manuscripts that failed to dazzle them with gold and colors. European collections, on the other hand, are full of unillustrated books of hours. Perusing these, one has the sense that owning a book of hours was a great social aspiration for many medieval believers, but that the book itself might grow in stages, and the owner only add images at a later stage when he or she could afford them. If so, then European collections—especially municipal and university libraries—contain many testaments to early deaths and unrealized goals.

Just as some manuscripts were originally produced without images and gained them only later, if ever, a production developed for images without books, which similarly met up with their hosts later. This section

---

5   Roger S. Wieck, *Time Sanctified: The Book of Hours in Medieval Art and Life*, 1st ed. (New York: G. Braziller in association with the Walters Art Gallery, Baltimore, 1988), p. 28.

is about images painted on single leaves that would be appropriate for insertion into private devotional books, including books of hours, but also prayerbooks with other texts besides the offices to be recited at the canonical hours. Above, in my discussion of a Southern Netherlandish manuscript for export to England (Cambridge, UL, Ms. Ff.6.8), I noted that the quires with suffrages comprise single-leaf images interleaved with single-leaf text pages. The manuscript was simply constructed that way. It is not a difficult leap to imagine that loose leaves—bearing images or texts—which were then in widespread circulation, could end up in other kinds of books. Because there is so often a disjoint between the text part of the manuscript and the image part, it can be very difficult to determine whether a leaf was original or added, or whether a book was embellished by the first, second, or subsequent owner. Fifteenth-century books of hours and prayerbooks often form a strange hybrid, partly mass-produced, partly bespoke.

1. Images for the most common offices

Many books of hours were sold bare with the expectation that the owner could add images later. As I have shown above, Northern and Southern Netherlandish book makers constructed their wares in order that textual incipits would begin on a fresh recto, so that a full-page miniature could easily be slotted in to face it. Images that accompany the major texts of the book of hours are the most common type of added leaves: the Annunciation (for the Hours of the Virgin), the Crucifixion (for the Hours of the Cross); Christ in Judgment (for the Seven Penitential Psalms); and the Mass for the Dead (for the Vigil for the Dead).[6] Image makers did a swift trade in these subjects. They also supplied saints on single leaves, such as those discussed earlier in Cambridge, UL, Ms. Ff.6.8. Artists who supplied these kinds of images, destined for books of hours made separately, included the Masters of the Pink Canopies, the Moerdrecht Masters, the Masters of the Gold Scrolls, and in the North, the Masters of the Suffrages and the Masters of the Dark Eyes. All of these artists have received thorough studies.[7] As one can see from this

---

6   The subjects of these cycles changed regionally and over time, for which see Vanwijnsberghe, "The Cyclical Illustrations of the Little Hours of the Virgin in Pre-Eyckian Manuscripts," and Vanwijnsberghe, "Le Cycle de l'Enfance des Petites Heures de la Vierge dans les Livres d'Heures des Pays-Bas Méridionaux."

7   Bernard Bousmanne, "Deux Livres d'Heures du Groupe aux Rinceaux d'Or," *Revue des archéologues et historiens d'art de Louvain* 20 (1986), pp. 119–44; and Bert

list, these artists often worked in groups, where the work of individual artists fades into a singular style. These artists must have aspired to a corporate style or brand in order to make interchangeable parts that could be slotted into off-the-shelf books. Although their work was formulaic, their wares made plain manuscripts somewhat richer and more "personalized."

Fig. 107 Christ Carrying the Cross, full-page miniature attributed to the Moerdrecht Masters, inserted into a book of hours. Tilburg, Universiteitsbibliotheek, Ms. KHS 12, fol. 39v-40r. Image © Tilburg Universiteitsbibliotheek, CC BY 4.0.

Cardon, "The Illustrations and the Gold Scrolls Workshop," in *Typologische Taferelen uit het Leven van Jezus: A Manuscript from the Gold Scrolls Group (Bruges, ca. 1440) in the Pierpont Morgan Library, New York, Ms. Morgan 649: An Edition of the Text, a Reproduction of the Manuscript, and a Study of the Miniatures*, ed. Bert Cardon, R. Lievens, and Maurits Smeyers, *Corpus van Verluchte Handschriften uit de Nederlanden = Corpus of Illuminated Manuscripts from the Low Countries* (Leuven: Peeters, 1985), pp. 119–204, have discussed the Masters of the Gold Scrolls, and their works contain references to earlier literature through which one could map the formation of this category in the twentieth century. Georges Dogaer, *Flemish Miniature Painting in the 15th and 16th Centuries* (Amsterdam: B. M. Israël, 1987), pp. 27–31; van Bergen, *De Meesters van Otto van Moerdrecht*; James Douglas Farquhar, "Identity in an Anonymous Age: Bruges Manuscript Illuminators and Their Signs," *Viator* 11 (1980), pp. 371–83; Farquhar, "Manuscript Production and Evidence for Localizing and Dating Fifteenth-Century Books of Hours: Walters Ms 239," *Journal of the Walters Art Gallery* 45 (1987), pp. 44–88; and Melanie E. Gifford, "Pattern and Style in a Flemish Book of Hours: Walters Ms. 239," *Journal of the Walters Art Gallery* 45 (1987), pp. 89–102 have discussed the Masters of Otto van Moerdrecht.

The Masters of Otto van Moerdrecht specialized in creating single-leaf miniatures to be inserted into books of hours. One such manuscript containing their added miniatures is Tilburg, UB, KHS 12 (fig. 107). It is a book of hours in Dutch, made in South Holland, and is dated 1434.[8] Fifteenth-century wooden boards covered in blind stamped brown leather still bind the manuscript. This binding is probably contemporary with the addition of the full-page miniatures, which were made by the Masters of Otto van Moerdrecht in the 1430s or 1440s. An early owner of the book therefore must have added them. In fact, the manuscript contains a fifteenth-century note of ownership of "Wendelmoed Iacobs dochter, Thomas Iacobsz. wijf, wonende inden Eynghel" (Wendelmoed the daughter of Jacob and the wife of Thomas Iacobsz, who lives in Eynghel [a town near Lisse]). It may have been she who added the miniatures.[9] This provides yet another example of my general observation that people who make one kind of addition (such as adding images) are likely to add several (such as adding inscriptions).

With features partway between "radishes" and "scallop," the penwork decoration is executed in a style that can be associated with Delft.[10] These ornaments contrast sharply, however, with the painted borders that the Moerdrecht masters supplied with the miniatures, so the resulting openings do not present a visually unified whole; one can clearly see the aesthetic seam where the new miniature meets the old text leaf. This book was not planned from the beginning to have miniatures, as the initials for the individual hours appear part-way down the page; according to the hierarchy of decoration, a full-page miniature should accompany an initial at the top of the page. As they stand, the images interrupt the text. For this reason the owner has had to violate the hierarchy, because there was no way to observe it given the manuscript as it stood, with its initials half-way down the page that didn't "match" the miniature. Technically, a full-page miniature should face a text page with the largest initial, situated at the upper left corner of the right-hand page. The owner could not adjust the existing decoration,

---

8   Gumbert, *Manuscrits Datés Conservés dans les Pays-Bas, T. 2 (Cmd-Nl 2)*, vol. II, p. 5, nt. 13, however, questions this date.

9   Tilburg, UB, KHS 12, fol. 262v.

10   Korteweg, *Kriezels, Aubergines en Takkenbossen: Randversiering in Noordnederlandse Handschriften uit de Vijftiende Eeuw*, pp. 56–67.

as the five-line initial *G* was already fixed on the page. Clearly, she was not satisfied with the moderate decoration of her book as received. The easiest way to rectify this was to add full-page miniatures, even if they disrupted the hierarchy. Adding value, color, and images were clearly more important to her than abiding by the rules of page layout. A vulgarian, she privileged decoration over design principles.

2. Images for indulgences

The second most common type of added leaf is that which helps the owner to earn indulgences, which sometimes required the presence of an image. The Mass of St. Gregory was frequently added to late medieval prayerbooks. A shift occurred in prayerbooks around the 1460s; before this time books of hours largely excluded the image of St. Gregory and its accompanying prayer. After this time, and in the last quarter of the fifteenth century, book owners demanded this prayer. I suspect that the exemplars copyists used often did not contain it, so that even manuscripts made in the latter part of the century lacked this desired text, and it was added later as an afterthought in a separate operation. Clearly, the prayer, with its enormous indulgence, offered solace to votaries who feared the fiery afterlife. The prayer and its image created a sudden and thorough demand.

The subject of this suddenly popular image depicts the origin of an indulgence called the Verses of St. Gregory. A legend motivated the prayer: Gregory the Great was performing Mass in the presence of an audience. At the moment when he elevated the host, that host miraculously turned into the Body of Christ, so that it was visible to those present. A micro-mosaic depicting Christ as Man of Sorrows and enshrined in the church of Sta Croce in Gerusalemme was said to have represented the vision that Gregory, and his audience, saw. In light of this experience, Gregory was said to have issued a prayer to the Passion — the Five Verses of St. Gregory — beginning *Adoro te in cruce pendentem* — and he attached a significant indulgence to anyone repeating the prayer in the presence of the image. Significantly, the indulgence was also valid if the reader performed it in front of a copy of the image. This is the same poem mentioned above that came in so many versions, with five, seven, nine or eleven verses: it was not only extremely popular, but it was ever-expanding (at least until the anti-indulgence climate of the Protestant Reformation marked its end).

Many manuscript owners added an image of the Mass of St. Gregory to their prayerbooks. The owner of HKB, Ms. 76 G 16, for example, added such an image to preface the Seven Verses of St. Gregory. All of the full-page miniatures and border decoration in this manuscript were executed by the Masters of the Dark Eyes, a group of illuminators who painted richly decorated prayerbooks, largely in South Holland from ca. 1480–1515. (I discuss them in some detail below in Part IV.) Their output was very large, which suggests that several painters were working together to create books in a house style, which was marked by thickly painted margins, a large stable of figurative images (some of which derived from prints), and a large amount of shell gold. None of the names of these painters has come down to us. They were apparently quite popular with members of the nouveaux riches. Some of them even went to England, where they became favorites of the nobility.[11] What interests me in the present context is the service they offered to book owners to update their older or plainer manuscripts.

These painters created the Mass of St. Gregory in a separate campaign of work from the rest of the miniatures, and clearly this image was not planned from the outset (HKB, Ms. 76 G 16; fig. 108).[12] This is apparent because the accompanying prayer, the *Adoro te*, does not begin on a fresh recto, does not begin with an 11-line initial, and its text block lacks the gold border found around texts elsewhere in the codex that have an accompanying full-page image. The normal situation demonstrating the proper hierarchy of decoration appears for example at the opening for the Seven Penitential Psalms in the same manuscript, where the borders on the left and right sides of the opening match, and the text begins with a large decorated initial at the top of the folio (fig. 109).[13] In other

---

11 Klara H. Broekhuijsen, *The Masters of the Dark Eyes: Late Medieval Manuscript Painting in Holland*, Ars Nova (Turnhout: Brepols, 2009), cat no. 6, pp. 95–96.

12 Masters of the Dark Eyes, Mass of St. Gregory, full-page miniature inserted into a book of hours. The Hague, Koninklijke Bibliotheek, Ms. 76 G 16, fol. 149v-150r http://manuscripts.kb.nl/zoom/BYVANCKB%3Amimi_76g16%3A149v_150r

13 Masters of the Dark Eyes, Opening at the Seven Penitential Psalms, with the Last Judgment on the left side of the opening, and the Psalms beginning with a large

words the opening with the *Adoro te* breaks the rules of the hierarchy of decoration. It is therefore clear that the full-page miniature was conceived after the *Adoro te* had already been inscribed and decorated. Perhaps the owner wanted an image in order to fulfill the demand of the accompanying rubric that the votary read in front of the *arma Christi* in order to earn 46,012 years' and 24 days' indulgence. While the Masters of the Dark Eyes would have supplied full-page miniatures for the major texts that constitute a book of hours (the Annunciation before the Hours of the Virgin, and the Last Judgment before the Seven Penitential Psalms, for example), perhaps the Mass of St. Gregory before the *Adoro te* was optional. If so, then perhaps the buyer chose to have the manuscript upgraded at the studio before taking it home.

Fig. 110 Mass of St. Gregory, opposite the incipit of the Adoro te in Middle Dutch. Brussels, Koninklijke Bibliotheek van België, Ms. IV 410, fol. 45v-46r. Image © Koninklijke Bibliotheek van België, all rights reserved.

decorated initial on the right. The Hague, Koninklijke Bibliotheek, Ms. 76 G 16, fol. 52v-53r. http://manuscripts.kb.nl/zoom/BYVANCKB%3Amimi_76g16%3A052v_053r

Fig. 111 The Mass of St. Gregory, facing the incipit of the Verses of St. Gregory.
The Hague, Koninklijke Bibliotheek, Ms. 133 E 22, fol. 186v-187r. Image
© Koninklijke Bibliotheek—the National Library of The Netherlands, CC BY 4.0.

People were so anxious to get an image of the Mass of St. Gregory into
their books that they would insert even an incomplete one (Brussels,
Koninklijke Bibliotheek, Ms. IV 410, fig. 110). This image is difficult to
localize, because its features have been painted with a broad brush, as
it were; the manuscript into which it has been inserted (Brussels, KB,
IV 410) is a book of hours in Dutch that contains penwork typical of
Brethren of the Common Life active in Den Bosch in the first quarter
of the sixteenth century.[14] The image that the owner added to this book
requires a leap of imagination to complete. Only a negative silhouette
defines the ghostly image of Christ looming on the altar. On the stark
back wall, the torturers lack any facial features, while the ecclesiastical
furnishings appear as abstract solids. At first I wondered whether
there were originally prints pasted to these voids, which had later been

---

14   Korteweg, *Kriezels, Aubergines en Takkenbossen*, pp. 154–65.

removed. Although this possibility cannot be ruled out, there is no glue residue on the void silhouettes. Even if there had been silhouetted prints pasted onto the parchment, it would not explain why the shapes throughout the sheet are underdeveloped (one of the faces has been painted with body color, and the altar has not been painted all). I must conclude that the owner preferred to have this strange and incomplete image, which was better than none, so strong was his desire to complete the indulgence with the relevant image.

A book of hours in Dutch introduced above (HKB, Ms. 133 E 22) with a French initial added to its back cover also has a single leaf miniature added near the end of the manuscript (fol. 186). It precedes a quire of four leaves, which form part of the original material of the book, but were inscribed by a different hand (fol. 187–190; fig. 111). One can see that they are part of the original parchment of the rest of the book, as they are similarly ruled for 20 lines, with double horizontal and vertical bounding lines. They were surplus in the original production and therefore left blank. I suspect that when the owner acquired it, he or she took the opportunity to commission a scribe to write a relevant prayer to accompany it: the Seven Verses of St. Gregory (fol. 187r/v). This prayer is inscribed in a different (and worse) hand from the rest of the manuscript. The unused parchment that came with the book was a powerful vacuum that the owner had to fill. He filled it with an indulgenced text, and while he was at it, added a relevant image—the Mass of St. Gregory—to activate the new prayer.

The accompanying rubric only comes at the end of the prayer:

rub: Pope Sixtus IV wrote the fourth and fifth verses of the seven little prayers that appear above, and with that he doubled all the indulgences previously given, so that the sum of the indulgences totaled 46,012 years and 40 days.

rub: Sixtus paus de vierde heft dit vierde ende vijfte gebet van desen seven voirscreven gebedekijns gemaect. Ende daer mede heft hi alle die oflaten hijf voir gegeven gedubbelliert. Alsoe dat die somme der oflaten maect tesamen xlvi dusent iaer xij iaer ende xl dagen. [HKB, Ms. 133 E 22, fol. 187v]

The script and decoration of this indulgence differ from that found in the rest of the manuscript. One can compare it, for example, to the incipit of the Vigil for the Dead, which is one of the core texts from the original part of the manuscript (fol. 102r; fig. 112).[15] Comparing the two reveals that the *Adoro te* clearly comes from a different campaign of work. Whereas the original parts of this manuscript were written in a much more refined and steady *textualis*, the added parts were inscribed in a much less elegant *textualis*. Differences in decoration also confirm their separate genesis. The incipit of the Vigil for the Dead has received painted and penwork decoration, which is lacking in the borders around the *Adoro te*. The full-page miniature depicting the Mass of St. Gregory likewise stems from a different campaign of work from the miniatures in the rest of the codex, such as the miniature depicting souls in the bosom of Abraham. Whereas five full-page miniatures in the original part of the manuscript were made in Utrecht, the Mass of St. Gregory added near the end, however, was made elsewhere, possibly in the Southern Netherlands. The image testifies to the international trade in the tools of salvation.

The initial of the added *Adoro te* has not been filled in, as this would have required that the freshly-inscribed quire be sent to a painter. So eager was the owner to have this prayer that he skipped the final step and simply imagined the opening letter every time he read the prayer. As often happens with added texts, the initials were never filled in, and the entire production looks half-baked. While the book is incomplete without the Mass of St. Gregory and its prayer, the prayer is also incomplete because the initials have not been painted. The added material could be as partial as the original book—completion is overall less important than the immediate need for a book, for something new in the book, for a particular prayer. Coming only at the end of the prayer (fol. 187v), the rubric reveals one of the motivations for adding the quire: to include a prayer that offered more than 46,000 years' indulgence. It is bound in sixteenth-century brown leather, blind stamped.

---

15 Souls in the bosom of Abraham, full-page miniature inserted to face the incipit of the Vigil for the Dead. The Hague, Koninklijke Bibliotheek, Ms. 133 E 22, fol. 101v-102r http://manuscripts.kb.nl/zoom/BYVANCKB%3Amimi_133e22%3A101v_102r

Fig. 113
Mass of St. Gregory, full-page miniature
inserted in a prayerbook. Copenhagen,
Royal Library, Ms. Thott. 129 octavo, fol. 49v.
© Royal Library Copenhagen, CC BY 4.0.

Fig. 114
Opening in a book of
hours, with a full-page
miniature of the Mass
of St. Gregory inserted
before the Verses of St.
Gregory. 's-Heerenberg,
The Netherlands,
Collection Dr. J. H.
van Heek, Huis Bergh
Foundation, Ms. 18, fol.
153v-154r. Image © The
Huis Bergh Foundation,
CC BY 4.0.

Fig. 115
Opening in a book of
hours, with a full-page
miniature of the Virgin
in Sole inserted before
the Hours of the Virgin.
's-Heerenberg, The
Netherlands, Collection
Dr. J. H. van Heek, Huis
Bergh Foundation, Ms. 18,
fol. 17v-18r. Image © The
Huis Bergh Foundation,
CC BY 4.0.

Users of a prayerbook from South Holland added only one full-page image to the prayerbook: the Mass of St. Gregory (Copenhagen, Royal Library, Thott 129 octavo; fig. 113). This manuscript has the look and feel of a book of hours but does not actually contain any offices; instead, it is a prayerbook, with a plethora of indulgenced texts. The manuscript has a slightly spikey script, of a variety one associates with Leiden, but it has marginal decoration consisting of half-length figures surrounded by blue text scrolls of a variety one associates with Delft. In fact, the manuscript may have been made for (or by) the Canonesses Regular of Saints Catharine and Barbara in Noordwijk, given the following features: St. Jeroen, the patron of Noordwijk is prominently featured; Saints Catherine and Barbara are first among the virgins in the litany; one of the statements at the end of the Vigil is a petition to "giving us alms," which would make sense only to those who asked for alms (chiefly those living in religious compounds); and finally the manuscript contains the Hundred Articles by Henry Suso (Seuse), a text closely associated with female religious (I know of only one copy of this text in a manuscript owned by a layperson). No other manuscripts have been associated with this convent, so it is impossible to compare Thott 129, 8° with other manuscripts attributed to the same monastery. Even so it is possible to draw a basic conclusion from this example: People in convents were not above the indulgence culture of the fifteenth century, but instead were vigorous patrons of manuscripts with indulgences and images that aided their acquisition.

A Mass of St. Gregory (fig. 114) and the Virgin in Sole (fig. 115), that is, the two most important indulgenced images, are the only miniatures that were added to 's Heerenberg, HB, Ms. 18.[16] The Mass of St. Gregory even shows souls being rescued from the fires of Purgatory in the foreground, thereby emphasizing the image's role as a tool for springing souls from the flames. While not enough manuscripts survive to be able to state confidently that the Mass of St. Gregory and the Virgin in Sole were the most frequently represented images toward the end of the fifteenth century, it can be stated confidently that sometimes they are

---

16 *Catalogue of Medieval Manuscripts and Incunabula at Huis Bergh Castle in 's-Heerenberg,* cat. 79, pp. 137–39.

the *only* images in a given devotional object or book. Votaries strongly desired to update their manuscripts in order to possess the most spiritually lucrative prayers. I suspect that books of hours were often made by copying earlier models made at a time before the indulgence craze. It is possible that the book makers peddled new texts and images to a market that was already flooded with books of hours. Such images also went viral as it were, and consumers wanted them as quickly as copyists and illuminators could supply them.

3. Portraits and personalizing details

Fig. 116 Opening in a book of hours, Southern Netherland or Northern France, ca. 1500, with a full-page image depicting a man being presented by John the Baptist, opposite the Crucifixion. Stockholm, National Library of Sweden, MS, A 233, fol. 56v-57r. Image © National Library of Sweden, CC BY 4.0.

Personalizing a book of hours proved another motivation for seeking extra single-leaf images that could be incorporated into that book. For example, a book of hours from Northern France or the Southern Netherlands had an early owner named John, possibly Jan de Trompes, who held several public functions in Bruges from 1498 to 1512.

Fig. 117 Woman in the garb of an Augustinian canoness (Lijsbett van Steengracht?)
in prayer before the Virgin and Child, full-page miniature inserted in a
prayerbook. Brussels, Koninklijke Bibliotheek van België, Ms. II 2348, fol.
130v-131r. Image © Koninklijke Bibliotheek van België, all rights reserved.

The owner had several images of himself added to the book of hours,
including a single leaf that he placed opposite a full-page Crucifixion,
so that it appears as a devotional diptych in the manuscript (Stockholm,
Royal Library, Ms. A.233; fig. 116).[17] He has himself represented as a
pilgrim, with the relevant badge visible on his arm. Clearly, this and
the other added leaves, which similarly show the male sitter with his
name saint at a number of shrines around the Holy Land, was designed
to reflect his personal religious accomplishments as they developed
through his life. Overall, the interest in adding pages to manuscripts
in order to personalize them crossed over social class and religious/
secular boundaries: the urge was widespread among those who owned
such books. Some owners, however—namely, wealthy patrons and the

---

17   Kathryn Rudy, "A Pilgrim's Book of Hours: Stockholm Royal Library A233," *Studies
in Iconography* 21 (2000), pp. 237–77; and "Addendum," *Studies in Iconography* 22
(2001), pp. 163–64.

religious—had access to a wider range and quality of materials for this project than the more ordinary book owner.

Lijsbett van Steengracht, a sister at Onze-Lieve-Vrouwgasthuis, a hospital in Geraardsbergen, chose to have her own likeness painted in a full-page miniature, and she inserted the leaf in her prayerbook to preface the rosary (BKB, Ms. II 2348; fig. 117). In the miniature the patron kneels with her book at the feet of a radiant Virgin and Child. The accompanying text begins with the *Ave Maria* in Latin, a refrain Lijsbett will repeat 50 times before she closes her book and folds the mirage of the Virgin away.

An easy way to accomplish this was to add a sheet at the beginning of the manuscript with one's coat of arms. The owner of a book of hours from Utrecht did just that (HKB, Ms. 133 E 17, fol. 1v; fig. 118).[18] While the manuscript was copied and decorated in South Holland around 1440–1460, the later owner near the end of the fifteenth century asserted his presence by adding a folio at the beginning of the book bearing a coat of arms, with two crossed swords on an arresting red background. The simplicity of the geometric design at the center appears at odds with the painterliness of the green, flower-strewn cloth behind the shield and the delicately shadow-casting gold acanthus in the border. On closer inspection, however, one can see that the simple swords have been painted over an earlier coat of arms, whose form leaks through the red paint. Thus: an early owner (the first or second?) added the coat of arms to a prominent place at the front of the book, and a subsequent owner (the second or third?) overpainted the shield with an anodyne symbol to erase evidence of the former ownership. An English owner of a Southern Netherlandish book of hours, introduced above, has likewise inserted a folio near the beginning of the book with an even more complicated coat of arms, one with three lobsters boiled a gules (Cambridge, UL, Ms. Ii.6.2; fig. 119).[19]

---

18   Coat of arms (overpainted), full-page miniature added to a book of hours. The Hague, Koninklijke Bibliotheek, Ms. 133 E 17, fol. 1v. http://manuscripts.kb.nl/zoom/BYVANCKB%3Amimi_133e17%3A001v

19   Added coat of arms. Cambridge, University Library, Ms. Ii.6.2, fol. 2v. http://cudl.lib.cam.ac.uk/view/MS-II-00006–00002/10

Fig. 120 Annunciation opening in the Hours of Jacobus Johannes IJsbrands.
Utrecht, Universiteitsbibliotheek, Ms. 15 C 5, fol. 15v-16r. Image © Utrecht
Universiteitsbibliotheek, CC BY 4.0.

Jacobus Johannes IJsbrands (d. 1504) accomplished several functions
simultaneously with the full-page images he commissioned for his book
of hours around 1460, which included his coats of arms (Utrecht, UB,
Ms. 15 C 5; fig. 120). As befitting a canon of the Cathedral in Utrecht,
he commissioned his book in Latin. Although the painted miniature
clashes with the penwork borders on the facing page, the two types of
decoration perform different roles. The penwork that brands the book
as a product of Utrecht: the Utrecht *draakjes* (dragons) that populate
many of the initials.[20] He enhanced the openings of the major texts with
painted miniatures attributed to one of the best painters in Utrecht,
the Master of Gijsbrecht van Brederode. With his paint, he performs
jobs that even the best calligraphers could not pull off. He has not only
depicted the patron in his robes that defined his status, but has turned

---

20 Anne Margreet W. As-Vijvers, ed. *Beeldschone Boeken: De Middeleeuwen in Goud
    en* Inkt (Zwolle and Utrecht: Waanders Uitgeverij & Museum Catharijneconvent,
    2009), pp. 36–39.

the patron's coat of arms, along with those of his family members, into decorative finials in the margins. Moreover, the painter has depicted the patron partially overlapping the frame as if entering the sacred space. Jacobus Johannes IJsbrands joins Gabriel and God in announcing the incarnation of Christ. This is a miniature that performs many functions at once.

4. Images for adding value

There was another reason to adopt elements of the modular method, which were not about increasing efficiency or decreasing costs, but rather about increasing the value of a manuscript beyond what a single-atelier system would allow. Let me explain. When Simon de Varie added images to his manuscript, his motivation was not just to personalize it (for the original illuminators had already accomplished this by depicting him in prayer before the Virgin) but to embellish it with the work of one of the most celebrated painters in the land: Jean Fouquet. In the modern era an unscrupulous dealer divided the Hours of Simon de Varie into two volumes. Parts of the manuscript are now in the Getty Museum in Los Angeles and in the Koninklijke Bibliotheek in The Hague. Piecing the manuscript together (virtually) reveals that it comprises illumination made in two campaigns of work.

A team of illuminators in Paris completed the main part of the work by 1455. At nearly the same time, or very shortly thereafter, Jean Fouquet, one of the few illuminators scholars can identify by name, supplied several added miniatures (HKB, Ms. 74 G 37a).[21] Jean Fouquet was apparently commissioned to create some more imagery for the luxurious manuscript that would specify Simon de Varie as its owner and depict him in the act of prayer. To this end, Jean Fouquet supplied a frontispiece with the coats of arms of Simon de Varie on the recto (HKB, Ms. 74 G 37a; fig. 121).[22] The patron's motto flutters from a loose banderol from the arms, and the object is represented against a

---

21 James H. Marrow and François Avril, *The Hours of Simon de Varie*, Getty Museum Monographs on Illuminated Manuscripts (Malibu: J. Paul Getty Museum in association with Koninklijke Bibliotheek, The Hague, 1994).

22 Coat of arms of Simon de Varie, full-page miniature added to the Hours of Simon de Varie. The Hague, Koninklijke Bibliotheek, Ms. 74 G 37a, fol. 1r. http://manuscripts. kb.nl/zoom/BYVANCKB%3Amimi_74g37a%3A001r

backdrop of floral trellis, a motif that will recur in other additions. On the verso of the leaf the artist depicted the Virgin and Child in half-length, appearing as a miniature altarpiece (fig. 122).[23] His execution is extremely delicate, with the Virgin's robe flowing over her child's head.

Fig. 123
Parisian miniaturist, Simon de Varie kneeling in devotion before the Virgin, in the Hours of Simon de Varie. The Hague, Koninklijke Bibliotheek, Ms. 74 G 37, fol. 1r. Image © Koninklijke Bibliotheek— the National Library of The Netherlands, CC BY 4.0.

The artist has again asserted his patron's identity by branding the image at the four corners with the repeated coat of arms of Simon de Varie, as if to show that the patron was ever in the presence of the Virgin. In fact, the illuminator responsible for the original campaign of work has already included an image depicting Simon de Varie kneeling in devotion before the Virgin (fig. 123). The added leaf, however, magnifies the imagery, adds his coat of arms (and with it, his status), and further personalizes the image with his motto. Indeed, the sheer quality of the painting of Jean Fouquet's image of the Virgin is sure to have impressed any who looked at the book, ensuring that no one could fail to associate

---

23   Opening of the Hours of Simon de Varie: Jean Fouquet, Virgin and Child, full-page miniature added to a book of hours with miniatures and marginal figures by artists in Paris. The Hague, Koninklijke Bibliotheek, Ms. 74 G 37a, fol. 1v-2r. http://manuscripts.kb.nl/zoom/BYVANCKB%3Amimi_74g37a%3A001v_002r

the image with its patron. But Fouquet worked in Tours, not in Paris, and he may have never seen the manuscript to which he was contributing. Paradoxically, he could personalize the book but remain remote from its production because of the component-based system of manuscript production. The patron is in the presence of the Virgin, but the artist was not in the presence of the patron.

A related set of concerns was at play in the Trivulzio hours, likewise a high-end production. Probably commissioned by a member of the court of Charles the Bold around 1469, the Trivulzio hours includes many single-leaf miniatures. Its owner apparently wanted images by some of the most famous and great names, but these were artists who lived in different cities.[24] The mechanics of the modular method allowed him to piece together a manuscript with many more full-page miniatures than most other books of hours have, and allowed him to sample the wares of several of several well-known painters, thereby turning his book of hours into a gallery for the best contemporary artists. But this is not because the patron could only afford to embellish his book in stages, but because he apparently desired to have images by several of the most famous artists alive, and they worked in different cities. Painters who supplied miniatures for the Trivuzio Hours were Simon Marmion from Valenciennes; the Vienna Master of Mary of Burgundy, who presumably worked in Ghent; and Lieven van Lathem, who worked in Ghent and then later in Antwerp. They apparently sent their images in, as it were, to be included in the project. So while the nobility—super-rich who had inherited wealth—could use the single-leaf image to possess examples of many famous artists in a single work, the nouveaux riches—who earned their wealth through business and trade—used them to add bling as funds allowed.

5. Images for missals

While some images were added because they represented new objects of devotion that an owner wanted to possess, others were added because their predecessors had worn out. For example, the users of the Gouda

---

24   Thomas Kren, "The Trivulzio Hours and the Interurban Network of Luxury Book Production in the Burgundian Netherlands," in *Conference in Celebration of Anne Korteweg's 65th Birthday* (The Hague, Koninklijke Bibliotheek: unpublished, 2007).

Missal (HKB, Ms. 135 H 45, introduced above) gave it a new Crucifixion miniature (fig. 124).[25] This is the image that the priest would kiss during the performance of the mass, so it is not surprising that the original one in this book wore out around 1500, prompting the owners to replace it. The replacement leaf, now fol. 101 (with the image on the verso) is a singleton that has been made expressly for a missal, which are larger than books for personal devotion. It is possible that the ateliers existed specifically to replace worn-out canon pages for missals.

Fig. 125 Masters of Otto van Moerdrecht, Crucifixion miniature inserted as a canon image in a missal copied in Delft. Heidelberg, Universitätsbibliothek, Ms. Trübner 21, fol. 96v-97r. Image © Heidelberg, Universitätsbibliothek, all rights reserved.

One such source for canon pages was the so-called Master(s) of Otto van Moerdrecht.[26] Their name comes from one of their earliest known patrons. Otto van Moerdrecht, canon of Utrecht Cathedral, presented a copy of a theological work, the *Postilla in Prophetas* by Nicolaus de Lyra,

---

25 Crucifixion and beginning of the canon, with a printed initial. The Hague, Koninklijke Bibliotheek, Ms. 135 H 45, fol. 101v-102r. http://manuscripts.kb.nl/ zoom/BYVANCKB%3Amimi_135h45%3A101v_102r

26 For an overview of these artists' works, see van Bergen, *De Meesters van Otto van Moerdrecht*.

to the monastery of Nieuwlicht near Utrecht in 1424. This manuscript has distinctive painted decoration (which has been attributed to the Master of Otto van Moerdrecht) that reappears in books of hours, missals, and prestigious commissions for the next five decades. A single person could not have accomplished the large output of works in this style, so the "Master" of Otto van Moerdrecht has become the "Masters." Saskia van Bergen has deduced that a number of artists working in a related style painted the miniatures in this rather substantial group of manuscripts, largely based on templates and models. Moreover, Hanns Peter Neuheuser has identified a number of large Crucifixion images that these artists have produced, which were destined for missals.[27] These include one miniature preserved in a missal (the winter part) that had been copied in Delft (Heidelberg, UB, Ms. Trübner 21; fig. 125).

This disparity between decoration styles on either side of the gutter in Trübner 21 reveals that miniature came from a different source than the text.[28] The text pages are decorated in a Delft style from the 1440s, with sprigs of green leaves running along a linear armature, whereas the decoration around the miniature has blue, yellow and orange leaves, as well as marginal angels that comment mournfully on the main image. One finds these little angels most often in manuscripts illuminated in Utrecht, which is where Otto van Moerdrecht lived and where he hired his eponymous master. However, the text pages were decorated and presumably copied in Delft. Feasts in red in the calendar include "Augustini patris nostri sollempne festum" (August 28), which suggests that it was made at an Augustinian convent. The manuscript was most likely copied by the sisters at the convent of St. Agnes in Delft, who had an active manuscript atelier in the mid-fifteenth century, and who are known to have copied and decorated other manuscripts in Latin, including the Fagel Missal, which they made for their own use in 1459–60.

Although the missal was made in Delft, it was adapted for a convent in Amsterdam: that of the convent of St. Mary Magdalene.[29] Their

---

27 Neuheuser, "Die Kanonblätter aus der Schule des Moerdrecht-Meisters," pp. 187–214.

28 Wilfried Werner, ed. *Cimelia Heidelbergensia: 30 illuminierte Handschriften der Universitätsbibliothek Heidelberg* (Wiesbaden: Reichert, 1975), , pp. 25–26.

29 Marian Schilder, ed. *Amsterdamse Kloosters in de Middeleeuwen* (Amsterdam: Vossiuspers AUP, 1997), cat. 38, p. 185.

note of ownership survives on the inner cover: "Istud missale hiemale pertinet sanctimonialibus sancte Marie Magdalene in aemstelredam." This had originally been a convent of Franciscan women, but they reformed, an act that always assumes moving toward a more highly controlled enclosure and a more stringent set of rules. In this case, they became a convent of Canonesses Regular, who followed the rule of St. Augustine; whereas Franciscan sisters largely used the vernacular in their devotional books, Canonesses used Latin. Their reform therefore meant re-education, and with it, a new set of authoritative books. They received some of these books from established Augustinian convents. The Utrecht calendar already had a red entry for "Augustini patris nostri sollempne festum" (August 28), but the Translation of St. Mary Magdalene was added to the calendar for March 9 to make the book appropriate for its new home in Amsterdam. The convent in Delft may have sent the manuscript to their newly-reformed sisters in Amsterdam.

An examination of the binding (brown leather, blind stamped, over boards) indicates it may be from the fifteenth century, and perhaps the book's second binding. At any rate, the book must have been rebound when it entered the convent in Amsterdam. Perhaps these changes were necessary to turn the manuscript from a bedraggled hand-me-down into a semi-bespoke luxurious gift. Several structural adjustments, which were made in the fifteenth century, required rebinding. I assess these below.

The full-page miniature—the Crucifixion folio—does not look as worn as the facing text folio, with the *Te igitur* incipit. That folio is worn from handling, and from moisture stains that may have resulted from being sprinkled with holy water. I propose that the Masters of Otto van Moerdrecht may have created this Crucifixion miniature in order to replace one that had been severely worn, and that the original image would have had wear matching that of the facing text folio. As the manuscript may not have been made expressly for the sisters in Amsterdam, but only adapted later for their use, it is possible that the book received a new Crucifixion miniature at the time it was given to the newly reformed canonesses. Thus, when the sisters in Amsterdam received their new missal, it might have been refreshed with a new miniature, one that hadn't yet been kissed and manhandled.

The first folio is a singleton sewn and glued to the beginning of the book; it consists of original parchment, with original ruling, but was harvested from elsewhere in the book. It has an enormous hole in the center, which is why the scribe avoided writing on it in the first instance. It provided, nonetheless, the physical support for a new dedication page, inscribed some time in the fifteenth century and mounted at the beginning of the book. It now bears testimony to a promise: the owners of the book have agreed to say masses for the members of a family every week. It reads:

> In primis servetur memoria Benefactorum dominus huius. Tem tenemur omni hebdomador ad quatuor missas scilitet inprimis ad tres pro magistro Johanne AEmilij et pro Elizabetha et Lobbrecht AEmilij duabus sororibus eius ad placitum legentis et ad unam missam pro Elisabetha Grebber et parentibus suis etiam ad placitum segmentis. Item senietur memoria ter in hebdomada cut collecta pro defunctis scilicet secunda quarta et sexta feria inprimis pro Juniore Jacobo Nicolai. Item sub eadem memoria pro Maria et Aleyde Johannis Godulphi et parentibus earum. Item pro Symone Jacobi et Katherina Nicolai uxore eius. Item pro Velsen Gerardi begutte benefactricis.

> Of primary importance, this [book] is to preserve the memory of its benefactors. The first three are held every week for four masses scilitet for Master Johan Emilij and two sisters Elizabeth and Lobbrecht Emilij his plea to the reader and one mass for Elizabeth Grebber and their parents to the right segments. Also senietur memory collected three times a week just for the dead, especially for the youngest, James, Nicholas, of course, Wednesdays and Fridays. Again, Mary and Aleyde of John Godulphi and under the same memory for their parents. Also for Simon James and Katherine Nicholas, his wife. Also for Velsen Gerard begutte benefactricis.

These benefactors have turned a used book into a tool for their memory and salvation. It is likely that the sheet was inscribed and attached to the book when it went to Amsterdam. The sisters there, who had previously been Franciscans, were now Augustinians, and therefore were required to function in Latin and to perform the daily offices. Their status as Augustinians made them more attractive to benefactors, who often considered the Latin prayers of more highly controlled Augustinians to have greater effect than those of more loosely controlled Franciscans.

Fig. 126 Masters of Otto van Moerdrecht, Crucifixion miniature inserted as a canon
         image in a missal copied in Hulsbergen (near Hattem). Enschede, Rijksmuseum
         Twenthe, inv. no. 381, fol. 125v-126r (photography James H. Marrow, Princeton
         University). Image © Rijksmuseum Twenthe, Enschede, CC BY 4.0.

Whether the Masters of Otto van Moerdrecht made the miniature
for the book when it was new or to replace a worn-out one, it is clear
that they were supplying loose canon pages for missals and did quite
a swift trade in them. They apparently made one for the Brothers of
the Common Life of St. Jerome (Hiëronymusberg) in Hulsbergen (near
Hattem) in 1457 (now Enschede, RMT, inv. no. 381; fig. 126). According
to a note on the first folio of that manuscript, the brothers made the
manuscript for the Tertiaries of St. Agnes in Amersfoort in 1457.[30] The
manuscript contains penwork initials with pen-flourishes in a style

---

30 Enschede, RMT, inv. no. 381, fol.1r: "Missale hoc pertinet conventui sororum
    domus sancte agnetis amersfordie. Scriptum in congregacione fratrum montis
    sancti Jheronimi prope hattem per manus Gherardi Amstel de arnem presbitri
    fratris eiusdem congregacionis. Procuratum cura et sollicitudine domini Augustini
    de varen de mechlinia. iiii rectoris et confessoris sororum domus sancte Agnetis
    prefate anno domini m° cccc° lvii. Cuius anima requiescat in pace Amen."

associated with the Brothers of the Common Life of St. Jerome. Such penwork appears, for example, on the *Te igitur* page across from the Crucifixion. In their penwork the brothers reveal no ability to depict the human figure, but only to make iterative abstract designs. For that reason, they relied on professional artists outside the monastery to provide the Crucifixion, the centerpiece of the missal. The Moerdrecht Masters supplied the miniature with a painted border. As with several examples I have analyzed above, here the brothers were not content to leave the painted decoration as is, clashing with their own penwork across the gutter. Their solution was to add some more penwork to the margins of the Crucifixion miniature. This made at least some show to integrate it visually, and at the same time it served a purpose: the ornate cruciform designs they added to the bottom and side margins gave the priest a target for his kiss during the ritual osculation of the image.

6. Other single-leaf miniatures

Fig. 127 Masters of the Delft Grisailles, Virgin and Child, full-page miniature inserted in a book of hours opposite the *Obsecro te.* Brussels, Koninklijke Bibliotheek van België, Ms. 21696, 116v-117r. Image © Koninklijke Bibliotheek van België, all rights reserved.

Fig. 128 Book of hours with text and decoration from Utrecht or the Eastern
Netherlands, and a miniature added later depicting St. Andrew, made by the
Masters of the Delft Grisailles. Nijmegen, Radboud Universiteit, Ms. 283, fol.
204v-205r. © Radboud Universiteitsbibliotheek, CC BY 4.0.

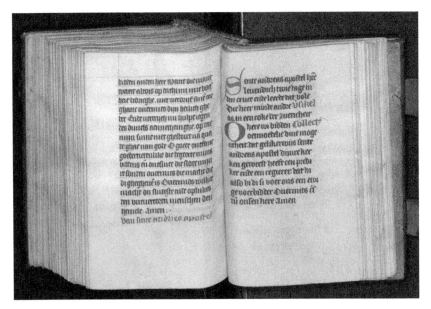

Fig. 129 Book of hours with text and decoration from Utrecht or the Eastern
Netherlands, and a miniature added later, inscribed on the back (204r) with a
prayer to St. Andrew. Nijmegen, Radboud Universiteit, Ms. 283 fol. 203v-204r.
© Radboud Universiteitsbibliotheek, CC BY 4.0.

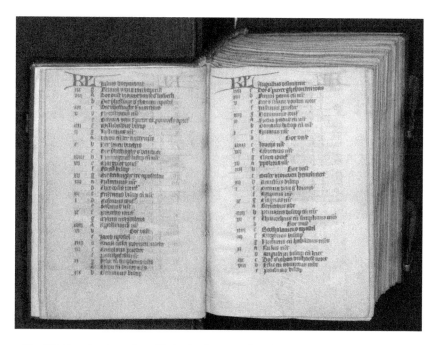

Fig. 130 Opening from the added calendar, revealing St. Hippolytus, patron of Delft, in red. Nijmegen, Radboud Universiteit, Ms. 283 fol. 4v-5r. © Radboud Universiteitsbibliotheek, CC BY 4.0.

A book of hours that can stylistically be attributed to the convent of St. Agnes in Delft tells a story in dirt. Like many books of hours, this one contains a copy of the *Obsecro te*. And like many copies of the *Obsecro te*, this one accompanies an image of the Virgin, a full-page miniature en grisaille attributed to the so-called Masters of the Delft Grisailles (Brussels, KB, 21696, 116v-117r; fig. 127).[31] One can see through the context of the book, however, that the image was not part of its original production. Whereas the text folio—the right side of the opening—has been thoroughly darkened through use, the image, while not in pristine condition, has been little handled. Therefore the owner inserted the image

---

31 A complete overview of these artists has yet to be written. Until then, consult Gloria K. Fiero, "Smith Ms. 36: A Study in Fifteenth Century Manuscript Illumination," *The Courier (Syracuse University Library Associates)* 13 (1976), pp. 3–27, who discusses a manuscript with Delft grisailles that is now HKB 79 K 1. See also Marta Osterstrom-Renger, "The Netherlandish Grisaille Miniatures: Some Unexplored Aspects," *Wallraf-Richartz-Jahrbuch* 44, pp. 145–73; and Anne Margreet W. As-Vijvers, *Tuliba Collection: Catalogue of Manuscripts and Miniatures from the Fifteenth and Sixteenth Centuries* (Hilversum: Tuliba Collection, 2014), no. 7, pp. 64–68.

well after reading the prayer dozens or even hundreds of times. Perhaps adding the image was a response to reading, an attempt to heighten the interest of a well-thumbed and very familiar prayer. Or perhaps the owner added images when he could afford them.

A book of hours introduced above, Nijmegen, UB, Ms. 283, also bears an added leaf made by the so-called Masters of the Delft Grisailles (fig. 128). These artists specialized in making single-leaf miniatures, blank on the back, that could be incorporated into books of hours. Originally made in Utrecht or the Eastern Netherlands, this book was probably brought to Delft for its updates. Whereas in the previous example, the image was left blank on the back, in this case the owner took advantage of the empty parchment that the grisaille afforded, and he or she treated the sheet as a page to be inscribed and integrated (fig. 129). A rubric was added in the bottom margin of the miniature (*van sente Johan Evangelist*), refers not to the picture, which represents St. Andrew, but rather to the prayer on the following folio. The mid-century scribe, probably from Delft, inscribed a prayer to St. Andrew on the back of his image. To make the integration complete, he or she has scratched out part of the rubric on fol. 203v and inscribed "Andries apostel" over the palimpsest. It is likely that the owner chose this particular spot in the manuscript to insert St. Andrew because it falls in a series of suffrages to male martyrs, and because and the previous text finishes at the bottom of the verso folio, which mean that an extra folio could easily be interpolated.

When the owner rebound the manuscript to incorporate the image of St. Andrew, he or she apparently also took the opportunity to give the manuscript a new calendar. The old one, with saints from Utrecht or further east, was discarded, and a new one for Delft was added. This added calendar, with one month per folio side, is written in very condensed script and with a different text block than the rest of the manuscript, which reveals that it was made in a different campaign of work (fig. 130). This calendar is nearly identical with one in HKB, Ms. 131 H 10, a manuscript probably made in the convent of St. Agnes in Delft in the 1420s. Sisters in this convent may also have updated the manuscript now in Nijmegen and inserted the grisaille miniature. If so, then both of my examples with miniatures added by these painters (BKB, Ms. 21696 and Nijmegen, UB, Ms. 283) can be associated with this convent, and the possibility must remain open that the grey miniatures originated there.

Another Delft book of hours was updated by the Masters of the Dark Eyes, who were probably secular professionals (for the manuscripts they made do not emphasize particular confessors, such as Francis or Augustine, that would reveal a monastic patron). This book of hours is now in Yale's Beinecke Library (Ms. 434).[32] Originally copied in Delft around 1480–1500, probably at one of the female convents in that city, the book has a calendar for Delft and distinctive red and blue Delft penwork (in the lower tiers of the hierarchy of decoration), plus painted border decoration (in the upper tiers). For example, the original painted decoration appears at the openings for the canonical hours, which also have five-line painted and gilt initials (fig. 131).[33] The original campaign of work also included painted nine-line initials at the openings to the major texts, such as the Hours of the Virgin, although it's unclear whether female monastics executed these, or whether they farmed them out to local professionals (fig. 132).

The convent that copied the book of hours and supplied this basic decoration, did not, however, create the full-page miniatures; rather, an early owner added these later, and their introduction caused a major disruption to the decorative program. For this manuscript, at least two different artists within the group called the "Masters of the Dark Eyes" painted highly colorful full-page miniatures complete with gold and painted border decoration involving trompe-l'oeil strewn flowers, and gold acanthus (fig. 132).[34]

32 Gerard Achten, Das Christliche Gebetbuch im Mittelalter: Andachts- und Stundenbücher in Handschrift und Frühdruck (Berlin: Staatsbibliothek Preussischer Kulturbesitz, 1987), p. 102. A description of the manuscript, including a collation, appears in Barbara A. Shailor, *Catalogue of Medieval and Renaissance Manuscripts in the Beinecke Rare Book and Manuscript Library, Yale University*, 3 vols. (Binghamton: Medieval & Renaissance Texts & Studies, 1984), vol. II, pp. 366–68. Shailor describes the manuscript's stratigraphy differently than I do. Where she sees three campaigns of work I see two: first, the historiated initials and penwork borders (1480–1500); and second, the full-page miniatures made by several Dark Eye Masters, who also executed the overpainted borders (ca. 1500–1510).

33 End of vespers of the Hours of the Virgin, with penwork border on one side (verso), and beginning of compline with a five-line painted and gilt initial and painted border on three sides (recto). Script and decoration applied in Delft. New Haven, Yale University, Beinecke Rare Book and Manuscript Library, Ms. 434, fol. 49v-50r. http://brbl-dl.library.yale.edu/vufind/Record/3592299

34 According to Broekhuijsen, *The Masters of the Dark Eyes: Late Medieval Manuscript Painting in Holland*, the added miniatures belong to the "Margaret of Austria" group within the Masters of the Dark Eyes.

Fig. 132 Opening at the incipit of the Hours of the Virgin, with the Adoration of the Magi (full-page miniature executed by the Masters of the Dark Eyes on added parchment), and a text folio with script, penwork decoration, and a historiated initial executed in Delft, with borders overpainted to match the facing folio. New Haven, Yale University, Beinecke Rare Book and Manuscript Library, Ms. 434, fol. 14v-15r. Image in the Public Domain.

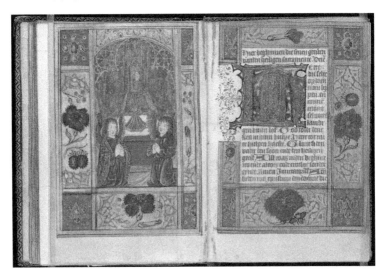

Fig. 133 Opening at the Seven Hours of the Holy Sacrament, with the Adoration of the Host by Angels (full-page miniature executed by the Masters of the Dark Eyes on added parchment), and a text folio with script, penwork decoration, and a painted and gilt initial executed in Delft, with borders overpainted to match the facing folio. New Haven, Yale University, Beinecke Rare Book and Manuscript Library, Ms. 434, fol. 55v-56r. Image in the Public Domain.

Fig. 134 Opening at the Vigil for the Dead, with the Raising of Lazarus (full-page miniature executed by the Masters of the Dark Eyes on added parchment), and a text folio with script, penwork decoration, and a painted and gilt initial executed in Delft, with borders overpainted to match the facing folio. New Haven, Yale University, Beinecke Rare Book and Manuscript Library, Ms. 434, fol. 149v-150r. image in the Public Domain.

When they added the miniatures around 1500–1510, suddenly the facing text pages were not decorated with sufficient grandeur, and the borders had to be overpainted in order to maintain visual continuity with the full-page miniatures. In other words, their intervention had elevated the miniatures, so they needed now to also elevate the borders in order to maintain the hierarchy. Original vines painted on the bare parchment still poke through the layer of fully-painted colorfields that the Masters of the Dark Eyes painted on top of them.

The addition of full-page miniatures disrupted the ecosystem of the book by shifting the hierarchy of decoration. When the Masters of the Dark Eyes added images, they had to raise the intensity of the decoration on the facing folios; otherwise, their bold blocks of color would have made the existing penwork decoration look extremely insubstantial. They systematically elevated the hierarchy of decoration throughout the codex. One opening they doctored up introduces a somewhat rare text, "The Seven Hours of the Holy Sacrament," whose incipit appears on fol. 56r (fig. 133). This text was copied by the monastic atelier in Delft, and then the Masters of the Dark Eyes supplied a relevant full-page miniature, in this case, one depicting angels adoring the sacrament in a monstrance on an altar. These masters delight in filling the page with color and gold, and do so by dividing the border space into compartments. I suspect that painting small, compartmentalized objects—strawberries, flowers, and jewels—took less effort than figurative painting would, and less effort than a continuous design would have. Making such compartments also allows the painter to break up the space into contrasting yellow and blue fields, thereby adding more color and visual interest to the page than a solid color would have. The artists added an analogous border on the facing text page, thereby overpainting the existing decoration.

The Masters of the Dark Eyes applied similar treatment to each of the four major texts in the manuscript. For the Vigil for the Dead, they added a miniature depicting Christ raising Lazarus (fig. 134). Here again the illuminators carefully coordinated the new decoration around the text folio so that it perfectly matches the decoration around the miniature, again relying on compartments in order to break their painting into smaller, easier-to-handle components. In each case, they left only a sprig of the original decoration—that immediately around the initial— because their linear, compartmentalized designs would have been difficult to fit around the jagged edge of the letter. The somewhat low quality of the painted border results in half-sized compartments with truncated jewels, as if the artists were pasting on wallpaper that came with motifs in fixed sizes. What they lacked in skill, they made up for with colorful exuberance. Their urban clientele must have appreciated this flamboyance.

One important question remains: did the owner of this book of hours take this manuscript to one of the Masters of the Dark Eyes and commission the added decoration? Or is it possible that the Masters of the Dark Eyes bought up used books of hours and then refurbished them, to add value and make them appealing to their socially mobile clientele? That question is unanswerable without further evidence. I can say, however, that the Masters of the Dark Eyes must have tested their market and responded by adding lots of color and gold quickly. They also understood the importance of visual unity across an opening, so that their large colorful miniatures would always be framed by even larger colorful borders.

7. Packages of images

Fig. 135 Opening at the Hours of the Holy Spirit in a book of hours inscribed in Delft, with an added full-page miniature depicting the Mass of St. Gregory. The Hague, Meermanno Museum, Ms. 10 F 2, fol. 133v-134r. Image © Meermanno Museum, CC BY 4.0.

Fig. 136 Opening at an indulgenced prayer to the Virgin in a book of hours inscribed in Delft, with a blank left for an image that was never filled in. The Hague, Meermanno Museum, Ms. 10 F 2, fol. 162v-163r. Image © Meermanno Museum, CC BY 4.0.

Fig. 137 Opening at the Hours of the Virgin, with an added full-page miniature depicting the Annunciation. The Hague, Meermanno Museum, Ms. 10 F 2, fol. 14v-15r. Image © Meermanno Museum, CC BY 4.0.

Some makers of full-page miniatures must have included the Mass of St. Gregory in "standard packages" of images to be sold off the shelf to owners of existing books. Evidence of such a package appears in a book of hours made in or around Delft in the fourth quarter of the fifteenth century (The Hague, Meermanno Museum, Ms. 10 F 2; fig. 135). This manuscript reveals not one set of post-production adjustments, but two. Different owners probably made the distinct sets of changes. The second of the two sets of changes involved the addition of the Mass of St. Gregory and other full-page images that are closely related stylistically. An analysis of the original parts of the manuscript and the two sets of additions reveals layers of personalization.

When the book was originally planned, the scribe had left blank folios on the versos before the major text divisions, which were ruled for the size of the anticipated images. These images were to be integral components of the book's structure, but these were never painted in (fig. 136). Instead, a later owner added a group of four images made in a different campaign of work: three standard subjects to preface the texts that define the book of hours—an Annunciation to face the Hours of the Virgin (fig. 137), a Crucifixion to face the Hours of the Cross, and

David playing his harp to face the Seven Penitential Psalms—and a full-page Mass of St. Gregory, which has been added to preface the Hours of the Holy Spirit (The Hague, Meermanno Museum, Ms. 10 F 2; fig. 135). Whereas the artist who supplied the images assumed that books of hours would contain the *Adoro te*, this book of hours lacks that text. The manuscript, which may have been made as early as 1460, was not supplied with a copy of the Verses of St. Gregory, but that did not stop the (later) owner from adding a full-page Mass of St. Gregory. The fact that the four images are all in the same style and have the same kind of border decoration suggests that the owner bought them as a group. Miniaturists made packages of full-page illuminations of standard subjects for books of hours, packets that patrons could buy to instantly illuminate their prayerbooks. Perhaps by 1460 or so, when these miniatures were made, the Mass of St. Gregory was simply considered a standard subject that no book owner would want to do without.

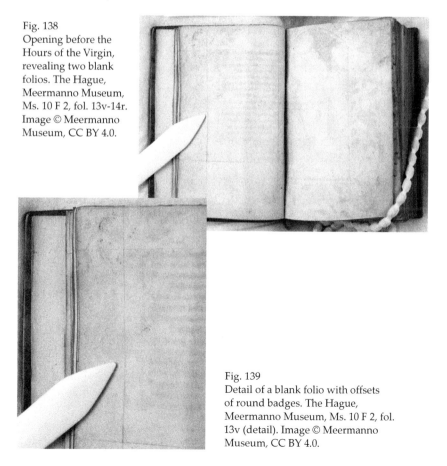

Fig. 138
Opening before the Hours of the Virgin, revealing two blank folios. The Hague, Meermanno Museum, Ms. 10 F 2, fol. 13v-14r. Image © Meermanno Museum, CC BY 4.0.

Fig. 139
Detail of a blank folio with offsets of round badges. The Hague, Meermanno Museum, Ms. 10 F 2, fol. 13v (detail). Image © Meermanno Museum, CC BY 4.0.

I suspect that the person who added these images was the book's second owner, for a previous owner had sewn badges to several blank folios that had previously prefaced these texts (fig. 138 and fig. 139).[35] Offsets from these badges, however, have not been imprinted on the backs of the miniatures. This indicates that someone removed the badges before adding the miniatures. Perhaps the second owner was trying to erase the signs of the previous owner's use and add her own instead.

8. Images removed from one manuscript and inserted into another

Sometimes it is clear that a miniature was simply not intended for its present manuscript. An Italian book of hours now in The Hague (HKB, Ms. 133 D 15, fol. 65v-66r) has miniatures made in the Southern Netherlands. Of course, it is perfectly conceivable that a manuscript made in one place could have images made in another. In fact, such combinations speak to the very essence of the separation of ateliers and division of labor at the heart of this study. However, the images now in this manuscript have obviously been removed from a different book. This is apparent from the relative amount of dirt visible on the left and right sides of the opening to the Office of the Dead (fig. 140).[36] The miniature has been thoroughly touched and handled, but not by the owner of the Italian book of hours, whose text leaves are pristine. Likewise, the miniature depicting the Visitation has been inserted as a recto, even though it has clearly been designed as a verso (as the wider border is on the left side of the miniature), which indicates that

---

35 On sewing badges into manuscript prayerbooks, see Asperen, *Pelgrimstekens op Perkament.* I would nuance van Asperen's claim implicit in the entire book that all such badges are "pilgrims' badges." Rather I believe many of the round badges bearing images of the Lamb of God, the Crucifixion, Resurrection, and other sacramental themes, were souvenirs of having taken the Eucharist and therefore have little to do with pilgrimage. See Kathryn M. Rudy, "Sewing the Body of Christ: Eucharist Wafer Souvenirs Stitched into Fifteenth-Century Manuscripts, Primarily in the Netherlands," *Journal of Historians of Netherlandish Art,* January 2016.

36 Mass of the Dead, full-page miniature made in the Netherlands, facing the incipit of the Office of the Dead, copied in Italy. The Hague, Koninklijke Bibliotheek, Ms. 133 D 15, fol. 65v-66r. http://manuscripts.kb.nl/zoom/BYVANCKB%3Amimi_133d1 5%3A065v_066r

its current position was not originally intended (fig. 141).[37] Someone has apparently cannibalized a Southern Netherlandish book of hours in order to provide the vital organs for this Italian book, which was designed—as the hierarchy of decoration shows—without full-page miniatures at the major openings.

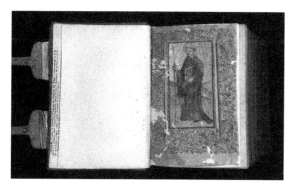

Fig. 142
Male saint, full-page miniature inserted as a frontispiece (1400–1450). 's-Heerenberg, The Netherlands, Collection Dr. J. H. van Heek, Huis Bergh Foundation, Ms. 11, fol. 1r. Image © The Huis Bergh Foundation, CC BY 4.0.

Fig. 143 Descent of the Holy Spirit, historiated initial, 1250–1300, pasted into a book's back cover. The Hague, Koninklijke Bibliotheek, Ms. 133 E 22. Image © Koninklijke Bibliotheek—the National Library of The Netherlands, CC BY 4.0.

---

37 Visitation, full-page miniature made in the Netherlands, facing the incipit of prime of the Hours of the Virgin. The Hague, Koninklijke Bibliotheek, Ms. 133 D 15, fol. 112v-113r. http://manuscripts.kb.nl/zoom/BYVANCKB%3Amimi_133d15%3A112v _113r

Images might come from a book that has, for whatever reason, lost its value. When such redistribution of images occurs, the miniatures land in a new context and take on a new role. Such is the case with an image depicting a standing male saint dressed in the garb of an abbot. It was removed from a manuscript, possibly a prayerbook, and inserted as a "frontispiece" to a different book, which is still in its medieval cover (fig. 142).[38] In other words, early modern collectors were not the first to cut apart manuscripts, but late medieval owners also cut images out of books. Likewise, a book of hours in Dutch (HKB, Ms. 133 E 22) was made in Utrecht in the third quarter of the fifteenth century and contains a package of full-page miniatures at the major openings (fig. above, 133 E 22, fol. 101v-102r). It has several other added things. One of the owners has pasted to the inside back cover a historiated initial made in France around 1250–1300 showing the Descent of the Holy Spirit over the assembled apostles, who grasp books and gasp (fig. 143). Before someone decided to trim it and append it to this manuscript, the image was already several hundred years old. As is the nature of such acts, this one is impossible to date with exactitude. One can imagine that a Dutch speaker who owned a thirteenth-century French prayerbook in Latin would have had limited use for it, if he read only Middle Dutch. The French images may have been like relics, to be divided from the body of the book and circulated around. At least one recipient decided to keep the loose treasure in his prayerbook to protect it.[39]

---

38 Korteweg, *Catalogue of Medieval Manuscripts and Incunabula at Huis Bergh Castle in 's-Heerenberg*, cat. 50, pp. 100–01.

39 In the context of discussing full-page miniatures and their placement, Kathleen L. Scott, "Design, Decoration and Illustration," in *Book Production and Publishing in Britain, 1375–1475*, ed. Jeremy Griffiths and Derek Albert Pearsall, *Cambridge Studies in Publishing and Printing History* (Cambridge and New York: Cambridge University Press, 1989), pp. 31–64, p. 56, n. 25, lists manuscripts with 3–47 images added at the front: "York Minster Library Ms Add. 2, with 47 pictures at the front [sic, kmr]; BKB IV 1095, with 21; Rennes BM, Ms. 22 and its detached part in London, British Library, Royal Ms 2.A.XVIII, with 16; London, British Library, Add. Ms 65100 (formerly Upholland College, Ms 42), with 15; Hours of the Duchess of Clarence (whereabouts unknown), with 8; Cambridge, Fitz, Ms. 3–1979, and NLW, Ms 17520, both with 7; Cambridge TC Ms B.11.7, with 3. Oxford, Bodleian Library, Ms Lat. Liturg. f. 2 has a group of six full-page miniatures at the front and five Memorials with pictures at the end as part of additional material to a Franco-Flemish core text." Some of the manuscripts Scott lists have become repositories for images removed from other books. To my mind, this explains why such images disrupt the hierarchy of decoration.

Fig. 144
Folio from the Murthly Hours, with a historiated initial enclosing a female patron kneeling before an altar. Edinburgh, National Library of Scotland, Ms. 21000, fol. 149v. Image © National Library of Scotland, all rights reserved.

Fig. 145
Folio from the Murthly Hours, formerly blank page, with a series of added inscriptions in French and Gaelic. Edinburgh, National Library of Scotland, Ms. 21000, fol. Iiv. Image © National Library of Scotland, all rights reserved.

Fig. 146
Lot's wife turning into a pillar of salt. English miniature repurposed for a French book of hours used in Scotland (the Murthly Hours). Edinburgh, National Library of Scotland, Ms. 21000, fol. 5r. Image © National Library of Scotland, all rights reserved.

Fig. 147
Entombment of Christ. English miniature repurposed for a French book of hours used in Scotland, with two curtains sewn to the margins (the Murthly Hours). Edinburgh, National Library of Scotland, Ms. 21000, fol. 21r. Image © National Library of Scotland, all rights reserved.

There were other motivations, too, for rehabilitating old miniatures. Sometimes old, discarded miniatures were of higher quality than anything that the book owner could now commission from scratch. That may have been the reason that the Scottish owner of the Murthly Hours harvested images from another book type (Edinburgh, NLS, Ms. 21000).[40] But they were not the only additions. The book has been Frankensteined together from several components of varying vintages. For instance, the main core of the texts that define the book of hours were copied in Paris in the 1280s, and exported to Scotland. These parts of the book contain original illuminations depicting a female patron in prayer. John Higgit argues that it was made for the supplicant pictured on fol. 149v, whom he identifies as an English woman named Joan de Valence (fig. 144). She married in or shortly after 1292. Her father, William de Valence (a half-brother of King Henry II of England), had been born in France and maintained ties there (he was in Paris in 1286, for example). I note, however, that the woman in prayer lacks a coat of arms or other sufficiently personalizing details to verify the status of the image as a portrait. As books of hours were often made as wedding gifts, it is unlikely that a book would be written so far advance of a marriage. Assigning ownership of the book to Joan de Valence is hasty.

While the book's earliest ownership remains obscure, the book provides some clues about its later owners. Obits in the calendar for Sir John Stuart (Stewart), lord of Lorne (d. 1421), and his wife Isabella, Lady of Lorne (d.1439) demonstrate that the book was brought to Scotland by the early fifteenth century. It also contains layers of additions on the blank flyleaves: an added prayer in French, followed by one of the earliest inscriptions in Gaelic, the latter were written in the late fourteenth or early fifteenth century and are contemporaneous with

---

40 John Higgitt, *The Murthly Hours: Devotion, Literacy and Luxury in Paris, England and the Gaelic West* (London: British Library and University of Toronto Press in association with the National Library of Scotland, 2000). For one analysis of the stratigraphy of the Murthly Hours, see De Kesel, "Use and Reuse of Manuscripts and Miniatures. Observations on Pasted-in, Recycled and Removed Miniatures and Text Leaves in Some Late Medieval Flemish Illuminated Manuscripts Related to 'La Flora,'" pp. 48–85, pl. 4–5; Stanton, "Design, Devotion, and Durability in Gothic Prayerbooks," considers the recycled images in the manuscript.

the additions in the calendar (fig. 145). These Gaelic additions further indicate that the manuscript was in Scotland at an early date.

Original parts of the manuscript include a calendar, the Hours of the Virgin, the Hours of the Holy Spirit, the Penitential Psalms, a Litany of the Saints, the Gradual Psalms and the Office of the Dead. An early owner—probably one in Britain—added a series of full-page miniatures to it, of the sort one associates with prefatory images to a psalter. Specifically this packet includes 23 full-page illuminations painted by three English artists, ca. 1260–1280 that were evidently made in a different campaign of work from the French body of the prayerbook. These illuminations may have been harvested from a psalter. They depict scenes from Genesis, the Infancy of Christ and the Passion, respectively. One of the miniatures—which shows Lot's wife turning into a pillar of salt as she looks back on Sodom—appears to have been torn rather violently from its original manuscript (fig. 146). Parchment is extremely tough, and it would have required considerable force to rend it asunder.

By applying the full-page miniatures to the book of hours, the owner was adding an image type associated with an earlier kind of prayerbook (the psalter) to a newer form of book. The owner(s) also considered the book as a site of expansion and experimentation. One owner has also sewn curtains to the top margins of all of the miniatures, thereby adding another physical layer to the book. Lifting the curtain to reveal the image below creates the tension and catharsis of revelation, and adds a new ritual to the acts of seeing, reading, and contemplating. However, the owner has treated one of the miniatures differently: the Entombment (fig. 147). Instead of sewing in a curtain only to the top, he or she has sewn a curtain at the bottom margin as well. It is as if, prompted by the actions of Christ's friends who wrap him in a shroud and tuck him into his sepulcher in the image, the user has swaddled the image in shrouds, so that he or she can draw the two textiles together and lay Jesus into manuscript bed.

Old images often found new homes in books of hours, which were essentially expandable and accommodating. To take another example, a book of hours whose core was written and illuminated in North Holland has full-page illuminations that were harvested from another book (Leiden, Ltk 289; fig. 148).

Fig. 148 Opening of a book of hours from Haarlem, with an inserted full-page miniature
          depicting the Virgin and Child with female donor. Leiden, Universiteitsbibliotheek,
          Ms. Ltk 289, fol. 13v-14r. © Leiden, Universiteitsbibliotheek, CC BY 4.0.

Fig. 149
Christ before Pilate, full-page
miniature, inserted in a book of
hours from Haarlem. Leiden,
Universiteitsbibliotheek, Ms. Ltk
289, fol. 71r. Image © Leiden,
Universiteitsbibliotheek, CC BY 4.0.

This manuscript was probably copied in Haarlem, where it was decorated with penwork and painted/gild borders at the major text openings. The penwork is similar to that found in the Missal of the Canons Regular of Haarlem, and the painted decoration has been classified as early "bunches-of-twigs" typical of Haarlem in the 1440s.[41] At some point in the fifteenth century an owner had the book taken apart in order to incorporate 11 full-page colored grisaille miniatures. Although grisaille miniatures later became a specialty associated with Delft, these miniatures appear to have been imported from the south, either from the Southern Netherlands or from Northern France. Miniatures from the south such as these became the models for the so-called Masters of the Delft Grisailles. In this case, however, they were removed from some other book in order to embellish this Haarlem book of hours.

A different manuscript had hosted the miniatures, and the owner (or the binder) harvested them from that book. Perhaps the miniatures were in a Latin book of hours, which somehow ended up in Haarlem, where few lay people could read Latin. Vernacular prayerbooks were the norm in the Northern Netherlands of the fifteenth century, but Latin prevailed in the Southern Netherlands and Northern France. Thus, the miniatures were the only valuable component of the book, so the rest was discarded.

In their original manuscript, the full-page grisaille miniatures were all bound as verso pages. One can see, for example, that the folio with the miniature depicting Christ before Pilate has now been inserted as a recto, but it previously had a different orientation to its book (Leiden, UB, Ms. Ltk 289; fig. 149). The vertical band of dirt along the outer edge has been deposited by the miniature's previous binding, where it was inserted as a verso. It is uncommon for miniatures to appear in a book as rectos. That they are rectos in this book is an indication that the book was not originally designed to have full-page miniatures. Not all of these miniatures ended up in ideal places, and some of the texts don't have a picture to preface the opening, and some of the images preface prayers that aren't quite right. For example, the Hours of the Virgin is prefaced by an image of the patron venerating the Virgin and Child, where one would expect to find an Annunciation. An image of

---

41   Korteweg, *Kriezels, Aubergines en Takkenbossen*, p. 107.

the Betrayal accompanies the Hours of the Cross (fol. 59v-60r) where one would expect the Crucifixion. Other Passion images are distributed throughout the rest of the book, without much regard to what texts they accompany. For example, the Agony in the Garden has been placed opposite the incipit of the Seven Penitential Psalms (fol. 121v-122r).

The manuscript from which the owner harvested the miniatures was slightly smaller than Ltk 289. Therefore the binder has added strips of parchment to some of the leaves in order to extend them. Such an extension is glued to the bottom of the image depicting a woman kneeling before the standing Virgin and Child (fol. 13v, as above). This image shows the woman wearing a French outfit and hairdo; she is different from the presumably Dutch owner of the new prayerbook. These are all indications that the images were not planned for this book, and that the book was not originally planned to have images, but that someone fitted them in later as best he could.

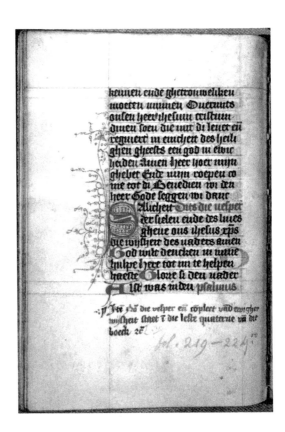

Fig. 150
Note written in the fifteenth century indicating where one can find the text for vespers and compline. Leiden, Universiteitsbibliotheek, Ms. Ltk 289, fol. 112v. © Leiden, Universiteitsbibliotheek, CC BY 4.0.

All these parts were bound in the late fifteenth century in a panel-stamped binding. Although one is tempted to call it an "original" binding because it is from the fifteenth century and therefore roughly contemporary with the book, it may well be the book's second binding. This would mean that the owner rebound it to accommodate the miniatures, but the binder has placed the quires out of order! One can see that this error was made already in the fifteenth century from a note written in a fifteenth-century hand on fol. 112v (fig. 150). The note reads: "vespers and complines of the Hours of Eternal Wisdom are in the last quire of this book." The quire to which the note refers has been attached after an added section (fol. 212–218), which contains suffrages. Rather than having the book rebound once again, the owner chose to simply add a note indicating where one could find the continuation of the text.

Fig. 151
Presentation of Christ in the Temple, full-page miniature on parchment, added to a later manuscript on paper. 's-Heerenberg, The Netherlands, Collection Dr. J. H. van Heek, Huis Bergh Foundation, Ms. 3 (inv. no. 301), fol. 4v-5r. Image © The Huis Bergh Foundation, CC BY 4.0.

A processional made for a community of friars reveals a different reason for harvesting older manuscripts ('s-Heerenberg, HB, Ms. 3). The friars may have made this manuscript themselves, for their own use in the first quarter of the sixteenth century. As it contains processions for "Beate Marie de Camberone" (fol. 50r), and prayers to St. Pharaïldis (fol. 64v), St. Gislenus (fol. 66v), and St. Hubert (fol. 67v), it may have been made by the friars of St. Truiden, which is equidistant from Cambron-Saint-Vincent and Saint-Hubert. The friars did the best they could with the skills and materials they had at hand. In the first quarter of the sixteenth century, printing was fast replacing hand-written books, and skills for making manuscript were on the decline. Parchment production may have also been declining, or else was simply overshadowed by the much cheaper material of paper whose production was stimulated by the printing industries. The friars made their new manuscript on paper, which has been bitten by the caustic iron gall ink. They applied red and blue penwork as best they could, but stiffly, and the results form networks of uninspired geometric forms. Making figurative imagery would have been hopeless. The book opens with the ceremonial procession for the purification of the Virgin, and instead of attempting to depict the Virgin afresh, they found a used image depicting the Presentation of Christ in the Temple (fig. 151).[42] This inserted image was made in the previous century (c. 1450–1460), on parchment not paper, and probably for a book of hours. Measuring 127x81 mm, it was about the same size as the processional and therefore worked in terms of scale.

One of the most dramatic cannibalized manuscripts involves the body of Christ. An early sixteenth-century printed missal needed a canon page. Rather than make one on paper—which is not very durable, and would wear out quickly under the repeated wear, as the priest kissed the image once during every mass—the printer or an early user has taken a much easier image of Christ crucified (fig. 152).[43] He has used a twelfth-century canon page. Paper had forced obsolescence built into its very material, which made it unsuitable for a missal. The early user realized this, and wanted a kissable image with proven endurance.

C. Adding quires

As I have shown above, singletons—if they have a tab that can fold around a quire and be stitched in with the other leaves—can be added into the binding of a book. A singleton with a tab can be thought of as a bifolium with most of one leaf cut off. A bifolium comprises the smallest possible complete quire. Although most scribes worked in terms of the four-bifolium quire (which provides eight pages with

---

42 *Catalogue of Medieval Manuscripts and Incunabula at Huis Bergh Castle in 's-Heerenberg*, cat. 67, p. 118.

43 Opening of a printed missal (early sixteenth century) revealing a full-page miniature on parchment depicting Christ crucified (twelfth century?) inserted as a canon page. Paris, Bibl. Sainte-Geneviève, inc. OE XV 698. http://bvmm.irht.cnrs.fr/consult/consult.php?mode=ecran&panier=false&reproductionId=13123&VUE_ID=1347929&carouselThere=false&nbVignettes=4x3&page=1&angle=0&zoom=petit&tailleReelle=

sixteen writing surfaces, and equals a complete piece of calf- or goatskin parchment, cut in half three times), they could also set out to inscribe an individual bifolium as a stand-alone unit. Some of these bifolia circulated separately. As I have argued elsewhere, a bifolium was a way to preserve and disseminate a word and image combination or to multiply a new devotion without having to make a whole new book.[44] Such bifolia could have circulated alone, outside a manuscript context; here I look at bifolia that were constructed expressly to be included in a book. Whereas some book owners added a prayer or two to an existing manuscript by filling blank parchment, others added entire quires containing indulgenced texts: these owners must have thought that adding them was good value.

1. Adding a bifolium

One of the earliest examples of enhancing a finished codex with a new bifolium occurs in the Egmond Gospels (HKB, Ms. 76 F 1).[45] Containing the four Gospels, the manuscript was written in Carolingian minuscule in Rheims in the third quarter of the ninth century with Northern French illumination executed at the same time. Extensive decoration appears at the canon tables and at the incipits of the four gospels (fig. 153).[46]

The book then made its way north to the Netherlands, where manuscript production was still undeveloped. Around 975, a hundred years after it was made, dedication images were made in Ghent in the form of a bifolium and added to the end of the book (fig. 154).[47] Dirk II, Count of Holland, and his wife Hildegard, presented the manuscript to Egmond Abbey at this time. These added images in fact commemorate

---

44 Rudy, *Postcards on Parchment*.
45 Adam S. Cohen, "Magnificence in Miniature: The Case of Early Medieval Manuscripts," in *Magnificence and the Sublime in Medieval Aesthetics: Art, Architecture, Literature, Music*, ed. C. Stephen Jaeger, *The New Middle Ages* (Basingstoke: Palgrave Macmillan, 2010), pp. 79–101, pl. 1–14, esp. pp. 89–90.
46 Evangelist portrait of Matthew, part of the original campaign of work in the Egmond Gospels, executed in the ninth century in Northern France. The Hague, Koninklijke Bibliotheek, Ms. 76 F 1, fol. 16v-17r. http://manuscripts.kb.nl/zoom/BYVANCKB%3Amimi_76f1%3Ans_016v_017r
47 Dedication miniatures, diptych made in Ghent ca. 975 and added to the Egmond Gospels. The Hague, Koninklijke Bibliotheek, Ms. 76 F 1, fol. 214v-215r. http://manuscripts.kb.nl/zoom/BYVANCKB%3Amimi_76f1%3Ans_214v_215r

this donation. Dirk and Hildegard also had the book covered in a gilt treasure binding sparkling with precious stones, which was lost in the sixteenth century. An inventory made in 1571 of the abbey's possession mentions the Egmond Gospels. Shortly thereafter, during the period of religious reform in Holland, the manuscript was transferred to the nearest city, Haarlem.

Bilaterally divided by the fold, the bifolium shows the two donors on the left side, each grasping the book and placing it on an altar with a tabernacle, the entire shrine decorated with tiered ornament and swags of drapery. Two arches (which also recall the forms of the canon pages elsewhere in the manuscript) and an ornate roof define the ecclesiastical space denoting "Egmond Abbey." On the facing folio Dirk II and Hildegard kneel before St. Adalbert, patron of Egmond Abbey. They are recognizable from the previous image, still wearing the same distinctive outfits. For his part, the saint turns to God, represented in a mandorla nestled in a green crenelated cloud. The image therefore reiterates the hierarchy of power, with Hildegard lying prostrate behind her husband and all subservient to God above. These images show the donation of the very book that the miniature has become part of. Self-referential, it was obviously made for this very book. Outside the context of its current frame, the Egmond Gospels themselves, the image would have little meaning. These added images were probably originally on a bifolium, but were apparently then separated before being sewn together during one of the restorations of the book.

Manuscripts that descend through a noble family's genealogy are often chosen as recipients for updates, for later rulers want to leave their marks on objects that reach deep into history, thereby legitimating their rules. When Charles V, King of France (1364–80) inherited the Hours of Blanche of Savoy, which had been written and illuminated ca. 1325–50, he added a bifolium full of imagery to it to make it his own (New Haven, Beinecke, Ms. 390).[48] The original part of the manuscript had been made at the French court in the second quarter of the fourteenth century. Several images in the original part of the manuscript show the

---

48 The Hours of Blanche of Savoy: New Haven, Beinecke Rare Book and Manuscript Library, Ms. 390. Written and illuminated ca. 1325–50, with additions commissioned by Charles V, King of France (r. 1364–80). Refer to the Beinecke's website for further literature.

donor, Blanche of Savoy, kneeling before figures from sacred history. In one of these, for example, she kneels before the Trinity (fig. 155).[49] In a quatrefoil frame bound in red, white, and blue, the image presents the patron in the same scale and in the same space as God the Father. A repeating design featuring the gold fleur-de-lis on a blue background forms a backdrop and identifies the patron as a member of the French nobility. Other decoration in the border also heralds the image: full baguette borders, inhabited by an angel swinging a censer, a soldier wielding a sword, and a pair of anthropomorphized creatures blowing horns in the bas-de-page, along with bunnies and birds and vine tendrils. These motifs visually heighten the page. When Charles V inherited the book, he had additions made that imitated these design features.

Charles V's illuminator carefully studied the earlier illumination before adding a bifolium in the third quarter of the fourteenth century. Paul de Winter has identified the copyist of the added section as Jean l'Avenant, who worked on several other royal commissions, including the Grandes Heures of Philip the Bold, now divided between Cambridge and Brussels.[50] The added bifolium was folded around one of the original bifolia and is therefore fully integrated with the existing manuscript. This added bifolium comprises fol. 1 and 4; it is wrapped around an older bifolium comprising fol. 2–3. There are four surfaces for texts and images in the added bifolium in the Hours of Blanche of Savoy: fol. 1r, 1v, 4r, and 4v. These additions were made to resemble the original manuscript, even though they were added a half-century later.

For example, the page layout of fol. 1v (added later) closely resembles that of its facing folio, 2r (original) (fig. 1v-2r, as above). The later artist has used a similar quatrefoil frame, which is a close approximation of, but is slightly less refined than, the original. He has framed the image

---

49   Opening from the Hours of Blanche of Savoy, including a miniature depicting Blanche of Savoy kneeling before the Trinity. New Haven, Yale University, Beinecke Rare Book and Manuscript Library, Ms. 390, fol. 1v-2r. http://brbl-media. library.yale.edu/images/10507295_quarter.jpg and http://brbl-media.library.yale. edu/images/10507296_quarter.jpg

50   Patrick M. de Winter, "The *Grandes Heures* of Philip the Bold, Duke of Burgundy: The Copyist Jean l'Avenant and His Patrons at the French Court," *Speculum* 57, no. 4 (1982), pp. 786–842, pp. 802–03. De Winter reproduces fol. 6r (fig. 20) and fol. 4r (fig. 21). He recognizes the hand of Jean l'Avenant in a two-volume *Bible historiale* (Hamburg, Kunsthalle, Ms. Fr. 1); and in the *Grandes Heures* of Philip the Bold (Cambridge, Fitzwilliam Museum, Ms. 3–1954 and BKB, Ms. 11035–37).

in red, white, and blue, but has reversed the order of the colors and has
thickened the lines. He has used a similar baguettes border on three
sides, but has changed the proportions of the borders. He has filled the
interstices with vines and birds but has colored them with a somewhat
more intense palette. He has populated the bas-de-page with fantastical
creatures that resemble those in the original part. In short: the later artist
has adopted a retardataire style so that the additions would blend in
with the original components.

Likewise, the new style stands across from the old in the opening
on fol. 3v-4r (fig. 156).[51] The left side of the opening (the original part)
brandishes a miniature with Blanche kneeling in prayer to St. Louis,
who was not only a saint, but also a symbol of French nationalism.
On the right sight of the opening is the added physical material. Jean
l'Avenant has supplied a facing folio in a similar style, this time with the
new patron, Charles V, showing his devotion to one of his chosen saints,
Anthony. In other words, Charles V has himself shown naturalized into
French history and into the fiber of the book. By using a retardataire
style, the illuminator has collapsed time, as if Charles V's reign were
already anticipated during the time of Blanche of Savoy, and indeed, in
the time of St. Louis and St. Anthony. The additions to this book and
their style form important political choices.

Charles V also recorded his presence in a new volume—a Bible in
French—by similarly employing extra inserted parchment. Guiard des
Moulins (b. 1251), a canon of St. Pier in Aire-sur-Lys, translated Petrus
Comestor's *Bible Historiale Complétée*, along selections of the Latin
vulgate into French, resulting in the first Bible in French. This text, often
highly illuminated, was made in copies for various noble libraries in
the fourteenth century. Raoulet d'Orléans copied one of these (now
HMMW, Ms. 10 B 23) in Paris, in 1371–72. The book begins with a splash
of color in a page-wide miniature showing God the father with the
four evangelists writing the Gospels, and the most famous of the Old

51 Opening from the Hours of Blanche of Savoy, including miniatures depicting
    Blanche kneeling before St. Louis, and Charles V before St. Anthony. New Haven,
    Yale University, Beinecke Rare Book and Manuscript Library, Ms. 390, fol. 3v-4r.
    http://brbl-media.library.yale.edu/images/10507299_quarter.jpg and http://brbl-
    media.library.yale.edu/images/10507300_quarter.jpg

Testament scenes, the fall from Paradise, in the bas-de-page (fig. 157).[52] On the next opening, the author Guiard des Moulins presents his work to William, archbishop of Sens (fig. 158).[53] The author genuflects before his patron, who is shown as an erudite man sitting at his desk with a book. Cordially the archbishop receives the gift, which is represented as a closed book connoting the finished translation by Guiard des Moulins. The rest of the manuscript is richly illuminated and numerous, with 247 column miniatures and 11 two-column miniatures, all of them in red, white and blue quatrefoil frames.

One illumination in the manuscript departs from this formula: the image at the very beginning of the book (fig. 159).[54] This miniature reiterates the scene on fol. 4v but with different characters. Instead of being just a column wide, it fills the entire folio. Instead of wearing loose robes, the presenter wears tight clothes fashionable for the 1370s. He presents not a closed book but an open one to a secular man on a throne, not an ecclesiastic. The open book features a full-page miniature on one side, thereby emphasizing the fact that the presented book is illuminated. In fact, the image represented in the opening of the depicted book shows God the father in a mandorla; in other words, it resembles the opening miniature of this very Bible. In the full-page presentation scene the repeated motif on the back wall is the French fleur-de-lis in gold against an ultramarine background, setting the scene as a French court. Rather than sitting at a desk reading, the recipient is sitting on a throne under a canopy connoting his power. All of these clues emphasize the gift of an illuminated book to a French monarch.[55]

---

52   Original frontispiece from Guiard des Moulins, Grande Bible Historiale Complétée, showing God the Father enthroned in a quatrefoil surrounded by angels, with the four evangelists and their symbols in the corners. Made in Paris in 1371–72. The Hague, Meermanno Museum, Ms. 10 B 23, fol. 3r. http://manuscripts.kb.nl/zoom/BYVANCKB%3Amimi_mmw_10b23%3A003r

53   Folio from from Guiard des Moulins, Grande Bible Historiale Complétée, with a column miniature depicting the author presenting his work to William, archbishop of Sens. Made in Paris in 1371–72. The Hague, Meermanno Museum, Ms. 10 B 23, fol. 4v. http://manuscripts.kb.nl/zoom/BYVANCKB%3Amimi_mmw_10b23%3A004v

54   Opening in Guiard des Moulins, Grande Bible Historiale Complétée, with a dedication of the manuscript by Jean de Vaudetar to King Charles V of France, and a full-page miniature depicting the presentation of the book to the king. The Hague, Meermanno Museum, Ms. 10 B 23, fol. 1v-2r. http://manuscripts.kb.nl/zoom/BYVANCKB%3Amimi_mmw_10b23%3A001v_002r

55   Erik Inglis, "A Book in the Hand: Some Late Medieval Accounts of Manuscript Presentations," *Journal of the Early Book Society* 5 (2002), pp. 75–97.

The presentation miniature forms a bifolium with a text page that identifies the recipient and the date: "In the year of our lord 1371 this work was painted according to a command for the honor of the illustrious prince Charles, King of France, when he was thirty-five and in the eighth year of his reign. John of Bruges, the aforesaid king's painter, has made this picture with his own hand" (Anno domini millesimo trecentesimo septuagesimo primo istud opus pictum fuit ad preceptam ac honorem illustri principis Karoli regis Francie etatis sue trecesimoquinto et regum sin octavo et Iohannes de Brugis pictor regis predicti fecit hanc picturam propria sua manu). This bifolium, with its outer faces (fol. 1r and 2v) blank, was made in a separate campaign of work from the rest of the manuscript, with a different ruling and script on the text side, and a different scale, palette and hand on the image side from what is found in the rest of the book. According to the inscription "this picture" (i.e., the presentation miniature) was made by Johannes of Bruges, otherwise known as Jean Bondol, official painter at the king's court. Jean de Vaudetar, chamberlain to the king, presents the manuscript in the image. The inscription indicates that the king commissioned the bifolium from his court painter, and the image commemorates the event of the king's chamberlain, Jean de Vaudetar, presenting the book to him. However, the bifolium is dated 1371, and the manuscript was not completed until the following year. Thus, the image on the bifolium anticipates the completion of the book (in a different atelier in Paris) and its presentation to the king. The quire is now mounted on a parchment strip that was probably added when the manuscript was rebound in the eighteenth century, but needle holes in the gutter of the bifolium indicate that it was originally sewn into the book. This bifolium attests to the fact that Charles V and his chamberlain Jean de Vaudetar went to some effort and expense to record the event of the book's presentation. Charles V added a bifolium with a presentation miniature and a dedicatory text to the *Bible Historiale* in order to document the performance of presentation. He also added a bifolium to the Hours of Blanche of Savoy in order to reinforce the continuity between Louis, Blanche and himself. In both cases he inserted himself into the books' respective histories through the operation of adding parchment.

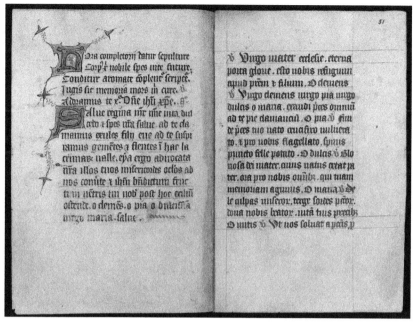

Fig. 160 Opening in a book of hours that reveals the fissure between two campaigns of work. Cambridge, University Library, Ms. Ee.1.14, fol. 50v-51r. Image © Cambridge University Library, all rights reserved.

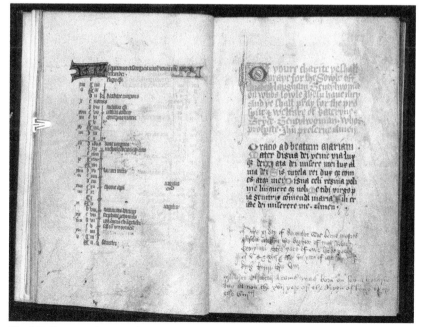

Fig. 161 Opening showing the end of the calendar, and a formerly blank folio filled with prayers in English and Latin by an early owner. London, British Library, Harley Ms. 2966, fol. 7v-8r. Image in the Public Domain.

Cambridge, UL, Ms. Ee.1.14, an English book of hours I discussed briefly above, contains a bifolium of prayers to the Virgin added to the end of the Hours of the Virgin (Cambridge, UL, Ms. Ee.1.14, fol. 51–52; fig. 160). One can immediately see that the bifolium was added, because 51r is ruled in a strong red pen, whereas the rest of the Hours of the Virgin (ending with 50v) was ruled in more subtle brown. The new scribe has maintained similar ruling size, text block, and letter size, and a similar textualis script, although he has decorated the gold, one-line initials with green ink that does not appear in the original parts of the book. He has tried to make the transition as smooth as possible. The motivation for adding extra physical material was to accommodate extra verses for the *Salve Regina*, which fill 51r. He then completes the rest of the bifolium with further prayers to the Virgin.

Above I discussed how manuscripts made in the Southern Netherlands for English export often had extra space in them. But when there wasn't enough space, the scrivener could add extra substrate. That is what happened in Harley 2966, another Southern Netherlandish manuscript used in England, to which a fifteenth-century English owner added a bifolium. Although there was plenty of blank space throughout this manuscript, the owner chose to have it taken apart and have a bifolium added to it, which wraps around the calendar, in order to create some blank parchment near the beginning of the book. The English owner(s) added texts to this fresh space (fig. 161).[56] A prayer in English copied in green ink appears at the top, followed by a prayer in Latin to the Virgin copied in brown ink. Owners may have commissioned scriveners to add these texts, as they have both been written in confident professional hands. A third text is slightly later and provides not a prayer but a piece of family history of the sort often inscribed in or around the calendar as a way of extending and personalizing the calendar's timekeeping function. I had suggested earlier that the blank space in the imported books of hours stimulated a desire to fill the space with personalized texts. Here the English owner felt that desire so strongly that he or she added even more space for personalization.

---

56 Opening showing the end of the calendar, and a formerly blank folio filled with prayers in English and Latin by an early owner. London, British Library, Harley Ms. 2966, fol. 7v-8r. http://www.bl.uk/catalogues/illuminatedmanuscripts/record.asp?MSID=8805

Fig. 162 Female patron and St. Mary Magdalene at her hermitage near Baune, devotional diptych added to a book of hours. Stockholm, National Library of Sweden, MS, A 233, fol. 1v-2r. Image © National Library of Sweden, CC BY 4.0.

A different motivation was at play in the pilgrim's hours introduced above (Stockholm A.233). Added parchment sheets feature a male owner, probably Jan de Trompes, who recorded his identity as a pilgrim within the pages.[57] This manuscript also has an added bifolium at the front of the manuscript (fig. 162). Half of the bifolium contains an image representing a woman, in half-length, in prayer directed to a representation of Mary Magdalene, who appears on the other side of the fold. This bifolium forms a diptych that shows a female sitter in half-length praying in perpetuity to Mary Magdalene. This saint was said to have taken up a hermitage at Beaune (France), where she, covered in hair, was elevated daily to heaven for her aural sustenance.[58] The sitter may be Mary Madeleine Cordier, Jan de Trompes' second wife, as Mary Magdalene would have been her name saint. Mary Madeleine Cordier died in 1510, and her husband survived until 1516. Perhaps he gave her

---

57   Rudy, "A Pilgrim's Book of Hours: Stockholm Royal Library A233," pp. 237–77; "Addendum," pp. 163–64.
58   Robert A. Koch, "La Sainte-Baume in Flemish Landscape Painting of the Sixteenth Century," *Gazette des Beaux-Arts* 66 (1965), pp. 273–82.

the book of hours at some point during their marriage, and she had it augmented in order to make her mark on the family prayerbook. This diptych has been inserted into the book as its first quire. Although her husband had made extensive additions to the book to display himself and his piety, she does not disrupt the quire structure, but layers her identity on top of his by placing her image at the very front of the book.

Adding a quire was a way to incorporate images and texts into a manuscript that had been omitted or had not yet been written or become popular when the manuscript was new. One book made in the eastern part of the Northern Netherlands, probably for a female Franciscan tertiary or Poor Clare, exemplifies this kind of addition (Paris, BnF, Cab. des Estampes, Ea 6 Rés).[59] This manuscript was copied on paper, and the copyist has illustrated the manuscript by pasting engravings into it, as Ursula Weekes has discussed.[60] It may have been collectively owned and used, or may have had a number of owners/keepers within the convent who made adjustments to it. One of these adjustments involved adding a bifolium of texts, now fol. 2–3. It contains a heavily indulgenced prayer based on the words from the INRI titulus, the piece of wood that Pilate was said to have nailed to the top of Christ's cross and that stated in three languages that he was "Jesus of Nazareth, King of the Jews."

The prayer announces:

Item, anyone who kneels before this Title of Triumph and prays with devotion in honor of the passion and death of Jesus Christ on the cross, with five *Pater Nosters* and five *Ave Marias* and one Credo, he will earn all of the indulgence that is to be found at the Church of Santa Croce in Rome, which indulgence has been tallied and counted by Gregory the Great and other popes, who have confirmed and increased it, one after the other. Item, Pope Sixtus IV gave, for the sake of reverence, 24,000 years' mortal sin, to whomever speaks the titulus in three languages, and to anyone who speaks it on a Friday, when one hears our lord's death sounding and sings *Tenebre*, from that each person earns 80,000 years' indulgence. Anyone who speaks it with devotion who is experiencing real sadness and pain will find in it merciful redemption. In this Church of Sta Croce, there is an indulgence every day of 48 years, as many quaternions, and one third of the forgiveness of all sins. Item, the Holy Father and Pope Sylvester, Gregory, Alexander, Nicholaus, Honorius

---

59   Weekes, *Early Engravers and Their Public*, pp. 100–19, and 294–301.
60   Ibid.

and Paglagius have given anyone who visits this church 1000 years. During Lent, Advent, and in the other high feasts, the indulgence is doubled. On the days listed below, all of the forgiveness from the pain and guilt of all sins is given, as in a jubilee year:
- on whit Friday
- on the day of the finding of the True Cross
- on the day of the raising of the holy cross
- on the day after St. Gregory's day (that is the 12th day of March). On that day the church is blessed.
- A few days after St. Gregory's day, that is after the vigil of St. Benedict, which is the 20th day of March. On that day the chapel called Jerusalem is blessed.
- on the second holy day [after] St. Cesarius's and St. Anastacius's day, who are lying bodily in this church. St. Cesarius's day is a most holy day, and St. Anastacius on the third day before St. Bartholomeus day.

Anyone who speaks, on the above-mentioned days before the title and with devotion, five Pater Nosters and five Ave Marias and one Credo will have forgiveness from all sins, from pain and guilt. Pope Sixtus IV has confirmed this indulgence, and after him, Pope Alexander VI. And so it continues through the year that a person earns 12,000 years' indulgence from mortal sin and two times that amount of venial sin.
- On Wednesdays and Fridays, the Holy Father, the pope, has given 24,000 years' indulgence. The faithful souls in purgatory may also earn this indulgence, if someone speaks five Pater Nosters and five Ave Marias and one Credo for them. If someone is too ill to kneel, he may pray the Pater Nosters sitting or lying down. Anyone who reads the following prayer in front of the martyrdom of our lord, for something for which he should burn in purgatory until final judgment day, God will transform it for him [into a lesser sentence]. I thank you, merciful dear lord Jesus Christ that you endured your martyrdom fully and stayed on the cross patiently and hung on the cross to the death and spoke sadly and cried bitterly and were completely broken. And that God let your blood out so that you mildly died a bitter death for my benefit. Dear lord, now I appeal to you by the depths of your endless mercy, I appeal to that heavenly kingdom that is synonymous with you. [Paris, BnF, Cab. des Estampes, Ea 6 Rés, fol. 2–3][61]

---

61   Paris, BnF, Cab. des Estampes, Ea 6 Rés, fol. 2–3: Item, wie voer desen titel der verwynningen knyet End emit aendacht bedet in betrachtingen der passion ende stervens Ihesu Christe aen deme cruce v pr nr ende v Ave Maria ende einen gelouwe, der verdient allen den aflaet den daer is te Romen inder kercken tot den heiligen cruce, welcker aflaet is an tale ende aen mate den Gregorius der groote ende ander paess me bestediget ende vermeerret hebben, der ein nae den anderen. Item, me paess Sixtus der vierde hevet gegeven om reverencien willen dis titels xxiiii^m iaer aflaetz dootlicker sunden, wie den titel spriect inden drien spraken

The copyist has inserted this bifolium, with its enormous and complicated indulgence, into a spot near the front of the manuscript. Although the manuscript may not be in its original order, and this bifolium may not be in its original place, clearly this bifolium forms a stand-alone unit. (It is currently near the calendar, which the indulgence text elucidates.) The owner adamantly wanted to include this indulgence, which has 570 words and was too long to be squeezed into any of the blank space in the manuscript. Including it required adding more physical material. As Ursula Weekes has ably discussed, the women who made this manuscript further personalized it by pasting hand-colored prints into

---

ende wie en spriect aenden vridach soe men ons heren doet luyt ende men *tenebre* singet, da van hevet eickelick minsche lxxx^m jaer afflaetz. Ende soe ein minsche den aendachtelicker spriect in aenbechtingen bedroefenisse ende liden verdient da van genadelicken verloest te vonden. In deser kercken tot den cruce is alle dage xlviiij iaer afflaetz. Soe vele karenen ende dat derde deil vergevinge alre sonden. Item, die heilige vader den paese Silvester [2v] Gregorius, Alexander, Nicholaus, Honorius ende Paglagius heft ein yegelicken gegeven m iaer einen yegelicken mynsche der dese kercke heymbesueket. Inder vasten inden advent ende inden anderen hochtijdelicken dagen is der aflaet tweevoldich. Aen desen dagen hier nae geschreven is allen wegen volcomen vergevinge alre sonden van pinen ende van scolt als in deme iubel iaere. Aen den wyssen vrijdach, aen des heiligen cruis dach der vindingen, aen des heiligen cruus dach der erhevingen, aenden neesten dach na sce Gregorius, dat is der xii^de dach des mertz. Aen den dage is die kirck geweit woerden. Aen den yedel dage nae sce Gregorius dach dat is nae sce Benedictus avont ende is der xx dach inden mertz. Aen den dage is die capelle die heischt Iherusalem geweit woerden. Aender tweer heiligen dach als sce Cesarius ende sce Anastacius de in deser kercken lychandelicken liget. Sce Cesarius is aen alre heligen dach Ende sce Anastarius aenden derden dach voer sce Bartholomeus dache. Ende wie aen desen dage voerschreven voer den titel mit andacht spriect v pater noster ende v ave marien ende einen gelouwen hevet vergevinghe alre sonden van pinen ende van scholt. Desen aflaet hevet bestedicht pais Sixtus der vierde ende na hem paes Alexander der vj^de. Ende aldus dorch dat gans [3r] iaer heft ein minsche alle dage daer van xij^m iaer aflaetz doorlicker sonden ende twee mael alsoe vele dagelicker sonden. Aen die midwech ende vrijdach xxiiij^m iaer aflaetz hebben gegeven de heilige vader de paesen. Desen aflaet mogen oech vercrigen de gelouwige zielen in deme vegevuer, alsmen v pr nr ende v Ave Maria ende einen gelouwe voer sij spriect. Ende off ein minsche soe cranck ware dat hij niet geknien ende[sic] conde, soe mach hij de pater noster sittende off liggende beden. Ende wie dit nagescreven gebet leest voer die martilie ons liefs heren waer dat sake dat hij soude beernen int vegevuer totten ioncxsten dage toe, dat wil god aen hem verwandelen. Ic dancke u gebenedide lieve here Ihesu Christe dattu din martilie begonstes crachtelick ende leetste anden cruus verduldelick ende hinges aenden cruus versmadelick ende sprakes droefflicken ende weendes bitterlicken ende woerdes te broken ganselicken ende gotes dijn bloet uut mildelicken ende storves om mijnen wil den bitteren doot. Lieve here nu bevele ich mij in die diepde dijnre grondeloser ontfermherticheit, ich bevele mij in dat hemelrijck dattu selver biste. Amen.

it to serve as "miniatures" and even painted borders around the prints to further embellish them and make the images seem more like fancy, bespoke miniatures. Additionally, the sisters must have added this textual bifolium, one that accommodates text that refers to the women's particular church and the relics it held and the indulgences available there on various days of the year. It mentions popes Sixtus IV (1471–84) and Alexander VI (1492–1503), thereby providing a *terminus post quem* for this added bifolium on 1492. While the sisters made this book for their own use, and therefore personalized it from the beginning, this indulgence was apparently added to the book after the indulgence was ratified.

Time and again, the texts that prayerbook owners desired to add were those containing indulgences. Such is also the case with Leiden, UB, BPL 3073, a book of hours in Dutch made in Utrecht or Delft in the 1420s. Its calendar has been lost, and the first folio reveals a highly worn incipit for the Hours of the Virgin, which suggests that the calendar had disappeared early in the book's career, as it wasn't there to protect the prayer text during the period of its heaviest use (fig. 163).[62] It has therefore been modified several times before it received its current binding, which is an early sixteenth-century brown leather, blind-stamped binding made in the Netherlands.

Texts in the original parts of the manuscript comprise various offices. Their incipits have plenty of decoration but offer no indulgences (fig. 164).[63] Toward the end of the fifteenth century (or possibly when the manuscript was rebound for the final time), an owner added a bifolium to the end of the book (Leiden, UB, BPL 3073, fol. 191–193; fig. 165).[64] This is written in a later script and represents an added prayer. According to these red words, the more the votary reads the prayer, the more sin it will eradicate. I contend that one of the reasons that owners inserted more physical material into their books (e.g., parchment bifolia) was to

---

62 Incipit of the Hours of the Virgin, with a historiated initial. Utrecht or Delft, ca. 1420s. Leiden, Universiteitsbibliotheek, Ms. BPL 3073, fol. 1r. https://socrates.leidenuniv.nl/ (then search for "BPL 3073")

63 Incipit from the original part of the manuscript, with decoration from Utrecht or Delft. Leiden, Universiteitsbibliotheek, Ms. BPL 3073, fol. 154v. https://socrates.leidenuniv.nl/ (then search for "BPL 3073")

64 Beginning of the added bifolium. Leiden, Universiteitsbibliotheek, Ms. BPL 3073, fol. 191r. https://socrates.leidenuniv.nl/ (then search for "BPL 3073")

accommodate indulgenced texts and prayers that would secure their position in the afterlife.

Fig. 166 Parchment diptych with the measurements of Christ's length and side wound, inserted into a French book of hours. Paisley, Renfrew District Museum and Art Gallery, Ms. 1, fol. 13–14 forming a diptych. Photo © Author, CC BY 4.0.

Another way they could sanctify their books was by inserting metric relics painted on parchment. The owner of a French book of hours has rebound the book to accommodate a parchment bifolium showing the wound in Christ's side, and the length of Christ's body (fig. 166).[65] These abstract shapes are enveloped in explanatory texts, in the form of short stanzas of rhyming French doggerel. They indicate that however humble the painted forms, they are true measurements of the savior, meaning that they are secondary contact relics of Jesus. The object itself folds so that the images and texts are on the inside, while the outside is blank. It forms a self-protecting autonomous unit, which, when inserted into a book of hours, brings that book closer to the body of Christ.

---

65 For a description, see N. R. Ker et al., *Medieval Manuscripts in British Libraries*, 5 vols. (Oxford: Clarendon Press, 1969–2002), vol. IV, pp. 1–2, where the author acknowledges that fols 13–14 form an added bifolium.

a. Adding new openings to old

Fig. 167 Monk praying for the release of souls from purgatory, full-page miniature made as part of a diptych and inserted into a book of hours. The Hague, Koninklijke Bibliotheek, Ms. 133 D 5, fol. 86v-87r. Image © Koninklijke Bibliotheek—the National Library of The Netherlands, CC BY 4.0.

Fig. 168 Opening in a book of hours, showing the original parchment and script (on the right side of the gutter) and the replaced incipit folio with text recopied in a different script (on the left side of the gutter). The Hague, Koninklijke Bibliotheek, Ms. 133 D 5, fol. 87v-88r. Image © Koninklijke Bibliotheek—the National Library of The Netherlands, CC BY 4.0.

Fig. 169
The pricking along the outer edge of the
bifolium only occurs on the added folios.
The Hague, Koninklijke Bibliotheek,
Ms. 133 D 5, detail of fol. 86–87. Image
© Koninklijke Bibliotheek—the National
Library of The Netherlands, CC BY 4.0.

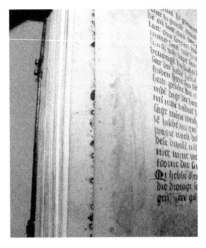

A medieval owner of HKB, Ms. 133
D 5, a book of hours made in South
Holland, was so worried about
purgatory that he commissioned a
full-page miniature showing souls
being released from it (fig. 167). The
cleric depicted in the image probably does not represent the medieval
owner, for the figure lacks specifying details, and furthermore, clerics
would be unlikely to use a book of hours, which was really in the purview
of the laity. Instead, a late medieval patron could have ordered an image
depicting a monk praying for his or her soul, for the image represents the
fulfillment of another transaction: perhaps the owner was a layperson
who had commissioned prayers from a local monastery. This owner did
not simply add the miniatures, but made more complicated interventions:
he or she added entire bifolia. That is, the opening folios were changed
to make new, and presumably more lavish, incipits. Replacing two folios
instead of one at each incipit was done in order to make the new full-
page miniatures match their respective facing folios. A book maker has
therefore cut out the existing incipit pages and replaced them with entire
bifolia. This technique has allowed the book maker to achieve entire
openings decorated in a unified style.

Only when one turns the page does one confront the rupture in style
(fig. 168). There one can see the original script on the right side, and on
the left the new script, which has been inscribed on the added bifolium.
In order to the replace the physical material, the scribe had to carefully
calculate the words so that the texts would join up. The added bifolia
are thicker than the other pages in the book; this causes the book to
spring open at these pages, where the parchment is less supple. When
he or she made these adjustments, the supple parchment of the original
book was not available, and the new components had to be made with
coarser material. These stiff bifolia also have disconcerting pricking

along the outer edge, which the original folios lack (fig. 169). By choosing to replace entire openings—entire two-page-spreads—the owner was quite clearly asserting that the decoration of his book mattered and that creating a visual unity across the entire opening was important enough for him to discard a perfectly good text page and remake it in a different style just to achieve this effect. The owner of this manuscript had the same desire as the owner of Beinecke 434 (discussed earlier): to add full-page images but maintain visual coherence across the entire opening. Whereas the miniaturist of Beinecke 434 preserved the existing parchment and simply painted over the old borders—which involved taking the book apart, and painting the new borders while the old quire was out of its binding, adding the full-page miniature, and rebinding— the craftsperson responsible for the changes to HKB, Ms. 133 D 5 did not rework any existing parchment, but rather replaced components.

2. Adding one or more full quires

Fig. 170
Cistercian breviary, made in the thirteenth century, photographed from the bottom to isolate a quire added in 1491. Perth, St. John's Kirk, Ms. 3. Photo © Author, CC BY 4.0.

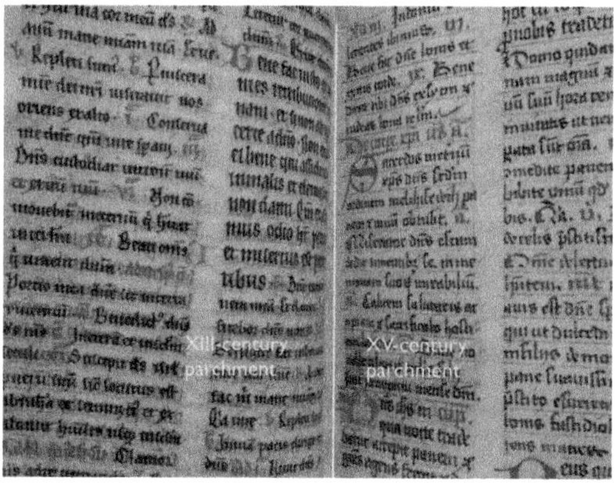

Fig. 171
Opening in a Cistercian breviary, with original thirteenth-century parts script and parchment on the left side of the gutter, and an added fifteenth-century quire on the right side of the gutter. Perth, St. John's Kirk, Ms. 3. Photo © Author, CC BY 4.0.

Fig. 172
Folio in a Cistercian breviary
showing two campaigns of
medieval foliation. Perth, St.
John's Kirk, Ms. 3, fol. 155r.
Photo © Author, CC BY 4.0.

A thirteenth-century example will reveal why it was so difficult to force manuscripts created before the modular method to accommodate new texts. Ms. 3 in the Kirk in Perth (Scotland) is a Cistercian breviary made in the thirteenth century with additions made in 1491.[66] Namely, fol. 52–58 forms an added quire (fig. 170). Clearly, this material was added in order to accommodate a new feast: that of Corpus Christi.[67] Its scribe has attempted to copy the earlier writing style but has not quite mastered it. His heavily ruled parchment also contrasts sharply with the much more subtle rulings of the thirteenth-century lines. These aesthetics aside, his structural problem was that the previous text did not finish neatly at the end of fol. 51v, and the reader would have to skip ahead, to fol. 59r, to read the last few lines of the text. This would have been impractical and inconvenient. Instead, the fifteenth-century scribe copied the last few lines of the previous text before starting the *Corpus Christi* (fig. 171). The fifteenth-century scribe easily fit the new text onto the new quire and then had some space left over on fol. 58v, on which he inscribed a sermon attributed to St. Ambrose. Where the thirteenth-century script resumes on fol. 59r, the scribe has then had to erase several lines of text, for he had already inscribed these at the beginning of the new quire. Thus, in order to accommodate the feast of *Corpus Christi* in approximately the correct place in the book, the scribe had to make adjustments at

---

66   Ibid., vol. IV, pp. 160–62. Ker describes the manuscript's stratigraphy, including some erasures, some discards, and the 41 leaves added in 1491.

67   Miri Rubin, *Corpus Christi: The Eucharist in Late Medieval Culture* (Cambridge and New York: Cambridge University Press, 1991).

both ends of the added quire, scraping and recopying text and finding a short text to serve as a quire filler. In the fifteenth century book makers obviated such problems by simply beginning new texts on fresh quires and then treating them as modular units. Incidentally, adding a quire disrupted the foliation from that point onward, and the fifteenth-century scribe added foliation in brown above the original foliation in red (fig. 172). Fifteenth-century scribes sidestepped this problem by simply not foliating the manuscript; very few fifteenth-century prayerbooks, books of hours, and breviaries are foliated. It's as if scribes were expecting future adjustments.

Calendars are never foliated, but that is not why I suspect that it was the calendar that gave book makers the idea to start making books out of packets, or pre-assembled parts. Rather, it's because calendars were made in separate operations. In most (semi-) liturgical books, the calendar is ruled separately from the rest of the book. It has a different number of lines per folio, and usually several columns. As the calendar had to be made in a separate operation, book makers in the Southern Netherlands may have begun specializing in making nothing but calendars. A book of hours made in Ghent or Bruges (HKB, Ms. 135 G 10), discussed above, was given to someone in the eastern Netherlands. It was at that time that someone probably removed the West Flemish calendar and replaced it with one for the diocese of Cologne. Below I give further examples of manuscripts that travelled far from where they were made. Their new owners found it easier to swap out the calendar than to rub out some saints and add others to make the calendar relevant for local feasts. Calendars could be exchanged because they were made on separate units.

The Gouda Missal (HKB, Ms. 135 H 45), presented several times above, also has an added quire, namely the canon (fol. 101–106). A full-page image depicting the Crucifixion, discussed above, initiates the new quire (fig. 124). Not only did the owners replace the image, but they replaced the entire quire containing the canon of the mass. Like a calendar, a canon was ruled and written differently from the rest of the manuscript and made in a different campaign of work. Whereas a missal contains multiple texts a priest would use when performing various kinds of masses over the course of the year, the canon of the mass was the text that was read at every mass. Copyists arranged the missal such that this text would fall at the very center of the book, so that the book would be open at its midpoint and balanced for this most important part of the ceremony. They also often copied this part of the book in larger script, so that the priest could read it easily from the distance of an arm's length away. Because the priest picked the book up and kissed the Crucifixion, which would also cause wear and tear to the binding, and then often sprinkled the altar with holy water, and flipped through these folios more quickly (because of the large letter size), this part of the book wore out most quickly.

Fig. 173 First folio of the Gouda Missal (from original part of the manuscript). The Hague, Koninklijke Bibliotheek, Ms. 135 H 45, fol. 10r. Image © Koninklijke Bibliotheek — the National Library of The Netherlands, CC BY 4.0.

As a canon is essential to the manuscript's function as a service book, the missal must have originally had one. This presumed canon would have been decorated in the same style as the other original parts of the manuscript, with red and blue initials and penwork (fig. 173). Perhaps it wore out from use, so that the old one was removed and replaced by a clean new one in the late fifteenth or early sixteenth century. When the Fraterhuis at Gouda was commissioned to replace the canon, they did so with the latest technology: they printed an image inside the initial, directly on the parchment folio, with a woodblock. They were on the forefront of printing technologies in the Netherlands, and they applied their skills in a novel fashion here[68] (fig. 174).[69]

Although some missals and service books were updated, it is in the realm of private prayerbooks and books of hours that owners often made considerable adjustments by adding entire quires. This adjustability was both a cause and an effect of the modular method of producing books. Not only was the possibility within reach, but there was considerable pressure to do so. The related production fact—that book components were increasingly being made remotely from the consumer—led owners to seek even more adjustments, as the remote producers had not perfectly anticipated their desires.

A book of hours made for use in the diocese of Utrecht ca. 1495 has a quire added to the front, before the calendar (HKB, Ms. 135 G 19). The added component accommodates a prayer to Christ, a prayer to Job, and a full-page image of a man kneeling in veneration before St. Jerome, who is in turn venerating a crucifix with the *Corpus Christi* in a landscape (fig. 175).[70] While the added section before the calendar is generally in the same style as the rest of the book, with similar scribal hand and image style, it is clear for two reasons that this first quire was an afterthought. First, it is highly unusual for such prayers to precede

---

68   Kok, "Een Houtsnede in een Handschrift."

69   *Te igitur* page in the Gouda Missal, with a wood-cut image of the Trinity printed directly on the page. The Hague, Koninklijke Bibliotheek, Ms. 135 H 45, fol. 102r. http://manuscripts.kb.nl/show/images/135+H+45

70   The patron with St. Jerome, full-page miniature added to the added quire at the beginning of a book of hours. The Hague, Koninklijke Bibliotheek, Ms. 135 G 19, fol. 4v-5r. http://manuscripts.kb.nl/zoom/BYVANCKB%3Amimi_135g19%3A004v _005r

the calendar. Second, the image, placed as it is on the right side of the opening, breaks the normal page layout.

While it's clear that the image was designed for its position (as the flower border is thicker on the outside than the inside), this sheet breaks the hierarchy of decoration established throughout the rest of the manuscript, whereby full-page miniatures appear on the left side of the opening and accompany gilt initials on the opposite recto. Indeed, the original scribe, illuminator, or planner establishes the hierarchy of decoration, and then later additions either conform with or violate it. In this first quire, the text, the image, and their layout are therefore quite eccentric, and must have been highly motivated by the man in the picture, presumably the patron. He wanted more of himself in the book, including a full-page miniature depicting himself in a position of prayer, in perpetuity. He apparently felt himself aligned with St. Jerome, who pounded his own chest with a rock, and with Job on his dung heap. This first added quire is his testament to his long, possibly self-inflicted suffering.

Other prayerbooks with added quires similarly testify to their owners' feelings and desires. A book of hours, made originally in Delft around 1440 but then updated later in the fifteenth century, has a quire added to the end of the book, the other most common place to insert something (HKB, Ms. 74 G 35, fol. 161v-162r; fig. 176).[71] The original parts of the manuscript were fitted with simple grisaille miniatures to mark the major text openings (fig. 177).[72] These original openings are also marked by painted decorated with gold baguettes. However, the added quire, which includes fol. 162r, has a different kind of border decoration, and the accompanying image is not a grisaille, but rather a full-color image. This suggests the following order of operations: begin with a basic book of hours; add grisaille miniatures; later add indulgenced prayers with

---

71   Face of Christ, full-page miniature added to an added quire at the end of a book of hours. The Hague, Koninklijke Bibliotheek, Ms. 74 G 35, fol. 161v-162r. http://manuscripts.kb.nl/zoom/BYVANCKB%3Amimi_74g35%3A161v_162r

72   So-called Masters of the Delft Grisailles, Angel, full-page miniature inserted before prayer to the personal angel. The Hague, Koninklijke Bibliotheek, Ms. 74 G 35, fol. 83v-84r. http://manuscripts.kb.nl/zoom/BYVANCKB%3Amimi_74g35%3A083v_0 84r

full-page miniatures from another source. Considering these additions in layers reveals several attempts at fulfilling desire.

The original part of 74 G 35, which represents a bare-bones book of hours, contains the Hours of the Virgin (fol. 15–53); the Hours of the Cross (fol. 54–59): Seven Penitential Psalms (fol. 60–79); and various Suffrages (fol. 80–104), and the Vigil for the Dead (105–141r). But the added quire (fol. 143–163) contains texts of a different nature:

143–145: *Adoro te* (7-verse version, indulgenced)

146r: indulgenced prayer to Virgin

146–149: non-indulgenced prayer to Virgin

150–152: Seven Last Words of Christ

152–155: Prayers to the Sacrament

156: Prayer to be read during elevation, indulgenced

157: Indulgenced prayer

158–160: O intemerata

161: blank

162–163: Prayer to the Face of Christ (indulgenced)

What is clear from this list is that most of the prayers that the early owner added were those that carried indulgences. By adding three quires to the end of the book, the owner made space for these prayers, which transformed the manuscript from a book of hours to a vehicle for purgatorial remission. As I have shown through research involving densitometry (measuring the amount of dirt on the page, as a way to indirectly measure intensity of reading), the added sections in both HKB, Ms. 74 G 35, and in HKB, Ms. 135 G 19 were among the most heavily used parts of the book. This is not surprising, as it stands to reason that an owner who would go to the trouble and expense to add particular texts would strongly desire those texts and then spend a disproportionally high amount of time with them. Owners of prayerbooks added not only individual images and prayers, but also entire groups of indulgenced texts.

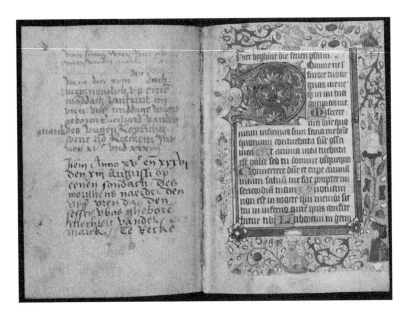

Fig. 178 Opening in a book of hours from Delft, written in Latin but with rubrics in Dutch. The owner has filled the quire with birth dates. Staatsbibliothek zu Berlin—Preußischer Kulturbesitz, Ms. Germ. Oct. 89, fol. 60v-61r. Image © Staatsbibliothek zu Berlin, CC BY 4.0.

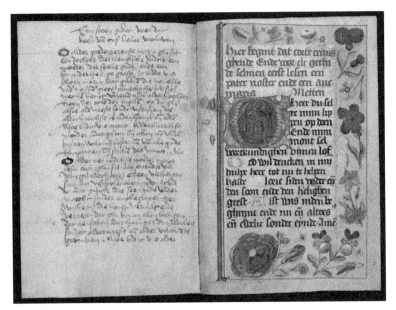

Fig. 179 Opening in a book of hours from Delft, showing an added module with the Hours of the Cross, and a prayer to be read before an image of the Virgin inscribed as a quire filler. Staatsbibliothek zu Berlin—Preußischer Kulturbesitz, Ms. Germ. Oct. 89, fol. 120v-121r. Image © Staatsbibliothek zu Berlin, CC BY 4.0.

The stratigraphy of a book of hours now in Berlin (Berlin, SPK, Germ. Oct. 89) clearly shows layers of hopes and fears barnacled onto a core manuscript.[73] That core was a book of hours written around the 1460s in the Northern Netherlands. These were written in Latin, but had some rubrics in the vernacular, which is a sign that the first owner found the Latin words more efficacious, but needed the Dutch rubrics to guide him through the book (fig. 178). Around the original parts the decoration is typical of Delft. One can see from the opening at the Seven Penitential Psalms (fol. 61r) that the book had contained blank folios, which the later owners used as a place to record family data. Specifically, the Van der Marck family of Reckem (Belgium) began adding these notes in 1525, more than a half-century after the book was first produced.

Of interest to the present discussion are the quires added to the beginning and end of the book in separate campaigns of work, not necessarily by members of the Van der Marck family. Clearly the series of owners considered the manuscript an expandable item, which could accordion outwards to accommodate desired prayers. One of the added sections in Oct. 89 (fol. 121–130), made around 1500, contains the Hours of the Cross (fig. 179). Abandoning the Latin, the new owner has opted for a vernacular version of the text, and has chosen to purchase the quire from an atelier that specialized in painting "Dutch strewn borders," which were bright and inoffensive. The script is amateurish. One can easily imagine that a medieval person, with a rudimentary training as a scribe and very low overhead, would start a business making quires such as this one, either as stand-alone booklets, or for purchasers to add to their existing book of hours.

The quire added at the beginning of the manuscript—before the calendar—provides insight into the fears and habits of one of the original owners. This quire (fol. 1–7) has provided space for a variety of texts and marks, including pen trials, notes of ownership, lone letters, once essential but now illegible notes, and small metal objects, which have left their offsets in the pliable parchment (fig. 180).

---

73 Hans Wegener, *Beschreibendes Verzeichnis der Miniaturen und des Initialschmuckes in den Deutschen Handschriften bis 1500. V: Die Deutschen Handschriften bis 1500*, 5 vols, Beschreibende Verzeichnisse der Miniaturen-Handschriften der Preussischen Staatsbibliothek zu Berlin (Leipzig: Weber, 1928), pp. 153–55, figs. 142, 143; Hermann Degering, *Kurzes Verzeichnis der Germanischen Handschriften der Preussichen Staatsbibliothek. III: Die Handschriften in Oktavformat und Register zu Band I-III*, 3 vols. (Leipzig: K. W. Hiersemann, 1925), p. 39; Achten, *Das Christliche Gebetbuch im Mittelalter: Andachts- und Stundenbücher in Handschrift und Frühdruck*, 13, no. 65, pl. 15.

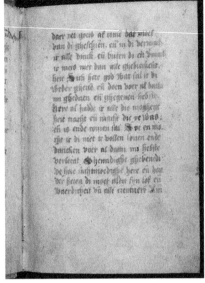

Fig. 180
First folio in an added section of a book
of hours whose core was made in Delft,
with offsets of small round metal objects.
Staatsbibliothek zu Berlin—Preußischer
Kulturbesitz, Ms. Germ. Oct. 89, fol.
1r. Image © Staatsbibliothek zu Berlin,
CC BY 4.0.

Fig. 181
Folio in an added section of a book of
hours whose core was made in Delft, with a
prayer to the Trinity, and needle holes from
formerly affixed objects. Staatsbibliothek
zu Berlin—Preußischer Kulturbesitz,
Ms. Germ. Oct. 89, fol. 2r. Image
© Staatsbibliothek zu Berlin, CC BY 4.0.

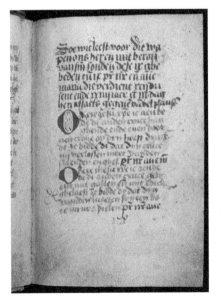

Fig. 182
Folio in an added section of a book of
hours whose core was made in Delft,
with an indulgenced prayer to the arma
Christi. Staatsbibliothek zu Berlin—
Preußischer Kulturbesitz, Ms. Germ. Oct.
89, fol. 3r. Image © Staatsbibliothek zu
Berlin, CC BY 4.0.

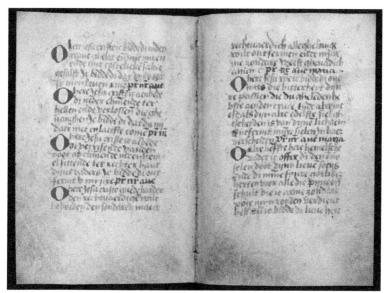

Fig. 183 Opening in an added section of a book of hours whose core was made in Delft, with the continuation of an indulgenced prayer to the arma Christi, revealing dirt and fingerprints from heavy handling. Staatsbibliothek zu Berlin—Preußischer Kulturbesitz, Ms. Germ. Oct. 89, fol. 3v-4r. Image © Staatsbibliothek zu Berlin, CC BY 4.0.

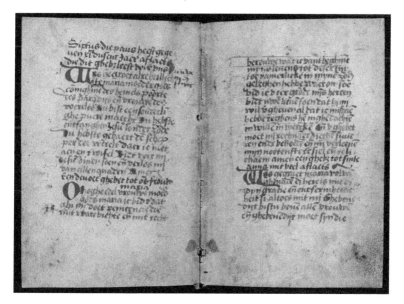

Fig. 184 Folio in an added section of a book of hours whose core was made in Delft, with an indulgenced prayer to the Virgin in Sole. Staatsbibliothek zu Berlin—Preußischer Kulturbesitz, Ms. Germ. Oct. 89, fol. 5v-6r. Image © Staatsbibliothek zu Berlin, CC BY 4.0.

Fig. 185
Folio in a book of hours whose core was
made in Delft: a full-page miniature
depicting Christ carrying the cross,
painted by a miniaturist in Delft.
Staatsbibliothek zu Berlin—Preußischer
Kulturbesitz, Ms. Germ. Oct. 89, fol.
44v. Image © Staatsbibliothek zu Berlin,
CC BY 4.0.

Additionally, this added quire contains:

1v-2v: a prayer to the Trinity (fig. 181);
3r-4v: the verses of St. Gregory, with nine verses and an indulgence
        for 92,000 years (fig. 182 and 183)
4v-5r: a prayer attributed to St. Bernard, to the Virgin
   5v: a prayer to the Virgin *in sole*, with an indulgence for 11,000 years
5v-6r: a prayer to the Virgin (fig. 184)
6r-6v: a prayer to St. Anne "with many indulgences"
   6v: a prayer to one's personal angel

As one can see from this list, three of the added prayers carried large
indulgences. Two further prayers, those to the Trinity and to one's
personal angel, promised personal protection. Indulgenced prayers
do not appear in the original core of the manuscript, and the book's
owner around 1500, when this quire was added, apparently deemed
this a shortcoming that had to be addressed. Even though the book was
already teeming with images, including full-page miniatures to mark
the canonical hours within the Hours of the Virgin, such as the Carrying
of the Cross on fol. 44v (fig. 185), the owner considered it wanting.

Adding a quire of indulgenced prayers to the beginning of the book helped to turn the book of hours into a vehicle for eternal transcendence. Moreover, as one can see from the dirt ground into the folios in this added section, the owner paid particular attention to the newly added prayers: they served an immediate need and were used heavily.

Fig. 186
Folio in the original part of the manuscript, copied and decorated in South Holland. Bruges, Stadsbibliotheek, Ms. 334, fol. 65r. Image © Bruges, Stadsbibliotheek, all rights reserved.

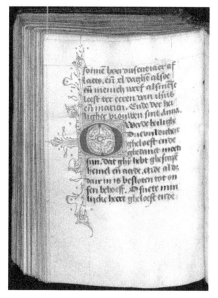

Fig. 187
Folio from a quire added and decorated around 1500 in the Southern Netherlands. Bruges, Stadsbibliotheek, Ms. 334, fol. 183v. Image © Bruges, Stadsbibliotheek, all rights reserved.

A book of hours introduced above, Bruges, Stadsbibliotheek, Ms. 334, was originally made in South Holland, and the core manuscript has red and blue penwork typical of South Holland, possibly Delft. However, the final two quires of the manuscript, beginning on fol. 183, were added later and have been inscribed by a different hand at the end of the fifteenth century. While the core of the manuscript was made in South Holland in the third quarter of the fifteenth century (fig. 186), the added quires were made around 1500 in the Southern Netherlands with less ornate red pen decoration (fig. 187). Such geographical layering in this manuscript suggests that the first or second owner had either moved south or sold it to someone in the south.

Not only is the decoration different in the two added quires of
Bruges, Stadsbibliotheek, Ms. 334, but so is the style of the script, the
accent of the vernacular language, and the type of prayer. The original
core of the manuscript contains the prayers one would expect to find in
a book of hours, including the Penitential Psalms, and the Long Hours
of the Cross. Instead of a normal long Hours of the Virgin, it has a
highly abbreviated version, in which the incipit for each hour presents
the events from the life of the Virgin as a rhyming couplet. This core
also contains the "Hundred Articles of Henry Suso," a text strongly
associated with female religious, and several prayers to be said before
an image of the Virgin. The later owner added: a prayer to the Virgin
of the Sun, with an indulgence of 71,000 years given by pope Sixtus IV
(fol. 183r-190v); another hand added a prayer to "the sweet name of
Jesus in the sun," which pope Sixtus IV indulgenced for 11,000 years
(fol. 191r-191v); and another prayer to the Virgin of the Sun, this time an
indulgence by Pope Sixtus for 11,000 years (fol. 191v). As Sixtus IV only
became pope in 1476, these additions must postdate that year. Clearly
what drove the new owner to add quires to the book was the strong
desire to include the newest and most heavily indulgenced prayers
available.

Time and again, the texts that owners added to existing books of
hours were those that carried more indulgences. This holds true for a
book of hours from Leiden in Middle Dutch (HKB, Ms. 76 G 13). The
original parts of the manuscript, made around 1490, have been inscribed
in the "spiky script" of Leiden, and they have blue acanthus border
decoration that also typifies production from that city (fig. 188).[74] The
full-page miniatures have a linear, graphic quality in which much of the
naked parchment is left exposed. They might even be characterized as
drawings heightened with wash.

Its original makers conceived of HKB, Ms. 76 G 13 as a series of the
simplest textual units marked by a splash of color at the major openings.
That the version of the Vigil for the Dead has only three lessons, rather
than the more rigorous nine, suggests that it was made for a lay person,
that is, someone who is not praying for others' souls as a livelihood. It

---

74 Opening in a book of hours made in Leiden, with the incipit of the Vigil for the Dead
    (three-verse version), and a full-page miniature depicting the Mass for the Dead.
    The Hague, Koninklijke Bibliotheek, Ms. 76 G 13, fol. 85v-86r. http://manuscripts.
    kb.nl/zoom/BYVANCKB%3Amimi_76g13%3A085v_086r

was perhaps this owner, or the manuscript's second owner not long thereafter, who added four quires and two full-page miniatures to the end of the manuscript after the Vigil for the Dead (HKB, Ms. 76 G 13, fol. 98–123). A date of ca. 1500 for these additions is reasonable. These have also been inscribed in a spikey hand, but not in the same hand as the original part of the manuscript. This suggests that the owner(s) lived in Leiden, purchased the manuscript there, and also had it updated there. These additions, as one might now expect, contain highly indulgenced prayers and begin with the Verses of St. Gregory, prefaced by a relevant full-page image of his vision (fig. 189).[75] Popular at the very end of the fifteenth century and beginning of the sixteenth, the nine-verse version of the Verses of St. Gregory promised enormous indulgences. According to the rubric, the suppliant would receive 92,000 years plus 24,000 years plus 80,000 days' indulgence, as confirmed "by many popes" (HKB 76 G 13, fol. 99r). Another prayer in this added section promises 7,000 years' indulgence, confirmed by Pope Boniface, for anyone who reads a short prayer in front of a crucifix (HKB 76 G 13, fol. 100v). This section of added material also includes another prayer to the Cross, marked by another full-page miniature depicting Christ on the Cross (fig. 190).[76]

Anonymous painters, called the Masters of the Suffrages for convenience, supplied the two full-page miniatures embedded in this added section. These artists were probably active in Leiden around 1500.[77] They seem to have specialized in making miniatures as upgrades for existing manuscripts, as is the case with the current example. Their bold, saturated colors contrast sharply with the watery tonalities of the painter who supplied the images in the original parts of the book. These painters often construct "strewn flower" borders and do so in a formulaic way,

---

75 Beginning of a group of quires added to a book of hours made in Leiden, with a full-page miniature depicting the Mass of St. Gregory (attributed to the Masters of the Suffrages) facing the Verses of St. Gregory. The Hague, Koninklijke Bibliotheek, Ms. 76 G 13, fol. 98v-99r. http://manuscripts.kb.nl/zoom/BYVANCKB%3Amimi_76 g13%3A098v_099r

76 Opening near the end of a book of hours made in Leiden, from an added section, with a full-page miniature depicting the Christ crucified (attributed to the Masters of the Suffrages) facing a prayer to the cross. The Hague, Koninklijke Bibliotheek, Ms. 76 G 13, fol. 105v-106r. http://manuscripts.kb.nl/zoom/BYVANCKB%3Amimi_ 76g13%3A105v_106r

77 A good study of these artists has not yet been written. In the mean time, consult A. W. Byvanck and G. J. Hoogewerff, *Noord-Nederlandsche Miniaturen in Handschriften der 14e, 15e en 16e Eeuwen* ('s-Gravenhage: M. Nijhoff, 1922–1925), no. 113.

filling the bottom corner with a large red rose in both cases. They show the flowers on a yellow background, which was much cheaper to paint than the gold backgrounds of the Southern Netherlandish miniaturists they are ultimately imitating. Their bold colors and designs must have appealed to a certain kind of urban consumer who wanted to make his or her book more showy and also more useful for new devotional tastes. Like the Masters of the Dark Eyes, discussed later, they seem to have also worked with scribes to make word-image ensembles with which owners could upgrade existing manuscripts.

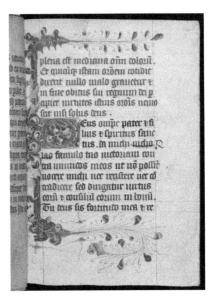

Fig. 191
Beginning of an added section of an enhanced book of hours. Cambridge, University Library, Ms. Ee.1.14, fol. 103r. Image © Cambridge University Library, all rights reserved.

Fig. 192
Folio in an enhanced book of hours, with a personalised prayer for "Nicholas," in which the name has been crossed out by a later user and replaced with the initial R. Cambridge, University Library, Ms. Ee.1.14, fol. 120r. Image © Cambridge University Library, all rights reserved.

An English book of hours introduced above also has entire quires with indulgences added to it, though these were modified over time to personalize the book (Cambridge, UL, Ms. Ee.1.14).[78] The original core of the manuscript was made in London around 1405. Some time

---

78	Binski, Zutshi, and Panayotova, *Western Illuminated Manuscripts: A Catalogue of the Collection in Cambridge University Library*, no. 191, pp. 180–81.

later a man whose name was evidently Nicholas was not satisfied with his book of hours when it came into his possession, as around 1440 he added several quires, which comprise fol. 51–52 and fol. 103–139. These additions were probably made in or around Bury St. Edmunds, and their style differs from that in the original parts of the book. Old and new sections appear side-by-side at fol. 103r (fig. 191). The additions were executed with a different style of script and decoration (complete with green penwork), on parchment ruled in bright red ink, whereas the original parts of the book were ruled in subtle brown.

The later owner was apparently disturbed by the lack of certain texts, such as the *Commendacio animarium* that initiates this added section, and sought to correct this lack. Into this packet of quires, he also added (or commissioned from a scribe) an indulgenced prayer personalized for himself: his name, Nicholas, has been worked into the body of the prayer text (fig. 192). A later (third?) owner crossed out the name of Nicholas and inserted his own initial, R, in the margin. Both layers of additions—the full quires of physical material, and the insertion of the letter *R*—were made to personalize the book to the new owner(s), and to turn the book into a machine for the salvation of specific souls.

In general, additions to prayerbooks were made to adjust the function of the book. Here I analyze a manuscript that is predominately a picture book, to which someone added more texts in several campaigns of work, including quires of indulgenced texts. The manuscript is a tiny prayerbook containing 66 full-page paintings by the Master of the Morgan Infancy Cycle (LBL, Add. 50005). The Master of the Morgan Infancy Cycle, who is named for a manuscript now in the Morgan Library and Museum in New York, was active in the second decade of the fifteenth century, when the core of this manuscript was written and painted.[79] Add. 50005 is one of the most fully illuminated prayerbooks made in the Northern Netherlands before the Master of Catherine of Cleves. It contains imagery that is iconographically creative as well as highly expressive (fig. 193).[80] However the original texts were a bit

---

[79] James Marrow named the Master of the Morgan Infancy Cycle after the artist in New York, Morgan Library and Museum, Ms. M. 866, for which see James H. Marrow, "Dutch Manuscript Illumination before the Master of Catherine of Cleves: The Master of the Morgan Infancy Cycle," *Nederlands Kunsthistorisch Jaarboek* 19 (1968), pp. 51–113.

[80] Master of the Morgan Infancy Cycle, Christ as Man of Sorrows, with the instruments of the passion. London, British Library, Add. Ms. 50005, fol. 133v. http://www.bl.uk/manuscripts/Viewer.aspx?ref=add_ms_50005_fs001r

sparse. This evidence, alongside the pictorial evidence, suggests that the book was used as a didactic booklet for a child, who would have chiefly used its pictures, which are each labeled at the bottom with inscriptions in red; the book also contains the simple texts taught to children: the *Pater Noster*, *Ave Maria*, and *Credo* (fig. 194).[81] The presence of these texts, in the original hand of the core manuscript, suggests that the book original functioned as a teaching tool to someone learning to read.

Later in the fifteenth century its owner augmented it. He or she added (or commissioned the addition of) new texts. The scribe first filled the backs of the miniatures, as well as the remaining blank parchment at the end of the core of the manuscript, and also added two quires of extra parchment beyond that. This means that the texts at the end of the manuscript (fol. 159v-179v) have been added chiefly in order to accommodate suffrages and indulgenced texts. Specifically, the added texts supply the manuscript with suffrages to various saints: Erasmus, Barbara, Catherine, the Eleven Thousand Virgins, Agatha, Stephen, Laurence, Jeroen, and Francis. This list of saints, which the new owner went to some length to include, may help to reveal who used the book. He or she probably lived in the County of Holland, where St. Jeroen was venerated, and may have had a Franciscan confessor. It is possible, for example, that the later fifteenth-century owner belonged to a community of tertiaries in a Franciscan milieu, in which Erasmus, Barbara, Catherine, Ursula, or Agatha was the patron saint. Tellingly, this person also added the seven-verse version of the Verses of St. Gregory (with an indulgence of 40,028 years and 40 days; fig. 195);[82] and a prayer to be said at the elevation of the Eucharist during mass, worth 2000 years' indulgence (LBL, Add. 50005, fol. 168r-169v and fol. 169v-171r, respectively). The late fifteenth-century owner, in other words, updated the manuscript with prayers to saints that must have held some personal interest, and with two heavily indulgenced prayers.

Here is one scenario that explains why the book looks the way it does: the manuscript was made for a child to aid in his mastery of reading and understanding the tenets of Christianity. When the child reached

---

81   Pater Noster, and beginning of the Ave Maria. London, British Library, Add. Ms. 50005, fol. 15v. http://www.bl.uk/manuscripts/Viewer.aspx?ref=add_ms_50005_fs001r

82   Verses of St. Gregory (added). London, British Library, Add. Ms. 50005, fol. 168r. http://www.bl.uk/manuscripts/Viewer.aspx?ref=add_ms_50005_fs001r

a certain age, he (or his confessor) wanted to increase his exposure to other texts, and therefore had the manuscript augmented. After all, the manuscript had a great deal of blank space available, on the backs of all of the miniatures. A scribe was commissioned not only to fill in these spaces, but also to add more material to the book, in the form of several quires, all filled with prayers, especially indulgenced ones.

A similar scenario may have been in play with a prayerbook made in the Southern Netherlands in the mid-fifteenth century (Harley 3828). That manuscript was apparently made for a young girl in order to learn to read, as it begins with a full-page miniature depicting an all-female classroom, facing the inscription of the alphabet in capital and lower-case letters (fig. 196).[83] The manuscript also contains other texts for a beginning learner, such as a rhyming prayer-poem, for which each stanza is dedicated to one of the *arma Christi*, pictured at the top of the folio (fig. 197).[84] These are easy to read and memorize (written as they are in rhyming vernacular), and they have been copied with almost no abbreviations that could have tripped up the young learner. Several quires were later added to the manuscript, including some with long rubrics and indulgences. These were written by a different hand in a different style, with more abbreviations and not images. It is possible that these were added when the child had matured, had advanced as a reader, and had entered the age when she could sin, and was therefore in need of indulgences to wipe the slate clean.

Owners also added components to a book in order to specify a foreign-made product. This occurred in England, as I have detailed above, but also in Scotland, which in the fifteenth century produced few luxury manuscripts. Scots of means often chose to buy manuscripts not from England, but rather from the Netherlands and France, Scotland's trading partners. Trade routes across the English Channel conveyed not only bulky items, such as wool, but also luxury items. In the act of trading commodities, parties also traded ideas, and the exact nature

---

83 Girls learning to read, a full-page miniature facing the alphabet, in a prayerbook probably made for a child. London, British Library, Harley Ms. 3828, fol. 27v-28r. http://www.bl.uk/catalogues/illuminatedmanuscripts/record.asp?MSID=4410

84 Rhyming prayer to Christ's robe and the dice of the arma Christi, with a miniature depicting these objects, in a prayerbook probably made for a child. London, British Library, Harley Ms. 3828, fol. 65v. http://www.bl.uk/catalogues/illuminatedmanuscripts/record.asp?MSID=4410

of those routes—with all the tangible and intangible items that flowed along them—was governed by political and market forces, as well as geography. Towards the end of the fifteenth century the harbor around Bruges silted up, and it lost its edge as a trading city. Antwerp on the River Schelde overtook it, and also became the center of art production. While Antwerp was the center of the printing industry in the Southern Netherlands, it also produced manuscripts, as did nearby Malines. It was probably from one of these two cities that James Brown, dean of Aberdeen, commissioned a manuscript prayerbook (Edinburgh, NLS, Ms. 10270).[85] From his home in Scotland, he might have used an agent to order the book, as he communicated some rather specific requests. The book contains a computational circle for calculating the date of Easter beginning in 1499, the probable date of production. It also contains a calendar with the obits of James Brown's parents, Elizabeth Lauder (11 June 1494) and Master Robert Brown (23 December 1460), an indulgenced prayer (the verses of St. Gregory) and a thaumaturgic prayer (extracts from St. John's Gospel); the Penitential psalms and litany, and the Office of the Dead. Everything in this book is about James Brown praying for the souls of his parents.

Fig. 198
Folio in the Prayer book of James Brown, with a full-page miniature depicting James Brown presented to the Virgin's altar. Edinburgh, National Library of Scotland, Ms. 10270, fol. 17v. Image © National Library of Scotland, all rights reserved.

---

85   David McRoberts, "Dean Brown's Book of Hours," *The Innes Review* xix (1968), pp. 144–67.

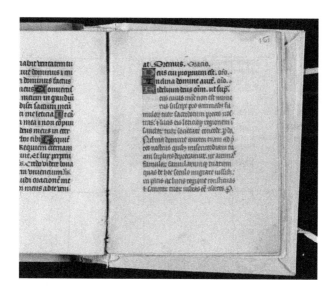

Fig. 199 Folio in the Prayer book of James Brown, with text added to existing parchment near the end of the manuscript. Edinburgh, National Library of Scotland, Ms. 10270, fol. 151r. Image © National Library of Scotland, all rights reserved.

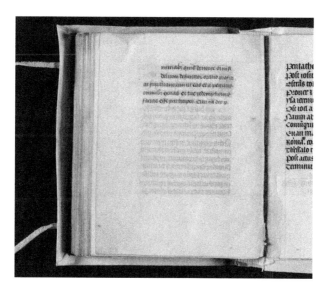

Fig. 200 Folio in the Prayer book of James Brown, with text added to existing parchment near the end of the manuscript. Edinburgh, National Library of Scotland, Ms. 10270, fol. 151v. Image © National Library of Scotland, all rights reserved.

Ms. 10270 contains four miniatures: James Brown presented by St. Augustine before an altar to Mary (fol. 17v; fig. 198); the Virgin and Child (fol. 50v); David in prayer, to preface the Penitential Psalms (fol. 90v); and the Raising of Lazarus to mark the beginning of the Vigil (fol. 111v). The portrait on fol. 17v shows the donor in prayer before a sculpted and polychromed image of the Virgin in a church, suggesting the patron's intense Marian devotion. Perhaps the illuminator was sketching the sitter from life when he depicted James Brown wearing an ermine wrap (fur on one side, silk on the other) terminating with little black tails on the floor, or perhaps he based this depiction on a verbal description. Either way, the painter was responding to the sitter's requests and particular aesthetic interests. Moreover, needle holes and fragments of textile indicate that the image was covered with green curtain. Lab tests would probably confirm that the curtain was made in silk. Did James Brown sew the curtains into his book? Or have them attached in Scotland? Or could one order a book, complete with silk curtains sewn in, directly from book makers in the Southern Netherlands?

The book was not entirely to his satisfaction, however, because upon receiving it, he had it augmented with local saints, including St. Andrew, and had a quire of prayers added to the end. The original Netherlandish book makers, although making the book to commission (as evidenced by the unusual combination of texts and the full-page miniature of the patron), had not used the right kind of Scottish calendar, but had copied a Netherlandish one instead. Among the saints in red, the calendar lists St. Macharius, a martyr whose relics were preserved in Ghent, but who would be utterly irrelevant to a dean from Aberdeen. The book's Scottish owner set out to adjust the manuscript to his needs by filling in the calendar and augmenting it with prayers and texts. Specifically, he filled in the empty parchment at the end of the Vigil (figs. 199 and 200). Someone has filled 151r with more prayer text in a very competent hand; another person, writing in a script that's nearly a Bourgogne, has made an addition on 151v. As these hands are distinctively not Scottish, either the patron found Netherlandish scribes who worked as scriveners in Scotland, or he had these additions made when he was abroad.

This blank parchment at the end of the Vigil did not however give him enough space, so he added a quire to the end of the book (fol. 152–157), which is ruled separately with narrower margins for less waste.

The items he was desperate to include in the book, which are copied in beginning on fol. 152r, are mnemonic verses for remembering the books of the Bible; a poem on the death of Elizabeth Lauder of the Bass (his mother); and a table for finding the date of Easter. Although the Netherlandish scribe had provided him with a computational circle for calculating the date, this chart was handier and did not require him to do any math. Considering that he had an ecclesiastical position in Aberdeen, one can see why he would want to know at least the books of the Bible. And the verses on his mother's death extend the function of the rest of the manuscript, to do what he could for the salvation of his mother's soul.

* * *

While parchment has a lifespan that far exceeds the lifetime—and possibly the imagination—of its maker, bindings wear out with heavy use. Moveable parts, such as leather and cords forced to function as hinges, crack and break, especially if they have been glued, as glue makes things brittle. Rebinding afforded book owners the possibility of making changes to their books. They could add new parchment modules such as single leaves, bifolia, and entire quires, or they could refurbish the decoration, cast off unnecessary parts (such as calendars made for elsewhere), or absorb images—old heirlooms or new miniatures— into their books. These adjustments were not seamless: quite literally this new physical material would be stitched, along with the original material, onto the cords that would be fixed into the book's new or reused covers. The seams were therefore on the inside of the book, deep within its gutter, and like the seams on well-hemmed trousers were largely out of sight.

Owners took the opportunity during rebinding to make changes to their books. The foregoing discussion has demonstrated that they sewed images in before major text openings, adding both color and devotional presence, while raising the value of their books. They added sheets with new prayers, especially those providing large indulgences that had come into circulation since the book was new. Owners often incorporated images of themselves, appended whole groups of images, or even harvested images stripped from another book. They could also incorporate longer prayers and texts, including recently devised feasts and new fashionable prayers copied onto bifolia or full quires. Indeed, copying prayers on flat sheets with a hard desk underneath must have been easier than copying them into an already bound book, as anyone who has ever attempted to write in a tightly bound diary can attest. After 1390 leaves with images circulated for this purpose, and I suspect that scriveners also copied short prayer texts into booklets, which owners could likewise bind into their books next time they had them rebound.

Some of these activities led to greater standardization in the processes of making books of hours. Throughout the fifteenth century in Northern Europe the standard was to be that all major texts began on a fresh quire, so that they left open the possibility that an owner could add an image either immediately or at a later date. Concomitantly, images were made on single leaves so they could be slotted into the book with the image on the left side of the opening. These forces also led to the rapid production of single-leaf images by fairly unskilled artists. The resulting images, especially those by the Masters of the Pink Canopies, are colored in with unmodulated paint, within lines drawn by simple geometric shapes, or based on simple models. Division of labor, plus the chance to train each contributor only to meet the demands of his small contribution, led to skill loss. Although few sale records survive that might indicate book costs over time, once suspects that modularly-made manuscripts came more cheaply to the consumer and widened the consumer base down-market.

Strangely enough, some of these same ideas were used at the opposite end of the quality spectrum. The mastermind behind the production of Simon de Varie's book of hours, for example, was able to assemble a book from component parts in Paris, including full-page miniatures made by Jean Fouquet who worked in Tours, precisely because making components modularly meant that one could make them remotely.

Adding new images often threw off the hierarchy of decoration and therefore required some other forms of upgrading. Such was the case in Beinecke Rare Book and Manuscript Library, Ms. 434. When the Masters of the Dark Eyes added full-page miniatures to an already complete book of hours, they added painted border decoration to match the images, thereby creating visually cohesive openings. One change begot another. The fact that the Masters of the Dark Eyes often created full-page images with rather unusual subjects suggests that they made upgrades for specific books, rather than using standard images that they had in stock. This observation is consistent with the additions they made to Beinecke 434, as well as for the leaf they added to the Fagel Missal, which could only have been made for this large missal. Thus, these artists were the ones to go to for lavishly colored bespoke miniatures. The Masters of the Dark Eyes return in Part IV, as they also specialized in rearranging books' contents so that the new entities hardly resembled the original parts from which they were made.

Part IV: Complicated interventions and complete overhauls

As the examples above demonstrate, people changed their books, adding physical material where necessary, in order to update older books to new situations. Scribes fitted texts into existing spaces. They wrote new texts on added quires. And owners were probably also able to buy quires of texts off the shelf to add. Of course, owners could also add images, largely in the form of single-leaf miniatures. Many of the manuscripts in the previous section had been introduced earlier in the current study, indicating that they had not one, but several different kinds of interventions.

Some books underwent complete overhauls and were changed structurally. Above I mentioned the Murthly Hours, which a late medieval owner had supplemented with a series of full-page miniatures, probably harvested from a psalter. Other ways of breaking up older books and redeploying their parts resulted in new book forms altogether. In this section, I consider bookish Frankensteins, pieces that have been stitched together into a new beast.

Building a book out of disparate quires

When it first catalogued its collection, the Royal Library in Brussels assigned each "booklet" within a composite volume a separate signature. This is why, for example, Brussels, KB, 4459–70, a miscellany made at the Cistercian monastery of Villers in the early fourteenth

    http://dx.doi.org/10.11647/OBP.0094.04

century, constitutes a manuscript within one set of covers but has a range of signatures. The cataloguer who assigned these signatures in the nineteenth century counted twelve distinct parts or modules within the binding and reflected that number in the new compound signature.[1]

Most libraries do not number composite volumes in this way, which means that scholars are much more likely to treat composites erroneously as single entities. Many prayerbooks, which at first glance seem to be homogenous volumes, in fact defy a single-stranded origin narrative. In this section I examine a few surprising examples. Of course the line between "a manuscript with some leaves or quires added later" and "a composite" is thin indeed. Regardless of what they are called, seeing them as stratified products can yield stories about layers of time and how medieval people treated, manipulated, and rescued the past.

A. An atelier in Bruges

Bruges in the fifteenth century had an advanced book-making culture. Whereas in the Northern Netherlands, convents played a significant role in manuscript production (including the Delft convents that loom large in this study, as well as convents in Gouda, Haarlem, Amsterdam, and elsewhere), in the Southern Netherlands, the organized and efficient production of manuscripts seems to have been in lay hands. Or at least, a large number of the resulting manuscripts do not reveal allegiance to a particular patron saint, particular confessor or rule and have not been "branded" by a convent. Important in Bruges instead were the rhetoricians' guilds, which produced all kinds of texts, including plays and personalized rhyming prayers. These played a role in book culture of late-fourteenth and fifteenth-century Bruges and stemmed partly from fashion at court, which had favored rhyming texts in the vernacular, because reading such texts aloud formed an integral part

---

1   These parts could be termed *booklets*. See Robinson, "The 'Booklet:' A Self-Contained Unit in Composite Manuscripts," pp. 46–67. For the manuscript, see Jean Baptist Gessler, *Jezus' Lijden en Zijdewonde in Woord en Beeld Verheerlijkt: Een Folkloristische Bijdrage tot de Kennis van de Godsvrucht Onzer Voorouders* (Leuven: Sint-Alfonsusdrukkerij, 1939), esp. pp. 13–22.

of courtly entertainment. Moreover, the strong court culture resulted in plenty of money for experimentation in the arts.

I have shown above that centers of manuscript production in the Southern Netherlands were early adopters of the single-leaf miniature and also of the modular method. Not only could they make new manuscripts out of component parts, but they could overhaul existing manuscripts by applying the same techniques. In this section I analyze one example: BKB, Ms. 19588.[2]

Upon first flipping through this manuscript, I thought it was homogenous, as if it were the product of a single organizing mind. But it is not. It begins with a calendar and has the look and feel of a book of hours, but it is rather a complicated object made in at least three campaigns of work, which I treat in turn.

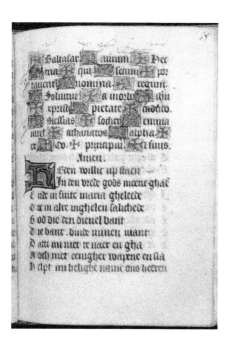

Fig. 201
Folio in a composite manuscript, with the end of an apotropaic text and the beginning of a versified vernacular Marian prayer in Middle Dutch. Brussels, Koninklijke Bibliotheek van België, Ms. 19588, fol. 68r. Image © Koninklijke Bibliotheek van België, all rights reserved.

---

2   For a description, see Maria Meertens, *De Godsvrucht in de Nederlanden. Naar Handschriften van Gebedenboeken der xvᵉ Eeuw*, 6 vols. ([n.p.]: Standaard Boekhandel, 1930–1934), vol. VI, no. 24.

Fig. 202 Annunciation painted by the Masters of the Gold Scrolls, with the beginning of the Hours of the Virgin in Latin, and a facing page in Middle Dutch in a different hand. Brussels, Koninklijke Bibliotheek van België, Ms. 19588, fol. 29v-30r. Image © Koninklijke Bibliotheek van België, all rights reserved.

Fig. 203
Last Judgement painted by the Masters of the Gold Scrolls, prefacing the Penitential Psalms in Latin. Brussels, Koninklijke Bibliotheek van België, Ms. 19588, fol. 84r. Image © Koninklijke Bibliotheek van België, all rights reserved.

Dating from 1410–15, the oldest part contains a calendar and some highly unconventional rhyming prayers and apotropaic texts primarily written in Dutch.[3] Their scribe is identical with one of the scribes of the Gruuthuse manuscript, a book made in Bruges that contains early rhymed vernacular texts in Middle Dutch.[4] In the early decades of the fifteenth century this city had a culture of advanced literacy stimulated by the court and chambers of rhetoricians, the rather high-falutin predecessors of poetry slam competitions. It appears, therefore, that this part of Ms. 19588, which contains dozens of rhyming prayers, was probably composed and copied in Bruges. Among these prayers, for example, one finds a versified vernacular prayer to Mary on fol. 68r, which was an avant-garde prayer, an attempt to rephrase an old sentiment in the mellifluous rhyming language of the Bruges literati (fig. 201). These oldest parts of the manuscript also contain talismanic texts, such as the prayer interspersed with crosses that ends on the same folio. These texts are written on quires of 16 lines per page, ruled in red, but with irregularly sized text blocks, as if the scribe were ruling the quires as he went. He used a rather thick parchment that has a velvety quality, which differs from the finer, thinner, more crumply parchment on which books of hours were usually copied. These qualities give the Dutch sections an experimental feel.

In the stratigraphy of this manuscript, the next layer comprises two modules of texts plus two loose images. These sections, which date from the 1440s, comprehend two of the texts that define a book of hours: the

---

3   Johan Oosterman, "Om de Grote Kracht der Woorden: Middelnederlandse Gebeden en Rubrieken in het Brugge van de Vroege Vijftiende Eeuw," in *Boeken voor de Eeuwigheid: Middelnederlands Geestelijk Proza*, ed. Th Mertens, *Nederlandse Literatuur en Cultuur in de Middeleeuwen* (Amsterdam: Prometheus, 1993), pp. 230–44, 437–44, esp. p. 440, no. 28; Johan Oosterman, *De Gratie van het Gebed: Middelnederlandse Gebeden, Overlevering en Functie: met Bijzondere Aandacht voor Produktie en Receptie in Brugge (1380–1450)*, 2 vols, Nederlandse Literatuur en Cultuur in de Middeleeuwen 12 (Amsterdam: Prometheus, 1995), vol. II, no. 2, 10, 29, 45, 66, 74, 77, 80, 93, 102, 110, 126, 137, 143, 148, 154, 175, 176, 190, 194, 202, 208, 209, 219, 244, 264, 269, 272, 273, 277, 289, 294, 339, 341, 359, 374; and Werner Verbeke, "'O Soete Cruce...' Een Berijmd Gebed in Handschrift Brussel, K. B, 19588," in *Serta Devota in Memoriam Guillelmi Lourdaux II: Devotio Windesheimensis*, ed. Werner Verbeke, et al., *Mediaevalia Lovaniensia, Series I / Studia xxi* (Leuven: Leuven University Press, 1995), pp. 297–313, have discussed some of the unique rhyming texts in this manuscript.

4   I owe this observation to Johan Oosterman. For the Gruuthuse manuscript (HKB, Ms. 79 K 10), see https://www.kb.nl/themas/middeleeuwen/het-gruuthusehandschrift

Hours of the Virgin (fig. 202) and the Seven Penitential Psalms (fig. 203). The parchment in these parts is fine, thin, and smooth, and the folios are ruled in brown for 18 lines per page. Thus, they are of a different campaign of work than the Dutch components. Whereas the Dutch parts are strange and unique, the Latin components are quite standard.

The scribe must have made these quires in collaboration with one or more artists called the "Masters of the Gold Scrolls" in modern literature, as the openings of the two modules each have column-wide miniatures painted by these masters. These artists worked in West Flanders and are known for recreating simple figurative and narrative miniatures with plain backgrounds enlivened by tendril-like geometric designs.[5] Dozens of books with their illuminations survive, and it is clear that they were several artists working in a common style in loose relationships with scribes.[6] This particular scribe-illuminator team in BKB, Ms. 19588 worked partly the old-fashioned way (with the illuminator painting directly on text pages for column-wide initials) and partly in the newer modular method (with full-page miniatures with blank backs prefacing texts produced in discreet packets). This suggests that while these masters made loose leaves for insertion into books of hours, they also worked with scribes to produce such pages. They were using some lessons gleaned from the Masters of the Pink Canopies (who preceded them by 50 years) but could also take specialty commissions as well. These artists were active in the post-Eyckian period in Bruges (and possibly in Ghent as well), from the 1440s. In total, Ms. 19588 contains four miniatures by these artists: two column-wide miniatures painted directly on the page (the Annunciation, the Last

---

5   Friedrich Winkler, *Die Flämische Buchmalerei des XV. und XVI. Jahrhunderts; Künstler und Werke von den Brüdern van Eyck bis zu Simon Bening* (Leipzig: E. A. Seemann, 1925), pp. 25–27 coined the name, the "Master of the Gold Scrolls" to describe a style of painting executed from ca. 1415–1460, probably in Bruges. The large size of the oeuvre quickly made it clear that multiple hands, rather than a single master, were painting miniatures in a similar style. For further studies about this group of artists, see Cardon, "The Illustrations and the Gold Scrolls Workshop;" Dogaer, *Flemish Miniature Painting in the 15th and 16th Centuries*, pp. 27–31; Bernard Bousmanne, Thierry Delcourt, and Ilona Hans-Collas, *Miniatures Flamandes, 1404–1482* (Paris; Brussels: Bibliothèque nationale de France; Bibliothèque royale de Belgique, 2011), pp. 140–42.

6   For an overview of workshop practices in the Southern Netherlands in this period, consult van Bergen, *De Meesters van Otto van Moerdrecht*.

Judgment) and two full-page miniatures (Crucifixion, Christ as Man of Sorrows). The manuscript also contains two full-page miniatures by these artists, which appear to be contemporary with these sections. Someone seems to have harvested these two modules—the Penitential Psalms and the Hours of the Cross—plus the two full-page miniatures from an existing book of hours. That person did not want the rest of the offices, but selected a range of peculiar and specific texts instead.

BKB, Ms. 19588 has been described as the product of collaboration between two scribes in the second decade of the fifteenth century.[7] But such a description does not really capture what is going on: two scribes did not set out to make this particular book. Two scribes indeed wrote the body of the text, but their labor did not overlap in time. In its current state this volume is the product of assembly, with 25 or 30 years separating the creation of the two components. A Dutch-speaking scribe in Bruges copied a number of obscure prayers, many of them rhyming, on parchment that he ruled as he went. He made a highly experimental object, not a standard commission. A patron could not have ordered the particular compendium of texts, because he would not have known they existed. In a totally separate process, scribes and illuminators worked together to make a boilerplate book of hours in Latin around 1440. Perhaps it was used until it fell apart, and someone salvaged some of the pieces to integrate them into what is now Ms. 19588. A few quires of texts, and two full-page miniatures were spared, and were applied to some existing quires of oddball Dutch texts. The scribe working in Latin was contemporary with the Masters of the Gold Scrolls, who post-date Jan van Eyck, and therefore the Latin section could not have been made in the 1410s.

However, when the textual components were put together, a new layer of adjustments took place. I think that the components only came together around 1480, decades after the texts were copied and the miniatures painted. The new owner of these disparate materials restructured and enhanced the fragments at hand. In all likelihood the miniature depicting the Crucifixion had prefaced the Hours of the Cross for the first forty-or-so years of its life before the new owner rebound it near the beginning of the manuscript (fig. 204).

---

7   Oosterman, *De Gratie van het Gebed*, p. 12.

Fig. 204 Crucifixion painted by the Masters of the Gold Scrolls, facing confession in Middle Dutch, with floral border decoration painted over a vine decoration. Brussels, Koninklijke Bibliotheek van België, Ms. 19588, fol. 13v-14r. Image © Koninklijke Bibliotheek van België, all rights reserved.

Fig. 205
Christ as Man of Sorrows painted by the Masters of the Gold Scrolls, full-page miniature with floral border decoration painted over a vine decoration, inserted so that it faces a Dutch text copied decades earlier. Brussels, Koninklijke Bibliotheek van België, Ms. 19588, fol. 143v-144r. Image © Koninklijke Bibliotheek van België, all rights reserved.

It now prefaces a confession, which the patron apparently wanted to emphasize, for she or he put it first, immediately after the calendar, and flagged it with a colorful miniature. Although the confession mentions Jesus (as most Christian prayers do) and could therefore be deemed relevant for the Crucifixion miniature, accompanying a confessional formula with an image of this subject is highly unusual. Its importance is further made visible by signs of wear. An owner of the image, perhaps the owner responsible for inserting it here, was extremely attached to this miniature. One can see this because Christ's face and torso have been rubbed repeatedly. Since no other part of the miniature is damaged, it was therefore, in all likelihood, damaged from veneration rather than from general wear. Furthermore, Christ's torso seems to be overpainted, and someone has added extra blood to Christ's wounds in a shade of red that is not part of the original artist's palette. In addition to the Crucifixion image, the new owner has placed an image of Christ as Man of Sorrows in the book so that it "illuminates" a text from the other campaign of work (fig. 205). The resulting organization reveals the owner's desire to draw attention to this text.

The late fifteenth-century owner who commissioned these changes may have been Yolente Doosterlinck, who inscribed her name in a shaky hand on the inside back cover, which is the manuscript's final medieval rebinding. It was possibly she who, in ca. 1480, placed the two loose miniatures before texts she wanted to emphasize. On the red background behind the Crucifixion (BKB, 19588, 13v) the letters

WK are repeated in blue, yellow, and white all over the back. This forms a variation to the Gold Scrolls Masters' normal approach to constructing backgrounds. A similar background with the same letters appears behind the Annunciation (fig. 202). The letters may refer to the original patron who ordered the image.[8] With the letters literally in the background, Yolente Doosterlinck was not bothered to have her own initials added during what may have been her campaign to overpaint the body of Christ and give him more blood.

She (or the late medieval owner, if not Yolente Doosterlinck) did, however, have the borders overpainted. Not only did she give the Crucifixion a prime position in the manuscript, kiss the body, enhance it with painted blood, but she may have been the one who upgraded the hairspray decoration on the openings with the miniatures and turned them into thickly painted flowers, a decorative style that had become popular in Ghent, Bruges and beyond by the end of the fifteenth century. Around all of the pages with illumination, one can see the old "hairspray" borders peeking out from under the newer opaque designs that (mostly) cover them. Overpainting the borders in the new style updated the book in terms of taste, brought visual coherence to it, and made it more colorful and sumptuous. The new owner lavished attention upon the book, as the new painted borders have been worn hard and have been considerably rubbed, suggesting that the person who went to all the trouble to salvage these fragments, upgrade, repaint, and rebind them, also handled the resulting manuscript and used it hard.

It may have been Yolente Doosterlinck who brought the disparate elements together, had the margins of the miniatures and some of the text folios repainted, and made for herself a personalized book upclycled from parts more than a half century old. At least she was the person who inscribed her name on the inside back cover of the new binding, as if laying claim to the binding job and to all the contents contained therein (fig. 206).

This discussion has shown that fifteenth-century book owners had a variety of choices to make for their books: what texts to include, how

---

8   *Cf* Baltimore, Walters Art Museum, W.239, fol. 13v, a Crucifixion, which has letters *L* and *A* repeated among a wall of wounds on the painted backdrop; these same letters appear on fol. 59v. On this manuscript, see Farquhar, "Manuscript Production and Evidence for Localizing and Dating Fifteenth-Century Books of Hours: Walters Ms. 239," pp. 44–88.

many images, and what kinds of borders, to name a few. They could change their minds about these choices even when their books were complete. They were also keen to re-use older book parts, and to take old books apart and upcycle their contents. They seemed to do so selectively, however. Saving some components means omitting others. When they made a new book out of pre-existing parts, they did not simply take all the components from A and follow them with all the components from B, and bind it all together. Instead, they selected and arranged carefully. In other words, they treated the broken-up books as modules that they could arrange according to their interests and desires.

B. Unica

Of course all manuscripts are unique, but some break severely with patterns and traditions. In this section I treat unica that are the results of complicated rearrangements and recombinations of physical material. A manuscript now in Heidelberg is the result of a *Biblia pauperum* that has been broken apart so that its folios could become full-page miniatures interleaved with a psalter and then stitched back together (Heidelberg, UB, Cod. Pal. Germ. 148).[9] The backs of the folios of the *Biblia pauperum* were blank, and most of them remain blank in the new hybrid; however, fol. 61 has *Biblia pauperum* on the recto and psalter on the verso, which demonstrates that the psalter scribe had the broken-up leaves of the *Biblia pauperum* when he began to write. A clue about the manuscript's origin appears at the front of the manuscript: a calendar for the bishopric of Eichstätt (in Bavaria). All the components were made there around 1430–50, with the *Biblia pauperum* slightly preceding the psalter.

A *Biblia pauperum* presents a typology, that is, stories from the New Testament explained as fulfillments of Old Testament prophecy and

---

9   I thank Thomas Lentes for bringing this manuscript to my attention and for sharing his thoughts about it. See also: Werner, *Cimelia Heidelbergensia: 30 illuminierte Handschriften der Universitätsbibliothek Heidelberg,* cat. 13, pp. 48–50; Maurus Berve, *Die Armenbibel: Herkunft, Gestalt, Typologie; Dargestellt Anhand von Miniaturen aus der Handschrift Cpg 148 D. Universitätsbibliothek Heidelberg,* Kult und Kunst (Beuron: Beuroner Kunstverlag, 1989); Siegfried Hofmann, *Der Ingolstädter Psalter: ein deutscher Psalter des Spätmittelalters aus der Universitätsbibliothek Heidelberg,* 1. Aufl. ed. (Regensburg: Schnell & Steiner, 2010); for an introductory study of the *Biblia pauperum,* based on a different manuscript, see Avril Henry, *Biblia Pauperum: A Facsimile and Edition* (Aldershot: Scolar Press, 1987).

precedent. This book type originated in the thirteenth century in a southern German monastery. Imagery is central to its endeavor. Each page serves as a "stand alone" unit, in which a New Testament story is depicted at the very center of the page, flanked by Old Testament prefigurations. Fol. 16v, for example, presents the story of Mary bringing the Christ child to the temple (fig. 207).[10] Four Old Testament prophets, who each wave a banderol bearing a textual reference to his respective prophecy, foresee this story. Further framing the image are two images depicting Old Testament events depicting mothers bringing their children to priests. Labels surround all of these images, so that each figure remains unambiguously named. These images and labels make the events clear, legible and didactic. Prose texts that nearly engulf the images form a further level of framing; they constitute explanations, showing how the Old Testament relates to the New Testament.

By taking this *Biblia pauperum* apart and integrating its leaves into a psalter, the binder was performing another act of exegesis. In effect, she or he was framing the psalter—the Old Testament text with the greatest currency as a devotional text—within a series of units that make the Old Testament relevant within the newer religion. Thus, the rebinding constituted an act of reframing and of interpretation. Bringing the two books together, the binder had to trim the *Biblia pauperum* down to the quick, as it had been copied onto larger folios than the psalter. Integrating the parts meant guillotining them, as the action of the knife forced them into a uniform page size. Imposing a new structure on the book asserted that the New Testament and the Old Testament were literally sewn together through prophecy. Not only did the book maker cut the *Speculum* apart and sew it into a new form, as full-page miniatures within a psalter, but an early user also sewed curtains to the tops of all of the *Speculum* folios. Although the curtains are no longer present, rows of needle holes at the tops of these folios attest to their former presence. Having to lift curtains in order to view the images must have given the owner an added layer of ritual, and allowed him or her to produce an act of revelation akin to the revelation depicted on the folios themselves: that the Old Testament is "revealed" in the New.

---

10   *Biblia pauperum* and psalter, interleaved. Heidelberg, Universitätsbibliothek, Cod. Pal. germ. 148, fol. 16v-17r. http://digi.ub.uni-heidelberg.de/diglit/cpg148

Fig. 208 Composite manuscript prayerbook made in France, fanned open to reveal signs of heavy use. 's-Heerenberg, The Netherlands, Collection Dr. J. H. van Heek, Huis Bergh Foundation, Ms. 2 (inv. 259). Image © The Huis Bergh Foundation, CC BY 4.0.

Fig. 209 An image module comprising two bifolia bound into a manuscript prayerbook compiled in France. 's-Heerenberg, The Netherlands, Collection Dr. J. H. van Heek, Huis Bergh Foundation, Ms. 2 (inv. 259). Image © The Huis Bergh Foundation, CC BY 4.0.

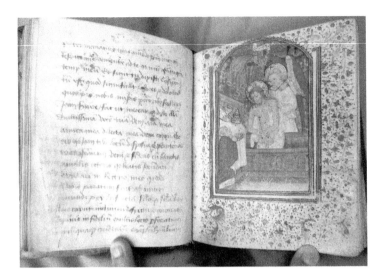

Fig. 210 Opening in a composite prayer book, with added prayers (left side), and a full-page miniature depicting the Mass of St. Gregory (right side). 's-Heerenberg, The Netherlands, Collection Dr. J. H. van Heek, Huis Bergh Foundation, Ms. 2 (inv. 259), fol. 40v-41r. Image © The Huis Bergh Foundation, CC BY 4.0.

Fig. 211 Opening in a composite prayer book, with two full-page miniatures, one depicting St. Francis receiving the stigmata, and one depicting the Nativity. 's-Heerenberg, The Netherlands, Collection Dr. J. H. van Heek, Huis Bergh Foundation, Ms. 2 (inv. 259), fol. 41v-42r. Image © The Huis Bergh Foundation, CC BY 4.0.

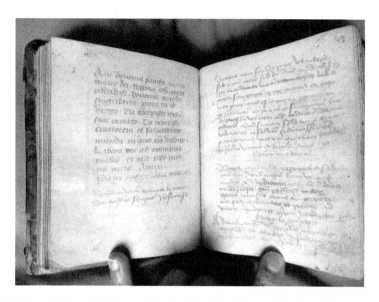

Fig. 212 Inscriptions added by two hands, filling the otherwise blank parchment.
's-Heerenberg, The Netherlands, Collection Dr. J. H. van Heek, Huis Bergh
Foundation, Ms. 2 (inv. 259), fol. 42v-43r. Image © The Huis Bergh Foundation,
CC BY 4.0.

Such acts of reframing took place in other contexts. A group of disparate
quires was brought together by late medieval owner in France to create
an unusual manuscript prayerbook ('s-Heerenberg, HB, Ms. 2, inv. no.
259).[11] The manuscript is a composite containing pieces of a calendar,
parts of at least two different books of hours (from the fifteenth century),
a single leaf with a prayer text probably copied in the sixteenth century,
and two bifolia with full-page miniatures. All of these elements were
bound together around 1500. Fanned open, the resulting volume
reveals its filthy pages, its margins that were trimmed for rebinding,
and the edges of the sixteenth-century binding (fig. 208). The owner
who gathered these elements and bound them together may have been
identical with the one who filled the blank space with more prayers. This
book provides an example of one that was heavily used and severely
altered. Those two activities often go together.

---

11   Korteweg, *Catalogue of Medieval Manuscripts and Incunabula at Huis Bergh Castle in
      's-Heerenberg*, cat. 49, pp. 98–100.

One unusual item that the owner has affixed is a module with images (fol. 40–43; fig. 209). I suspect that this packet circulated separately as a small picture book before it was integrated into the composite volume around 1500. Formed of two nested bifolia, its top and bottom surfaces were left blank so that it served as a natural cover to the booklet. (These spaces later provided writing surface for an enthusiastic owner.) These outer folios protected the contents, which consisted of images only and no words. Was this a book for the illiterate? Although that is unknowable, what is clear is that the booklet presented a non-textual, images-only form of piety.

The images painted on the internal surfaces present the idea of the Body of Christ in three different ways, each according to a different miraculous vision. The first image in the module is a Mass of St. Gregory in which the diminutive pope sees the body of Christ before him (fig. 210). This emphasizes the body at the center of the image, framed by an angel. With all the clothing and the bright blue background, Christ's naked body, spattered with blood, holds the center. Turning the page reveals a different manifestation of the body: Christ as a red-winged angel coming to impress his stigmata onto St. Francis. The third image shows the Nativity, the birth of the physical manifestation of Jesus on earth, according to the vision of St. Bridget of Sweden (fig. 211). This particular combination of images is unusual. Is it possible that the booklet was made for someone with a Franciscan confessor, who wanted to remember taking the Eucharist, celebrate a Corpus Christi feast, or otherwise commemorate an event centered on the body of Christ?

Several different people have added prayers to the blank space comprising the booklet's "covers." One wrote a Marian prayer in a fine late fifteenth-century hand on the back of the Nativity, choosing this location in order to be as close to Mary as possible (fig. 212). Another person, writing in a quick bookhand of the sixteenth century, added another prayer to the rest of this formerly blank opening. But this was not the first addition made to fol. 43r. A row of needle holes along the outer edge, and a circle of needle holes near the modern folio number "43" suggest that two objects were formerly stitched to this folio: a tall rectangular object, and a small round object. Did they date from a time when the picture booklet was still loose and unbound to a book of hours?

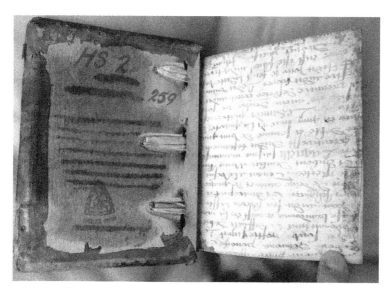

Fig. 213 Flyleaf and inner board of binding. 's-Heerenberg, The Netherlands, Collection Dr. J. H. van Heek, Huis Bergh Foundation, Ms. 2 (inv. 259). Image © The Huis Bergh Foundation, CC BY 4.0.

Fig. 214 Family kneeling before St. John the Baptist [?], 's-Heerenberg, The Netherlands, Collection Dr. J. H. van Heek, Huis Bergh Foundation, Ms. 2 (inv. 259), fol. 147r. Image © The Huis Bergh Foundation, CC BY 4.0.

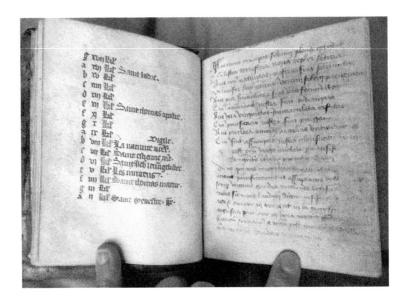

Fig. 215 Single leaf with prayers added at the end of the calendar.
's-Heerenberg, The Netherlands, Collection Dr. J. H. van Heek, Huis
Bergh Foundation, Ms. 2 (inv. 259), fol. 12v-13r. Image © The Huis
Bergh Foundation, CC BY 4.0.

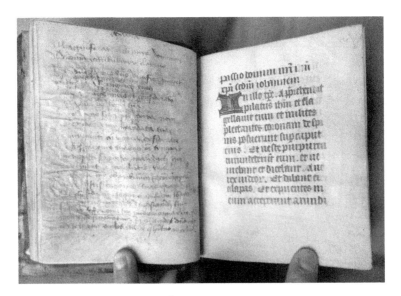

Fig. 216 A single leaf with prayers, and the incipit of the Passion according to
St. John. 's-Heerenberg, The Netherlands, Collection Dr. J. H. van Heek,
Huis Bergh Foundation, Ms. 2 (inv. 259), fol. 13v-14r. Image © The
Huis Bergh Foundation, CC BY 4.0.

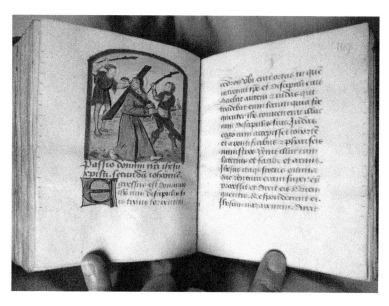

Fig. 217   The incipit of an illustrated Passion tract in Latin. 's-Heerenberg, The
Netherlands, Collection Dr. J. H. van Heek, Huis Bergh Foundation, Ms. 2 (inv.
259), fol. 166v-167r. Image © The Huis Bergh Foundation, CC BY 4.0.

This volume—the entity now known as 's-Heerenberg, HB, Ms. 2 (inv.
259)—comprehends the picture booklet, as well as a number of other
sections that were made in distinct campaigns of work:

1. Flyleaves made parchment of ca. 1500, which are contemporary with the
   binding (fig. 213);

2. Part of a book of hours in Latin, copied in France, possibly in Troyes,
   which consists of a calendar (fol. 1–12), the beginning of the Gospel
   of St. John, the Hours of the Virgin, and other prayers, some of them
   rhyming (fol. 44r-153v), in a production made in France c. 1400–25, with
   illuminations painted directly on the folios. This campaign of work
   includes a column-wide miniature depicting a secular family, who
   appears kneeling before John the Baptist (fig. 214). Their dress suggests
   that this part of the book was made in the 1420s. They may represent
   the family that commissioned this campaign of work. (The calendar was
   copied by a different scribe, but all these parts are ruled the same way,
   and have the same kinds of initial decoration, and therefore belong to
   the same layer in the book's stratigraphy);

3. A single leaf with prayers (fol. 13; fig. 215);

4. Part of a book of hours in Latin, copied in France, c. 1425–75 (fol. 14–39, 154–65) (fig. 216);

5. The picture booklet, with three full-page miniatures, made in France c. 1425–50, discussed earlier (fol. 40–43) (figs. 209–211);

6. An illustrated Passion tract in Latin, with nine miniatures painted directly on the folios, made in France c. 1475–1500 (fol. 166–207; fig. 217). This is ruled for a text block of 85x65 mm, 15 lines, *littera hybrida.*

The calendar (Item 2) has feasts in red including St. Sabiniani (March 2), St. Helena (April 4), the Translation of St. Lupus (May 10), the Translation of the Crown (August 11); these feasts are appropriate to Troyes and indicate that Item 2 was either made or used there. This section also contains a family portrait, likely the donors. Of course these observations about possible origins do not extend to the origins of the other parts.

Fig. 218 Opening in a composite prayer book, with a parchment painting depicting the Face of Christ pasted in, opposite the incipit of the Hours of the Virgin. 's-Heerenberg, The Netherlands, Collection Dr. J. H. van Heek, Huis Bergh Foundation, Ms. 2 (inv. 259), fol. 45v-46r. Image © The Huis Bergh Foundation, CC BY 4.0.

What follows is one scenario that accounts for the elements in this volume. Before 1500 someone in France acquired or inherited a number of well-worn and rather broken prayerbooks made earlier in the fifteenth century. He or she took these apart, and made a selection of the quires they contained, choosing a calendar from this one, a group of quires from that one, and an entire Passion tract of recent vintage that formed a booklet on its own. This person also incorporated a thin booklet of just two bifolia, which contained three images to commemorate the Eucharist. Either this collector of objects, or an earlier owner, stuck an image of Christ's face on Veronica's towel into the book, where there was some blank parchment (fig. 218). The collector then assembled these modules, together with a single sheet of prayers, and brought them to a binder, who bundled them together and bound them in the binding that currently protects them. This blind-stamped brown leather binding was made around 1500. In this binding the modules continued to receive hard wear in the sixteenth century, and the owner, or series of owners, filled much of the blank parchment with short prayers. This was accomplished over time, as the owner(s) took the book to various scriveners who make these additions in various hands. The book was made in layers over the course of a century, with physical material from multiple campaigns of work, and additional texts written in even more campaigns of work. The book, as it has survived in its binding, is a serendipitous encounter between many hands and many desires over a century.

The two cases just analyzed have revealed unique products cobbled together out of disparate parts for a particular set of circumstances. The Bavarian experiment in illustrating a psalter with typology may have been a one-off, and the French book of hours resulted from someone's collecting a particular group of parts. Owners and binders responded to specific, received sets of physical material units as springboards for new and experimental books. In these examples, and in many examples discussed above, owners also responded to blank parchment by succumbing to the desire to fill it.

While these examples were one-offs, other refurbishings followed a more general taste. In the late fifteenth century certain ateliers tapped into people's desire to overhaul older books and specialized in just that. Each of these transformations was unique and based on the available material at hand. Many such ateliers may have existed, but here I want to concentrate on two monastic ateliers plus one that was probably secular and staffed by urban professionals. I will revisit in greater detail

Netherlandish workshops I briefly introduced above, to explore in more detail how they operated.

C. The convent of St. Ursula

In the second half of the fifteenth century, convents in the Northern Netherlands not only made manuscripts but began specializing in updating older manuscripts in order to make them more relevant to their users. Convent sisters used sophisticated methods of adding modules to both new and used manuscripts, and could vary the degree of illumination according to an owner's budget. At least two convents (the Franciscan convent of St. Ursula and the Augustinian convent of St. Agnes, both in Delft) specialized in restructuring old manuscripts. I have identified three books of hours that the scriptorium of Franciscan tertiary sisters of St. Ursula augmented: Oxford, Bodleian Library, Ms. Rawl. Liturg. E.9*; HKB, Ms. 132 G 38; and Uppsala, Universitetsbiblioteket, Ms. C 517 k, which I treat here in turn. Those from the Augustinian convent I treat later in this section. Whereas the Franciscan convent specialized in adding new, indulgenced prayers to plain prayerbooks, the Augustinian convent specialized in adding lavish decoration to them.

1. Oxford, Bodleian Library, Ms. Rawl. Liturg. E.9*

Oxford, Bodleian Library, Ms. Rawl. Liturg. E.9* (hereafter: Rawlinson) is a book of hours that originally came from North Holland, to judge by its particular brand of rather coarse penwork (fig. 219).[12] Writing on thick parchment of low quality, the scribe copied the most basic offices from Geert Grote's translation: a calendar, Hours of the Virgin, Hours of the Holy Spirit, Hours of the Cross, Hours of Eternal Wisdom, the Seven Penitential Psalms and Litany, and the Vigil for the Dead. The North Holland scribe wrote only a few extra prayers as quire filler after

---

12 Opening in a book of hours at the incipit of the Hours of the Holy Spirit, with penwork from North Holland. Oxford, Bodleian Library, Ms. Rawlinson Liturgical e.9*, fol. 43r.

the Short Hours of the Cross (63r-68r). These quire fillers (fol. 68v-70v) comprise a prayer to the Wounds of Christ, to St. Francis, to Mary, to one's personal angel, and to St. Sebastian (fig. 220).[13] There are no prayers before and after taking the sacrament, and no extra collects in the Vigil for the Dead for friends and family, and no indulgences to fill out this book. This was a basic, bare-bones construction.

Either the original owner ordered the book of hours in North Holland, or else this person bought the rather generic book of hours there already complete. Its original decoration has no personalizing features that would suggest a bespoke product. The crudeness of the decoration makes it difficult to date, but the third quarter of the fifteenth century is a reasonable guess. One of the manuscript's subsequent owners wrote his name on the flyleaf in the late fifteenth or early sixteenth century: Pieter Willemsz of Goeree. He might have been the one who brought the manuscript to an atelier in Delft to have more prayers added to it.

Treating the manuscript structurally reveals its phased genesis and shows how the original parts of the manuscript interact with the added parts. Rawlinson and many other books of hours made after ca. 1450 were constructed using the modular method. As the collation diagram reveals, each major text has been copied onto a number of discrete quires. The scribe would begin each major text on a fresh quire, fill as many quires as needed to inscribe the entire text, and then often leave the rest of the quire blank. Often he or she would use a final quire of two, four, or six leaves rather than the usual eight if he perceived that the end of the text was near, so as to reduce wasted, uninscribed parchment. He would then begin the next text on its own fresh quire. Thus the individual texts were produced in units, which could then be assembled into books of hours with the texts in any order. This system also enabled a stationer or binder to add full-page miniatures to preface the major texts, as these could be inserted to the front of a module. One of the consequences of this method was that it often left some blank but ruled parchment at the end of each module.

---

13 Folio in a book of hours that falls at the end of a module, which was filled by the original scribe in North Holland for prayers to one's personal angel and to St. Sebastian. Oxford, Bodleian Library, Ms. Rawlinson Liturgical e.9*, fol. 70r.

Oxford, Bodleian Library, **Ms. Rawl. Liturg. E.9***: structure and content
Book of hours with modular structure and additions; Ms foliated 1–124

	Physical composition				Textual contents	
quire	structure of quire	includes folios	physical material from **Phase I** (North Holland) or **Phase II** (Delft-Ursula convent)	folios added or removed	contents	Written by Hand from North Holland (NH) or Delft-Ursula convent (DU)?
I	6	ff. 1–6	I		**calendar**	NH
II	6	ff. 7–12	I			NH
III	8	ff. 13–20	I		**Hours of the Virgin** (13r–42r)	NH
IV	8	ff. 21–28	I			NH
V	8	ff. 29–36	I			NH
VI	8	ff. 37–42	I			NH
VII	8	ff. 43–50	I		**Hours of the Holy Spirit** (43r–51v);	NH
VIII	2	ff. 51–52	I		quire filler added by DU (51v–end of quire)	NH + DU
IX	8 (-1)	ff. 53–59 (catchword on 59v)	II	fol. before 53 cut out probably because it had a decorated initial	**Verses of St. Gregory;** Prayers for the Sacrament, etc.	DU
X	2 (+1)	ff. 60–62	II			DU

XI	8	ff. 63–70	I		**Short Hours of the Cross** (63r-68r); NH hand added quire filler 68v-70v	NH
XII	8	ff. 71–78	I		**Hours of Eternal Wisdom** (71r-86v)	NH
XIII	8	ff. 79–86	I			NH
XIV	8 (-1)	ff. 87–93	I	fol. before 87 cut out probably because it had a decorated initial	**Seven Penitential Psalms and Litany** (86r-97v)	NH
XV	4	ff. 94–97	I			NH
XVI	8 (-1)	ff. 98–104	I	fol. before 98 cut out probably because it had a decorated initial	**Vigil of the Dead with 9 lessons** (98r-123v)	NH
XVII	6 (+1)	ff. 105–111	I			NH
XVIII	10	ff. 112–121	I			NH
XIX	2 (+1)	ff. 122–124	I, II	f. 124 (former pastedown) is from Delft		NH + D

Key	Original physical material from North Holland
	Physical material supplied by the Ursula convent in Delft

In Rawlinson, the later scribe from Delft has topped up Quire VIII with text, and then added Quires IX and X. These added texts are:

> Verses of St. Gregory (nine-verse version)
>
> Prayers to the sacrament (The folio containing the rubric that would have prefaced the prayers to the Sacrament has been cut out, probably because it was decorated)
>
> Prayers to be read in front of the Virgin's image for 30 days
>
> Prayer to the Virgin in the Sun, with an indulgence of 11,000 years
>
> Prayer to St. Erasmus to prevent sudden death, with a post-script rubric promising an indulgence of 140 days
>
> Prayers and privileges of St. Anne.[14]

One can see from this list that most of the prayers added to the manuscript provided indulgences, promised to prevent sudden death, or, in the case of the privileges of St. Anne, guaranteed riches. These privileges demanded that the reader look upon an image of St. Anne and perform "honor" by giving alms or lighting a candle, presumably in front of her image. It is no wonder that the manuscript's owner would have gone to great lengths to have his book taken out of its binding, have extra folios added to it, and have it rebound.

A close look at the structure of the added material reveals a great deal about the Delft scribe's method. Original parts of the manuscript (those written in North Holland) are inscribed in a *littera textualis*, ruled for a text block of 102x70mm. The North Holland scribe only ruled the block, and not the individual lines, but wrote 19 lines per folio using some other type of guide system. However the Delft scribe was not used to writing in an unlined text block. She took the manuscript out of its binding, then ruled the blank parchment at the bottom of fol. 51v and the recto and verso sides of fol. 52 (fig. 221).[15] When doing this, she matched the size of the new text block as closely as possible to the

---

14   These unusual prayers are nearly identical to those inscribed in BKB, Ms. IV 312, fol. 97v-98v.

15   Opening in a book of hours with the last 6 lines of the Hours of the Holy Spirit written by scribe from North Holland, and the rest of fol. 51v and 52r ruled and written by scribe from Delft, to fill the quire. Oxford, Bodleian Library, Ms. Rawlinson Liturgical e.9*, fol. 51v-52r.

existing one. She also matched the script size as closely as possible, although she wrote in a *textualis*, which was the "corporate" style of the convent of St. Ursula.

Some features of the added sections make it possible to connect this manuscript to a group of books of hours made for and/or by the Franciscan tertiary sisters of St. Ursula in Delft, a house that formed in 1454 or 1457, which produced many surviving manuscripts.[16] Several different scriptoria in Delft, which can be associated with various convents in that city, wrote manuscripts and decorated them with distinctive red and blue penwork, which is also present in the added sections of Rawlinson, such as on fol. 53v (fig. 222).[17] The convent sisters of St. Ursula probably listed Ursula as the first virgin in the litany in the books of hours they produced, and they also featured St. Ursula in red in the calendar. Many of the manuscripts in this group have ruling similar to that found in the added parts of Rawl. Liturg. e. 9*. Manuscripts I have localized to the convent of St. Ursula have catchwords that are written in script the same size as the text itself, and placed just to the right of the vertical ruling in the lower margin. An example appears in a book of hours now in The Hague (HKB, Ms. 135 E 18, fol. 107v; fig. 223).[18] Among manuscripts made in Delft, only those connected to the convent of St. Ursula (as determined by the calendar and decoration) contain these distinctive catchwords. A similar catchword appears on fol. 59v of Rawlinson, which connects the added parts of the manuscript to the St. Ursula group (fig. 224).[19]

It is also possible that this convent had a relationship with a particular binder. When the scribes from Delft—possibly sisters of St. Ursula—finished their augmentations and reassembled the quires of

---

16 Until a fuller study of manuscripts from this convent appears, consult: Kathryn Rudy, "De Productie van Manuscripten in het Sint-Ursulaklooster te Delft," *Delf: Cultuurhistorisch magazine voor Delft* 12, no. 2 (2010), pp. 24–27.

17 Folio in a book of hours inscribed by a Delft scribe, with typical red and blue penwork from Delft. Oxford, Bodleian Library, Ms. Rawlinson Liturgical e.9*, fol. 53v.

18 Folio in a book of hours with Delft decoration and a catchword, which is a codicological feature associated with manuscripts from the convent of St. Ursula in Delft. The Hague, Koninklijke Bibliotheek, Ms. 135 E 18, fol. 107v. http://manuscripts.kb.nl/zoom/BYVANCKB%3Amimi_135e18%3A107v

19 Opening with a catchword in a book of hours whose core was made in North Holland before extensive additions were made in Delft. Oxford, Bodleian Library, Ms. Rawlinson Liturgical e.9*, fol. 59v-60r.

this manuscript, they added a protective leaf to the end, which would become the back paste-down (it was lifted later when the spine was repaired). A scribe had obviously discarded the leaf after making an unrecoverable error (fig. 225).[20] Only one side is inscribed, and the copyist binned the leaf before writing on the other side or adding the initials in red and blue. This workshop for manuscript updates, which, after all, recuperated every line and every centimeter of space on the written surface to convey prayers, simply did not waste parchment. Instead, someone in the atelier used this mistake page as binding material.

Salvaged from the garbage heap, the protective leaf is inscribed in a controlled *textualis* of the variety that the convent of St. Ursula produced and is close in style to the leaf from HKB, Ms. 135 E 18, the one with the distinctive catchword mentioned above. That the stub of the leaf wraps around to the front of the previous quire indicates that the leaf was integrated into the structure of the book at the time of rebinding. Perhaps the convent of St. Ursula had its own bindery. Perhaps they sold or gave their scraps to the bindery. Perhaps the scribes were not members of the house of St. Ursula at all, but belonged to a professional atelier in Delft that wrote and bound manuscripts then sold them to the convent of St. Ursula. This third option, however, is unlikely, since several of the manuscripts in this group have collects in the Vigil for the Dead "for those who give us alms," a statement that strongly suggests that the manuscripts originated in a monastic context.

Nevertheless, the scribe has used a male noun "arm sondaer" in a rubric added to Rawlinson, which suggests that the added prayers were commissioned by a man, or that the sisters were updating and older manuscript to be sold in the open market, and therefore used the generalized male pronouns. This is also consistent with the note of ownership inscribed at the beginning of the book, indicating that it belonged to Pieter Willemszn of Goeree. Perhaps he wanted a book of hours with the latest prayers, but rather than buying a new one from scratch, he chose a much less expensive option, namely, buying a used, homely, no-frills book of hours, then having it augmented and rebound.

---

20 The inside back cover and the last folio of a book of hours (formerly a paste-down), which may have been waste material from the St. Ursula scriptorium in Delft. Oxford, Bodleian Library, Ms. Rawlinson Liturgical e.9*, fol. 124v and inside back cover.

2. The Hague, Koninklijke Bibliotheek, Ms. 132 G 38

A book of hours originally made in South Holland (HKB, Ms. 132 G 38) contains two layers of additions. Likely made in Delft around 1480, it has an Utrecht calendar with feasts in red including St. Hippolytus (13 August, who was venerated in Delft) and St. Jeroen (17 August, venerated in parts of South Holland). Although the manuscript may have been produced in Delft, it was not originally made in the convent of St. Ursula, for the first confessor in the litany is St. Martin, and the first virgin is St. Agnes. Where exactly within South Holland it was created remains unclear. Following its completion, one layer of changes was executed by the same monastic scriptorium that updated the Rawlinson manuscript—that of St. Ursula in Delft. The other layer was added in Leiden. Both Leiden and Delft are in South Holland, so all three stages of production occurred in close proximity. These layers of additions, worked into the fiber of the original manuscript, attest to an owner's (or two owners') desires to make the book more colorful and to fill it with new prayers, including indulgenced texts. An atelier in Leiden added more decoration, as well as full-page miniatures, and subsequently the convent sisters added numerous prayer texts to the book and decorated some of them. Below I have included a chart providing an overview of these two campaigns of work. The changes wrought at the Ursula convent were similar to, but far more complicated than, the interventions in Rawlinson and require some explanation.

HKB, Ms. 132 G 38 originally contained the normal texts associated with a book of hours: a calendar, the Hours of the Virgin, the Seven Penitential Psalms, the Short Hours of the Cross, the Verses of St. Gregory (five-verse version), and the Vigil for the Dead, along with a few suffrages and texts associated with St. Francis. Like Rawlinson, this manuscript was also constructed in modular units, but they are arranged somewhat differently here. (The Hours of the Virgin and the Seven Penitential Psalms, for example, comprise one unit, and the offices are organized in a different sequence.) This original part of the manuscript dates from about 1480 and was written somewhere in South Holland, possibly Delft. For the sake of abbreviation, I have called these sections "SH" (for South Holland) in the chart below. All of these original folios were written in a rather loose *hybrida* script and have quire notations in a small Gothic script on the recto side of the first four folios of each quire. Some simple penwork decoration appears on the original folios (although these were largely overpainted).

Hague, KB 132 G 38 (Book of Hours from South Holland, with additions).
Ms foliated I-XIII, 1–139

| | Physical construction | | | | Inscribed and painted content | |
quire	structure of quire	includes folios	Phase I (South Holland); Phase II (Leiden); Phase III (Ursula convent)	summary of added leaves	textual contents: written/painted by **South Holland scribe** (SH), **Leiden painter** (L), or **St. Ursula scribe** (U)	
I	6	ff. I-VI	I		calendar	SH
II	6	ff. VII-XII	I			SH
III	8 (+1)	ff. XIII-8	I+II	full-page miniature, Annunciation (fol. XIIIv) added in Leiden	**Hours of the Virgin** (1r-50r)	SH + L
IV	8	ff. 9–16	I			SH + L
V	8	ff. 17–24	I			SH + L
VI	8	ff. 25–32	I			SH + L
VII	8	ff. 33–40	I			SH + L
VIII	8	ff. 41–48	I			SH + L
IX	8 (+1)	ff. 49–57	I+II	full-page miniature, Last Judgment (52v) added in Leiden	filler added by St. Ursula scribe (bottom of 50r-50v); prayer inscribed by Hand SH (51r); filler added by St. Ursula scribe added by St. Ursula scribe (bottom of 51-51v)	SH + U + L
X	8	ff. 58–65	I		**Seven Penitential Psalms and Litany** (53r-71v);	SH + L

Quire	Folios	Structure	Addition	Content	Hands
XI	ff. 66–73	8	I		quire filler added by St. Ursula scribe (bottom of 71v–72r); quire filler inscribed by original SH hand (72v); quire filler by St. Ursula scribe (bottom of 72v–73v)	SH + L + U
XII	ff. 74–82	8 (+1)	I+II	full-page miniature, Crucifixion (74v) added in Leiden	**Short Hours of the Cross** (75r–82v); instructions for offering up penance (82v); quire filler by St. Ursula scribe (bottom of 82v)	SH + L + U
XIII	ff. 83–93	8 (+3)	I+II+III	full-page miniature, Mass of St. Gregory (83v) added in Leiden;	**Verses of St. Gregory**, written by both SH and U hands (84r–86v);	SH + L + U
				85, 87 inscribed added at the Ursula convent in Delft	Original SH hand: Prayers for the Sacrament (86r–86v); Additional prayers to Sacrament by Ursula hand (86v–87v); prayer to St. Francis and other Franciscan prayers by original SH hand (88r–91v); suffrages to Sts. Quirin, Sebastian, and the personal angel by original SH hand (91v–93v); prayer to Jesus by Ursula hand, as quire filler (bottom 93v)	SH + U
XIV	ff. 94–101	8	III	quire inscribed and added at Ursula convent in Delft	Prayers to the Virgin (94r–101r); to St. Erasmus (101r–102v);	U
XV	ff. 102–105	4	III	quire inscribed and added at Ursula convent in Delft	to St. Christopher (102v–103v); suffrages to Sts. Ursula, the 11,000 Virgins, Katherine, and Barbara (104r–105v)	U
XVI	ff. 106–114	8 (+1)	I+II	full-page miniature, Mass of the Dead (106v) added in Leiden	**Vigil of the Dead** (107r–124v);	SH + L

Hague, KB 132 G 38 (Book of Hours from South Holland, with additions). Ms foliated I-XIII, 1–139, cont.

	Physical construction				Inscribed and painted content	
quire	structure of quire	includes folios	Phase I (South Holland); Phase II (Leiden); Phase III (Ursula convent)	summary of added leaves	textual contents: written/painted by South Holland scribe (SH), Leiden painter (L), or St. Ursula scribe (U)	
XVII	8	ff. 115–122	I			SH + L
XVIII	8	ff. 123–130	I		prayers to Mary (125r-128v) and St. Anne (129r); prayer to be read before an image of the Virgin added by St. Ursula scribe as quire filler (bottom of 129v through end of quire)	SH + U
XIX	8	ff. 131–138	I		prayer to St. Anthony (131r-133r); condensed and indulgenced Hours of the Passion (133r-135r); prayer to Christ's 7 Last Words (135v-136v); indulgenced prayer to the Virgin added by St. Ursula scribe (136v); Prayer to the Virgin (137r-138r);	SH + L + U
XX	2 (-1)	ff. 139	III		prayer to and privileges of St. Anne added by S. Ursula scribe (138r-139v)	U
XXI	2	ff. 140-back pastedown	III		Notes of ownership	early owners

All original folios (from the first phase of production) have quire notations on the lower right recto.
None of the leaves or quires added in Delft has quire notations.
Only quire XIV, written by the scribe from the convent of St. Ursula, has a catchword (on 101v).

Key	Contains only original material support (parchment) supplied in a South Holland atelier
	Contains material support (parchment) from Leiden in addition to parchment from a South Holland atelier
	Contains only material support (parchment) added at the Ursula convent in Delft

Even though this book of hours was originally copied with extra texts, suffrages and some indulgences, its early owner was not completely satisfied with it and commissioned a series of full-page miniatures for it. This was easy to do, since most new texts began on the first folio of a new quire: the manuscript was made according to the "modular method" described above. The five added full-page miniatures now comprise fol. 13v (Annunciation), fol. 52v (Last Judgment), fol. 74v (Crucifixion), fol. 83v (Mass of St. Gregory), and fol. 106v (Mass for the Dead). Adding full-page miniatures therefore involved taking the manuscript out of its binding and slipping the edges of the painted folios around the back of these quires. Artists working in Leiden (the so-called Masters of Hugo Jansz. Van Worden) produced the miniatures, and the particular kind of painted border decoration associated with them is known as "Leiden blue acanthus."[21] The painters who provided these miniatures also supplied the incipit text folios with painted borders, so that the openings would form visually coherent ensembles.

added decoration to match
facing folio (from Leiden)

added parchment, with miniature and
painted decoration (done in Leiden)

original parchment, text and penwork
decoration (from S. Holland), and
overpainted decoration (done in Leiden)

Fig. 226 Opening in a book of hours at the incipit of the Verses of St. Gregory, with two campaigns of work: the script, penwork, and painted initials were executed in the original campaign of work, and the full-page miniature was added later, along with painted decoration around the text folio to make it match. The Hague, Koninklijke Bibliotheek, Ms. 132 G 38, fol. 83v-84r. Image © Koninklijke Bibliotheek — the National Library of The Netherlands, CC BY 4.0.

---

21 Added miniatures and border decoration like these are closely related to painting in Berlin, SBB-PK, Germ. qu. 18, a book of hours in which the miniatures are integral, rather than being tipped in.

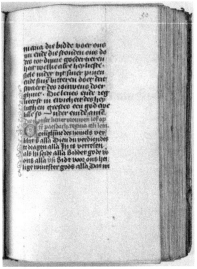

Fig. 227
Folio in a book of hours, on which a painter applied "Leiden blue acanthus" border decoration over the top of the existing penwork decoration. The Hague, Koninklijke Bibliotheek, Ms. 132 G 38, fol. 133v. Image © Koninklijke Bibliotheek— the National Library of The Netherlands, CC BY 4.0.

Fig. 228
Folio in a book of hours, to which a scribe from the convent of St. Ursula in Delft added a prayer and Delft penwork to the blank parchment at the lower part of the folio. The Hague, Koninklijke Bibliotheek, Ms. 132 G 38, fol. 50r. Image © Koninklijke Bibliotheek—the National Library of The Netherlands, CC BY 4.0.

For example, the original manuscript, copied somewhere in South Holland, contained the Five Verses of St. Gregory (fig. 226). A rubric and incipit for this text appears on fol. 84r, in the loopy *hybrida* of the original South Holland scribe. A painted four-line initial, alternating red and blue one-line initials, and penwork decoration, were also included in the original production. When the owner had it upgraded with miniatures in Leiden, he or she ordered images for the major text openings and for this indulgenced text. The loose single-leaf miniature had painted border decoration characterized by thin blue acanthus, typical of Leiden in the second half of the fifteenth century. These would have clashed with the simple penwork flourishes on the text pages. To give the opening a harmonious unity, the owner therefore added analogous blue border decoration painted onto the facing text page. (I have shown several examples above where adding miniatures meant also adding decoration to the facing page.)

The owner evidently asked the Leiden illuminator to add decoration throughout the book. On other folios, the illuminator painted over the top of existing penwork decoration (fig. 227). He or she did this to raise the hierarchy of decoration by an increment, as four-line initials under the new scheme should have painted borders, not penwork borders, which belong to a lower echelon. This painted decoration was apparently added in Leiden, probably by a professional artist who specialized in "Leiden blue acanthus" decoration.[22]

Next the owner then had yet another set of additions made, this time textual. Some of these involved adding more physical material, and some exploited areas of parchment left empty in the first phase of execution. These added texts can be easily distinguished from the original texts in the manuscript written elsewhere in South Holland. I believe that the same atelier that added prayers to Rawlinson inscribed these additions: the Franciscan convent of St. Ursula in Delft. In order that no blank parchment would remain, the scribes there delighted in filling up the ends of quires with short texts. A St. Ursula scribe did just this, for example, on fol. 50r (fig. 228), where she squeezed in a text of "Onser liever vrouwen lof" (*Regina celi*) to be read on Easter day. In order to add this, she first re-ruled the bottom of the folio in dark brown ink, with condensed lines so that she could fit in more text. She wrote in the neat *textualis* that was the house style of the Ursula convent and did not try to match the script of the existing book. She has also given the two-line initial a red and blue flourish in a style unmistakably from Delft and which typify production at the Ursula convent.

---

22   The artists who work in this style have been called the Masters of Hugo Jansz. van Woerden. Related examples of this style appear in approximately 30 other manuscripts. For an overview of the style, see Defoer et al., *The Golden Age of Dutch Manuscript Painting,* pp. 287, 297.

Fig. 229 Opening in a book of hours. The 3.5 lines on the left side of the gutter and all of the script and penwork on the right side are part of the original production (written somewhere in South Holland); an indulgenced prayer with a rubric mentioning Pope Sixtus IV, added as quire filler, was inscribed at the convent of St. Ursula in Delft. The Hague, Koninklijke Bibliotheek, Ms. 132 G 38, fol. 136v-137r. Image © Koninklijke Bibliotheek—the National Library of The Netherlands, CC BY 4.0.

Fig. 230 Opening in a book of hours. The 14.5 lines on the left side of the gutter are part of the original production (written somewhere in South Holland). The rubric on fol. 71v-72r, the prayer that follows, and the penwork decoration, were added at the convent of St. Ursula in Delft. The Hague, Koninklijke Bibliotheek, Ms. 132 G 38, fol. 71v-72r. Image © Koninklijke Bibliotheek—the National Library of The Netherlands, CC BY 4.0.

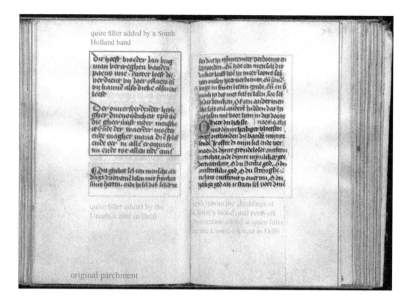

Fig. 231 Opening in a book of hours showing quire fillers added in two campaigns of work: 13 lines of red text on the left side of the gutter were inscribed in the first campaign of work, somewhere in South Holland; the final three lines on the left, and all of the text on the right side of the gutter (a prayer about the sheddings of Christ's blood), plus the blue and red penwork, were inscribed later at the convent of St. Ursula in Delft. The Hague, Koninklijke Bibliotheek, Ms. 132 G 38, fol. 72v-73r. Image © Koninklijke Bibliotheek—the National Library of The Netherlands, CC BY 4.0.

Fig. 232 Opening in a book of hours, with original parchment on the left, and the back of an added leaf on the right. The text comprises quire filler added at the convent of St. Ursula in Delft: the end of the sheddings of Christ's blood, followed by a saying of St. Augustine. The Hague, Koninklijke Bibliotheek, Ms. 132 G 38, fol. 73v-74r. Image © Koninklijke Bibliotheek—the National Library of The Netherlands, CC BY 4.0.

Likewise, a scribe from the Ursula convent could not bear to leave nearly
a folio's worth of empty lines on fol. 136v, which precedes some Marian
prayers (fig. 229). Instead, she copied a short, indulgenced prayer into
the space. It has a rubric that declares:

> *rub:* Pope Sixtus IV has given anyone who reads this prayer 11,000 years'
> indulgences. *inc:* Hail, most holy mother of God, Mary, queen of heaven…

> *rub:* Sixtus die vierde paeus heeft gegeven all den genen die dit gebet
> lesen xi^m iaer oflaet. *inc:* Wes gegruet alre heilichste Maria moeder gods
> coninghine des hemels. [HKB, Ms. 132 G 38, fol. 136v]

This scribe from St. Ursula's convent thereby updated the book of hours
with a prayer that she carefully chose for this location: it relates to the
Marian theme of this section of the book, is short enough to fit into the
remaining space on the page, and it carries an enormous indulgence.

The scribe from the Ursula convent filled several more blank but
ruled original folios with additional texts. Several folios had been left
blank by the original scribe at the end of the Penitential Psalms and
litany in Quire XI. These blank but ruled folios begin at the bottom of
fol. 71v (fig. 230). The Ursula scribe filled these blank lines with several
prayers, beginning with one to be read while looking the Face of Christ,
This prayer is a corrupted version of the *Salve Sancta Facies,* whose prayer
text has drifted into a fiery emotional outburst, which I transcribe here
in full. Prefatory and postscript rubrics, each promising different results
for the devotion, top and tail the prayer:

> *rub:* Whoever looks upon that image of the Veronica with devotion will
> have 300 days' indulgence from the pope of Rome. Moreover, he will not
> die within 10 days from an unforeseen or sudden death. You should also
> read the following prayer with devotion. *inc:* I greet you, blessed face
> of our lord Jesus Christ. O, lord, I beg you from the depths of my heart
> that you look at me [literally: *throw your blessed eyes on me*], and protect
> me from the enemy from hell and from all evil people and from wild
> ferocious beasts, and from all the evils that may hinder me, body and
> soul. After this miserable life, give me the joy and rapture of everlasting
> life. Amen. *rub:* Item, any woman in labor who looks upon that image of
> the Veronica will be gladdened and comforted in her time of need. [HKB,
> Ms. 132 G 38, fol. 71v-72r]

That the image returns the viewer's gaze is implied by the prayer; by
extension, the image would protect the votary by keeping an eye on her.
The prayer both addresses Jesus directly in a dialogue, and acknowledges

his presence in the conversation through the image. Several promises about the technical benefits of looking at the image are made by the prefatory rubric, and the post-script rubric claims that looking at the image will help a woman in childbirth. The prayer text itself positions the reader to ask for several other benefits, mostly involving protection from hellhounds and the like. Both a spiritual benefit redeemable in Purgatory for a shortened sentence, as well as an earthly and analgesic benefit, are promised by the rubrics.

Plenty of space remained at the end of this quire for the St. Ursula scribes to fill (fig. 231). Some more opportunistic inclusions were invited by the blank folios, and one scribe has copied two short texts in red at the top of fol. 73v. A St. Ursula scribe has left a respectful distance and copied another indulgenced prayer, with this rubric:

> *rub:* A person shall read this prayer every day three times with devotion in his heart. He shall know for certain that he will never again be damned. The more often a person reads this, the more benefit he shall earn from our lord, and especially during his final days. If he is not able to read this himself, he can just think it, or another person shall pray it for him, that another person will pray it for him in the case of mortal peril. **Prayer:** O, lord, you have unbound the chains of my sins with your holy sheddings of blood...[HKB, Ms. 132 G 38, fol. 72v-73v][23]

Even this prayer did not fill all of the available space, and four lines remained at the end of fol. 73v (fig. 232). A very short text, a prayer attributed to St. Augustine, was used by the St. Ursula scribe to fill these lines, so that no blank lines remained. In short, the scribe used the open spaces from fol. 71v-73v opportunistically. One of the core values at the convent of St. Ursula must have been to leave no blank parchment. Such choices were not completely random; rather, the St. Ursula scribe selected by theme and by length, as she copied the prayer to the "blood sheddings of Christ" so that it would immediately precede the Crucifixion. The sisters must have also had a selection of short texts available on an exemplar that they could copy into small spaces of parchment.

---

23   HKB, Ms. 132 G 38, fol. 72v-73v: *rub:* Dit ghebet sel een mensche alle dage driewerven lesen mit ynnicheit sijns herten. Ende hi sel des seker we[73]sen dat hi nymmermeer verdoemt en sel worden. Ende hoe een mensch dit dicker leest, hoe hi meer loons sel van onsen heer verdienen ende sonderlinge in sinen lesten eynde, ende en vermach hi des niet self te lesen, soe sel hi dat dencken, of een ander mensche selt enen anderen bidden, dat hi dat lesen wil voor hem in des dootsnoot. Gebet. *inc:* O, heer, du hebste mit dijnre heiliger bloetstortinge ontbonden die banden mijnre sonden.

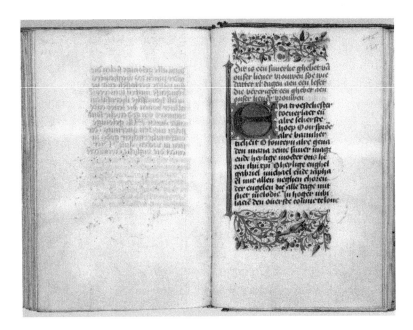

Fig. 233 Opening in a book of hours, with a blank area formerly filled with sewn-on badges. The Hague, Koninklijke Bibliotheek, Ms. 132 G 38, fol. 124v-125r. Image © Koninklijke Bibliotheek—the National Library of The Netherlands, CC BY 4.0.

Fig. 234 Opening in a book of hours at the Verses of St. Gregory, with a diagram showing the arrangement of original and added parchment; the additions transform the prayer from a 5-verse version into a 9-verse version with a larger indulgence. The Hague, Koninklijke Bibliotheek, Ms. 132 G 38, fol. 84r-85v. Image © Koninklijke Bibliotheek—the National Library of The Netherlands, CC BY 4.0.

Fig. 235 Opening in a book of hours, with original and added parchment. Fol. 86r is part of the
original manuscript (made in South Holland) and has a prayer to the sacrament. Fol. 85
was inscribed at the convent of St. Ursula in Delft and added later; fol. 85v contains the
ninth and final Verse of St. Gregory, and a postscript rubric indicating that reading the
previous prayer is worth 92,042 years' & 80 days' indulgence. The Hague, Koninklijke
Bibliotheek, Ms. 132 G 38, fol. 85v-86r. Image © Koninklijke Bibliotheek—the National
Library of The Netherlands, CC BY 4.0.

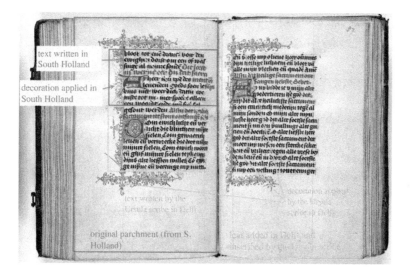

Fig. 236 Opening in a book of hours, with original and added parchment. Fol. 86 is part of the
original manuscript (made in South Holland). The first 9.5 lines, including the red letter
A with its few strokes of whispy penwork, were inscribed by the original scribe and are
typical of the original production. A scribe at the convent of St. Ursula in Delft filled
the rest of fol. 86v with a prayer to the sacrament, added bold red and blue penwork
decoration, and extended the existing penwork into the upper margin; she continued
the prayer on added parchment (fol. 87), on which she inscribed another prayer to
the sacrament. The Hague, Koninklijke Bibliotheek, Ms. 132 G 38, fol. 86v-87r. Image
© Koninklijke Bibliotheek—the National Library of The Netherlands, CC BY 4.0.

The Sisters of St. Ursula left only one area of parchment blank: that on fol. 124v (fig. 233). Someone had stitched small round objects to the bottom of this folio. Needle holes are still visible in the parchment, arranged in circles, and the round, toothed offsets of these objects appears on fol. 125r, indicating that they were made of metal that bit into the soft parchment. Given that the sisters of St. Ursula held as one of their values the filling up of parchment, I conjecture that the owner had already sewn in the badges before she brought the manuscript to the convent for textual updates. By turning it into a repository for small, round badges, the owner had already amended her book in her own amateurish way; now she was commissioning professional updates to it. Rather than remove the badges, the sisters simply avoided writing on the same page, as the badges would have formed obstacles to the scribe.

Three kinds of interventions were made in HKB, Ms. 132 G 38 by the sisters at the Ursula convent. First, as I have shown, they added texts to the blank but ruled spaces in the manuscript, thereby making use of otherwise wasted rulings. Second, they added some single leaves of text, specifically fol. 85 and 87, in order to extend existing prayers. I want to look at more closely at the section of the manuscript that contains these folios, because they reveal this scribe's *modus operandi*. Third, they added several quires to the manuscript (quires XIV, XV, and XX). These were not simply added to the end of the manuscript, but were worked into logical places in the middle and at the end. In this way, these added quires resemble the one in Rawlinson. I treat these below.

How and why the single leaves were added? Physical evidence can help to answer this. The opening fol. 83v-84r (fig. 226) has an original text page with the *Adoro te in cruce pendentem* in Dutch, plus one of the added full-page miniatures showing the Mass of St. Gregory, designed to accompany this prayer. A simple rubric prefaces the prayer:

> *rub:* Anyone who reads this on his knees in front of this figure and is free of mortal sin will earn 20,000 years' indulgence and 14 days' indulgence from Callistus. [HKB, Ms. 132 G 38, fol. 84r-84v]

Presenting the five-verse version of the prayer, the prayer text finishes at the bottom of fol. 84v. But the owner was not satisfied with this short version of the prayer. Like the owner of the Tongeren/Tienen manuscript (HKB, Ms. 75 G 2) discussed above, the owner wanted the longer, later version of the prayer with the more munificent indulgence. Owners sometimes added the text of the *Adoro te* as well as the image that would activate it, inscribed on a separate quire. They then inserted these new modules into books that were already complete (although in its owner's opinion, deficient). In this case, the scribe has added an extra leaf, fol. 85, in order to add four more verses to the prayer, thereby turning the five-verse *Adoro te* into the nine-verse version (fig. 234). Not only that, but the scribe has given the prayer a second rubric, this one at the end of the prayer, which promises even more indulgences:

> *rub:* Anyone who speaks nine *Pater Nosters* and nine ave Marias with contrition in his heart before the *arma Christi*, will earn 92,024 years and 80 days' indulgence. Really. [HKB, Ms. 132 G 38, fol. 85v; fig. 235][24]

By adding a leaf, the scribe was able to turn a prayer worth 20,000 years' indulgence into one worth more than 92,000 years. Although careful inspection reveals that fol. 85 is written in a different hand than fol. 84, the scribe has gone to some effort to work this added text seamlessly into the pre-existing book. For example, she has ruled the additional pages for 19 lines to match the original text pages, and she has used the same sized text block. However, the penwork applied to the added sections reveals its Delft origins and contrasts with the nondescript South Holland penwork in the original sections.

Fol. 87 also comprises a singleton added to the manuscript. A diagram overlaying fol. 86v-87r shows how the scribe added the material but also integrated the new text and decoration with the old (fig. 236). Continuing writing right where the previous text ended, she used the existing space, and added even more physical material, to make room for prayers to the sacrament, which fill fol. 87r/v.

---

24   HKB, Ms. 132 G 38, fol. 84r-85v, 5 Verses of Saint Gregory (in original hand from South Holland), augmented with 4 more verses (in hand from Delft), *rub:* Soe wie op sinen knien dit gebet leest buten doit sonden, die verdient xx^m jaer ende xiiii dage oflaets voir dese figuer van Calixtus. *inc:* O, heer Jhesu Christe, ic aenbede di inden cruce…. [85v] *rub:* So wie mit berou des herten spreect voort wapen ons heren ix *Pater nosteren* ende ix *Ave Marien*, die verdient xcii^m jaer xxiiii jaer ende lxxx dagen oflaets. Waerachtich.

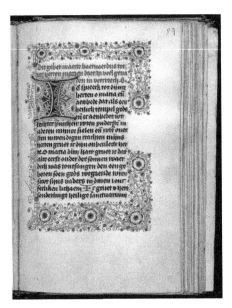

Fig. 237
Folio in a book of hours from a
section added at the convent of St.
Ursula in Delft. Gaps in the penwork
border decoration are for small
painted figures, which have not been
filled in. The Hague, Koninklijke
Bibliotheek, Ms. 132 G 38, fol. 94r.
Image © Koninklijke Bibliotheek—the
National Library of The Netherlands,
CC BY 4.0.

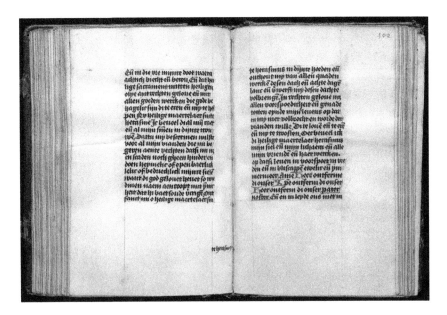

Fig. 238 Opening in a book of hours from an added section, at the division between
two added quires, revealing the large catchword typical of production at the
convent of St. Ursula in Delft. The Hague, Koninklijke Bibliotheek, Ms. 132 G 38,
fol. 101v-102r. Image © Koninklijke Bibliotheek—the National Library of The
Netherlands, CC BY 4.0.

Fig. 239 Opening in a book of hours from an added section, with one prayer to St. Ursula and one to her 11,000 virginal companions; fol. 104r is decorated with penwork typical of Delft on three sides of the text block. The Hague, Koninklijke Bibliotheek, Ms. 132 G 38, fol. 103v-104r. Image © Koninklijke Bibliotheek—the National Library of The Netherlands, CC BY 4.0.

Furthermore, the atelier at St. Ursula's in Delft added entire quires of parchment to expand the text-writing area. These are quires XIV, XV and XX and they are written in the neat corporate *textualis* that I associate with the convent of St. Ursula in Delft. The red and blue "block" penwork that has been associated with Delft manuscript production appears on the opening folio of quire XIV (fol. 94r); I believe this was executed at the convent of St. Ursula in Delft (fig. 237). There is a gap in the decoration, however, which has surely been left open for a figure, probably one bearing a blue scroll.[25] However, this has not been filled in. I suspect that the convent of St. Ursula did not have a painter who could add figures, but that the sisters only copied texts and added penwork decoration. In this case the sheet was never sent to the painter to be completed.

Another codicological feature reveals quires XIV and XV as products of the St. Ursula convent. Just as in Rawlinson and in most of the

---

25   Kathryn M. Rudy, "Margins and Memory: The Functions of Border Imagery from a Delft Manuscript," in *Manuscript Studies in the Low Countries. Proceedings of the 'Groninger Codicologendagen' in Friesland 2002* (Groningen: Egbert Forsten, 2008), pp. 216–38.

manuscript production from the convent of St. Ursula, the scribe used a large catchword where she produced entire quires (in this case, on HKB, Ms. 132 G 38, fol. 101v; fig. 238). None of the original leaves of HKB, Ms. 132 G 38 has catchwords.

Texts in the added quires further point to the convent of St. Ursula as the place where this manuscript was augmented. Quires XIV and XV, both added, contain a prayer to the Virgin (94r-101r); a prayer to St. Erasmus (101r-102v); a prayer to St. Christopher as well as his "privileges" (102v-103v); and prayers to Sts Ursula, the Eleven Thousand Virgins, Katherine, and Barbara (104r-105v). Because the St. Ursula was the patron of the convent where I believe the work was carried out, the choice of these added female saints is significant. The other, older convent of female Franciscans in Delft was dedicated to St. Barbara, a convent of which St. Ursula may have formed a satellite, though one with a larger footprint and presumably a scriptorium. Moreover, within this section of prayers to saints, the prayer to St. Ursula receives extra decoration, with penwork on three sides of the page (fig. 239). This emphasis on St. Ursula strengthens my hypothesis that these manuscript updates in HKB, Ms. 132 G 38 and Rawl. Liturg. e. 9* were made in the convent of St. Ursula in Delft.

Moreover, the scribe from St. Ursula's has also inscribed the Privileges of St. Anne into HKB, Ms. 132 G 38 at the very end of the manuscript (fol. 139r/v). She had to add an extra bifolium of parchment—a blank sheet possibly salvaged from the scrap heap—to the end of the book (now fol. 139–140) in order to make room for the privileges of St. Anne.[26] I have only found this text in two other manuscripts: Oxford, Bodleian Library, Ms. Rawl. liturg. e. 9*, fol. 61v-62v, discussed immediately above, and BKB, Ms. IV 312, fol. 97v-98v, which also belongs to the same group of books of hours written in Delft, probably at the convent of St. Ursula.[27] BKB IV 312 also shares a similar layout and decoration as the others in the "Ursula" group. While BKB IV 312 only partially survives and is missing its calendar, its litany lists Ursula as the first virgin and Martin as the first confessor, making it likely that this manuscript also originated at the convent of St. Ursula in Delft.

Evidence I have presented in this section suggests that book owners would bring their books of hours to the convent of St. Ursula in Delft to

---

26   Fol. 139 (the added, final folio) has only 18 lines, whereas the rest of KB 132 G 38 has 19 lines, suggesting that this final folio was taken from another manuscript.

27   For the texts and localization of this manuscript, see the BNM (http://www.bibliotheek.leidenuniv.nl/bijzondere-collecties/handschriftenarchievenbrieven/bnm.html#database).

have their manuscripts updated with highly beneficial prayers, including indulgenced prayers and the Privileges of St. Anne, which promised health and riches. While the scribe who added the prayers to Rawlinson may not be the same as the scribe who added prayers to HKB 132 G 38, they write in a very similar corporate hand, that is, a house style designed to smooth over individual scribes' personal hands and replace them with something interchangeable. One of the values the sisters of St. Ursula exhibited was frugality. In manuscripts they made from scratch, they filled every available line of parchment with prayers. They likewise filled up the books of hours they updated by filling all of the spaces that had been left blank during the original production. As I have show earlier, ateliers that used the modular method would often leave parts of quires unfinished. The sisters of St. Ursula filled these up with richly useful prayers. They squeezed more texts into the blank areas of the book. They sometimes added single leaves, or even entire quires in order to accommodate desired texts. Whereas the leaves added in Leiden accommodated full-page images, those added at the Ursula convent only contained text. One might surmise that the convent did not have an artist, but only scribes who could copy text and add pen flourishes. They "branded" their products by inscribing prayers to their patron saint, Ursula.

For whom did the sisters of St. Ursula update manuscripts? The two examples I have examined above started out as quite different objects. Whereas the Rawlinson manuscript was of low quality and was quite humble, HKB 132 G 38 was a large illuminated book of hours with images and painted borders. One possibility is that lay sisters brought these books with them when they entered the Ursula convent, and then the conventual scriptorium brought the disparate books into a common form by adding certain texts. More likely however is that private lay owners brought their used manuscripts in for refurbishing. Evidence for this appears in two notes of ownership at the end of HKB 132 G 38, from a woman named Diewer Goes and another named Josina van Sijdenburch.[28] Neither identifies herself as *zuster*.

While I suspect that they refurbished the books of hours for lay customers outside the conventual walls, they also revamped books for their own use, which is the subject of the next section.

---

28   The notes of ownership, written on the last flyleaf, read: "Diet bock hoert toe Diewer Goes. Diet vint die brnttet weder ter recten hant," and: "Dit bock hoert toe IJosina van Sijdenburch aensien doet ghedencken sijt gheduerich ijn liefden vierich." For a full description, see Asperen, *Pelgrimstekens op Perkament*, cat. 46, pp. 327–28.

3. Uppsala, Universitetsbiblioteket, Ms. C 517 k

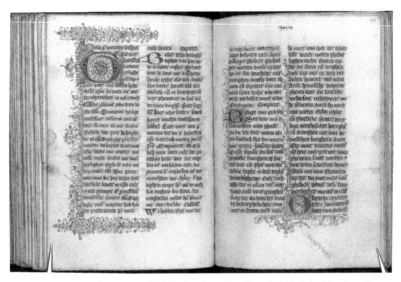

Fig. 240 Opening in a lay breviary in Middle Dutch with offices inscribed in Utrecht, where modest penwork decoration was applied in a block around the initials; this penwork was extended into the margins in Delft. Uppsala, Universitetsbiblioteket, Ms. C 517 k, fol. 216v-217r. Image © Uppsala Universitetsbiblioteket, CC BY 4.0.

Fig. 241 Opening at the incipit of the psalter in a lay breviary made in Utrecht and upgraded in Delft. Fol. 35 is from the original manuscript, inscribed in Utrecht, with a historiated initial depicting David playing his harp (painted in Utrecht); fol. 34 is from a section added in Delft. Illuminators in Delft added more border decoration to fol. 35r: block penwork and a painted bird with a scroll. Uppsala, Universitetsbiblioteket, Ms. C 517 k, fol. 34v-35r. Image © Uppsala Universitetsbiblioteket, CC BY 4.0.

Fig. 242 Folio at the incipit of the psalter in a lay breviary, with David playing his harp (painted in Utrecht), with Utrecht penwork extended in the margin with Delft penwork. Uppsala, Universitetsbiblioteket, Ms. C 517 k, fol. 35r. Image © Uppsala Universitetsbiblioteket, CC BY 4.0.

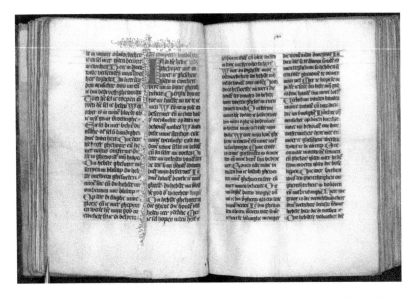

Fig. 243 Opening in a lay breviary made in Utrecht and upgraded in Delft. A scribe in Delft has added red and blue penwork to the upper and intercolumnar margins, thereby extending the modest blue penwork originally applied around the letter *I* in Utrecht. The new penwork extends into the upper and lower margins of fol. 49v but does not fill the space completely, and therefore maintains the hierarchy of decoration dictated by the 4-line *I*. Uppsala, Universitetsbiblioteket, Ms. C 517 k, fol. 49v-50r. Image © Uppsala Universitetsbiblioteket, CC BY 4.0.

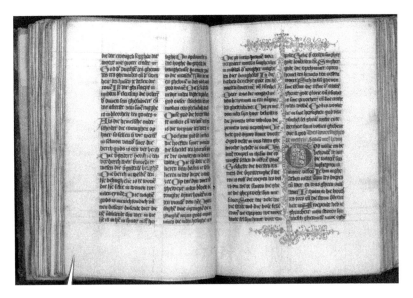

Fig. 244 Opening in a lay breviary made in Utrecht and upgraded in Delft, with Delft penwork added to Utrecht penwork. The new penwork extends into the upper and lower margins of fol. 71r but does not fill the space completely, and therefore maintains the hierarchy of decoration dictated by the 4-line *G*. Uppsala, Universitetsbiblioteket, Ms. C 517 k, fol. 70v-71r. Image © Uppsala Universitetsbiblioteket, CC BY 4.0.

Fig. 245 Opening in a lay breviary made in Utrecht and upgraded in Delft, with Delft penwork added to Utrecht penwork. The new penwork fills the upper and lower margins of fol. 132v, and therefore maintains the hierarchy of decoration dictated by the 5-line G. Uppsala, Universitetsbiblioteket, Ms. C 517 k, fol. 132v-133r. Image © Uppsala Universitetsbiblioteket, CC BY 4.0.

The sisters of St. Ursula may have offered a service to laypeople to update their manuscripts, but they may also have taken older manuscripts and updated them for their own use. A case in point is Uppsala, Universitetsbiblioteket, Ms. C 517 k, a lay breviary in Dutch with added components, where the core of the manuscript consists of a psalter (fol. 35r-115v), Canticles (fol. 115v-123v); Litany and Collects (fol. 124r-128r); Office of the Dead (fol. 128r-132v); Office for the Dedication of a Church (fol. 132v); Office for Good Friday (fol. 139v); Prayers for Communion and to Mary (fol. 144r-150v); Offices of the Trinity (fol. 150v), prayers to St. Augustine (fol. 160r) and St. Francis (fol. 167v); Common of Saints (fol. 173v-216r); Offices of various saints (fol. 216v-322v; fig. 240); Office of the Crown of Thorns (fol. 323r-330v). All of these parts were written by a single hand (or several people working in a corporate style), probably in Utrecht in the mid-fifteenth century.

The original parts of the manuscript were also decorated in Utrecht, in a ho-hum style of the mid-fifteenth century. For example, a historiated initial with David playing his harp marks the beginning of the psalter (fig. 241 and 242). Modest red and blue penwork was applied to the initial at that time, in a style associated with Utrecht, marked by rows of little circles. Perhaps someone used the manuscript in or around Utrecht for some time.

It may have been in a bad state of repair after several years of use when someone brought to Delft, where it was renewed and updated. Specifically, textual and penwork evidence suggest that it was brought to the Franciscan convent of St. Ursula in Delft, where various things were done to it. Blue and red decoration in a style typical of Delft were added it to the initials that were already there. For example, the historiated initial with David has a border made of blue and red penwork in a Delft style on the upper, lower, and right sides, and a Utrecht border on the left border. Similarly, the Delft illuminator added penwork decoration to the existing Utrecht penwork on several folios, including fol. 49v (fig. 243) and fol. 71r (fig. 244). The decorator in Delft has applied the additional decoration carefully, extending it from the existing penwork in order to blend it in. He (or more likely she) has also adjusted the hierarchy of decoration so that four-line initials (which alternate in red and blue and in Utrecht had merely received a small amount of penwork in the opposite color) are elevated in Delft so that they receive two colors of decoration that spills into the border. Apparently, "updating" the book not only meant imposing some local color, but also adding more decoration to a modestly decorated book. Four-line initials suddenly received decoration that filled a margin and spilled out at the top and bottom (as on fol. 49v, 71r), and five-line initials with some gold were elevated so that they received red and blue "block" penwork on three sides (fig. 245). In addition to augmenting the existing penwork with more penwork in a Delft style, the atelier in Delft also added entire quires to the manuscript. I summarize these additions in this table:

Uppsala, Universitetsbiblioteket, Ms. C 517 k

Textual contents	Quire	Written by hand from Utrecht or Delft?	Structure of quire	Includes folios	Folios added or removed	Notes and summary of added leaves and hands
Indulgentiae urbis Romae (fol. 2r-5v)	I	D1 and D2	6 (-2) (wants 1 and 3)	fol. 1-4		5v written by a different Delft scribe
calendar (fol. 6r-11v)	II	D	6 (+1) (fol. 11)	fol. 5-11		
Offices of the Purification of the Virgin (12r), the Visitation (17v), the Birth of the Virgin (23v) and Mary Magdalene	III	D2	8	fol. 12-19		catchword on 19v
	IV	D2	8	fol. 20-27		catchword on 27v
	V	D2	6 (+1)	fol. 28-34	fol. 34 added	
psalter (35r-115v)	VI	U	8	fol. 35-42		
	VII	U	8	fol. 43-50		
	VIII	U	8	fol. 51-58		
	IX	U	8	fol. 59-66		
	X	U	8	fol. 67-74		
	XI	U	8	fol. 75-82		
	XII	U	8	fol. 83-90		
	XIII	U	8	fol. 91-98		
	XIV	U	8	fol. 99-106		
	XV	U	8	fol. 107-114		

Uppsala, Universitetsbiblioteket, Ms. C 517 k, cont.

Textual contents	Quire	Written by hand from Utrecht or Delft?	Structure of quire	Includes folios	Folios added or removed	Notes and summary of added leaves and hands
Canticles (115v-123v); Litany and Collects (fol. 124r-128r); Office of the Dead (fol. 128r-132v); Office for the Dedication of a Church (132v); Office for Good Friday (139v); Prayers for Communion and to Mary (fol. 144r-150v); Offices of the Trinity (150v), St. Augustine (160r) and St. Francis (167v); Common of Saints (fol. 173v-216r); Offices of various saints (fol. 216v-322v); Office of the Crown of Thorns (fol. 323r-330v)	XVI	U	8 (+1)	fol. 115–123	116 added	
	XVII	U	8	fol. 124–131		
	XVIII	U	8	fol. 132–139		
	XIX	U	8	fol. 140–147		
	XX	U	8	fol. 148–155		
	XXI	U	8	fol. 156–163		
	XXII	U	8	fol. 164–171		
	XXIII	U	8	fol. 172–179		
	XXIV	U	8	fol. 180–187		
	XXV	U	8	fol. 188–195		
	XXVI	U	8	fol. 196–203		
	XXVII	U	8	fol. 204–211		
	XXVIII	U	8	fol. 212–219		
	XXIX	U	8	fol. 220–227		

XXX	U	8	fol. 228–235		
XXXI	U	8	fol. 236–243		
XXXII	U	8	fol. 244–251		
XXXIII	U	8	fol. 252–259		
XXIV	U	8	fol. 260–267		
XXXV	U	8	fol. 268–275		
XXXVI	U	8	fol. 276–283		
XXXVII	U	8	fol. 284–291		
XXXVIII	U	8	fol. 292–299		
XXXIX	U	8	fol. 300–307		
XL	U	8	fol. 308–315		
XLI	U	8 (-1)	fol. 316–322	fol. after 322 removed, probably blank	
XLII	D	8 (+1)	fol. 323–331	fol. 331 added	Hymn of the Cross (fol. 331rv)

The original "Utrecht" part of the manuscript begins on fol. 35r, with the psalter. Because the original scribe foliated this section, the psalter begins with a Roman numeral (*ii*). The Delft atelier added 34 folios of front matter, including an unusual calendar and several offices (fol. 12r-34v). Whether the manuscript had a calendar when it traveled from Utrecht to Delft is unknowable but likely, as calendars formed an important part of the breviary. The new owners in Delft must have found it easier to begin afresh rather than to add some saints and scrape out others from a received, foreign calendar. They therefore added five quires to the beginning of the book. These quires contain the following texts:

> fol. 2r: **The bull of Pope Sixtus IV (1481) describing an indulgence for Franciscans who visit the Seven Principal Churches in Rome, physically or virtually** (*rub:* Dit is die bulle vanden nagescreven oflaten. In den iaer ons heren M.CCCC. ende lxxxi des xv. dages inden wintermaent des morgens vroe ter sevender uren, so heeft onse alre heilichste vader in Christo paeus Sixtus die vierde inden namen om beden wille des eerlikcn broeder engel van Clanasio [sic: Clavasio] ter tijt een geemeen vicarious den mynre brueders oorden vanden observancien heft verleent ende gegeven den mynre borders, den claren, ende den broderen ende den susteren vander derder rugulen sinte Franciscus volcomen oflaet van allen sonden in sonderlingen steden als die comen so sellen si alleen dencken op die kercken te romen ende bidden watsi willen. Ende verdienen daer mitten oflaet recht of sit e roem waren. *rub:* Aldus selmen daer in treden. Item, alle die geen die hem tot desen oflaet vogen willen die sellen ten eersten tot eenre tijt spreken xv pr nrn drie warf. Die eerste xv pr nosteren selmen offeren god ter eren ende te love voorden geesteliken vader den paeus sixto die vierde die dit oflaet gegeven heft. Die ander xv pr nrn selmen offeren gode te love ende ter eren voor die dit oflaet verworven hebben. Die derde xv pr nosteren selmen offeren voor alle die geheel kerstenheit ende dit gebet selmen niet dan eens doen tot eenre tijt als wanneerment eerst beginnen sel...;

> fol. 2r-5r: **How to visit the Seven Churches of Rome** (*rub:* Hoemen die kercken visitieren sel). Het is te weten dat binnen romen syn iiii.ᶜ kerken ende liiii. daermen alle dage misse in doet, van welker kercken sijn seven principael kercken boven alle den anderen geprivileert mit gracien ende heilicheden...);

fol. 5v: **Key to the letters in the calendar, and how they correspond to the churches of Rome** (*rub:* Dit is die bedudenisse vanden letteren ende vanden crucen. Item, die letteren die voor die seven kercken staen, als A.B.C., Daer selmen bi vinden inden kalendier in wat kercken men die heiligen eren sel alsmen dat oflaet verdienen wil dat op die heiligen haer dagen geteykent staet...)

fol. 6r-11v **Calendar for the bishopric of Utrecht, with letters A-G that refer to the Seven Principal Churches of Rome and indulgences associated with each station** (fig. 246). Entries in red include Agniet ioncfrou (January 21), Maria Magdalena (July 22), Marien inden snee (August 5), Ipolitus maertelaer (August 13), Jeroen priester (August 17), Franciscus confessoor (October 4), Die xi.^m maechden (October 21), and Kathrina ioncfer (November 25). These dates are consistent with production at the convent of St. Ursula in Delft.

fol. 12r-34v **Various offices**. Office of the Purification of the Virgin (12r), the Visitation (17v), the Birth of the Virgin (23v) and Mary Magdalene (29r)

Fig. 246 Opening in a lay breviary made in Utrecht and upgraded in Delft, in a section of quires added in Delft, with the end of the calendar and the beginning of the Mass of the Purification of the Virgin. Uppsala, Universitetsbiblioteket, Ms. C 517 k, fol. 11v-12r. Image © Uppsala Universitetsbiblioteket, CC BY 4.0.

Fig. 247 Opening in a lay breviary made in Utrecht and upgraded in Delft, with Delft
penwork added to Utrecht penwork. The new penwork added to four of the
initials G fills half of the margin, and therefore maintains the hierarchy of
decoration dictated by the 3-line initials. The opening also reveals a large
catchword inscribed in the manner typical of the Ursula convent in Delft.
Uppsala, Universitetsbiblioteket, Ms. C 517 k, fol. 27v-28r. Image © Uppsala
Universitetsbiblioteket, CC BY 4.0.

The added texts strongly reveal the interests and identity of the convent
that added them. The texts copied on fol. 2r-5v, which describe the
Stations and Indulgences of the Principal Churches in Rome (*Indulgentiae
urbis Romae*),[29] are specifically designated for Franciscans, and the added
calendar is specific to Franciscan sisters dedicated to St. Ursula in Delft.
The added offices represent those that were celebrated by the Franciscan
sisters that did not appear in the original part of the manuscript acquired
from Utrecht.

It is clear codicologically that the five quires comprising the front
matter were added in Delft, not imported from Utrecht. First, the

---

29 See Nine Robijntje Miedema, *Die 'Mirabilia Romae:' Untersuchungen zu ihrer
Überlieferung mit Edition der Deutschen und Niederländischen Texte*, Münchener Texte
und Untersuchungen zur Deutschen Literatur des Mittelalters (Tübingen: M.
Niemeyer, 1996).

decoration in these first five added quires was entirely executed in a Delft style, not layered over an Utrecht style. Second, the added calendar closely resembles the calendars made at this convent of St. Ursula in Delft. It is very close to Oxford, Bodleian Library, Ms. Rawl. liturg. f. 8; and also to Leiden, University Library, Ltk 287. Third, the front matter is written in the corporate style of the convent of St. Ursula in Delft. Its features include a *textualis* that is not overly fussy, with barbed ascenders. Fourth, it has a codicological particularity of St. Ursula in Delft, namely large catchwords inscribed in full size at the right side of vertical bounding line (fol. 19v, 27v); they are fairly high on the page, so that they frequently survive trimming (fig. 247). Such catchwords can be associated with the convent of St. Ursula in Delft, but are not a feature of manuscripts made in Utrecht.

The litany of the saints, which is in the original (Utrecht) part of the manuscript, lists Martin as the first confessor and Mary Magdalene as the first virgin. These are the "neutral" choices for a litany made within the diocese of Utrecht, where St. Martin was the patron saint of the cathedral in Utrecht. Nearly all of the manuscripts that originated at the convent of St. Ursula in Delft have a litany that features Martin as first confessor and Ursula as first virgin. However, the convent in Delft did not deem it essential to excise the existing litany and replace it with a more familiar one, despite its rather extensive overhaul of the manuscript's textual and decorative program.

The three manuscripts analyzed in this section (Oxford, Bodleian Library, Ms. Rawl. Liturg. e.9*; HKB, Ms. 132 G 38; and Uppsala, Universitetsbiblioteket, Ms. C 517 k) were all made in disparate regions of the Northern Netherlands. All three manuscripts were brought to the convent of St. Ursula in Delft, where they were further embellished, and updated with textual additions made to the existing parchment, and with more parchment added to make room for even more textual additions. As the Franciscan sisters apparently used the breviary as part of their daily ritual of prayer, the breviary was probably made for the Franciscans' own use. Likewise, the books of hours could have been made for a sister within the convent. Perhaps sisters from Amsterdam and Leiden entered the Delft convent, and brought books with them, which were deemed lacking. They performed book surgery on them in order to bring them in line with the corporate norm, as it were.

Alternatively, laypeople outside the convent could have brought their older, used book of hours, including items they had bought second hand or had inherited, to the Franciscans in Delft to have them updated and embellished. Part of this procedure meant adding extra indulgenced texts, prayers to the sacrament, and other desirable prayers that were beyond the bare-bones book of hours. The sisters also left their stylistic marks in these books, writing and applying penwork decoration in their highly recognizable corporate style. This must have been much cheaper than ordering a new book to be made from scratch.

In sum: the sisters at the convent of St. Ursula expressed their values of saving parchment when they undertook to recycle the manuscripts analyzed in this section. At the close of the fifteenth century Christians were demanding prayers that offered them indulgences; these were frequently prayers that were to be read in the presence of images. Other prayers, such as those to Anne, promised riches. All three manuscript witnesses to the Privileges of St. Anne came from Delft, probably from the same scriptorium at the convent of Franciscan tertiaries. It is possible that these privileges were connected to a brotherhood or cult image of St. Anne that was in Delft, and that the sisters offered a service to readers to augment their existing prayerbooks with items that would make them rich.[30] They might have told customers that St. Anne's ministrations would offset the costs of the scribal adjustments and rebinding.

D. The convent of St. Agnes in Delft

The convent of St. Ursula was not the only convent in Delft that updated older manuscripts. I argue here that the convent of St. Agnes in Delft, which was across the street from the Ursula convent, also engaged in this practice, with even more astonishing results. A prayerbook with extensive decoration in conflicting styles (HKB, Ms. BPH 148; hereafter: BPH 148) tells the story of multiple phases of execution, including a later phase undertaken at the Agnes convent. When the manuscript came

---

30 There was also a convent dedicated to St. Anne in Delft; this convent was Augustinian after 1468, and the manuscripts associated with this house are usually in Latin and quite distinct in terms of parchment type, layout, script, and decoration. It is unlikely that the three manuscripts presented here with the "Privileges of St. Anne" originated from that convent.

up for sale, dealer Heribert Tenschert described it as "ein rätselhaftes Hauptwerk der holländischen Buchmalerei" (a puzzling masterpiece of Dutch book painting).[31] According to Tenschert the text was written and the border decoration was applied in a scriptorium in Delft. I disagree with this view, and analyze the book's stratigraphy in order to propose a different and more complicated etiology. This manuscript, including the calendar, was copied by one hand (except for some much later additions made on the blank parchment near the end of the codex). Several codicological features suggest that this took place around 1440 in the Southern Netherlands. Its unusual calendar does not firmly localize it. Heribert Tenschert described the calendar as "Utrecht(?)." Likewise, Charlotte Lacaze saw that the manuscript contained different styles of decoration, but assigned the entire production to Delft, including the calendar.[32] This view is too simple. Anne Korteweg was correct when she stated that the manuscript was copied in the Southern Netherlands (probably in Bruges) and partly decorated there, using miniatures painted by the Masters of Zweder from Culemborg who were active in Utrecht, and that additional decoration was added in Delft.[33] Below I unpack this.

---

31 This manuscript does not appear in MMDC or on the website of the KB. The dealer Heribert Tenschert sold the manuscript in 1990 to the Bibliotheca Philosophica Hermetica (Amsterdam), where it had the signature BPH 148. In 2010 most of the manuscripts from this collection, including BPH 148, were transferred to the Koninklijke Bibliotheek. For a manuscript description, consult H. Tenschert and E. König, *Leuchtendes Mittelalter III: Das Goldene Zeitalter der Burgundischen Buchmalerei 1430–1560, Sammlung Carlo de Poortere U.A*, Katalog / Antiquariat Heribert Tenschert (Rotthalmünster: Heribert Tenschert, 1991), no. 27, pp. 311–25. Miranda Bloem, *De Meesters van Zweder van Culemborg: Werkplaatspraktijken van een Groep Noord-Nederlandse Verluchters, ca. 1415–1440* (PhD thesis, University of Amsterdam, 2015), pp. 361–69 and passim, places the manuscript in the corpus of the Zweder Masters.

32 Charlotte Lacaze, "A Little-Known Manuscript from the Workshop of Master Pancraz," in *Masters and Miniatures: Proceedings of the Congress on Medieval Manuscript Illumination in the Northern Netherlands (Utrecht, 10–13 December 1989)*, edited by K. van der Horst and Johann-Christian Klamt (Doornspijk: Davaco, 1991), pp. 255–63, treats the manuscript in an article-length study, but I question several of her conclusions.

33 Helen Wüstefeld and A. S. Korteweg, *Sleutel tot licht: Getijdenboeken in de Bibliotheca Philosophica Hermetica* (Amsterdam: In de Pelikaan, 2009), cat. 7, pp. 110–11 (written by Korteweg).

Fig. 248 Opening in a prayer book, showing September-October calendar pages inscribed in the Southern Netherlands, with the *KL* painted and gilt in the Southern Netherlands, and the penwork applied in Delft. The Hague, Koninklijke Bibliotheek, Ms. BPH 148, fol. 9v-10r. Image © Koninklijke Bibliotheek—the National Library of The Netherlands, CC BY 4.0.

Fig. 249 Opening in a prayer book, showing text folios inscribed in the Southern Netherlands, with one-, two-, and four-line initials gilt and painted in the Southern Netherlands (probably Bruges), with Delft penwork decoration added later. The Hague, Koninklijke Bibliotheek, Ms. BPH 148, fol. 24v-25r. Image © Koninklijke Bibliotheek—the National Library of The Netherlands, CC BY 4.0.

Fig. 250 Opening in a prayer book, with a full-page miniature painted on a bifolium (fol. 111&118) by the Masters of Zweder of Culemborg depicting St. Nicholas; the bifolium has been ruled, inscribed, and incorporated into the prayerbook. The Hague, Koninklijke Bibliotheek, Ms. BPH 148, fol. 118v-119r. Image © Koninklijke Bibliotheek — the National Library of The Netherlands, CC BY 4.0.

Fig. 251 Opening in a prayer book, with a full-page miniature depicting Christ as Man of Sorrows and an angel border on the right, painted by the Masters of Zweder van Culemborg, and border decoration around the miniature applied by a painter in the Southern Netherlands. The Hague, Koninklijke Bibliotheek, Ms. BPH 148, fol. 138v-139r. Image © Koninklijke Bibliotheek — the National Library of The Netherlands, CC BY 4.0.

Although the calendar contains entries in red for Utrecht saints, including the translation of St. Martin, patron of the cathedral of Utrecht (11 November), which is one of the defining features of a calendar for Utrecht, it also contains many entries in black for many saints from the Southern Netherlands and France that do not appear in Utrecht calendars (fig. 248).[34] Which is more likely? That a scribe from Utrecht would copy a local exemplar but include minor southern saints? Or that a scribe from Bruges would copy a local exemplar but include important northern saints? The latter, of course. As the calendar and the rest of the manuscript (except fol. 166, which I discuss later) were copied by one hand, this evidence suggests that the manuscript was copied in the Southern Netherlands, possibly in Bruges, for a Northern Netherlandish client. In this way, the scribe used a local model but adjusted it slightly by including the most important saints from the bishopric of Utrecht in red.

In other ways, the manuscript is much more consistent with a production in Bruges than in Utrecht. Its script, a version of *littera hybrida*, is much more at home in the southern Netherlands, as *littera textualis* was the norm for devotional books made in Utrecht in the 1430s and 40s. In fact, this script owes some of its qualities to a *bâtarde* that one might associate with Francophone Burgundian court culture. The fact that it is in Latin also points to the Southern Netherlands, as the majority of prayerbooks made in the North were in the vernacular. Some of its painted decoration also hails from the Southern Netherlands (fig. 249). One-line initials alternate between blue and gold and fall anywhere in the text line. Larger initials are more ornate and are always pushed to the left edge of the text block. In other words the original decoration, applied in the Southern Netherlands, is internally consistent.

While the scribe was writing in the Southern Netherlands, he incorporated 12 full-page miniatures painted by the Masters of Zweder of Culemborg as part of the original planning. Because the manuscript is a prayerbook and not a book of hours, it lacks Passion and Infancy

---

34 According to Hermann Grotefend, *Taschenbuch der Zeitrechnung des Deutschen Mittelalters und der Neuzeit* (Hannover: Hahnsche Buchhandlung, 1960) [hereafter: GTZ], saints in BPH 148 that do not appear in calendars for Utrecht include: Macharius, whose relics were in Ghent (9 May); Quiricus and Julitta, martyrs (16 June) [GTZ: Paris]; Vincent, confessor (14 July) [GTZ: Cambrai]; Christopher, martyr (24 July) [Paris, Bruges, but usually on 27 July]; Timothy and Apollinaris martyrs (23 August) [Paris, Bruges]; Genesius, martyr (25 August) [Paris]; Bertin, abbot, confessor (5 September) [GTZ: northern France]; Theodard, bishop (of Maastricht), martyr (10 September) [GTZ: Liège]; Gengulf, martyr (10 December) [GTZ: Tournai]; Caprasius, martyr (20 October) [GTZ: Trier, Liège, France]; Rumoldus, bishop, martyr (27 October) [GTZ: Liège].

cycles that would accompany the standard Hours. Instead the Zweder Masters supplied it with iconic rather than narrative imagery (fig. 250). The Masters of Zweder van Culemborg, a group of illuminators associated with the city of Utrecht, take their name from a missal they illuminated that belonged to Zweder van Culemborg, bishop of Utrecht, who died in 1433 at Basel (Bressanone/Brixen, Seminario maggiore, Ms. C 20).[35] Miranda Bloem has convincingly attributed the miniatures in BPH 148 to the Bressanone Master within the Zweder group. Perhaps the Northern Netherlandish client transported these miniatures from Utrecht to Bruges, which was a well-travelled route.[36]

At a time when miniatures were largely being made as singletons that were blank on the back and were only slipped into place before binding, this manuscript, unusually, displays a different way of constructing the book. Namely, the miniatures are integral with the quire structure and inscribed on the back. In other words, the illuminators painted on bifolia rather than on singletons. Additionally, two of the Zweder miniatures (fol. 19v and 55v) were worked in as singletons, although these, too, were inscribed on the back by the original hand and were therefore planned from the beginning; they may have begun as bifolia that the scribe for some reason trimmed down.

I propose, therefore, that the scribe had a stack of bifolia with illuminations, and then ruled their backs and integrated them into the manuscript as he was writing. In every case, the image is on the left side of the opening. This means that the bifolia supplied by the Zweder Masters each had an image on the left side of the centerline, on one side of the parchment. The scribe could fold these bifolia so that the image was either on the inside of the bifolium (if the image fell in the first half of the quire), or the outside (if the image fell in the second half of the quire). Either way, the image would always fall on the left side of the opening. No bifolium contains more than one miniature; however, the Zweder Masters did execute border decoration on one folio: the angel

---

35   Defoer et al., *The Golden Age of Dutch Manuscript Painting*, pp. 12, 98, 104, 106, 109; Miranda Bloem, *De Meesters van Zweder van Culemborg*, pp. 321–29 and *passim*. Bloem identifies the hand of the artist in BPH 148 as the Bressanone master, who was active in Utrecht.

36   For a discussion of another manuscript containing painting from both Bruges and Utrecht (HKB, Ms. 77 L 45), see Rudy, *Postcards on Parchment*, pp. 29–33. Van Bergen, *De Meesters van Otto van Moerdrecht*, discusses at greater length manuscript illuminators who moved from Utrecht to Bruges, where labor conditions in the book industry were more favorable in the mid-fifteenth century.

border on fol. 139r (fig. 251). Borders such as this are typical of the work of the Zweder Masters, who often painted sorrowing angels around text folios opposite Passion iconography, for example, in HKB, Ms. 79 K 2 (fig. 252).[37] This opening in BPH 148 (138v-139r), with its dramatic and sorrowful paratext, is formed of a single bifolium at the center of the quire, with Christ as Man of Sorrows on the left of the fold, and a text page with an angel border on the right, all painted by the Masters of Zweder van Culemborg. It is clear that the border around BPH 148, fol. 139r was executed by North Netherlandish artists, because the angel in the lower border holds a banderol inscribed in small, neat *textualis* letters that typify Northern scribes and contrast sharply with the large script of the body of the page, written in a form of *bâtarde* that typifies the Southern Netherlands. Moreover, the palette of the angels, including the one with the soft green garment, matches that in the Zweder miniature, which includes an angel with an analogous robe, but this color contrasts with the border around the miniature on 138v, which uses a darker kelly green. That the miniatures and one of the borders were painted first, and that the work of the scribe came second, marks an experimental reversal of the normative processes of book production.

This was a book project led by the illuminator rather than scribe. The images in BPH 148, plus the border of fol. 139r, were probably painted in the 1430s in the Northern Netherlands (in Utrecht), but then must have travelled to the Southern Netherlands, where they were inscribed and integrated into this prayerbook. Alternatively, the Bressanone Master may have executed the miniatures while he was in or around Bruges. Either way, the bifolia, furnished with miniatures, were handed to a scribe in the Southern Netherlands, who built the rest of the manuscript around these images. The scribe then supplemented this parchment with many more bifolia, which he ruled with upper, lower, and lateral bounding lines that conformed to the size of the miniatures. In other words, the miniaturist dictated the size of the text block. This situation is fundamentally different from the older method of making a manuscript, which began with a scribe copying a text and leaving room for miniatures and initials. BPH 148, on the other hand, began with the images, onto and around which the scribe wrote.

---

37 Opening in a book of hours, with a full-page miniature depicting the Deposition from the Cross opposite a text page with sorrowing angels, painted by the Masters of Zweder van Culemborg. The Hague, Koninklijke Bibliotheek, Ms. 79 K 2, pp. 170–171, http://manuscripts.kb.nl/show/images/79+K+2

Fig. 253 Opening in a prayer book, with a full-page miniature depicting the Virgin and Child with St. John, painted on a singleton (fol. 55) by the Masters of Zweder van Culemborg, with border decoration aroud the miniature applied by a painter in the Southern Netherlands. The Hague, Koninklijke Bibliotheek, Ms. BPH 148, fol. 55v-56r. Image © Koninklijke Bibliotheek—the National Library of The Netherlands, CC BY 4.0.

Fig. 254 Opening in a prayer book, with a long rubric used as a space filler; Delft penwork decoration added to text folios inscribed in the Southern Netherlands. The Hague, Koninklijke Bibliotheek, Ms. BPH 148, fol. 54v-55r. Image © Koninklijke Bibliotheek—the National Library of The Netherlands, CC BY 4.0.

Fig. 255 Opening in a prayer book, with a suffrage to St. Erasmus (112r), written in the Southern Netherlands on the reverse of the miniature depicting St. Lawrence, painted by the Bressanone Master; later, Delft penwork decoration was added to both text folios. The Hague, Koninklijke Bibliotheek, Ms. BPH 148, fol. 111v-112r. Image © Koninklijke Bibliotheek—the National Library of The Netherlands, CC BY 4.0.

Fig. 256 Opening in a prayer book, with a full-page miniature depicting St. Lawrence painted by the Bressanone Master (112v), and a suffrage to St. Lawrence (113r), with painted border decoration applied in the Southern Netherlands; the suffrage is inscribed on the reverse of a miniature depicting St. Christopher. The Hague, Koninklijke Bibliotheek, Ms. BPH 148, fol. 112v-113r. Image © Koninklijke Bibliotheek—the National Library of The Netherlands, CC BY 4.0.

Fig. 257 Opening in a prayer book, with a full-page miniature depicting St. Christopher painted by the Bressanone Master (113v), and a suffrage to St. Christopher (114r), with painted border decoration applied in the Southern Netherlands. The Hague, Koninklijke Bibliotheek, Ms. BPH 148, fol. 113v-114r. Image © Koninklijke Bibliotheek—the National Library of The Netherlands, CC BY 4.0.

Fig. 258 Opening in a prayer book, with a full-page miniature depicting St. George, with painted border decoration typical of that executed by the sisters of St. Agnes in Delft. The Hague, Koninklijke Bibliotheek, Ms. BPH 148, fol. 165v-166r. Image © Koninklijke Bibliotheek—the National Library of The Netherlands, CC BY 4.0.

What challenged the scribe was to cause incipits of texts to fall opposite their relevant images. This involved making some adjustments. For one, he had to make sure that the image of Christ as Man of Sorrows, with the angel border, fell at the center of a quire so that the two halves of the sheet would face each other. To do that, he wrote the preamble to the litany on fol. 131r-138r, but stopped short of actually listing the saints, so that the sorrowing Christ opening could fall at 138v-139r. Elsewhere in the book he made further accommodations, as one can see around the *O Intemerata* (fig. 253). This text was written to accompany a miniature depicting the Virgin and St. John. The previous text finished near the top of fol. 55r. The scribe was therefore confronted with considerable blank space on the rest of the page. He filled much of it by writing a long rubric to preface the *O Intemerata* (fig. 254). These adjustments became more intense around the suffrages of the saints, the most densely illustrated section of this prayerbook. As I showed earlier, some book makers in Bruges interleaved singletons containing prayers with singletons containing miniatures. This generated undesirable blank space and caused waste. Contrariwise, the scribe of BPH 148 obviated this problem by using the backs of the miniatures as surfaces for text. For example, the suffrage to St. Erasmus (fol. 112r; fig. 255) is inscribed on the back of the image depicting St. Lawrence (fol. 112v, fig. 256). And the suffrage to St. Lawrence is written on the back of the full-page illumination depicting St. Christopher (fol. 113v, fig. 257). Into the interstices between these images, the scribe wrote suffrages to the minor saints, those without full-page images. For example, the suffrage to St. Stephen (lacking a miniature) has been copied onto fol. 111v, squeezed between two saints—Peter and Lawrence—who do receive full-page miniatures. All of this indicates that the scribe began with bifolia prepared with the full-page paintings when he began to write, and he elected to write on the inviting surfaces of the backs of the miniatures. It also means that the arrangement of the images, rather than the importance of the saints, determined their sequence in the suffrages.

After the scribe copied the texts around the miniatures and onto the supplementary bifolia, he sent most—although not all—of the bifolia to an illuminator in the Southern Netherlands (probably Bruges) who applied the gilt and painted two-, three-, and four-line initials. These are done in gold and opaque paint in a South Netherlandish style. He also sent most—although not all—of the Zweder master's bifolia to this atelier, where painted border decoration was also applied to the full-page miniatures and facing text pages.

Some of the folios, for one reason or another, were not sent to the Bruges decorator. Twenty years later, around 1460, the manuscript was still incomplete: the St. George miniature and other folios and lacked borders, and some of the large initials were not painted. By this time the manuscript was in the Northern Netherlands. Its owner decided not only to complete the missing decoration, but to have the manuscript's decorative program upgraded on nearly every page. This involved taking the manuscript to Augustinian convent of St. Agnes in Delft, where the sisters were known to have written and illuminated manuscripts.[38] They must have disbound the book and worked on it intensively with a variety of techniques, including penwork, painting, and gilding. They completely overhauled the decorative program.

One folio that the Agnes sisters embellished was a full-page miniature that had been added as an afterthought: that depicting St. George fighting the dragon, painted by the Masters of the Gold Scrolls. These artists were associated with the city of Bruges in the 1440s through the 1460s, and it is likely that this miniature was added when the manuscript was still in Bruges and before it returned to the Northern Netherlands. Because the image was added later, after the text was inscribed, the book maker was not able to work this image logically next to the suffrage to St. George and merely appended this image at the end of the manuscript (fol. 165v; fig. 258). It is clear that the accompanying prayer was added as an afterthought. It must have been added after the Bruges decorator had already finished embellishing the folios. The Agnes sisters painted the border with bold forms and copious gold. They favored designs with radially symmetrical flowers, and bulbous botanical forms. They also applied another kind of decoration to the bottom of the folio: vines with green leaves and red and gold balls. This motif appears in their work throughout the 1450s and 1460s, for example, in the Fagel Missal, fol. 192r.

---

38   For the convent of St. Agnes and illumination in Delft, see Defoer et al., *The Golden Age of Dutch Manuscript Painting*, pp. 185–97.

Fig. 259 (left)
Folio in a prayer book,
embellished by the sisters of
St. Agnes with a depiction of
a chicken head. The Hague,
Koninklijke Bibliotheek, Ms.
BPH 148, fol. 61v. Image
© Koninklijke Bibliotheek—the
National Library of The
Netherlands, CC BY 4.0.

Fig. 260 (below)
Full-page penwork decoration
added to fill a blank folio. The
Hague, Koninklijke Bibliotheek,
Ms. BPH 148, fol. 77r. Image
© Koninklijke Bibliotheek—the
National Library of The
Netherlands, CC BY 4.0.

Most notably, the sisters added penwork decoration to nearly every text folio of BPH 148. They globally adjusted the hierarchy of decoration so that the one-, two-, and three-line initials received pen work flourishes. For the one-line initials buried within the text block, this meant that the penwork artist had to extend the decoration through the interlineal space and out to the margin. Such flourishes, quite unusually, creep among and between the words before erupting in the margin.

Painted border decoration was also part of the sisters' repertoire. In the opening on fol. 24v-25r one can also see that the initials four lines and higher also received painted flourishes (fig. 249). Examples appear on fol. 24v, 29r, 32r. The canonesses also employed marginal figures, often birds, with banderols, or short religious aphorisms in the margins, usually inscribed in blue ink. One of these appears in the lower margin on fol. 24v, and another at the side margin of the St. George miniature (fig. 258 above). Such figures with banderols became a hallmark of Delft illumination and typify Delft manuscript manufacture.[39] Most distinctively, they included a severed chicken's head among the marginal embellishments (fig. 259). Such a chicken head also appears in the Fagel Missal, but does not appear outside the atelier of the sisters of St. Agnes.

Illuminators in Delft, including the sisters of St. Agnes, often used their signature form of penwork, applied in red and blue. Various convents in Delft adopted variations of the red-blue penwork, as if to capitalize on the successful brand that the Augustinian sisters had developed. One of the most astonishing folios in BPH 148 is one of the few folios that had been blank when the sisters received it (fig. 260). They filled it with penwork. Whereas penwork normally emanates only from an initial and reiterates the hierarchy of the page by presenting the appropriate degree of decoration for the size of the initial, here the penwork is untethered to script altogether. It presents a radially symmetrical design in red and blue penwork and green wash. One might consider it a piece of independent abstract art.

Fig. 261
Bird with message in beak, a motif typical of the St. Agnes convent in Delft. The Hague, Koninklijke Bibliotheek, Ms. BPH 148, fol. 33v. Image © Koninklijke Bibliotheek — the National Library of The Netherlands, CC BY 4.0.

---

39   Until a more complete study is written, consult C. W. de Kruyter, "The Emblematic Character of the Border Ornaments in Delft Codices," *Quaerendo* 3 (1973), pp. 211–16.

Fig. 262
Folio in a book of hours written
an illuminated at the convent
of St. Agnes in Delft, with
border decoration including
a bird with scroll in its beak
bearing the words "Iste liber
scriptus et perfectus est in
monasterio vallis iozaphat."
Krakow, Czartoryski, Ms. 2946,
fol. 25v. The manuscript is the
property of the XX. Czartoryski
Foundation in Krakow. Image
© XX. Czartoryski Foundation,
all rights reserved.

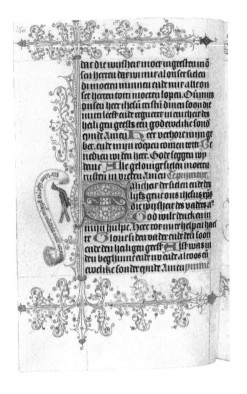

The other penwork borders, executed on every text page, are in a style that typifies Delft in mid-century; the motifs are identical to those known to have been executed at the St. Agnes convent in Delft. These include the birds and fantastical creatures bearing messages inscribed on unfurling banderols (fig. 261). Manuscripts that the sisters of St. Agnes are known to have illuminated contain analogous imagery. One such bird, painted in a book of hours now in Krakow, has a banderol in its beak announcing "Iste liber scriptus et perfectus est in monasterio vallis iozaphat" [This book was written and perfected (embellished) in the monastery of the Valley of Iosaphat] (fig. 262). They called themselves the sisters of St. Augustine, dedicated to St. Agnes, and lived in a monastery they dubbed "the Valley of Josaphat" (even though their monastery was in the center of Delft). The bird is clearly announcing that the book was written and illuminated in this monastery. The sisters applied penwork to the BPH 148 that is closely analogous to the penwork they signed in Krakow. For example, the penwork on fol. 17v-18r (fig. 263) closely resembles that applied to the book in Krakow. One difference, though, is that the Krakow book of hours only has penwork that emanates from initials, whereas BPH 148 has penwork on all four sides, and extra painted decoration on folios with an initial.

Fig. 263 Delft penwork decoration added to text folios inscribed in the Southern Netherlands. The Hague, Koninklijke Bibliotheek, Ms. BPH 148, fol. 17v-18r. Image © Koninklijke Bibliotheek—the National Library of The Netherlands, CC BY 4.0.

Fig. 264 St. James, full-page miniature and suffrage, with border decoration painted by the Sisters of St. Agnes in Delft. The Hague, Koninklijke Bibliotheek, Ms. BPH 148, fol. 106v-107r. Image © Koninklijke Bibliotheek—the National Library of The Netherlands, CC BY 4.0.

Fig. 265
Folio in the Fagel Missal, showing the incipit for the feast of St. Agnes with extra decoration, illuminated by the sisters of St. Agnes in Delft, 1459–60. Dublin, Trinity College, Ms. 81, fol. 192r. Reproduced with kind permission of the Board of Trinity College Dublin. Image © Trinity College Library Dublin, all rights reserved.

On the opening with a full-page miniature depicting St. James, they added the most astonishing embellishment (fig. 264). While the Zweder masters painted the central miniature, the border can be none other than the work of the sisters of St. Agnes. The design is based on abstracted, fleshy flowers arranged on a gold bar armature, with banderols winding around the armature. The same motif appears in the Fagel Missal, a manuscript signed by the sisters of St. Agnes. They wrote and illuminated the Fagel Missal in 1459 and 1460. They exhibited a wide range of illuminating styles in this manuscript, but reserved this style to the embellishment around their patron saint, Agnes, on fol. 192r (fig. 265). They also used this same kind of decoration around the opening of the book of Matthew, the first of the Gospels, in a large manuscript now in Copenhagen (Ms. Thott 11 folio; fig. 266). They reserved this form of corkscrewing painted and gilt decoration for the most important folios, to heighten their importance with gold and a burst of color. It is possible that the book's original owner singled this saint out for special treatment, but it is more likely that the bifolium (fol. 106–107) was simply not sent to the Bruges decorator. Evidence for this appears on the back of the St. James leaf (fol. 106r; fig. 267). Whereas the Bruges decorator painted the initials on fol.

105v, the sisters of St. Agnes painted those on fol. 106r. Apparently it fell to the sisters to apply all the minor decoration to the bifolium 106–107.

Fig. 266 Folio in a Gospel manuscript, showing the opening for the Book of Matthew, with painted decoration executed by the sisters of St. Agnes in Delft, made ca. 1459–60. Copenhagen, Royal Library, Ms. Thott 11 folio, fol. 4r. Image © Royal Library Copenhagen, CC BY 4.0.

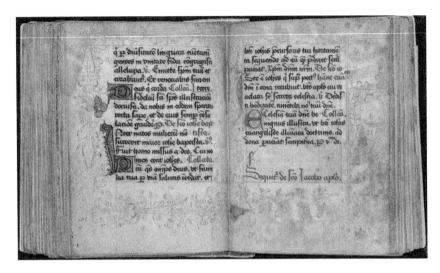

Fig. 267 Opening with short suffrages to St. John the Baptist and St. John the Evangelist, and a rubric for the suffrage to St. James. The Hague, Koninklijke Bibliotheek, Ms. BPH 148, fol. 105v-106r. Image © Koninklijke Bibliotheek—the National Library of The Netherlands, CC BY 4.0.

Fig. 268 Opening with painted and penwork border decoration executed by the sisters of St. Agnes in Delft. The Hague, Koninklijke Bibliotheek, Ms. BPH 148, fol. 86v-87r. Image © Koninklijke Bibliotheek—the National Library of The Netherlands, CC BY 4.0.

Fig. 269 Opening with an extended rubric left of the gutter, and an incipit with a simple blue initial right of the gutter. The Hague, Koninklijke Bibliotheek, Ms. BPH 148, fol. 68v-69r. Image © Koninklijke Bibliotheek—the National Library of The Netherlands, CC BY 4.0.

Fig. 270 Opening with a Pietà (full-page miniature made by the Bressanone Master, with border decoration executed in the Southern Netherlands), facing a text folio with an initial overpainted in the Northern Netherlands. The Hague, Koninklijke Bibliotheek, Ms. BPH 148, fol. 19v-20r. Image © Koninklijke Bibliotheek—the National Library of The Netherlands, CC BY 4.0.

Finally, the sisters of St. Agnes applied painted decoration to text folios. One of these has the incipit of a prayer to the heart of the Virgin (fig. 268). This folio may have had an underwhelming blue initial, like the one the sisters left untouched on fol. 69r (fig. 269). For the heart prayer the sisters have raised the level of decoration by filling the border with painted and gilt decoration, even though it does not surround or face a miniature. They were therefore registering their esteem for this prayer, or responding to the patron's request to add more decoration here. They have painted monumental versions of the succulent flowers with cones, which appear at a smaller scale on fol. 109r (above).

They may have also repainted other initials, such as one that appears on the folio opposite the Pietà (fig. 270). A sinuous magenta dragon, whose body erupts in acanthus, fills the interior of the letter *D*. Such dragons are a well-known symbol of Utrecht and embellish many manuscripts made there.[40] Several other features are odd about this initial: its blue paint is flaking off, it juts into the left margin, and there is a curious blank margin immediately above the frame of the *D*. Here is a scenario that explains these particularities: fol. 22r was inscribed in the Southern Netherlands, where it received a nine-line initial *D*, similar to the *O* on fol. 69r (fig. 269). Such a plain initial did not satisfy the owner, who wanted to raise the decorational level of fol. 69r to befit a folio facing a full-page miniature. Either the sisters of St. Agnes, or a painter in Utrecht, built a gold frame around the letter, but this frame had to be shifted to the left to cover up the mediocre penwork on the left side of the initial; they also scraped out the penwork immediately above the letter, leaving behind a clean strip between the letter and the border decoration. They filled the interior of the initial with a dragon and covered the blue *D* with white tracery, fragments of which remain. Perhaps because of the particular mixture of blue paint, it didn't adhere to the parchment very well. Since such dragons do not form part of the repertory of imagery made by the Bruges illuminator, nor by the sisters of St. Agnes, this and the related initials , in this manuscript point to yet another atelier where localized work was carried out on this manuscript over a course of several decades. This is a complicated explanation, but indeed, the potpourri of imagery in this opening calls for some layered thinking.

---

40   As-Vijvers, *Beeldschone Boeken: De Middeleeuwen in Goud en Inkt*, pp. 36–39.

The manuscript reveals again that it was the product of stages of production. I have proposed here that the miniatures, made as bifolia by the Masters of Zweder van Culemborg in Utrecht in the 1430s, travelled to the Southern Netherlands, expressly for a book destined for a client in the bishopric of Utrecht. A scribe in the Southern Netherlands, possibly in Bruges, carried out the copying, and sent many of the bifolia to a local painter to be embellished with initials and border decoration. Two decades later, when the manuscript and possibly its owner had returned to Utrecht or its environs, the book received additional embellishment, possibly in two different workshops. One of those workshops was that of the convent of St. Agnes in Delft, where the entire manuscript received extensive penwork decoration and a variety of painted decoration. In its complicated career, the manuscript had owners that cared deeply about the amount and extent of decoration. As the additional decoration was so extensive, it could only have been applied with the book apart. Prayerbook owners who sought upgrades to their books had a variety of choices about whom to hire. They had at least two choices in Delft for upgrades, the convents of St. Ursula and St. Agnes, with the latter providing much more lavish and gilt decoration.

Interventions of the kind seen in the manuscripts discussed above receive their most complicated and advanced manifestation in the work of the Masters of the Dark Eyes, a discussion of whom is taken up in the next section.

E. The Masters of the Dark Eyes

In the discussion above regarding HKB, Ms. 132 G 38, I showed that an atelier in Leiden and the sisters of St. Ursula in Delft both made changes to the manuscript: they added new texts in the available spaces; added decoration and raised the hierarchy of the decoration (by elevating areas of penwork only to areas of painted decoration); added single leaf-miniatures to preface certain texts and added text leaves in order to augment prayers, namely, the Verses of St. Gregory, turning it from a five-verse version into a nine-verse version); and added entire quires full of texts. I proposed that the convent of St. Ursula in Delft had executed some of these changes, and that the sisters there specialized in updating older books to make them appropriate for continued use. The Masters of the Dark Eyes, whom I introduced above, seem to be professional artists unconnected to a religious house, who similarly made interventions to existing manuscripts, including adding single leaves and entire quires. They also took manuscripts apart, made major structural and cosmetic changes, and then reassembled them. Whereas the Sisters of St. Ursula specialized in adding texts and modest decoration, and the sisters of St. Agnes specialized in supplying elaborate penwork, painted, and gilt decoration, the Masters of the Dark Eyes specialized in adding both texts and images, plus exuberant painted border decoration in saturated colors.

1. Alongside the Master of Gijsbrecht van Brederode

One of the most dramatic examples of manuscript augmentation appears in a book of hours, which was made in two distinctive campaigns of work that were executed over a half-century (HKB, Ms. BPH 151).[41] The core of manuscript was made in Utrecht around 1465, at which time it was complete and viable as a vehicle for private devotion. It contained only standard texts for a book of hours: a calendar, the Hours of the Virgin, the Hours of the Holy Cross, the Hours of the Holy Spirit, some suffrages, the Seven Penitential Psalms, Litany, and the Vigil for the Dead. Shortly after these core texts were copied, the Master of Gijsbrecht van Brederode executed the decoration for them. This painter probably worked in Utrecht.

A half-century later, however, the manuscript's new owners desired to possess new prayers that would reflect the changing fashion and taste in prayer. The Masters of the Dark Eyes, a group of artists active in the decades surrounding 1500 possibly based in South Holland, wrought these changes.[42] These artists, none of whom can be identified by name, can however be identified by their style. They specialized in applying copious amounts of colorful illumination to books of hours and prayerbooks and apparently represented good value per square

---

41   The manuscript was in the Bibliotheca Philosophica Hermetica in Amsterdam (Ms. 151) until 2011, when most of the manuscripts from that collection were deposited at the National Library (Koninklijke Bibliotheek) in The Hague.

42   Broekhuijsen, *The Masters of the Dark Eyes: Late Medieval Manuscript Painting in Holland.*

centimeter of applied decoration. In addition to illuminating new prayerbooks, they may have even specialized in updating existing manuscripts, as several prayerbooks with their augmentations survive.[43] Analyzing these updates reveals the extent to which devotion had changed in the course of the second half of the fifteenth century. The added prayers are precisely those devotions that had become fashionable at the end of the century, and were generally added to manuscripts made two, three, or more decades earlier. (See the chart below for a summary of the changes to the manuscript.) The manuscript's second or third owner apparently commissioned a stationer who had access to parchment, scribes, binders, and illuminators—namely, the Masters of the Dark Eyes—to supply the additional images.

Whereas the interventions discussed in the previous section were probably made at the convent of St. Ursula in Delft, the interventions discussed below were probably made in a professional, that is, non-monastic atelier.[44] While the Masters of the Dark Eyes sometimes worked with monasteries or monastic books, they appear overwhelmingly to have worked for private secular patrons, and the manuscripts they produced (largely books of hours and prayerbooks) reveal no allegiance to any particular saint, order, or religious community. Unlike the various sisters and nuns updating manuscripts in Delft, the Masters of the Dark Eyes were apparently secular professionals.

---

43 The Masters of the Dark Eyes also added sections to Liège, UB, Wittert 34 (discussed below); Oxford, Bodleian Library, Douce 381; Dublin, Trinity College, Ms. 81, fol. 186 (the Fagel Missal, with an added Mass for St. Anne, discussed above); Rome, Bibliotheca Casanatense, Ms. 4216, fol. 221; London, British Library, Harley Ms. 2887, fol. 3 (a *Salvator Mundi* added into an older book of hours); and London, British Library, Harley Ms. 1892 (with several interventions by the Masters of the Dark Eyes). These are listed in Ibid., p. 271 and point to a larger pattern in which these masters were hired to augment existing books. These artists and the copyists with whom they worked therefore made adjustments to far more manuscripts than I can treat here.

44 It should be noted, however, that the boundary between "monastic" and "professional" production may be a permeable one, considering that the convent of St. Ursula, for example, may have also taken private commissions to create new manuscripts and update old ones, and secular urban illuminators may have supplied illuminations for manuscripts inscribed in monastic ateliers. At the very least, more research is needed to explore the relationships between monastic and non-monastic manuscript ateliers in the fifteenth century.

The Hague, KB, BPH 151: structure and textual content

	Physical construction				Inscribed content	
quire	structure of quire	includes folios	Phase I (ca. 1465) or Phase II (ca. 1510)	Notes on construction and summary of added leaves	textual contents: written by Utrecht scribe (U), or scribe working alongside the Masters of the Dark Eyes (MDE)	Inscribed content
I	6	f. 1-6	I	Stitching between 3-4	**calendar**	U
II	8 (-1)	f. 7-13	I	Stitching between 10-11	calendar	U
III	8 (+2)	f. 14-23	I, II	Stitching between 19-20; 14, 15 are single leaves, added ca. 1510.	**Hours of the Virgin**	U, MDE
IV	8	24-31	I	Stitching between 27-28	Hours of the Virgin	U
V	8 (-1)	32-38	I	Stitching between 35-36; final folio (after 38) cut out, with loss of text	Hours of the Virgin	U
VI	8	39-46	I	Stitching between 42-43	Hours of the Virgin	U
VII	8	47-54	I	Stitching between 50-51	Hours of the Virgin	U
VIII	8 (+1)	55-63	I, II	Stitching between 58-59; 60 is single leaf, added ca. 1510.	Hours of the Virgin (through 59v); **Hours of the Cross begins 61r**	U, MDE
IX	8	64-71	I, II	Stitching between 67-68; 64 and 71 are singletons (64 from 1465, and 71 from ca. 1510)	Hours of the Cross (through 65r, line 11); indulgenced prayers (65r, line 12-70v)	U, MDE
X	8	72-79	I	Stitching between 75-76	**Hours of the Holy Spirit**	U
XI		80-87	I	Stitching between 83-84	Hours of the Holy Spirit	U
XII		88-95	I, II	Stitching between 91-92	**Suffrages**	1465 [88-93v, line 1]; 1510 [93v, line 2-95v]; thus, the hand from 1510 fills in the rest of the blank

Quire	Leaves	Folios	Group	Stitching and construction notes	Contents	Production notes
XIII		96–104	II	Stitching between 100–101; folio cut out after 103 (but without loss of text); 96 and 104 are full-page added miniatures; 104 is glued to 95; 96–103 comprise a separate booklet, which was formerly glued into the book between 95 and 104.	**Prayer to the Seven Sorrows**	97–102 ruled differently from the rest of the text, in reddish brown ink, with horizontal and vertical bounding lines, thus it was made in a different campaign of work; 97–100 are numbered "1–4" in a 16th-century hand, brown ink, lower right
XIV	8 (-1)	105–111	I	Folio cut out before 105 (which would have had the incipit for the Seven Penitential Psalms); Stitching between 107–108	7 Psalms & litany	
XV	8	112–119	I	Stitching between 115–116	7 Psalms & litany	
XVI	8 (+1)	120–128	I, II	Stitching between 124–125; 120 is a single leaf [from 1465], joined to 128; 121 is full-page miniature [from 1510]	**Indulgenced prayers**	U [fol. 120r–120v line 9]; MDE [120v line 10–128v]
XVII	6	129–134	II	Stitching between 131–132	Added prayers	MDE in 1510
XVIII	6 (+1)	135–141	II	Stitching between 137–138; 141 added full-page min	Suffrages, filler prayer to the cross	MDE in 1510
XIX	8 (-1)	142–148	I	Stitching between 145–146; folio missing after 148	**Vigil of the Dead**	U
XX	8	149–156	I	Stitching between 152–153	Vigil of the Dead	U
XXI	8	157–164	I	Stitching between 160–161	Vigil of the Dead	U
XXII	2	165–166	I	Stitching between 165–166	Vigil of the Dead	U

Key	
	Quires made, inscribed and decorated ca. 1465 in Utrecht
	Quires made all or partly ca. 1510 by bookmakers associated with the Masters of the Dark Eyes

Fig. 271 Opening at the incipit of the Hours of the Holy Spirit, with the Coronation
of the Virgin (full-page miniature by the Masters of the Dark Eyes on added
parchment, made ca. 1510), and the Descent of the Holy Spirit (historiated initial
painted by the Master of Gijsbrecht van Brederode, made as part of the original
campaign of work ca. 1465, with painted border decoration of the same era). The
Hague, Koninklijke Bibliotheek, Ms. BPH 151, fol. 71v-72r. Image © Koninklijke
Bibliotheek—the National Library of The Netherlands, CC BY 4.0.

As the table shows, two distinctive campaigns of work appear in this
book. Openings for the major texts reveal the old and the new work,
side by side. At the opening for the Hours of the Holy Spirit (HKB, Ms.
BPH 151, fol. 71v-72r; fig. 271), for example, the original campaign of
work appears on the right side of the opening, and the work of the
Masters of the Dark Eyes on the added parchment on the left. Original
parts include historiated initials painted by the Master of Gijsbrecht van
Brederode, who executed the Pentecost initial. This painter, working
with delicate brushstrokes and a minute brush, gave each apostle
different facial features to convey a range of psychological responses
to the descent of the Holy Spirit. As the borders are somewhat unusual
and are encrusted with red, blue, green, and pink paint as well as leaf
gold, one can see that the painter applied pigment directly to the text
folios and coordinated decoration carefully with the text block.

The style, palette and subject matter of the Master of Gijsbrecht van
Brederode clash quite severely with what has been added to the left

side of the opening: a full-page miniature depicting the Coronation of the Virgin. While the Master of Gijsbrecht van Brederode probably completed his illumination around 1465, one of the Masters of the Dark Eyes completed the Coronation around 1500 or shortly thereafter. In comparison to the earlier illumination in the initial, the full-page miniature has been executed much more quickly, with a thicker brush, and very little attention to differentiating the faces. The Masters of the Dark Eyes completed the full-page miniature with a border painted with liquid gold applied over a ground treated first with gesso, which provides a three-dimensional ground for the gold. It also provides an entirely different visual effect from the more labor-intensive gold foil that the Master of Gijsbrecht van Brederode used in the original sections of the manuscript. More research into these materials is necessary, but I suspect that the gold paint of the Masters of the Dark Eyes was cheaper than the gold foil of the Master of Gijsbrecht van Brederode.

Fig. 272 Opening at the incipit of the Hours of the Virgin, with the Annunciation (full-page miniature by the Masters of the Dark Eyes on added parchment, made ca. 1510), and Virgin and Child (historiated initial painted by the Master of Gijsbrecht van Brederode, made as part of the original campaign of work ca. 1465, with painted border decoration of the same era). The Hague, Koninklijke Bibliotheek, Ms. BPH 151, fol. 15v-16r. Image © Koninklijke Bibliotheek — the National Library of The Netherlands, CC BY 4.0.

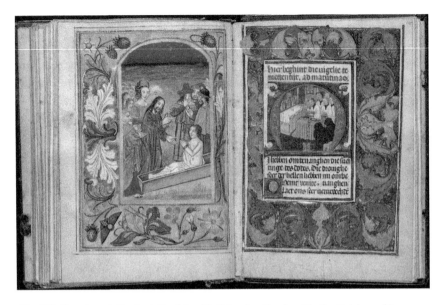

Fig. 273 Opening at the incipit of the Vigil for the Dead, with the Raising of Lazarus (full-page miniature by the Masters of the Dark Eyes on added parchment, made ca. 1510), and Mass of the Dead (historiated initial painted by the Master of Gijsbrecht van Brederode, made as part of the original campaign of work ca. 1465, with painted border decoration of the same era). The Hague, Koninklijke Bibliotheek, Ms. BPH 151, fol. 141v-142r. Image © Koninklijke Bibliotheek—the National Library of The Netherlands, CC BY 4.0.

The Masters of the Dark Eyes transformed all of the major text openings in a similar way, so that they are visually loud and brash and call attention to the beginning of each incipit. For example, they have added a full-page miniature depicting the Annunciation to the opening of the Hours of the Virgin (fig. 272). They have tried to match the borders in size and chromatic intensity by duplicating the thick gold and bold painted colors, dominated by blue flowers, from the earlier part of the production.

Even without the interventions executed around 1500, the manuscript would have been complete.[45] Expanding the imagery in the book—adding more pictures—meant finding alternative themes for some of the openings. For the Vigil for the Dead, the original artists had supplied an image of the Mass for the Dead in the historiated initial (fig. 273). Therefore, the Masters of the Dark Eyes chose an alternative subject for the added full-page miniature, specifically, the Raising of Lazarus.

---

45   In fact, the original parts of The Hague, Koninklijke Bibliotheek, Ms. BPH 151 are very close to those in Liège, UB, Ms. Wittert 34. Both manuscripts have historiated initials and border decoration in the same style. BPH 151 would have looked very much like Wittert 34 before it received its augmentations.

Because the original parts of the manuscript contained no indulgenced prayers, the person who bought or inherited the book at the end of the fifteenth century deemed its texts and images insufficient, and felt compelled to make a number of adjustments to it. The additional texts, which will be discussed more fully below, consist overwhelmingly of indulgenced prayers and prayers that were to be read in conjunction with images. They were able to create images by painting them on full-page sheets, which could then be bound together with the existing manuscript to books of hours and prayerbooks.

Given the intricacies of the amendments, one might assume that a planner, or *libraire*, oversaw them. This *libraire* had to come up with a new program based on what was already present in the manuscript and what the new owner desired. He had to coordinate the work of both the copyists and the illuminators, who were also closely integrated with each other, since many of the added textual sections also contain small miniatures. Someone at the atelier, such as a *libraire,* might have begun by taking the manuscript apart and ruling the blank folios. In planning the additions, the planner attempted to smooth the seams between the old and the new, for example, by ruling the additions with the same dimensions as the original parts.

Fig. 274 Opening from a section added by the Masters of the Dark Eyes ca. 1510, with a miniature depicting the Crucifixion and an indulgence. The Hague, Koninklijke Bibliotheek, Ms. BPH 151, fol. 65v-66r. Image © Koninklijke Bibliotheek—the National Library of The Netherlands, CC BY 4.0.

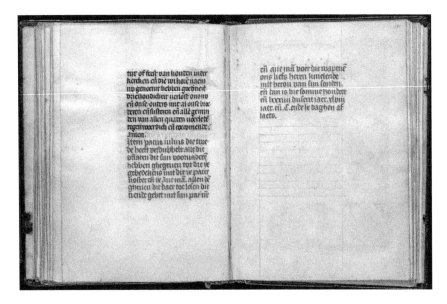

Fig. 275 The end of a prayer written around 1465 in black on fol. 120v (part of the original parchment of the book), and a rubric added ca. 1510 to the bottom of fol. 120v, which continues on 121r (on added parchment). Note that the back of the miniature has been ruled with the same dimensions as the original text pages. The Hague, Koninklijke Bibliotheek, Ms. BPH 151, fol. 120v-121r. Image © Koninklijke Bibliotheek — the National Library of The Netherlands, CC BY 4.0.

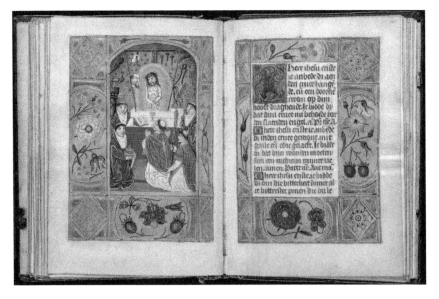

Fig. 276 Opening from a section added by the Masters of the Dark Eyes ca. 1510, with a full-page miniature depicting the Mass of St. Gregory facing the Verses of St. Gregory. The Hague, Koninklijke Bibliotheek, Ms. BPH 151, fol. 121v-122r. Image © Koninklijke Bibliotheek — the National Library of The Netherlands, CC BY 4.0.

The scribes making additions to the already-complete manuscript inscribed the new prayers on bits of the parchment left at the end of a quire; when that parchment was exhausted, they added additional sheets of parchment and inscribed those. The same holds true in BPH 151. For example, the Short Hours of the Cross—one of the original texts—filled an entire quire of the original book, plus part of the next quire; the fifteenth-century scribe left the rest of the quire unwritten. The sixteenth-century scribe filled that blank space at the end of the quire, beginning on fol. 65r, with a new prayer—an indulgenced prayer to be read before a crucifix—where he found a bit of ruled parchment, then continued copying this text onto the verso side of the folio, but then added several more folios to accommodate the rest of the prayer (fig. 274). In this way, nearly all of the older ruled parchment is filled, and the new parts are interdigitized with the old parts. Furthermore, the added text about the cross fits thematically with the text to which it was appended, the Hours of the Cross. Added physical material made space for new texts. The contents of those texts is extremely revelatory for understanding the sixteenth-century patron's desires. Two main texts fill the quire: a prayer to be read "in front of an image of the crucifix," for which the reader would earn as many days' indulgence as Christ had wounds on his body; and a prayer that yielded 100,000 years' indulgence and 90 quadragenes and ensured that its reader would not die without the sacrament.[46] The later scribe found some space at the end of Quire XII (fol. 95r/v), and added to it an indulgenced prayer worth 80,000 years.[47]

---

46   BPH 151, fol. 65–67v: *rub:* Dese bedinge salmen lesen voer een beelt des crucifix. Ende so wiese mit devocien leest, verdient also veel daghen af[65v]laets als Cristus menighe wonde had in sinen lichaem in sijnre passien. Welcken aflaet heeft ghegeven die paus Gregorius die derde uut beden eenre koninginne van Ingelant. *inc:* Ic bidde di alre beminste here Jhesu Criste om der over groter liefden wil daer ghi dat menschelike... 68v-70v: *rub:* Die dit navolgende gebet leest verdient c^m jaer aflaets ende xc karenen. Daer toe seit sint Jan Guldemont, so wie dat dagelix leest, en sal niet sterven ongebiecht noch sonder dat heilige sacrament. *inc:* In die tegenwoordicheit dijns heiligen lichaems ende dijns heiligen dierbaren bloets...

47   BPH 151, fol. 94v-95v: Indulgenced prayer, *rub:* Die dit navolgende gebet lesen mit berou van sijn sonden, die verdient [95r] lxxx^m jaeren aflaets. *inc:* O here Jhesu Criste levende gods soen...

The sixteenth-century studio also added entire quires, such as fol. 120–128. This quire contains, among other items, a copy of the 10-verse version of the *Adoro te* along with a full-page miniature depicting the Mass of St. Gregory (fig. 275 and 276). This text and miniature have been slotted in just after the Seven Penitential Psalms and Litany of the Saints, which fill two fifteenth-century quires (BPH 151, fol. 105–111, 112–119). The sixteenth-century scribe ruled the otherwise blank back of the miniature of the Mass of St. Gregory and planned to inscribe the prayer's rubric on the back of the image. But he must have realized that the long rubric would not fit on a single folio. He therefore found a single text page from the earlier part of the manuscript on which the end of another prayer had been written but which still had several ruled but blank lines. He appended this fifteenth-century leaf (fol. 120) to the beginning of the sixteenth-century quire, and used these blank spaces to start the rubric, which is then continued on the back of the miniature. In this way, the fifteenth century parchment is integrated with the sixteenth-century additions; the back of the miniature (BPH 151, 121r) has been ruled so that it has the same ruling dimensions as the rest of the book; a minimum of new material has been added; and the blank spaces in the original sections of the manuscript have been filled with text; and the sixteenth-century scribe who added the rubric attempted to imitate the earlier script. Those scribes and artists who made amendments to this book, in other words, went to great lengths to integrate their work with what was already there. But they also went to great lengths to add indulgences and new devotional images that had come into vogue.

The additions supplied the newest, most highly indulgenced versions of the prayers circulating around 1500. For example, the added rubric accompanying the 10-verse version of the *Adoro te* reads:

> *rub:* Item, Pope Julius II doubled all of the indulgences that his forefathers had given to the nine little prayers with the nine *Pater Nosters* and nine *Ave Marias* to anyone who will read this tenth prayer with its *Pater Noster* and *Ave Maria* in front of the *arma Christi,* kneeling with contrition for his sins. This is a sum of 184,048 years and 160 days of indulgence. [BPH 151, fol. 120v-124v]

rub: Item, paeus Julius die tweede heeft verdubbelt alle die oflaten die sijn voorvaderen hebben ghegeven tot die ix gebedekens mit die ix *Pater noster* ende ix *Ave Maria* allen den ghenen die daer toe lesen dit tiende gebet mit sijn *Pater noster* [121r] ende *Ave Maria* voer die wapenen ons liefs heren, knielende mit berou van sijn sonden. Ende dan is die somme hondert ende lxxxiiii dusent jaer xlviii jaer ende c ende lx daghen aflaets. [BPH 151, fol. 120v-124v]

Not only is the new rubric-prayer-image added to the older manuscript, but the rubric itself is about accretions, both the growth of the prayer, from nine to ten verses, and also the concomitant accretion in indulgences. One of the most indulgenced prayers in the later Middle Ages was the Verses of St. Gregory. This prayer accompanies a large, clear, full-page miniature depicting the Mass of St. Gregory, with the *arma Christi* filling the space around the altar. It has been made to match the text block and border of the incipit of the prayer, which indicates that the illuminators and the copyists of the added parts of the manuscript were highly coordinated. The mention of Pope Julius also provides an indication for the date of these additions. Julius II was pope from 1503–1513, so these additions could not have been made before 1503.

Immediately after winning an indulgence for 80,000 years, the reader can go on to the next heavily indulgenced prayer:

BPH 151, fol. 124v: *rub:* Item, Pope Julius II changed the *Prayer for the conception of our dear Lady* and doubled the indulgence, so that anyone who reads it in front of an image of Our Dear Lady in the Sun, kneeling, who is in a state of grace, earns 22,000 years.

124v: *rub:* Item, paeus Julius die twede heeft dat *Gebedeken van die ontfangenis van onser liever vrouwen* dus verandert ende heft die aflaten verdubbelt. Soe wie dat leest voer dat beelt van onser liever vrouwen in die sonne, knielende, staende in state van gracien xxii^m jaer. *inc:* Weest ghegruet alre heylichste joncfrouwe…

Older versions of this prayer carried an indulgence of only 11,000 years. Julius II was probably the reigning pope when these additions were made. The illuminators and the scribes with whom they worked were in this way underscoring the novelty of their wares.

Fig. 277 Opening from a section added by the Masters of the Dark Eyes ca. 1510, with a miniature depicting the Virgin in Sole and a prayer with an indulgence for 92,000 years. The Hague, Koninklijke Bibliotheek, Ms. BPH, fol. 124v-125r. Image © Koninklijke Bibliotheek—the National Library of The Netherlands, CC BY 4.0.

Fig. 278 Opening from a section added by the Masters of the Dark Eyes ca. 1510 with a miniature depicting the Virgin accompanying an indulgenced prayer. The Hague, Koninklijke Bibliotheek, Ms. BPH 151, fol. 125v-126r. Image © Koninklijke Bibliotheek—the National Library of The Netherlands, CC BY 4.0.

Fig. 279 Opening from a section added by the Masters of the Dark Eyes ca. 1510 with a miniature depicting the Lactation of St. Bernard. The Hague, Koninklijke Bibliotheek, Ms. BPH 151, fol. 128v-129r. Image © Koninklijke Bibliotheek—the National Library of The Netherlands, CC BY 4.0.

Fig. 280 Opening from a section added by the Masters of the Dark Eyes ca. 1510 with a miniature depicting Mary and Jesus, to accompany the *O intemerata*. The Hague, Koninklijke Bibliotheek, Ms. BPH 151, fol. 130v-131r. Image © Koninklijke Bibliotheek—the National Library of The Netherlands, CC BY 4.0.

Fig. 281 Opening from a section added by the Masters of the Dark Eyes ca. 1510 with a
         miniature depicting St. Anne, Mary and Jesus, to accompany an indulgenced
         prayer to St. Anne. The Hague, Koninklijke Bibliotheek, Ms. BPH 151, fol.
         133v-134r. Image © Koninklijke Bibliotheek—the National Library of The
         Netherlands, CC BY 4.0.

Fig. 282 Opening from a section added by the Masters of the Dark Eyes ca. 1510 with
         a miniature depicting an angel, to accompany a prayer to the personal angel.
         The Hague, Koninklijke Bibliotheek, Ms. BPH 151, fol. 134v-135r. Image
         © Koninklijke Bibliotheek—the National Library of The Netherlands, CC BY 4.0.

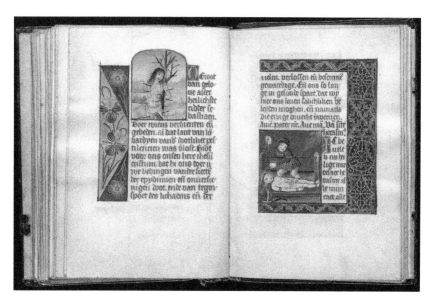

Fig. 283 Opening from a section added by the Masters of the Dark Eyes ca. 1510 with miniatures depicting St. Sebastian and St. Erasmus, to accompany prayers to those saints. The Hague, Koninklijke Bibliotheek, Ms. BPH 151, fol. 136v-137r. Image © Koninklijke Bibliotheek—the National Library of The Netherlands, CC BY 4.0.

In summary, the Verses of St. Gregory initiate an entire section of indulgenced prayers added in the sixteenth century. These fill three added quires (fol. 120–141), which contain the following:

– the 10 Verses of St. Gregory, with an indulgence for 84,068 years' and 160 days' indulgence and a full-page miniature to accompany it, depicting the Mass of St. Gregory (120v-124v);

– the prayer to the Virgin of the Sun, with an indulgence doubled by Julius II to 22,000 years' indulgence for reading the prayer in the presence of the image, accompanied by a miniature depicting the Virgin and Child in the sun and standing on the sliver of moon (124v-125v; fig. 277);

– another indulgenced prayer to the Virgin, promising that she will appear to the reader before his death to tell him when he will die, which is also accompanied by an image of the Virgin and Child, who are wearing an enormous string of coral beads (fol. 125v-129r; fig. 278);

– a prayer attributed to St. Bernard, which is accompanied by a miniature depicting the Virgin squirting breast milk into the saint's mouth (fol. 129r-130v; fig. 279);

– a translation of the *O intemerata*, with an image depicting Christ appearing to his mother after his resurrection (fol. 130v-133v; fig. 280);

– a prayer to be read while kneeling in front of the image of St. Anne three times, which yields an indulgence of 10,000 years of mortal sin and 20,000 years of venial sin, which accompanies a contrafact of the *Ave Maria* adjusted for St. Anne, and a miniature depicting the female trinity (fol. 133v-134r; fig. 281);

– another prayer to St. Anne (134r-135r)

– a prayer to one's personal angel, with an image of an angel (fol. 135r; fig. 282);

– illustrated suffrages to St. Sebastian (fol. 136r/v), St. Erasmus (fol. 137r; fig. 283), St. Anthony (fol. 138r), St. Margaret (fol. 138v), and St. Dorothy (fol. 139v);

– and finally, to fill the quire, a rubric promising 1000 days' indulgence to anyone who reads a short prayer in front of the cross.

This list contains all that had become fashionable between 1465 and 1510: prayers that connected images with indulgences, prayers to St. Anne and to the personal angel, and suffrages to saints associated with bodily protection.

2. Leeds, Brotherton Ms. 7 with an added booklet

The sixteenth-century atelier made one last important addition, which was separate from the additions listed above. Working together with a different artist but one within the circle of the Masters of the Dark Eyes, a scribe produced an independent illustrated booklet with a devotion to the Virgin of the Seven Sorrows. This written part of the booklet comprises an entire quire of six folios (BPH 151, fol. 97–102) that was probably added to the manuscript in the early sixteenth century at the same time the other image-centered and indulgenced prayers were added.[48] These folios were ruled differently from the rest of the additions, namely, with reddish brown ink, and single upper, lower, left and right bounding lines (whereas the rest of the manuscript has no horizontal boundary lines). A different copyist inscribed this booklet.

---

48   This booklet was formerly glued into the book between fol. 95 and fol. 104 (which is how I found it in 2009). It was apparently removed for the BPH exhibition of 2009–2010 so that it could be displayed separately, and it is now tucked into the book loosely.

Fig. 284 Opening from an autonomous booklet added to the book of hours; the booklet was made by the Masters of the Dark Eyes ca. 1510 and includes a painting depicting the Virgin of the Seven Sorrows to accompany the booklet-length prayer to the Virgin's sorrows. The Hague, Koninklijke Bibliotheek, Ms. BPH 151, fol. 96v-97r. Image © Koninklijke Bibliotheek—the National Library of The Netherlands, CC BY 4.0.

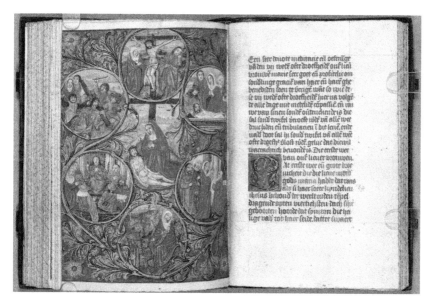

Fig. 285 Opening from an autonomous booklet added to the book of hours; the booklet was made by the Masters of the Dark Eyes ca. 1510 and includes a painting depicting the Virgin of the Seven Sorrows to accompany the booklet-length prayer to the Virgin's sorrows. Leeds, University Library, Ms. Brotherton 7, fol. 142v-143r. Reproduced with the permission of Special Collection, Leeds University Library. © Leeds University Library, CC BY 4.0.

Fig. 286 Autonomous booklet with the prayer to the Seven Sorrows of the Virgin,
formerly glued into The Hague, Koninklijke Bibliotheek, Ms. BPH 151. Image
© Koninklijke Bibliotheek—the National Library of The Netherlands, CC BY 4.0.

In addition to the six folios of text, the booklet is prefaced by an image
depicting the Seven Sorrows (BPH 151, fol. 96v; fig. 284). This image
differs from the other full-page illuminations in the book. It is based
on a diagrammatic organization of the page, with Mary at the center
surrounded by roundels recounting the events of her Sorrows. It is the
only image in the book not framed by a rectilinear border. It was made
in a separate campaign of work, by one of the Masters of the Dark Eyes,
but not necessarily one coordinated in the larger image campaign of the
book.

A second, very similar sixteenth-century booklet has survived within
another book of hours which was also written in the fifteenth century,
then similarly updated by the Masters of the Dark Eyes in the early
sixteenth century (Leeds, Brotherton Ms. 7). Like BPH 151, the Brotherton
manuscript contains added prayers and full-page miniatures that have
been integrated into an existing manuscript in order to augment it
with new and fashionable devotions. The Seven Sorrows booklet in
the Brotherton manuscript contains a nearly identical prefatory image
(Leeds, Brotherton 7, fol. 142v; fig. 285). In both manuscripts, the Seven

Sorrows booklet has been written by a scribe different from the one who produced the other sixteenth-century additions. In their content and structure, the similarity of these two booklets, suggests that the booklets were made by an atelier in series, as a marketable product, which consumers could then integrate into a book of hours. In fact, the booklet in BPH 151 was only glued in, not sewn, and it has now come loose (fig. 286). If this is the case, then such booklet-makers must have worked closely with illuminators working in the circle of the Masters of the Dark Eyes, who produced the relevant imagery depicting the Seven Sorrows of the Virgin.

Perhaps the booklets were originally sold in such a way that the painted image remained unconnected from the textual packet. Close examination of the structure of the manuscript supports this hypothesis. In the Leeds manuscript, the image depicting the Seven Sorrows is wider than the other miniatures; so wide, in fact, that the outer edge has been trimmed severely so that it would fit into the manuscript. The Seven Sorrows images in both manuscripts have no trace of border decoration, and both are bound in such a way that they have a very small inner border so that the image extends nearly to the gutter. The dimensions suggest that the leaf was not designed to be inserted into a manuscript at all, but rather that votaries were meant to mount their image of the Seven Sorrows on the wall or to hold it in their hands while they followed the Virgin through her sorrows outlined in the text. In this way, votaries could have an inexpensive replica of a full-sized painted altarpiece, such as the one found in the church of Onze-Lieve-Vrouw in Bruges.

The two paintings on parchment depicting the Seven Sorrows share with the panel what might be termed an "altarpiece aesthetic," whereby individual scenes are arranged around a central devotional image within the framework of fictive microarchitecture. At the level of production, it is possible that the Masters of the Dark Eyes drew their compositional model from a monumental altarpiece; and analogously, at the level of reception, it is possible that owners treated these paintings on parchment as private altarpieces, rather than as manuscript illuminations. Perhaps the supplicant read the prayer while continually referring back to the unbound image, which was held apart from the text and formed a miniature parchment altarpiece.

Although the booklet in Leeds has a rubric, which does not appear in the BPH manuscript, the prayer text in both booklets is otherwise identical. Did patrons have to pay extra for the version with the rubric? In the Leeds manuscript it reads:

> *rub:* A very devout meditation and exercise about the seven sorrows or lamentations of our dear lady Mary, which is very good and rewarding for obtaining special grace from her and her blessed son, so that anyone who contemplates these following seven sorrows or lamentations each day with compassion and pity and contrition for his sins, he shall without a doubt be consoled from all the pain, tumult and tribulation in this life. After his death he shall without a doubt be released from all sorrows or lamentations. The first sorrow of our dear Lady. [Leeds, Brotherton Ms. 7, fol. 143r]

The rubric weaves a parallel relationship between the life of the votary and that of Mary, so that contemplating Mary's sorrows will relieve the votary of his or her own sorrows. The prayer itself leads the reader through the Seven Sorrows, in chronological order, beginning with the circumcision that is pictured at the lower right of the accompanying image. The structure of the image is reminiscent of images for the rosary devotion, in which a prayer text is structured around a series of images, and each image receives sustained contemplation in turn. The difference, however, is that the rosary structures the recitation of a short prayer that the votary had committed to memory and could therefore repeat while looking at the image, while the votary probably did not memorize the text of the Seven Sorrows, and would have to toggle between the cognitive fields of reading and seeing.

* * *

The Masters of the Dark Eyes formed a loose group of anonymous illuminators who worked in a similar style. The discussion above suggests that they must have collaborated with a group of scribes. Their very large output in the decades around 1500 provides some indication of the size of the group of scribes and illuminators. They created books of hours and prayerbooks from scratch, and this at a time when copying texts was increasingly separated from making images. This is not to say that individual masters worked both as scribes and illuminators, but rather that the group included scribes as well as illuminators. They must have also offered a service to update existing prayerbooks. In this they may have been copying a business model from two convents in Delft, the Augustinian convent of St. Agnes, and later the Franciscan convent of St. Ursula, which moved in across the street. Just as both conventual and secular (professional) workshops made books of hours for the growing literate market, they also repaired and updated manuscripts.

The Southern Netherlands and Northern France also had advanced book-making cultures in the fifteenth century, but they were dominated by secular professionals rather than by female monastics. They not only produced books, but also performed extensive upgrades. The owners of BKB, Ms. 19588, and 's-Heerenberg, HB, Ms. 2, treated existing components as building blocks for a new book.

One can imagine that updating older manuscripts was lucrative and in demand, as patrons could modify an heirloom with all the new devotions they desired. Bookmakers such as the Masters of the Dark Eyes and the convent sisters of St. Ursula in Delft apparently supplied modular units. It is not clear whether they worked with certain binders, as an insufficient number of original (or second) bindings has survived to ascertain this. They were more than happy to comply with the desires of patrons, who wanted the newest prayers imported from the south, the prayers with the largest indulgences, prayers that were image-centered, and plenty of images. They wanted, in short, to be fashionable, free of pain in the afterlife, and surrounded by color and gold. Their motivations were multifold, and I provide an overview of them in the next and final part.

Part V: Patterns of desire

This study has analyzed book production at a time before forced obsolescence. Manuscripts could have useful careers for decades or even centuries. Medieval book makers were in the business of creating something of duration. This conformed to a particular style of reading, for which an individual would read—and re-read—selected texts over the course of days, weeks, or years. While the conservatism of the religious culture demanded that certain texts span generations, other elements of book-making and reading culture reveal the dynamism of the religious literature. Book makers responded to fashions in devotional behavior and to the ever-more important spiritual economy of indulgences. They responded to these shifts by physically expanding the book to accommodate such novelties. Books also responded to the increasing prosperity of the urban merchant classes, both by becoming more affordable and numerous, and by being capable of receiving more decoration when the book owner could eventually afford it.

Codices filled with liturgical, paraliturgical and devotional texts, including books of hours and prayerbooks, assume that Christian ether will prevail far into the future, in fact, into eternity. The fifteenth-century legal notices added to sixth-, seventh-, and eighth-century gospels books, including the Book of Kells, presume that the gospel book constituted a permanent safe-haven for their amanuensis and land transfer records. That the book would someday no longer have authoritative value was unfathomable. Parchment manuscripts were good for record keeping because they embodied a combination of authority and permanence. But that permanence was not rigid: the medium of the parchment book was alive and could grow. Developments in book-making technology

    http://dx.doi.org/10.11647/OBP.0094.05

meant that the parchment book could grow even more easily in the fifteenth century, just before the era of the printing press's hegemony. Unlike the printed book, which is fixed and rigid, the manuscript was expandable.

Manuscripts could be personalized because they were handmade. Book owners who began with complete and serviceable manuscripts nonetheless deemed them insufficient and in need of adjustment. A medieval person was likely to have a book that either used to belong to somebody else, including a selection of prayers he never used, was so old as to be outdated, or did not reflect his current social status. Though the books were often hand-me-downs, people expected their books to adapt to reflect their world, even as the books themselves had incredible longevity. What to do? Augment. Improve.

I have asked in this study: how did later users register their opinions that a book considered perfectly acceptable by its previous owners was for them somehow incomplete, and by what means did they express their discontent? How can their acts of recycling and upcycling be interpreted? The kinds of augmentations owners made to books reveal certain patterns of desires, which I enumerate here.

A. Desire to personalize the book

People often wrote notes of ownership in books, usually at the beginning or ending flyleaves. Writing one's name on the front of the book or among its folios, adding one's name saint to the calendar, or crossing out the name of a previous owner can all be accomplished on the blank or existing parchment. Sometimes subsequent owners crossed out previous notes before adding their own. Other times, they simply added their names to the list, thereby showing themselves as just one owner in a growing provenance. One suspects that the impulse to eradicate previous owners is inversely correlated to the sentimentality and family bonds with those people. One wouldn't cross out a grandmother.

While many of the forms of personalization in this study have not involved rebinding the book, others went beyond the superficial. These include the updates that involved adding images of the new owner. The Hours of Blanche of Savoy was taken apart and reconfigured for its new owner. Simon de Varie had his book of hours furnished with full-page miniatures depicting the Virgin and his coat of arms. The anonymous male owner of HKB, Ms. 135 G 19 added a quire to the beginning of his book of hours, including a full-page miniature depicting him in prayer before St. Jerome. I suspect that many people who could afford personalized portraits would have been people who would have commissioned books from scratch. If someone makes elaborate changes to an old prayerbook, such as the case with the Hours of Blanche of Savoy, the motivation must certainly be to show the new owner in continuity with the former owner, a form of ancestor worship through objects.

B. Desire to commemorate a changed family situation

When owners added birth, death, and marriage information to the interstices of the manuscript, they were turning it into a personalized volume that would have lasting relevance as a record of family history. They also added names of family members to calendars, thereby putting those family members on the same level as saints. Religious houses, likewise, added the names of the dead to calendars so that dead patrons, like saints, could be commemorated annually. I also speculated above that those who had books for their children to teach them to read could have upgraded those books with indulgences when the children reached their teenaged years, at which time they could sin with abandon. Several examples above show that book owners made small adjustments to their books to turn them into more effective didactic tools.

C. Desire to store small precious objects

Owners pasted or stitched small paintings on parchment into their book so that they could keep precious objects safe in an equally precious location. Such small objects were often gifted or traded among monastics, who could then store them in their prayerbooks, for the image would embellish the book, just as the book would protect the image. This operation added a function of the manuscript, namely, to turn it into a treasure chest for items of both intrinsic and extrinsic value. Owners could stitch in prints, pilgrims' souvenirs, images that commemorated the Eucharist.[1] They could also sew curtains into the book, nearly always stitching the curtain to the upper margin of the page.[2] The curtain itself, if silk, could be a precious object, but it also enhanced and framed the image that it veiled. Adding such a curtain would imply adding a new layer of ritual to the book, for the curtain would have to be lifted each time the viewer gazed upon the image.

D. Desire for more embellishment

Some additions did not personalize the book at all. For example, in Ltk 289, a later owner who added full-page illuminations harvested from a different book, including a miniature depicting the patron of that book in prayer before the Virgin. The owner of the Dutch prayerbook was thus adding an image of someone he or she may not have known or been related to.

Many of the examples above reveal that owners wanted to embellish folios in order to unify the hierarchy of decoration across the entire book, or to raise the level of decoration. Often when new images were added, they affected the overall decoration program, which had to be smoothed over with another layer of decoration. The owner of the Beinecke 434 did just that, in part because the Masters of the Dark Eyes offered this service. Studios specializing in embellishing existing books were not confined to urban (male?) professionals; convents in Delft would provide such services, too. After all, they were illuminating words to praise God.

E. Recycling and refurbishing

Above I have hypothesized that certain missals received new canons because this was the most heavily used part of the manuscript and

---

1   Rudy, *Postcards on Parchment: The Social Lives of Medieval Books* analyzes many small autonomous paintings added to manuscripts. For metallic badges added to manuscripts, consult Asperen, *Pelgrimstekens op Perkament*; Megan Foster-Campbell, "Pilgrimage through the Pages: Pilgrims' Badges in Late Medieval Devotional Manuscripts," in *Push Me, Pull You: Imaginative and Emotional Interaction in Late Medieval and Renaissance Art*, ed. Sarah Blick and Laura Deborah Gelfand, *Studies in Medieval and Reformation Traditions* (Leiden: Brill, 2011), pp. 227–74; Rudy, "Sewing the Body of Christ: Eucharist Wafer Souvenirs Stitched into Fifteenth-Century Manuscripts, Primarily in the Netherlands."
2   Sciacca, "Raising the Curtain on the Use of Textiles in Manuscripts."

therefore would age faster than the rest. This phenomenon might have been quite common, but is hard to study from the twenty-first century, because the dirty parts are likely to have been discarded. Because they reveal themselves by their absence, they often go undetected. The examples enumerated here will have to stand for a larger phenomenon.

Owners harvested the best stuff from other manuscripts to flesh out their own book. They would break up obsolete manuscripts, including those in foreign languages that the new owner did not read, or those that had been received in a damaged state. Recycling and repurposing older images provided a way to maintain links with the past. It produced precious goods out of otherwise discarded waste.

F. Desire to make foreign-produced manuscripts locally relevant

Sometimes books passed into new regions with different local saints. So that local saints would be reflected in the calendar and litany, the new owners added them in what space they could find. In the case of the Uppsala breviary, the sisters of St. Ursula discarded the old calendar and replaced it with a new one altogether, in a move that required rebinding.

Books of hours made in the Southern Netherlands had large amounts of empty space built into them, by virtue of the method by which they were made. Foreign recipients—that is, English buyers—found space in them to add things, primarily prayers in the vernacular, in this case English. The new methods for making manuscripts out of modules, many of them as small as a single leaf, were mirrored at the level of reception by a new habit of filling the ample blank spaces with personal, local prayers.

G. Desire to incorporate new prayers

New prayers were continually written in the late Middle Ages, and new feasts ratified. For example, the celebration of the feast of *corpus Christi*, which was already made official in 1264, became extremely popular in the fifteenth century. Prayers to the sacrament are among those frequently copied on separate quires in fifteenth-century ateliers. For example, the feast of *corpus Christi* was added to prayerbooks, such as the Cistercian breviary in Perth. This required adding physical material to accommodate the lengthy text. Lay book owners likewise added prayers to the host, which often appear clustered in a single added quire.

Urbanites began demanding prayers based on clock-time rather than on the canonical hours. They added prayers to be recited when they woke in the morning and went to bed at night. These were at odds with the ways in which the offices structured time. People's tastes toward the end of the fifteenth century also turned to more image-based prayers. Groups of artists such as the Masters of the Dark Eyes were eager to meet their needs with their commercial products.

Another prayer added to a wide range of religious books were those to St. Anne, who had an active cult in the fourteenth century, which became extremely popular in the late fifteenth. One can see some of the material spoils of her cult in the Curtius Museum in Liège, which contains a room with dozens of polychromed carved wooden sculptures depicting St. Anne, all dating from the decades flanking 1500. This sudden surge of interest is also reflected in prayerbooks bearing augmentations from those decades.

H. Fear of hell

The desire to include more indulgences was the single-most pronounced reason that a patron upgraded a prayerbook. I have enumerated many instances in which patrons added the *Adoro te*, or upgraded a short version of that prayer for a longer version that promised more indulgences. Because older books generally did not have this prayer, it had to be added. This is the single-most frequently added prayer to books of hours in the late fifteenth century. Illuminators also responded by making images of the Miraculous Mass of St. Gregory, the narrativized version of Christ as Man of Sorrows that most frequently accompanied the prayer.

The intense interest in the Verses of St. Gregory and the prayer to the Face of Christ, along with their accompanying images, suggest that prayers were also subject to fashion. Votaries were clearly driven to employ these prayers because they were highly indulgenced, but it is also clear that owners treasured their visuality, their image dependency.

I. Desire to reflect wealth

Those who used their books of hours and prayerbooks in semi-public settings, such as in a church or chapel, were displaying their piety as well as the lavishness of their accouterments. A colorful manuscript was highly visible. Painted colors are visible from several meters, and the coruscations of burnished gold from even farther away. On the continuum between flashy and demure, it must have been somewhere on the acceptable end. Book owners marked their changes in status by commissioning images and decoration, which reflected their wealth. They could even dress their books in silk velvet chemise bindings, which would make them appear sumptuous even when closed.

How the nouveaux riches displayed their wealth remained distinct from how the nobility did. Whereas the former went for quantity, the latter went for quality. New wealthy urbanites wanted wall-to-wall color, applied by anonymous masters, while the rich nobility wanted nameable artists, perhaps several of them in the same book. For example, for the Trivulzio Hours it was probably a male noble in the circle of Charles the Bold who assembled an array of single-leaf miniatures, each made in a distinctive style by a namable artist. These miniatures were commissioned expressly for this patron and depict him several times. Contrariwise, the Masters of the Dark Eyes took a very different approach in making products for the nouveaux riches. These artists, who produced thickly gilded, visually noisy manuscript paintings, largely worked for patrons who lacked coats of arms. Whereas the nobility wanted delicate painting, the recently moneyed wanted as much color as possible. As if to respond to this desire, the Masters of the Dark Eyes often made much larger books of hours than those made in previous generations. They also worked in ways to increase efficiency: they formed a conglomeration of artists who worked in a corporate style, in which individual style was erased so that the individual artists became interchangeable. One can compare these artists with the artist who upgraded the Hours of Simon de Varie, who worked around the same time and was also interested in bringing magnificence, color and gold to the page, but who executed paintings with painstaking precision.

J. Changes, social and codicological

In this study I have argued that around 1390 a structural change occurred in the way in which books were made. People had been making amendments to manuscripts as long as manuscripts had been made: change a word, a letter, add an image. But the modularization of the book suddenly facilitated post-production changes of this kind, both large and small, and even anticipated future adjustments.

Copying the text in one kind of atelier, and making the images in a different kind of atelier, had several implications. Division of labor allowed individuals to specialize, and therefore to streamline production and bring costs down. Dividing and separating labor meant that a new layer of management—the person who brought the components together—would take on new importance. Very little is currently known about such people, sometimes called *stationers*. The value they add seems to be about organizing labor. When labor is divided, then the singular workers no longer have an overview of the whole. Each is only making his component. In order to create interchangeable parts, as it were, book makers regionally settled on some general standards. Modularization led to increased standardization, and for the copyists and illuminators, increased routinization. It created a need for management, and therefore removed the producers from the consumers by a step. I wouldn't be surprised if these early managers were money-grubbing, self-important and exploitative, but there's no way to prove it, short of a séance.

Making images separately from copying texts means that text pages would not have had images, and image pages would not have had text, as that would have required more coordination, planning, and therefore time and effort. The modular method led to the growing importance of the full-page miniature as the main unit of pictorial embellishment. Small images were probably sold on rather large sheets of parchment, so that they could be trimmed to meet the needs of any sized book: this was yet another way in which increased labor efficiency created increased material waste. As full-page miniatures rose in importance, with equal and opposite force, historiated initials became a design unit of the past. While decorated initials remained common and integral to the hierarchy of decoration, historiated initials became much less common, because they required the unfinished book to travel between workshops.

This study has explored the intersection between the material framework of the book, the social framework in which it operated, and the individual desires of its owner. It has demonstrated that medieval book owners, particularly those in the Netherlands, applied a variety of methods to keep their older, inherited, and second-hand books personal and relevant. In short, the evidence I have gathered here shows that market forces shaped the new book of hours, and then human recipients shaped its adjustments.

The ideas I have discussed in this book include how high-volume production quickly slides into modularization, with an attendant skill-loss. This is highly visible in the world I currently inhabit. Ikea showrooms often lurk near airports far out of town where the real estate is cheap. I see them when I arrive in various cities to look at manuscripts. Based in Sweden, Ikea sells modular furniture overseas. It is responding of course to a need: the quick population boom of the decades around 2000, and all those new upwardly mobile humans who needed a place to sit. They are also responding to a clutter-free aesthetic by providing cheap cabinetry where unsightly stuff can be hidden behind opaque doors. But then as now, people react to receiving modularized, low-quality standardized products by trying to enhance them. Entire books and websites are dedicated to "Ikea hacks," ideas for modifying the dull furniture.

Ultimately the printing press responded to the demand for cheap books, and this changed everything. Printed editions had a finality and fixedness that manuscripts did not. Manuscripts were always somehow provisional. One could always scribble in the margins, add more material, or make major changes during rebinding. This was partly due to their material. Manuscripts on parchment were built to last but also to breathe, and therefore had to be able to absorb changes over time. Printed books on paper, on the other hand, were friable. Depending on the sort of paper from which they were made, their edges might simply give up with extensive use. One could bind up a group of printed booklets together, but the material did not invite adjustments to the text and decorative program to the same extent that parchment did.[3] Whereas parchment can have objects (badges, curtains, images) sewn to it, can have words scraped out with a knife, can be kissed by priests at ten thousand masses, printed books can have none of it. The fact that comparatively few incunables survive compared to the number that must have been produced suggests that early owners already considered them ephemeral.[4]

The book was a repository of authority and is understood as such even in the modern day. Modern readers therefore think of the status of the medieval book as fixed. But in fact it was standard to alter the book. Doing so was perhaps a pleasurable transgression. Moreover, in order to maintain its authority in a culture of changing devotions and shifting relationships to the text—and particularly one where relationships to texts were personalized via specific saintly devotions, name saints, the calendar, etc.—a book that was to maintain its authority could not in fact remain pristine. It needed updating in order to maintain its position as conduit for effective devotion, to keep up with new (or newly emphasized) feasts such as the Corpus Christi, or with new papal indulgences, new cult images, precisely those elements that the Reformation culture, steeped in printing, abhorred. The culture of devotion in the fifteenth century was anything but static. For this reason, people were hungry to have books that fit their needs and took every opportunity to outfit the book as needed over time. Manuscript producers would have been fools not to create a method for creating manuscripts that allowed for the different devotional demands of various clients and markets.

What distinguishes the fifteenth century from the current era is the duration of goods. Somewhere along the way, a particularly cruel and clever capitalist invented forced obsolescence. Implicit in this study lies a comparison between the parchment world of the Middle Ages and the digital world we are currently in the throes of adopting. I do not wish to be sentimental about the past but would like to learn from it. Although a circular economy for manuscripts functioned well in the

---

3   The exceptions can be highly amusing. See Adam Smyth, "'Shreds of holinesse:' George Herbert, Little Gidding, and Cutting Up Texts in Early Modern England," *English Literary Renaissance* (2012), pp. 452–81.

4   Kok, *Woodcuts in Incunabula Printed in the Low Countries* provides statistics and analysis about incunabula in her introduction.

parchment era, it is not something I would wish to return to, for several reasons. Keeping books in circulation for decades or even centuries was a necessity because they were so expensive that a literate person might only own one book. A more literate culture demands access to more reading material. But another, and perhaps even more important reason that this model will no longer work is that medieval reading was fundamentally repetitive and therefore demanded durable materials that could withstand daily recitation over a period of years, decades or even centuries. Such were the habits borne of an essentially conservative religious culture. Circular reading—repetitious recitation—therefore had its parallel in the circular economy of manuscript. Manuscript owners, employing the techniques I have catalogued in this study, could amend their books to keep up with changing devotional fashion—such as the increased importance of indulgences—, but only up to a point: no manuscript could expand quickly or effectively enough to absorb the range of new ideas that belong to a pluralistic secular society. The manuscript is the wrong medium for the polymath, the atheist, the skeptic, the browser, or the seeker of broad knowledge. These readers consume many texts rapidly and sequentially, one time through or perhaps twice, after selecting from a boundless variety of choices. Theirs is a type of reading that electronic media serve well, even better than the printed books once did.

Another thread in my argument has been that manuscripts could be expanded and they even invited expansion in a way that printed books did not. Yet I began this story a few hundred pages ago with a story about the printed Soviet Encyclopedia, which seems to undermine my claims, for it, too, was updated post-production with glue to accommodate a new political situation. I have never laid my hands on a Soviet Encyclopedia adjusted with a long article about the Bering Strait, and chances are you haven't either. However, you can imagine it, the way it looks and feels. You can picture the dutiful Soviet book owner slathering spatulas of off-white paste on the back of the replacement sheet, then squaring it up, and pressing it into the book in the designated place. You can imagine how cool the paper feels as the moisture is absorbed into it and then evaporates, lowering the surface temperature. You can imagine how wrinkly the paper becomes as it wicks up the moisture. The encyclopedia owner closes the book so that the pages themselves act as a press flattening out the wrinkly new page. The replacement is fixed to its new position. Beria's biography buried underneath paper and paste would become a layer in the cellulose rubble of history. But afterwards, when the glue had dried, you would be able to tell that something was amiss. The page with the pasted article would be stiff. That double-thick and stiffened page will now be the one to which the book will now always fall open. In the brittle printed book, the silent addition would scream attention to itself. In the animal manuscript, on the other hand, the stitched-in additions would become part of an organic whole. In fact, this is why cataloguers often miss them. The main operation holding the manuscript, with its additions, together is the needle and thread. The parchment manuscript is sutured into its binding, and the seams can be ripped open, the book enlarged, and the package sewn back up again, but the stitches inside are largely invisible. When the world of parchment, needle and thread gave way to the world of paper, moveable type and glue, with that shift came a brittleness that resisted organic expansion. The paper book was purchased, read and discarded. It was, in short, consumed.

Bibliography

Achten, Gerard. *Das Christliche Gebetbuch im Mittelalter: Andachts- und Stundenbücher in Handschrift und Frühdruck*. Ausstellungskataloge / Staatsbibliothek Preussischer Kulturbesitz (Berlin: Staatsbibliothek Preussischer Kulturbesitz, 1987).

Alexander, J. J. G. *Medieval Illuminators and Their Methods of Work* (New Haven: Yale University Press, 1992).

Areford, David S. "The Image in the Viewer's Hands: The Reception of Early Prints in Europe." *Studies in Iconography* 24 (2003), pp. 5–42.

As-Vijvers, Anne Margreet W., ed. *Beeldschone Boeken: De Middeleeuwen in Goud En Inkt*. (Zwolle and Utrecht: Waanders Uitgeverij & Museum Catharijneconvent, 2009).

As-Vijvers, Anne Margreet W. *Tuliba Collection: Catalogue of Manuscripts and Miniatures from the Fifteenth and Sixteenth Centuries* (Hilversum: Tuliba Collection, 2014).

Ashley, Kathleen M. "Creating Family Identity in Books of Hours." *Journal of Medieval and Early Modern Studies* 32, no. 1 (2002), pp. 145–66. http://dx.doi.org/10.1215/10829636–32-1-145

Asperen, Hanneke van. *Pelgrimstekens op Perkament: Originele en Nageschilderde Bedevaartssouvenirs in Religieuze Boeken (ca 1450-ca 1530)*. (PhD thesis, Radboud Universiteit Nijmegen, 2009).

Bennett, A. "Devotional Literacy of a Noblewoman in a Book of Hours of ca. 1300 in Cambrai." In *Manuscripts in Transition: Recycling Manuscripts, Texts and Images: Proceedings of the International Congres [sic] Held in Brussels (5–9 November 2002)*, edited by Brigitte Dekeyzer and Jan van der Stock, pp. 149–205 (Leuven: Peeters, 2005).

—, "The Transformation of the Gothic Psalter in Thirteenth-Century France." In *The Illuminated Psalter: Studies in the Content, Purpose and Placement of Its Images*, edited by F. O. Büttner, pp. 211–21 (Turnhout: Brepols, 2004).

Berve, Maurus. *Die Armenbibel: Herkunft, Gestalt, Typologie; dargestellt anhand von Miniaturen aus der Handschrift Cpg 148 D. Universitätsbibliothek Heidelberg.* Kult und Kunst, 4 (Beuron: Beuroner Kunstverlag, 1989).

Biemans, J. A. A. M. *Middelnederlandse Bijbelhandschriften: Verzameling van Middelnederlandse Bijbeltekstencatalogus* (Leiden: Brill, 1984).

Biernoff, Suzannah. *Sight and Embodiment in the Middle Ages* (The New Middle Ages) (Basingstoke and New York: Palgrave, 2002). http://dx.doi.org/10.1057/9780230508354

Binski, Paul. "The Illumination and Patronage of the Douce Apocalypse." *The Antiquaries Journal* 94 (2014), pp. 1–8. http://dx.doi.org/10.1017/s0003581514000602

Binski, Paul, P. N. R. Zutshi, and Stella Panayotova. *Western Illuminated Manuscripts: A Catalogue of the Collection in Cambridge University Library* (Cambridge and New York: Cambridge University Press, 2011). http://dx.doi.org/10.1017/cbo9780511780479

Blick, Sarah, and Laura Deborah Gelfand, eds. 2 vols., *Push Me, Pull You: Imaginative and Emotional Interaction in Late Medieval and Renaissance Art* (Leiden: Brill, 2011). http://dx.doi.org/10.1163/9789004215139

Bloem, Miranda. *De Meesters van Zweder van Culemborg: Werkplaatspraktijken van een Groep Noord-Nederlandse Verluchters, ca. 1415–1440* (PhD thesis, University of Amsterdam, 2015).

Bousmanne, Bernard. "Deux Livres d'Heures du Groupe aux Rinceaux d'Or." *Revue des archéologues et historiens d'art de Louvain* 20 (1986), pp. 119–44.

Bousmanne, Bernard, Thierry Delcourt, and Ilona Hans-Collas. *Miniatures Flamandes, 1404–1482.* Catalogue de l'exposition présentée à la bibliothèque royale de Belgique à Bruxelles du 30 septembre au 30 décembre 2011 puis à la BnF à Paris du 6 mars au 10 juin 2012 (Paris and Brussels: Bibliothèque nationale de France; Bibliothèque royale de Belgique, 2011).

Braekman, Willy Louis. "Enkele Zegeningen en Krachtige Gebeden in een Vlaams Devotieboek uit de Vijftiende Eeuw." *Volkskunde* 79 (1978), pp. 285–307.

—, *Middeleeuwse Witte en Zwarte Magie in het Nederlands Taalgebied: Gecommentarieerd Compendium van Incantamenta tot Einde 16de Eeuw.* Reeks VI, nr 127 (Gent: Koniklijke Academie voor Nederlandse Taal- en Letterkunde, 1997).

Brandhorst, J. P. J. "The Hague, Koninklijke Bibliotheek Ms 76 F 5: A Psalter Fragment?" *Visual Resources* 19 (2003), pp. 15–25. http://dx.doi.org/10.1080/0197376031000078558

Broekhuijsen, Klara H. *The Masters of the Dark Eyes: Late Medieval Manuscript Painting in Holland.* Ars Nova, 10 (Turnhout: Brepols, 2009).

Brown, Michelle. *The Lindisfarne Gospels: Society, Spirituality and the Scribe.* British Library Studies in Medieval Culture (London: British Library, 2003).

Buettner, Brigitte. "Past Presents: New Year's Gifts at the Valois Courts, Ca. 1400." *Art Bulletin* 83, no. 4 (2001), pp. 598–625. http://dx.doi.org/10.2307/3177225

Byvanck, Alexander Willem, and G. J. Hoogewerff, *Noord-Nederlandsche Miniaturen in Handschriften der 14e, 15e en 16e Eeuwen* ('s-Gravenhage: M. Nijhoff, 1922–1925).

Cardon, Bert. "The Illustrations and the Gold Scrolls Workshop." In *Typologische Taferelen uit het Leven van Jezus: A Manuscript from the Gold Scrolls Group (Bruges, Ca. 1440) in the Pierpont Morgan Library, New York, Ms. Morgan 649: An Edition of the Text, a Reproduction of the Manuscript, and a Study of the Miniatures,* edited by Bert Cardon, R. Lievens and Maurits Smeyers. Corpus van Verluchte Handschriften uit de Nederlanden = Corpus of Illuminated Manuscripts from the Low Countries, pp. 119–204 (Leuven: Peeters, 1985).

Claassens, G. H. M., and Werner Verbeke, eds. *Medieval Manuscripts in Transition: Tradition and Creative Recycling,* Mediaevalia Lovaniensia, vol. ser 1, studia 36 (Leuven: Leuven University Press, 2006).

Clemens, Raymond, and Timothy Graham. *Introduction to Manuscript Studies* (Ithaca: Cornell University Press, 2007).

Cohen, Adam S. "Magnificence in Miniature: The Case of Early Medieval Manuscripts." In *Magnificence and the Sublime in Medieval Aesthetics: Art, Architecture, Literature, Music,* edited by C. Stephen Jaeger. The New Middle Ages, pp. 79–101, pl. 1–14 (Basingstoke: Palgrave Macmillan, 2010).

Cyrus, Cynthia J. *The Scribes for Women's Convents in Late Medieval Germany* (Toronto: University of Toronto Press, 2009).

De Hamel, Christopher. *Glossed Books of the Bible and the Origins of the Paris Booktrade* (Woodbridge: D. S. Brewer, 1984).

—, *Cutting up Manuscripts for Pleasure and Profit,* The Sol M. Malkin Lecture in Bibliography 11 (Charlottesville: Book Arts Press, 1996).

De Kesel, Lieve. "Use and Reuse of Manuscripts and Miniatures. Observations on Pasted-in, Recycled and Removed Miniatures and Text Leaves in Some Late Medieval Flemish Illuminated Manuscripts Related to 'La Flora.'" *Bulletin du bibliophile,* no. 1 (2011), pp. 48–85, pl. 4–5.

de Kruyter, C. W. "The Emblematic Character of the Border Ornaments in Delft Codices." *Quaerendo* 3 (1973), pp. 211–16. http://dx.doi.org/10.1163/157006973x00219

de Winter, Patrick M. "The *Grandes Heures* of Philip the Bold, Duke of Burgundy: The Copyist Jean l'Avenant and his Patrons at the French Court." *Speculum* 57, no. 4 (1982), pp. 786–842. http://dx.doi.org/10.2307/2848764

Defoer, H. L. M., A. S. Korteweg, Wilhelmina C. M. Wüstefeld, and Introduction by James H. Marrow. *The Golden Age of Dutch Manuscript Painting.* Exh. Cat. Rijksmuseum Het Catharijneconvent, Utrecht and the Pierpont Morgan Library, New York. 1st ed. (Stuttgart: Belser, 1989).

Degering, Hermann. *Kurzes Verzeichnis der Germanischen Handschriften der Preussichen Staatsbibliothek. III: Die Handschriften in Oktavformat und Register zu Band I-III.* 3 vols. (Leipzig: K. W. Hiersemann, 1925).

Dekeyzer, Brigitte, and Jan van der Stock, eds. *Manuscripts in Transition: Recycling Manuscripts, Texts and Images: Proceedings of the International Congres* [Sic: kmr] *Held in Brussels (5–9 November 2002),* Corpus of Illuminated Manuscripts, vol. 15 (Leuven: Peeters, 2005).

Delaissé, L. M. J. "The Importance of Books of Hours for the History of the Medieval Book." In *Gatherings in Honor of Dorothy E. Miner,* edited by Ursula E. McCracken, Lilian M. C. Randall and Richard H. Randall, pp. 203–25 (Baltimore: Walters Art Gallery, 1974).

—, "Towards a History of the Medieval Book." In *Codicologica: Towards a Science of Handwritten Books, Vol. 1, Théories et Principes,* edited by Albert Gruys and J. P. Gumbert, pp. 75–83 (Leiden: Brill, 1976).

Derolez, Albert. "Masters and Measures. A Codicological Approach to Books of Hours." *Quærendo* 33, no. 1 (2003), pp. 83–95. http://dx.doi.org/10.1163/157006903322348188

Dogaer, Georges. *Flemish Miniature Painting in the 15th and 16th Centuries* (Amsterdam: B. M. Israël, 1987).

Donovan, Claire. *The De Brailes Hours: Shaping the Book of Hours in Thirteenth-Century Oxford.* Toronto Medieval Texts and Translations, 7 (Toronto and Buffalo: University of Toronto Press, 1991).

—, "The Mise-en-Page of Early Books of Hours in England." In *Medieval Book Production: Assessing the Evidence; Oxford, July 1988,* edited by Linda L. Brownrigg. Proceedings of the Conference of the Seminar in the History of the Book to 1500, pp. 147–61 (Los Altos Hills: Anderson-Lovelace, 1990).

Drogin, Marc. *Anathema! Medieval Scribes and the History of Book Curses* (Totowa: Allanheld & Schram, 1983).

Dückers, Rob, and Ruud Priem. *The Hours of Catherine of Cleves: Devotion, Demons and Daily Life in the Fifteenth Century* ([Antwerp]: Ludion, 2009).

Duffy, Eamon. *Marking the Hours: English People and Their Prayers 1240–1570* (New Haven and London: Yale University Press, 2006).

Evans, Mark L. *The Sforza Hours* (London: British Library, 1992).

Farquhar, James Douglas. "Identity in an Anonymous Age: Bruges Manuscript Illuminators and Their Signs." *Viator* 11 (1980), pp. 371–83. http://dx.doi.org/10.1484/j.viator.2.301514

—, "The Manuscript as a Book." In *Pen to Press: Illustrated Manuscripts and Printed Books in the First Century of Printing,* edited by Sandra Hindman and James Douglas Farquhar, pp. 11–99 (College Park: Art Dept., University of Maryland, 1977).

—, "Manuscript Production and Evidence for Localizing and Dating Fifteenth-Century Books of Hours: Walters Ms 239." *Journal of the Walters Art Gallery* 45 (1987), pp. 44–88.

Fawtier, Robert. *La Bible Historiée Toute Figurée de la John Rylands Library* (Paris: Pour les Trustees et gouverneurs de la John Rylands library, 1924).

Fiero, Gloria K. "Smith Ms. 36: A Study in Fifteenth Century Manuscript Illumination." *The Courier (Syracuse University Library Associates)* 13 (1976), pp. 3–27.

Foster-Campbell, Megan. "Pilgrimage through the Pages: Pilgrims' Badges in Late Medieval Devotional Manuscripts." In *Push Me, Pull You: Imaginative and Emotional Interaction in Late Medieval and Renaissance Art*, edited by Sarah Blick and Laura Deborah Gelfand. Studies in Medieval and Reformation Traditions, pp. 227–74 (Leiden: Brill, 2011). http://dx.doi.org/10.1163/9789004215139_008

Freedberg, David. *The Power of Images: Studies in the History and Theory of Response* (Chicago: University of Chicago Press, 1989).

Geddes, Jane. *The St. Albans Psalter: A Book for Christina of Markyate* (London: British Library, 2005).

Gerritsen-Geywitz, Gisela. "Kaarsvet en Kerkwijding." In *Rapiarijs: Een Afscheidsbundel voor Hans van Dijk*, edited by S. Buitink, A. M. J. van Buuren and I. Spijker, pp. 45–47 (Utrecht: Instituut de Vooys voor Nederlandse taal-en letterkunde, 1987).

Gerry, Kathryn. "Cult and Codex: Alexis, Christina and the St. Albans Psalter." In *Der Albani-Psalter. Stand und Perspektiven der Forschung / the St. Albans Psalter. Current Research and Perspectives*, edited by Jochen Bepler and Christian Heitzmann. Hildesheimer Forschungen, Band 4, pp. 69–95 (Hildesheim, Zürich and New York: Georg Olms, 2013).

Gessler, Jean Baptist. *Jezus' Lijden en Zijdewonde in Woord en Beeld Verheerlijkt: een Folkloristische Bijdrage tot de Kennis van de Godsvrucht Onzer Voorouders* (Leuven: Sint-Alfonsusdrukkerij, 1939).

Gifford, Melanie E. "Pattern and Style in a Flemish Book of Hours: Walters Ms. 239.'" *Journal of the Walters Art Gallery* 45 (1987), pp. 89–102.

Gladwell, Malcolm. *The Tipping Point: How Little Things Can Make a Big Difference* (Boston: Little, Brown & Co., 2000).

Grotefend, Hermann. *Taschenbuch der Zeitrechnung des Deutschen Mittelalters und der Neuzeit*, 10th ed. (Hannover: Hahnsche Buchhandlung, 1960).

Gumbert, J. P. *The Dutch and Their Books in the Manuscript Age* (London: British Library, 1990).

—, *Manuscrits Datés Conservés dans les Pays-Bas; Catalogue Paléographique des Manuscrits en Écriture Latine Portant des Indications de Date; T. 1. Manuscrits d'Origine Étrangère, 816-c. 1550. T. 2. Manuscrits d'Origine Néerlandaise (XIVe-XVIe Siècles), et Supplément au Tome Premier (Cmd-Nl 2)*. 2 vols. (Leiden: Brill, 1988).

—, "Times and Places for Initials." *Quaerendo* 39 (2009), pp. 1–24. http://dx.doi.or g/10.1163/001495209x12555713997411

—, "Codicological Units: Towards a Terminology for the Stratigraphy of the Non-Homogenous Codex." *Segno e testo* 2 (2004), pp. 17–42.

—, "Codicologische Eenheden—Opzet Voor een Terminologie." *Koninklijke Nederlandse Akademie van Wetenschappen. Mededelingen van de Afdeling Letterkunde, Nieuwe Reeks* 67, no. 2 (2004), pp. 5–38.

Hanna III, Ralph. "Booklets in Medieval Manuscripts: Further Considerations." *Studies in Bibliography*, 39 (1986), pp. 101–12.

Harjula, Janne. "Underground Literature: Archaeological Finds of Books and Book Elements from Finnish Churches." *Mirator* 16 (2015), pp. 160–90.

Hasenohr, Geneviève. "L'Essor des Bibliothèques Privées aux XIVe et XVe Siècles." In *Histoire Des Bibliothèques Françaises, Vol. 1: Les Bibliothèques Médiévales du Vie Siècle à 1530*, edited by André Vernet, pp. 215–63 (Paris: Éditions du Cercle de la Librairie, 1989).

Hathaway, Neil. "Compilatio: From Plagarism to Compiling." *Viator* 20 (1989), pp. 19–44.

Henry, Avril. *Biblia Pauperum: A Facsimile and Edition* (Aldershot: Scolar Press, 1987).

Higgitt, John. *The Murthly Hours: Devotion, Literacy and Luxury in Paris, England and the Gaelic West* (London: British Library and University of Toronto Press in association with the National Library of Scotland, 2000).

Hindman, Sandra, Michael Camille, Nina Rowe, and Rowan Watson. "Reconstructions: Recuperation of Manuscript Illumination in Nineteenth- and Twentieth-Century America." In *Manuscript Illumination in the Modern Age: Recovery and Reconstruction*, edited by Sandra Hindman and Nina Rowe, pp. 215–74 (Evanston: Northwestern University, 2001).

Hoek, Klaas van der. "The North Holland Illuminator Spierinck: Some Attributions Reconsidered." In *Masters and Miniatures: Proceedings of the Congress on Medieval Manuscript Illumination in the Northern Netherlands (Utrecht, 10–13 December 1989)*, edited by K. van der Horst and Johann-Christian Klamt, pp. 275–80 (Doornspijk: Davaco, 1991).

Hofmann, Siegfried. *Der Ingolstädter Psalter: ein Deutscher Psalter des Spätmittelalters aus der Universitätsbibliothek Heidelberg* (Regensburg: Schnell & Steiner, 2010).

Hull, Caroline S. "Rylands Ms French 5: The Form and Function of a Medieval Bible Picture Book." *Bulletin of the John Rylands University Library of Manchester* 77, no. 2 (1995), pp. 3–24.

Hülsmann, Margriet. "Penwerk: een Eigen Vorm van Boekdecoratie in Vijftiende-Eeuwse Noordnederlandse Handschriften." In *Middeleeuwse Handschriftenkunde in de Nederlanden 1988; Verslag van de Groningse Codicologendagen 28–29 April 1989*, edited by Jos M. M. Hermans, pp. 13–28 (Grave: Alpha, 1989).

—, *Tronies, Baardmannen en Hondenkoppen. Noord-Hollandse Boekdecoratie uit Derde-Orde-Conventen aangesloten bij het Kapittel van Utrecht (ca. 1430–1480).* (PhD thesis, Amsterdam, Vrije Universiteit, 2009).

Inglis, Erik. "A Book in the Hand: Some Late Medieval Accounts of Manuscript Presentations." *Journal of the Early Book Society* 5 (2002), pp. 75–97.

James, M. R. *A Descriptive Catalogue of the Manuscripts in the Library of Corpus Christi College, Cambridge.* 2 vols. (Cambridge: University Press, 1912).

—, *The Western Manuscripts in the Library of Trinity College, Cambridge: A Descriptive Catalogue.* 4 vols. (Cambridge: Cambridge University Press, 1900). http://dx.doi.org/10.1017/cbo9780511702471

Ker, N. R., A. J. Piper, Andrew G. Watson, and Ian Campbell Cunningham. *Medieval Manuscripts in British Libraries.* 5 vols. (Oxford: Clarendon Press, 1969–2002).

Koch, Robert A. "La Sainte-Baume in Flemish Landscape Painting of the Sixteenth Century." *Gazette des Beaux-Arts* 66 (1965), pp. 273–82.

Kok, Ina. "Een Houtsnede in een Handschrift." In *Manuscripten en miniaturen: studies aangeboden aan Anne S. Korteweg bij haar afscheid van de Koninklijke Bibliotheek*, edited by J. A. A. M. Biemans, Klaas van der Hoek, Kathryn Rudy and Ed van der Vlist. Bijdragen tot de Geschiedenis van de Nederlandse Boekhandel, pp. 231–42 (Zutphen: Walburg Pers, 2007).

—, *Woodcuts in Incunabula Printed in the Low Countries*, transl. by Cis van Heertum, 4 vols. (Leiden: Brill, 2013).

Korteweg, A. S. *Catalogue of Medieval Manuscripts and Incunabula at Huis Bergh Castle in 's-Heerenberg* ('s-Heerenberg: Stichting Huis Bergh, 2013).

—, ed. *Kriezels, Aubergines en Takkenbossen: Randversiering in Noordnederlandse Handschriften uit de Vijftiende Eeuw*, Exh. Cat. (The Hague, Rijksmuseum Meermanno-Westreenianum. Zutphen: Walburg Pers, 1992).

Kren, Thomas. "The Trivulzio Hours and the Interurban Network of Luxury Book Production in the Burgundian Netherlands." In *Conference in Celebration of Anne Korteweg's 65th Birthday* (The Hague, Koninklijke Bibliotheek: Unpublished Lecture, 2007).

Kresten, O. and G. Prato. "Die Miniatur des Evangelisten Markus im Codex Purpureus Rossanensis: eine spätere Einfügung." *Römische historische Mitteilungen* 27 (1985), pp. 381–403.

Kwakkel, Erik. "The Cultural Dynamics of Medieval Book Production." In *Manuscripten en Miniaturen: Studies Aangeboden aan Anne S. Korteweg bij haar Afscheid van de Koninklijke Bibliotheek*, edited by J. A. A. M. Biemans, Klaas van der Hoek, Kathryn Rudy and Ed van der Vlist. Bijdragen tot de Geschiedenis van de Nederlandse Boekhandel, pp. 243–52 (Zutphen: Walburg Pers, 2007).

—, "Towards a Terminology for the Analysis of Composite Manuscripts." *Gazette du livre médiéval* 41 (2002), pp. 12–19.

Lacaze, Charlotte. "A Little-Known Manuscript from the Workshop of Master Pancraz." In Masters and Miniatures: Proceedings of the Congress on Medieval Manuscript Illumination in the Northern Netherlands (Utrecht, 10–13 December 1989), edited by K. van der Horst and Johann-Christian Klamt. Studies and Facsimiles of Netherlandish Illuminated Manuscripts, 3, pp. 255–63 (Doornspijk: Davaco, 1991).

Legaré, Anne-Marie. "Livres d'Heures, Livres de Femmes: Quelques Examples en Hainaut." *Eulalie* 1 (1998), pp. 53–68.

Leson, Richard A. "Heraldry and Identity in the Psalter-Hours of Jeanne of Flanders (Manchester, John Rylands Library, Ms Lat. 117)." *Studies in Iconography* 32 (2011), pp. 155–98.

Loerke, William. "Incipits and Author Portraits in Greek Gospel Books: Some Observations." In *Byzantine East and Latin West: Two Worlds of Christendom in Middle Ages and Renaissance Studies in Ecclesiastical and Cultural History*, edited by Deno John Geanakoplos, pp. 377–81 (New York: Harper & Row, 1966).

Lowden, John. "The Beginnings of Biblical Illustration." In *Imaging the Early Medieval Bible*, edited by John Williams. Penn State Series in the History of the Book, pp. 9–60 (University Park: Pennsylvania State University Press, 1999).

Maniaci, Marilena. *Terminologia Del Libro Manoscritto* (Rome and Milan: Istituto centrale per la patologia del libro & Editrice Bibliografica, 1996).

Marrow, James H. "Dutch Manuscript Illumination before the Master of Catherine of Cleves: The Master of the Morgan Infancy Cycle." *Nederlands Kunsthistorisch Jaarboek* 19 (1968), pp. 51–113.

—, "Text and Image in Two Fifteenth-Century Dutch Psalters from Delft." In *Spiritualia Neerlandica: Opstellen voor Dr. Albert Ampe hem door vakgenoten en vrienden aangeboden uit waardering voor zijn wetenschappelijk werk*, pp. 341–52 (Antwerp: UFSIA-Ruusbroecgenootschap, 1990).

Marrow, James H., and François Avril. *The Hours of Simon de Varie*. Getty Museum Monographs on Illuminated Manuscripts (Malibu: J. Paul Getty Museum in association with Koninklijke Bibliotheek, The Hague, 1994).

McKendrick, Scot. *Flemish Illuminated Manuscripts, 1400–1550* (London: British Library, 2003).

McRoberts, David. "Dean Brown's Book of Hours." *The Innes Review* xix (1968), pp. 144–67.

Meertens, Maria. *De Godsvrucht in de Nederlanden. Naar Handschriften van Gebedenboeken der XVe Eeuw.* 6 vols. ([n.p.]: Standaard Boekhandel, 1930–1934).

Miedema, Nine Robijntje. *Die 'Mirabilia Romae:' Untersuchungen zu ihrer Überlieferung mit Edition der Deutschen und Niederländischen Texte*, Münchener Texte und Untersuchungen zur Deutschen Literatur des Mittelalters, Bd 108 (Tübingen: M. Niemeyer, 1996).

Minnis, Alastair J. "Late-Medieval Discussions of Compilatio and the Role of the Compilator." *Beiträge zur Geschichte der deutschen Sprache und Literatur* 101 (1979), pp. 385–421.

Mockridge, Diane. "The Order of the Texts in the Bodley 34 Manuscript: The Function of Repetition and Recall in a Manuscript Addressed to Nuns." *Essays in Medieval Studies* 3 (1986), pp. 207–16.

Moll, Willem. "De Boekerij van het St. Barbara-Klooster te Delft, in de Tweede Helft der Vijftiende Eeuw: eene Bijdrage tot de Geschiedenis der Middeleeuwsche Letterkunde in Nederland." *Kerkhistorisch archief* IV (1866), pp. 209–86 (24–28).

Neuheuser, Hanns Peter. "Die Kanonblätter aus der Schule des Moerdrecht-Meisters." *Wallraf-Richartz-Jahrbuch* 64 (2003), pp. 187–214.

Oliver, Judith. *Gothic Manuscript Illumination in the Diocese of Liège (c. 1250-C. 1330).* Corpus van verluchte Handschriften uit de Nederlanden = Corpus of Illuminated Manuscripts from the Low Countries. Vol. 2–3 (Leuven: Peeters, 1988).

—, "Reconstruction of a Liège Psalter-Hours." *The British Library Journal* 5, no. 2 (1979), pp. 107–28.

Oosterman, Johan. *De Gratie van het Gebed: Middelnederlandse Gebeden, Overlevering en Functie: met Bijzondere Aandacht voor Produktie en Receptie in Brugge (1380–1450).* Nederlandse Literatuur en Cultuur in de Middeleeuwen. 2 vols. Vol. 2 (Amsterdam: Prometheus, 1995).

—, "Om de Grote Kracht der Woorden: Middelnederlandse Gebeden en Rubrieken in het Brugge van de Vroege Vijftiende Eeuw." In *Boeken voor de Eeuwigheid: Middelnederlands Geestelijk Proza*, edited by Th Mertens. Nederlandse Literatuur en Cultuur in de Middeleeuwen, pp. 230–44, 437–44 (Amsterdam: Prometheus, 1993).

Orchard, Nicholas. *The Leofric Missal.* Vol. v (Woodbridge and London: Boydell Press for the Henry Bradshaw Society, 2002).

Orme, Nicholas. *Medieval Children* (New Haven and London: Yale University Press, 2001).

Orr, Michael T. "Hierarchies of Decoration in Early Fifteenth-Century English Books of Hours." In *Tributes to Kathleen L. Scott: English Medieval Manuscripts: Readers, Makers and Illuminators*, edited by Marlene Villalobos Hennessy, pp. 171–95 (London: Harvey Miller, 2009).

Osterstrom-Renger, Marta. "The Netherlandish Grisaille Miniatures: Some Unexplored Aspects." *Wallraf-Richartz-Jahrbuch* 44 (1983), pp. 145–73.

Panayotova, Stella, and Andrew Morris. *The Macclesfield Psalter: "A Window into the World of Late Medieval England"* (Cambridge: Fitzwilliam Museum, 2005).

Parkes, M. B. "The Influence of the Concepts of Ordinatio and Compilatio on the Development of the Book." In *Medieval Learning and Literature: Essays Presented to Richard William Hunt*, edited by J. J. G. Alexander and M. T. Gibson, pp. 115–41 (Oxford: Clarendon Press, 1976).

Pelteret, David Anthony Edgell. *Slavery in Early Mediaeval England: From the Reign of Alfred until the Twelfth Century*. Studies in Anglo-Saxon History, 7 (Woodbridge: Boydell, 1995).

Plummer, John. *Liturgical Manuscripts for the Mass and the Divine Office* (New York: Pierpont Morgan Library, 1964).

Poleg, Eyal. "The Bible as Talisman: Textus and Oath-Books." In *Approaching the Bible in Medieval England*. Manchester Medieval Studies, pp. 59–107 (Manchester: Manchester University Press, 2013).

Reinburg, Virginia. *French Books of Hours: Making an Archive of Prayer, c. 1400–1600* (Cambridge and New York: Cambridge University Press, 2012). http://dx.doi.org/10.1017/cbo9781139030496

Reynolds, Catherine. "The Undecorated Margin: The Fashion for Luxury Books without Borders." In *Flemish Manuscript Painting in Context*, edited by Thomas Kren and Elizabeth Morrison, pp. 9–26 (Los Angeles: J. Paul Getty Museum, 2006.

Robinson, Pamela R. "The 'Booklet:' A Self-Contained Unit in Composite Manuscripts." *Codicologica: Towards a Science of Handwritten Books* 3 (1980), pp. 46–67.

Rogers, Nicholas. *Books of Hours Produced in the Low Countries for the English Market in the Fifteenth Century* (M. Litt. thesis, Cambridge University, 1982).

—, "Patrons and Purchasers: Evidence for the Original Owners of Books of Hours Produced in the Low Countries for the English Market." In *Als Ich Can: Liber Amicorum in Memory of Professor Dr. Maurits Smeyers*, edited by Bert Cardon, Jan van der Stock, Dominique Vanwijnsberghe and Katharina Smeyers. Corpus of Illuminated Manuscripts = Corpus Van Verluchte Handschriften, pp. 1165–81 (Leuven: Peeters, 2002).

Rouse, Richard H., and Mary A. Rouse. "The Book Trade at the University of Paris, c. 1250-C. 1350." In *La Production du Livre Universitaire au Moyen Age: Exemplar et Pecia: Actes du Symposium Tenu au Collegio San Bonaventura de Grottaferrata en Mai 1983*, edited by Louis J. Bataillon, Bertrand G. Guyot and Richard H. Rouse, pp. 41–123 (Paris: Editions du Centre national de la recherche scientifique, 1983).

Rubin, Miri. *Corpus Christi: The Eucharist in Late Medieval Culture* (Cambridge and New York: Cambridge University Press, 1991).

Rudy, Kathryn. *Postcards on Parchment: The Social Lives of Medieval Books* (New Haven and London: Yale University Press, 2015).

—, "Sewing the Body of Christ: Eucharist Wafer Souvenirs Stitched into Fifteenth-Century Manuscripts, Primarily in the Netherlands." *Journal of Historians of Netherlandish Art* (January 2016), unpaginated.

—, "The Birgittines of the Netherlands: Experimental Colourists." In *Printing Colour 1400–1700: Histories, Techniques, Functions and Reception*, edited by Elizabeth Upper and Ad Stijnman, pp. 82–90 (Leiden: Brill, 2014).

—, "Kissing Images, Unfurling Rolls, Measuring Wounds, Sewing Badges and Carrying Talismans: Considering Some Harley Manuscripts through the Physical Rituals They Reveal." *eBLJ (The Electronic British Library Journal)* special volume: Proceedings from the Harley Conference, British Library, 29–30 June 2009 (2011).

—, "De Productie van Manuscripten in het Sint-Ursulaklooster te Delft." *Delf: Cultuurhistorisch magazine voor Delft* 12, no. 2 (2010), pp. 24–27.

—, "Dirty Books: Quantifying Patterns of Use in Medieval Manuscripts Using a Densitometer." *Journal of Historians of Netherlandish Art* 2, 1 (2010). http://dx.doi.org/10.5092/jhna.2010.2.1.1

—, "Margins and Memory: The Functions of Border Imagery from a Delft Manuscript." In *Manuscript Studies in the Low Countries. Proceedings of the 'Groninger Codicologendagen' in Friesland 2002*, pp. 216–38 (Groningen: Egbert Forsten, 2008).

—, *Sint Anna in de Koninklijke Bibliotheek: ter Gelegenheid van de Vijfenzestigste Verjaardag van Anne S. Korteweg* (Amsterdam and The Hague: Buitenkant & Koninklijke Bibliotheek, 2007).

—, "An Illustrated Mid-Fifteenth-Century Primer for a Flemish Girl: British Library, Harley Ms 3828." *Journal of the Warburg and Courtauld Institutes* 69 (2006), pp. 51–94.

—, "A Pilgrim's Book of Hours: Stockholm Royal Library A233." *Studies in Iconography* 21 (2000), pp. 237–77; and "Addendum." *Studies in Iconography* 22 (2001), pp. 163–64.

Rudy, Kathryn M., and Ed van der Vlist, "Het Geschreven Boek in Nederland tot omstreeks 1400: Continuïteit en Emancipatie." *Jaarboek voor Nederlandse boekgeschiedenis* 17 (2010), pp. 15–51.

Rudy, Kathryn M., and René Stuip. "'Martin Fights in July, and He Strikes St. Vaast with the Font.' A Cisiojanus and a Child's Alphabet in Oxford, Bodleian, Ms Rawlinson Liturgical E 40." *Cahiers de Recherches Médiévales et Humanistes / A Journal of Medieval and Humanistic Studies* 19 (2010), pp. 493–521. http://dx.doi.org/10.4000/crm.12029

Saenger, Paul Henry. "Books of Hours and the Reading Habits of the Later Middle Ages." In *The Culture of Print: Power and the Uses of Print in Early Modern Europe*, edited by Alain Boureau and Roger Chartier, pp. 141–73 (Cambridge: Polity, 1989).

—, *Space between Words: The Origins of Silent Reading* (Stanford: Stanford University Press, 1997).

Sand, Alexa. "*Cele Houre Memes*: An Eccentric English Psalter-Hours in the Huntington Library." *Huntington Library Quarterly* 75, no. 2 (2012), pp. 171–211. http://dx.doi.org/10.1525/hlq.2012.75.2.171

—, "A Small Door: Recognizing Ruth in the Psalter-Hours 'of Yolande of Soissons.'" *Gesta* 46, no. 1 (2007), pp. 19–40. http://dx.doi.org/10.2307/25067147

—, "Vision, Devotion, and Difficulty in the Psalter Hours 'of Yolande of Soissons.'" *The Art Bulletin* 87, no. 1 (2005), pp. 6–23.

Sandler, Lucy Freeman. "Notes for the Illuminator: The Case of the *Omne Bonum*." *The Art Bulletin* 71, no. 4 (1989), pp. 551–64. http://dx.doi.org/10.2307/3051269

—, *The Psalter of Robert De Lisle in the British Library* (London and New York: Harvey Miller/Oxford University Press, 1983).

Sandler, Lucy Freeman. *Illuminators & Patrons in Fourteenth-Century England: The Psalter & Hours of Humphrey de Bohun and the Manuscripts of the Bohun Family* (London: The British Library, 2014).

Schier, Volker, and Corine Schlief. "Seeing and Singing, Touching and Tasting the Holy Lance: The Power and Politics of Embodied Religious Experiences in Nuremberg, 1424–1524." In *Signs of Change: Transformations of Christian Traditions and Their Representation in the Arts, 1000–2000*, edited by Nils Holger Petersen and Nicolas Bell, pp. 401–26 (Amsterdam and New York: Rodopi, 2004).

Schilder, Marian, ed. *Amsterdamse Kloosters in De Middeleeuwen* (Amsterdam: Vossiuspers AUP, 1997).

Sciacca, Christine. "Raising the Curtain on the Use of Textiles in Manuscripts." In *Weaving, Veiling, and Dressing: Textiles and Their Metaphors in the Late Middle Ages*, edited by Kathryn M. Rudy and Barbara Baert. Medieval Church Studies, pp. 161–90 (Turnhout: Brepols, 2007).

Scott, Kathleen L. "Design, Decoration and Illustration." In *Book Production and Publishing in Britain, 1375–1475*, edited by Jeremy Griffiths and Derek Albert Pearsall. Cambridge Studies in Publishing and Printing History, pp. 31–64 (Cambridge and New York: Cambridge University Press, 1989).

Shailor, Barbara A. *Catalogue of Medieval and Renaissance Manuscripts in the Beinecke Rare Book and Manuscript Library, Yale University*. 3 vols. (Binghamton: Medieval & Renaissance Texts & Studies, 1984).

Skemer, Don C. *Binding Words: Textual Amulets in the Middle Ages*. Magic in History (University Park: Pennsylvania State University Press, 2006).

Smeyers, Maurits. *Naer Natueren Ghelike: Vlaamse Miniaturen Voor Van Eyck (Ca. 1350-Ca. 1420)* (Leuven: Davidsfonds, 1993).

Smyth, Adam. "'Shreds of holinesse:' George Herbert, Little Gidding, and Cutting Up Texts in Early Modern England," *English Literary Renaissance* (2012), pp. 452–81. http://dx.doi.org/10.1111/j.1475–6757.2012.01113.x

Stanton, Anne. "Design, Devotion, and Durability in Gothic Prayerbooks." In *Manuscripta Illuminata: Approaches to Understanding Medieval and Renaissance Manuscripts*, edited by Colum Hourihane, pp. 87–107 (University Park: Penn State Press, 2014).

—, "Turning the Pages: Marginal Narratives and Devotional Practice in Gothic Prayerbooks." In *Push Me, Pull You: Imaginative and Emotional Interaction in Late Medieval and Renaissance Art*, edited by Sarah Blick and Laura Deborah Gelfand. Studies in Medieval and Reformation Traditions, pp. 75–122 (Leiden: Brill, 2011). http://dx.doi.org/10.1163/9789004215139_004

Stanton, Anne Rudlofol. "The Psalter of Isabelle, Queen of England 1308–1330: Isabelle as the Audience." *Word & Image: A Journal of Verbal/Visual Enquiry* 18, no. 4 (2002), pp. 1–27. http://dx.doi.org/10.1080/02666286.2002.10404973

Stirnemann, Patricia. "The King of Illuminated Manuscripts: The Très Riches Heures." In *The Limbourg Brothers: Nijmegen Masters at the French Court, 1400–1416*, edited by Rob Dückers and Pieter Roelofs. Exh. cat., Museum het Valkhof, Nijmegen, pp. 113–19 (Ghent: Ludion, 2005).

—, "Fils de la Vierge. L'initiale à Filigranes Parisiennes: 1140–1314," *Revue de l'Art* 90 (1990), pp. 58–73.

Stooker, Karl, and Theo Verbeij. *Collecties op Orde: Middelnederlandse Handschriften uit Kloosters en Semi-Religieuze Gemeenschappen in de Nederlanden*. Miscellanea Neerlandica, 15–16. 2 vols. (Leuven: Peeters, 1997).

Stuard, Susan Mosher. *Gilding the Market: Luxury and Fashion in Fourteenth-Century Italy* (Philadelphia: University of Pennsylvania Press, 2006).

Tenschert, Heribert, and Eberhard König. *Leuchtendes Mittelalter III: Das Goldene Zeitalter Der Burgundischen Buchmalerei 1430–1560, Sammlung Carlo de Poortere U. A.* Katalog / Antiquariat Heribert Tenschert, 27 (Rotthalmünster: Heribert Tenschert, 1991).

Tufte, Edward R. *The Visual Display of Quantitative Information*. 2nd ed. (Cheshire: Graphics Press, 2001).

van Bergen, Wilhelmina Saskia. *De Meesters van Otto van Moerdrecht. Een Onderzoek naar de Stijl en Iconografie van een Groep Miniaturisten, in Relatie tot de Productie van Getijdenboeken in Brugge Rond 1430* (PhD thesis, University of Amsterdam, 2007).

—, "The Production of Flemish Books of Hours for the English Market: Standardization and Workshop Practices." In *Manuscripts in Transition: Recycling Manuscripts, Texts and Images: Proceedings of the International Congres* [Sic] *Held in Brussels (5–9 November 2002)*, edited by Brigitte Dekeyzer and Jan van der Stock. Corpus of Illuminated Manuscripts, pp. 271–83 (Leuven: Peeters, 2005).

Vanwijnsberghe, Dominique. "The Cyclical Illustrations of the Little Hours of the Virgin in Pre-Eyckian Manuscripts." In *Flanders in a European Perspective: Manuscript Illumination around 1400 in Flanders and Abroad: Proceedings of the International Colloquium, Leuven, 7–10 September 1993*, edited by Maurits Smeyers and Bert Cardon, pp. 285–96 (Leuven: Peeters, 1995).

—, "Le Cycle de l'Enfance des Petites Heures de la Vierge dans les Livres d'Heures des Pays-Bas Méridionaux." In *Manuscripten en Miniaturen: Studies Aangeboden aan Anne S. Korteweg bij haar Afscheid van de Koninklijke Bibliotheek*, edited by J. A. A. M. Biemans, Klaas van der Hoek, Kathryn Rudy and Ed van der Vlist. Bijdragen tot de Geschiedenis van de Nederlandse Boekhandel, pp. 355–65 (Zutphen: Walburg Pers, 2007).

Verbeke, Werner. "'O Soete Cruce...' Een berijmd Gebed in Handschrift Brussel, K. B., 19588." In *Serta Devota in Memoriam Guillelmi Lourdaux II: Devotio Windesheimensis*, edited by Werner Verbeke, M. Haverals, R. de Keyser and J. Goossens. Mediaevalia Lovaniensia, Series I / Studia XXI, pp. 297–313 (Leuven: Leuven University Press, 1995).

Vertongen, Susie. "Herman Scheerre, the Beaufort Master and the Flemish Miniature Painting: A Reopened Debate." In *Flanders in a European Perspective: Manuscript Illumination around 1400 in Flanders and Abroad: Proceedings of the International Colloquium, Leuven, 7–10 September 1993*, edited by Maurits Smeyers and Bert Cardon. Corpus van Verluchte Handschriften = Corpus of Illuminated Manuscripts, pp. 251–65 (Leuven: Peeters, 1995).

Vezin, Jean. "Les Livres Utilisés Comme Amulettes et Comme Reliques." In *Das Buch als Magisches und als Repräsentationsobjekt*, edited by Peter Ganz. Wolfenbütteler Mittelalter-Studien, pp. 101–15 (Wiesbaden: Harrassowitz, 1992).

Watson, Rowan. "The Illuminated Manuscript in the Age of Photographic Reproduction." In *Making the Medieval Book: Techniques of Production: Proceedings of the Fourth Conference of the Seminar in the History of the Book to 1500, Oxford, July 1992*, edited by Linda L. Brownrigg, pp. 133–43 (Los Altos Hills and London: Anderson-Lovelace & Red Gull Press, 1995).

—, *Vandals and Enthusiasts: Views of Illumination in the Nineteenth Century: An Exhibition Held in the Henry Cole Wing of the Victoria and Albert Museum, 31 January-30 April 1995* (London: Victoria and Albert Museum, 1995).

Watteeuw, Lieve. "...Pour Avoir Nettoyé et Relyé Ij Grans Livres Appartenant à Monseigneur... Documentation Concerning the Fifteenth-Century Care of Manuscripts in the Burgundian Library." In *Manuscripts in Transition: Recycling Manuscripts, Texts, and Images*, edited by Brigitte Dekeyzer and Jan van der Stock, pp. 241–51 (Paris and Dudley: Peeters, 2005).

Weekes, Ursula. *Early Engravers and Their Public: The Master of the Berlin Passion and Manuscripts from Convents in the Rhine-Maas Region, ca. 1450–1500* (London: Harvey Miller, 2004).

Wegener, Hans. *Beschreibendes Verzeichnis der Miniaturen und des Initialschmuckes in den Deutschen Handschriften bis 1500. V: Die Deutschen Handschriften bis 1500.* Beschreibende Verzeichnisse der Miniaturen-Handschriften der Preussischen Staatsbibliothek zu Berlin. 5 vols. (Leipzig: Weber, 1928).

Werner, Wilfried, ed. *Cimelia Heidelbergensia: 30 illuminierte Handschriften der Universitätsbibliothek Heidelberg* (Wiesbaden: Reichert, 1975).

Wieck, Roger S. "Folia Fugitiva: The Pursuit of the Illuminated Manuscript Leaf." *The Journal of the Walters Art Gallery* 54, Essays in Honor of Lilian M. C. Randall (1996), pp. 233–54.

—, "The Primer of Claude De France and the Education of the Renaissance Child." In *The Cambridge Illuminations: The Conference Papers*, edited by Stella Panayotova, pp. 167–72 (London: Harvey Miller, 2007).

—, "Special Children's Books of Hours in the Walters Art Museum." In *Als Ich Can: Liber Amicorum in Memory of Professor Dr. Maurits Smeyers*, edited by Bert Cardon, Jan van der Stock, Dominique Vanwijnsberghe and Katharina Smeyers. Corpus of Illuminated Manuscripts = Corpus van Verluchte Handschriften, pp. 1629–39 (Leuven: Peeters, 2002).

—, *Time Sanctified: The Book of Hours in Medieval Art and Life* (New York: G. Braziller in association with the Walters Art Gallery, Baltimore, 1988).

Winkler, Friedrich. *Die Flämische Buchmalerei des XV. und XVI. Jahrhunderts; Künstler und Werke von den Brüdern van Eyck bis zu Simon Bening* (Leipzig: E. A. Seemann, 1925).

Wüstefeld, Helen, and A. S. Korteweg. *Sleutel tot licht: Getijdenboeken in de Bibliotheca Philosophica Hermetica* (Amsterdam: In de Pelikaan, 2009).

List of illustrations

234 Opening in a book of hours at the Verses of St. Gregory, with a   262
     diagram showing the arrangement of original and added parchment;
     the additions transform the prayer from a five-verse version into a
     nine-verse version with a larger indulgence. The Hague, Koninklijke
     Bibliotheek, Ms. 132 G 38, fol. 84r-85v. Image © Koninklijke
     Bibliotheek—the National Library of The Netherlands, CC BY 4.0.

235 Opening in a book of hours, with original and added parchment. Fol.   263
     86r is part of the original manuscript (made in South Holland) and
     has a prayer to the sacrament. Fol. 85 was inscribed at the convent
     of St. Ursula in Delft and added later. Fol. 85v contains the ninth
     and final Verse of St. Gregory, and a postscript rubric indicating
     that reading the previous prayer is worth 92,042 years' & 80 days'
     indulgence. The Hague, Koninklijke Bibliotheek, Ms. 132 G 38, fol.
     85v-86r. Image © Koninklijke Bibliotheek—the National Library of
     The Netherlands, CC BY 4.0.

236 Opening in a book of hours, with original and added parchment.   263
     Fol. 86 is part of the original manuscript (made in South Holland).
     The first nine and a half lines, including the red letter *A* with its few
     strokes of whispy penwork, were inscribed by the original scribe and
     are typical of the original production. A scribe at the convent of St.
     Ursula in Delft filled the rest of fol. 86v with a prayer to the sacrament,
     added bold red and blue penwork decoration, and extended the
     existing penwork into the upper margin; she continued the prayer
     on added parchment (fol. 87), on which she inscribed another prayer
     to the sacrament. The Hague, Koninklijke Bibliotheek, Ms. 132 G 38,
     fol. 86v-87r. Image © Koninklijke Bibliotheek—the National Library
     of The Netherlands, CC BY 4.0.

237 Folio in a book of hours from a section added at the convent of St.   266
     Ursula in Delft. Gaps in the penwork border decoration are for
     small painted figures, which have not been filled in. The Hague,
     Koninklijke Bibliotheek, Ms. 132 G 38, fol. 94r. Image © Koninklijke
     Bibliotheek—the National Library of The Netherlands, CC BY 4.0.

238 Opening in a book of hours from an added section, at the division   266
     between two added quires, revealing the large catchword typical
     of production at the convent of St. Ursula in Delft. The Hague,
     Koninklijke Bibliotheek, Ms. 132 G 38, fol. 101v-102r. Image
     © Koninklijke Bibliotheek—the National Library of The Netherlands,
     CC BY 4.0.

239 Opening in a book of hours from an added section, with one prayer   267
     to St. Ursula and one to her 11,000 virginal companions; fol. 104r
     is decorated with penwork typical of Delft on three sides of the
     text block. The Hague, Koninklijke Bibliotheek, Ms. 132 G 38, fol.
     103v-104r. Image © Koninklijke Bibliotheek—the National Library
     of The Netherlands, CC BY 4.0.

247 Opening in a lay breviary made in Utrecht and upgraded in Delft,   280
    with Delft penwork added to Utrecht penwork. The new penwork
    added to four of the initials *G* fills half of the margin, and therefore
    maintains the hierarchy of decoration dictated by the three-line
    initials. The opening also reveals a large catchword inscribed
    in the manner typical of the Ursula convent in Delft. Uppsala,
    Universitetsbiblioteket, Ms. C 517 k, fol. 27v-28r. Image © Uppsala
    Universitetsbiblioteket, CC BY 4.0.

248 Opening in a prayer book, showing September-October calendar
    pages inscribed in the Southern Netherlands, with the *KL* painted
    and gilt in the Southern Netherlands, and the penwork applied in
    Delft. The Hague, Koninklijke Bibliotheek, Ms. BPH 148, fol. 9v-10r.
    Image © Koninklijke Bibliotheek—the National Library of The
    Netherlands, CC BY 4.0.

249 Opening in a prayer book, showing text folios inscribed in the   284
    Southern Netherlands, with one-, two-, and four-line initials gilt
    and painted in the Southern Netherlands (probably Bruges), with
    Delft penwork decoration added later. The Hague, Koninklijke
    Bibliotheek, Ms. BPH 148, fol. 24v-25r. Image © Koninklijke
    Bibliotheek—the National Library of The Netherlands, CC BY 4.0.

250 Opening in a prayer book, with a full-page miniature painted on   285
    a bifolium (fol. 111&118) by the Masters of Zweder of Culemborg
    depicting St. Nicholas; the bifolium has been ruled, inscribed,
    and incorporated into the prayerbook. The Hague, Koninklijke
    Bibliotheek, Ms. BPH 148, fol. 118v-119r. Image © Koninklijke
    Bibliotheek—the National Library of The Netherlands, CC BY 4.0.

251 Opening in a prayer book, with a full-page miniature depicting Christ 285
    as Man of Sorrows and an angel border on the right, painted by the
    Masters of Zweder van Culemborg, and border decoration around
    the miniature applied by a painter in the Southern Netherlands. The
    Hague, Koninklijke Bibliotheek, Ms. BPH 148, fol. 138v-139r. Image
    © Koninklijke Bibliotheek—the National Library of The Netherlands,
    CC BY 4.0.

252 Opening in a book of hours, with a full-page miniature depicting   288
    the Deposition from the Cross opposite a text page with sorrowing
    angels, painted by the Masters of Zweder van Culemborg. The
    Hague, Koninklijke Bibliotheek, Ms. 79 K 2, pp. 170–171. http://
    manuscripts.kb.nl/show/images/79+K+2

253 Opening in a prayer book, with a full-page miniature depicting the   289
    Virgin and Child with St. John, painted on a singleton (fol. 55) by the
    Masters of Zweder van Culemborg, with border decoration around
    the miniature applied by a painter in the Southern Netherlands. The
    Hague, Koninklijke Bibliotheek, Ms. BPH 148, fol. 55v-56r. Image
    © Koninklijke Bibliotheek—the National Library of The Netherlands,
    CC BY 4.0.

Index

This book need not end here…

At Open Book Publishers, we are changing the nature of the traditional academic book. The title you have just read will not be left on a library shelf, but will be accessed online by hundreds of readers each month across the globe. OBP publishes only the best academic work: each title passes through a rigorous peer-review process. We make all our books free to read online so that students, researchers and members of the public who can't afford a printed edition will have access to the same ideas.

This book and additional content is available at:
http://www.openbookpublishers.com/isbn/9781783742332

Customize

Personalize your copy of this book or design new books using OBP and third-party material. Take chapters or whole books from our published list and make a special edition, a new anthology or an illuminating coursepack. Each customized edition will be produced as a paperback and a downloadable PDF. Find out more at:

http://www.openbookpublishers.com/section/59/1

Donate

If you enjoyed this book, and feel that research like this should be available to all readers, regardless of their income, please think about donating to us. We do not operate for profit and all donations, as with all other revenue we generate, will be used to finance new Open Access publications.

http://www.openbookpublishers.com/section/13/1/support-us

Like Open Book Publishers f

Follow @OpenBookPublish 🐦

Read more at the Open Book Publishers BLOG

You may also be interested in…

The Sword of Judith: Judith Studies Across the Discipline
Edited by Kevin R. Brine, Elena Ciletti and Henrike
Lähnemann

http://dx.doi.org/10.11647/OBP.0009
http://www.openbookpublishers.com/product/28

*From Dust to Digital: Ten Years of the
Endangered Archives Programme*
Edited by Maja Kominko

http://dx.doi.org/10.11647/OBP.0052
http://www.openbookpublishers.com/product/283

*Text and Genre in Reconstruction: Effects of Digitalization
on Ideas, Behaviours, Products and Institutions*
Edited by Willard McCarty

http://dx.doi.org/10.11647/OBP.0008
http://www.openbookpublishers.com/product/64

Lightning Source UK Ltd.
Milton Keynes UK
UKOW07f0311191016

285633UK00003B/7/P

9 781783 742332